IF THE SNAKE
もし蛇が

Edited by Anne Stenne

Verlag der Buchhandlung Walther und Franz König, Köln
Roulette Russe, Denmark

IF THE SNAKE is an entity, a being-milieu affecting the city through invisible presences, different intelligent forms, chemical, biological, and algorithmic processes. Each feature within this situated entity has inherently dynamic qualities that, due to the conditions of their co-presence, endlessly grow as particular and contingent modes of continuity.

This infant, complex milieu is a prompt for spontaneous order, self-generating, material with consciousness, and shifting meaning, constantly modifying its plasticity in total indifference to any potential witness. The exhibition appears as merely one hypothesis of its existence amidst many.

A pool the color of a cosmetic product reflects a frog, a live simulation unfolding over the course of an annual orbit. Hands in endless movement try to contain the animal floating in zero gravity. Sometimes, humans inside the pool ripple the surface of its abstract body. Moving around a sandy yard infused with artificial scents and radiation-mutated flowers, one person emits sound while the other responds with discreet movements. Nearby, a subject has been cut out from a shining pedestal.

It's morning; an algorithmic snake moves along the sand. In the vicinity, private thoughts reconstructed as mental images are generating chimeras of ideas in reaction to human presence and noisy swarms of crows flying above. In the adjacent building, an experiment is unfolding: a diagrammatic drawing, depicting its uncertain state in a biome host, grows malignant through electro-chemical reaction.

In the year 4936, in an abandoned school, the last mortals hold hostage immortal humans who tried to escape an Earth being dismantled by the acceleration of its rotation. This has been repeated every day over 3000 years, with no one in a position to know its origin. The union of a mortal and an immortal has given birth not to a child but to the Infant, containing all the possibilities within itself at the same time. A Deepfake technology transforms objects and spaces into a mutating newborn. What occurs self-edits and generates in real time, changing shape with each iteration. Everything is bound by the void.

Ever-changing sounds permeate from an interconnected set of materials and flow past sonic cooperatives. Instruments are animated by objects, objects by electricity, and electricity by sound. These semi-autonomously lie between continuity and contingency: one object being flying insects, whose accidental death by electrocution causes the power system to shut down temporarily, in an odd synchronicity.

An artificial lifeform in the shape of a chimeric, branching serpent, learning and evolving by itself, adapts to stimuli from the extradiegetic world. Right now it adjusts to the actual presence of a young person embodying a Manga character, speaking of its condition, abandoned by its maker. They are at times in a non-causal relationship, though occasionally modify one another's behavior.

On the river, floating devices are harvesting the river's microbiome. Extracted DNA of unknown and unnamed organisms, adapted to different chemicals, propagates decontamination by distributing its memory to other locations. The same water circulates in a complex network of glass objects, engineered to delay its flow and time. Heat generated by a device warms the water, which contains a soft robotic manta ray. Silica dioxide, silicon, silicone.

Outside and everywhere, there is an ominous sound of a Geiger machine, punctuated sporadically by blooms of an unknowable scent, inhaled without knowledge or consent. Molecular structures are transmuted to different consumable forms of artificial flavor. The mood of an entire city appears after dark, in the volatile shape of a smoke plume. Every night, different faces and voices involved in an intimate fictional scene reenact the moment preceding the murder of a poet and are interrupted by their own thoughts.

There is some kind of shipwreck, a navigation in a virtual airplane, frozen in time, a raw, digital Pompeii of a sort in which sleeping bodies have been captured. Unpredictably, the snake slithers as a naked body furtively dances through the site, both gaining their kinetic energy from that which they encounter. They add a corporeal memory to the asperity of these other worlds. One of these worlds is a hallucination: an animation depicting, in ecstatic carnage, one possible realization of entangled utopian visions.

In views from the anti-world, conversations, the production of diagrams, and the use of software aim at enacting operations of thought. Inside, the surface of a wall punctured by nozzles exhales wind in contiguity with a pool of coagulating black liquid matter, learning and reacting to personal data. A device, in a dark landscape of powdered bones, lends human fevers to the building.

IF THE SNAKE is not a portrait, comprised of various facets. Nor is it a ghost in the machine, an animism whose sensible presence relies exclusively on human attribution or values. It is self-presenting and still eschews representation. It is the naturalization of odd, artificial otherness: the constitution of a weirding, sensible subject made of many.

Departing from consensual reality—a reality bound by the "known"—requires the speculative aspect of fiction in order to reach worlds thought of as impossible, to playfully imagine what they could be, and to actualize them. This pointless topology is an overflow of porous fictions, a crossfade in a state of uncertainty, a continuum of unstable formalizations of possibilities.

PIERRE HUYGHE, ARTISTIC DIRECTOR OKAYAMA ART SUMMIT 2019

TAREK ATOUI

MATTHEW BARNEY

ETIENNE CHAMBAUD

PAUL CHAN

IAN CHENG

MELISSA DUBBIN &
AARON S. DAVIDSON

JOHN GERRARD

FABIEN GIRAUD & RAPHAËL SIBONI

GLASS BEAD

ELIZABETH HÉNAFF

PIERRE HUYGHE

EVA L'HOEST

FERNANDO ORTEGA

SEAN RASPET

LILI REYNAUD-DEWAR

PAMELA ROSENKRANZ

TINO SEHGAL

MIKA TAJIMA

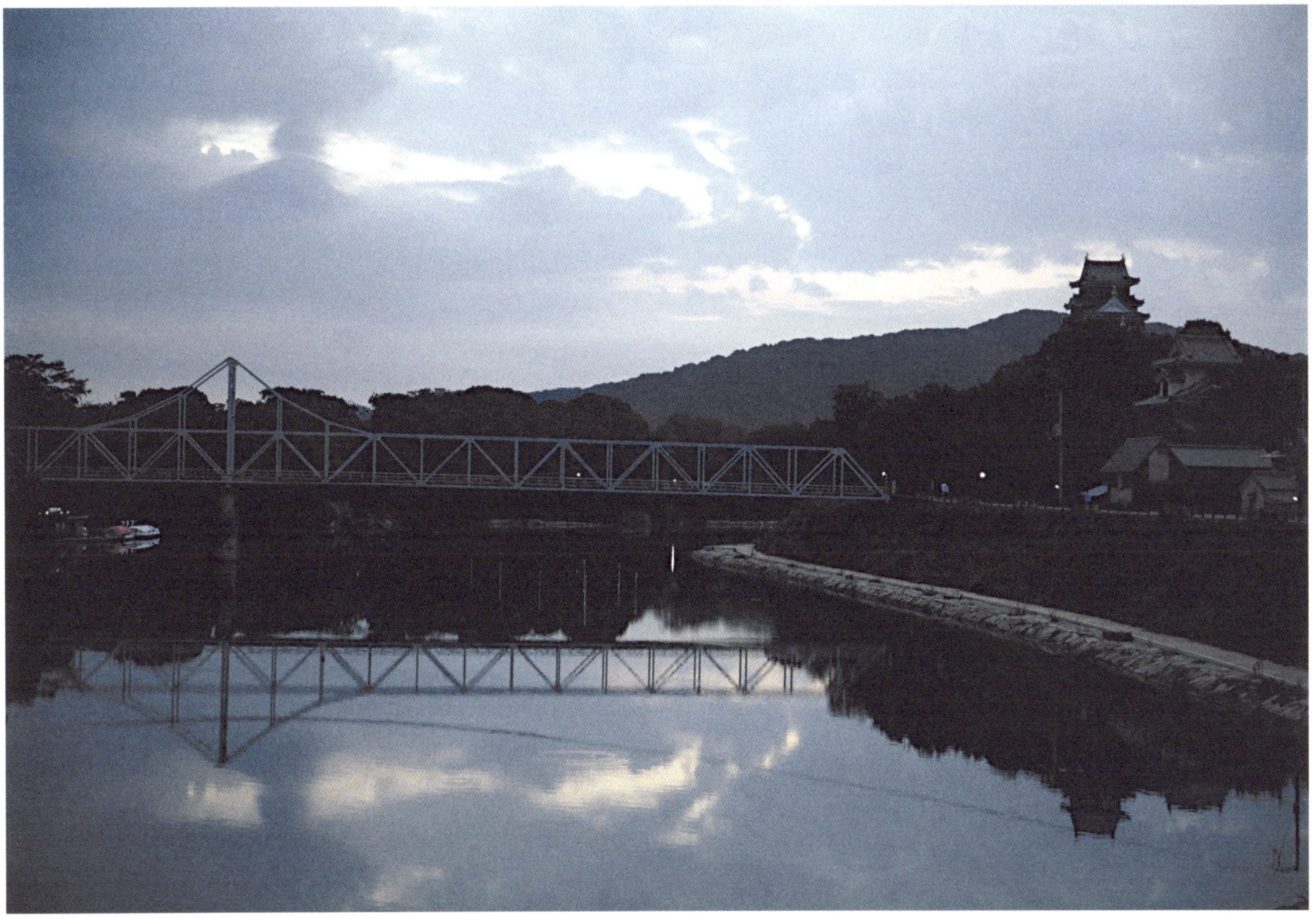

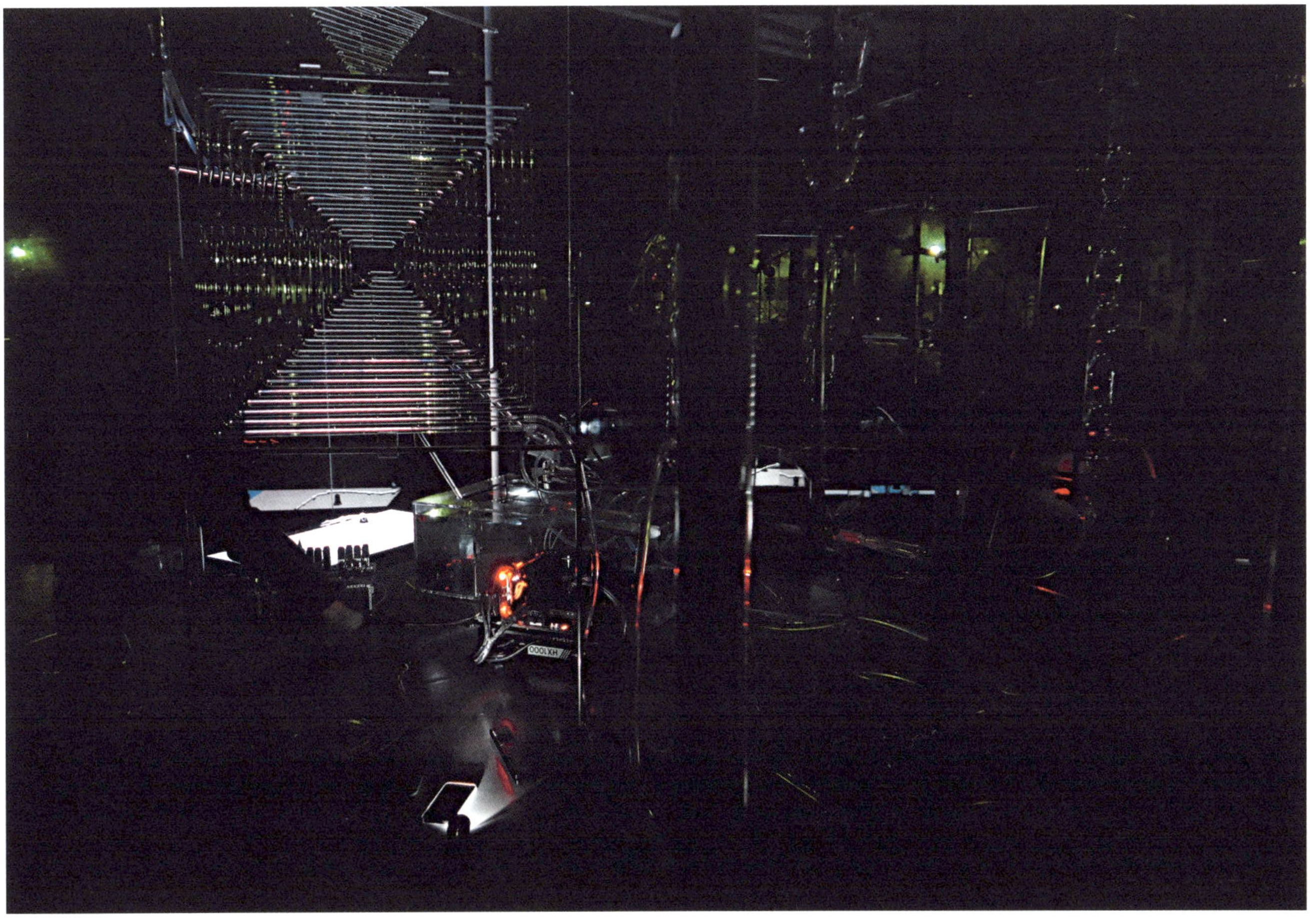

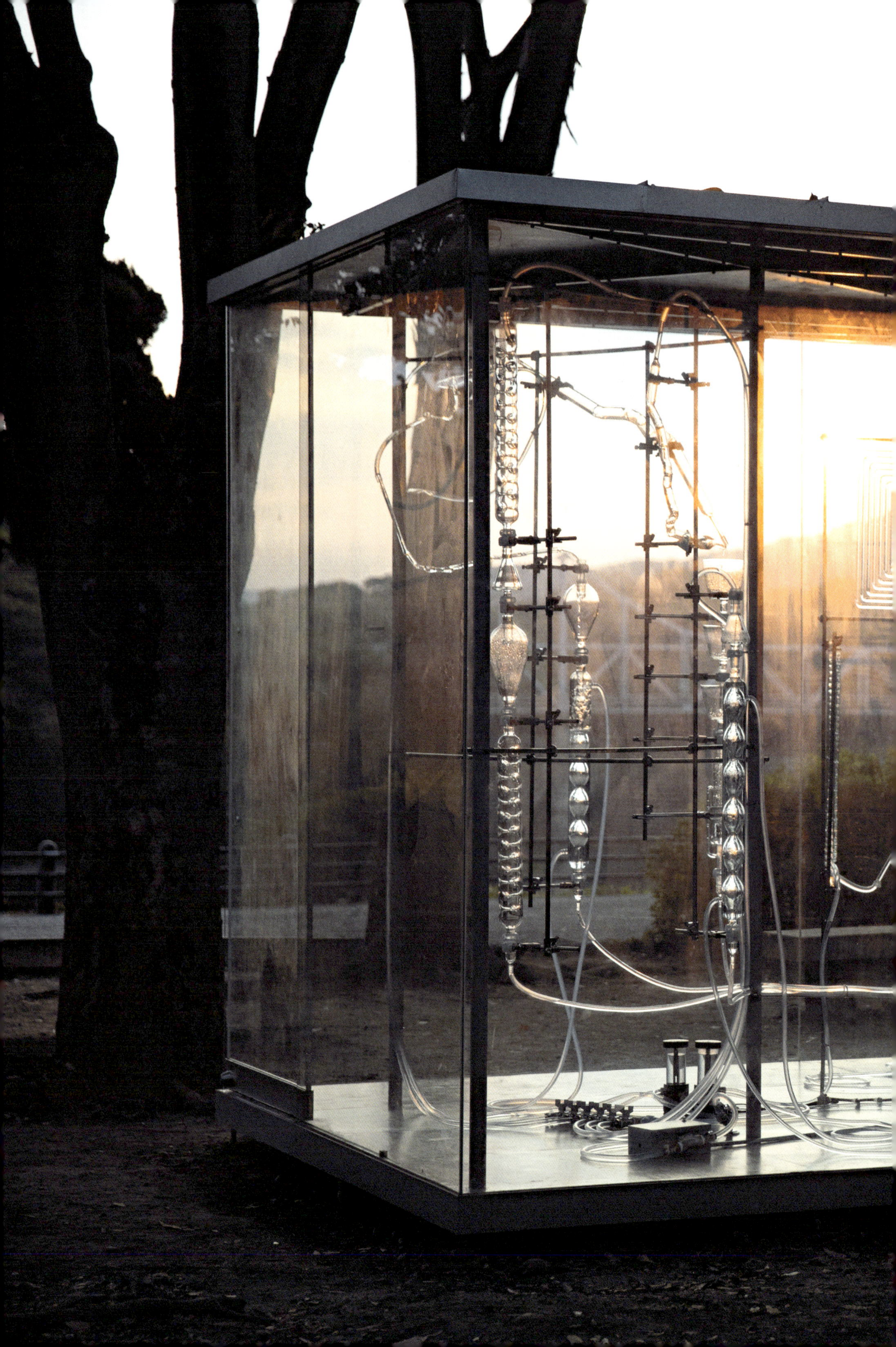

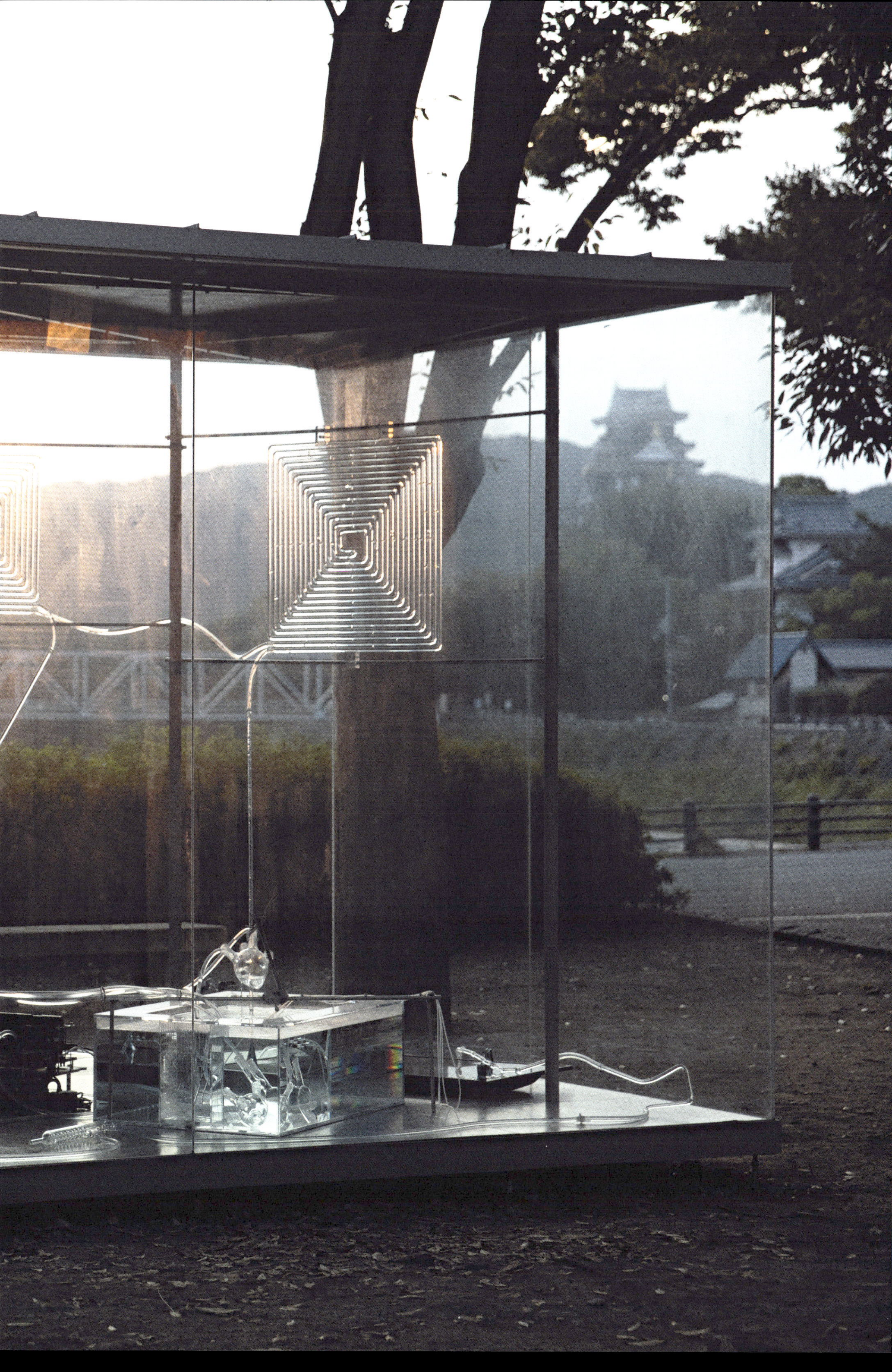

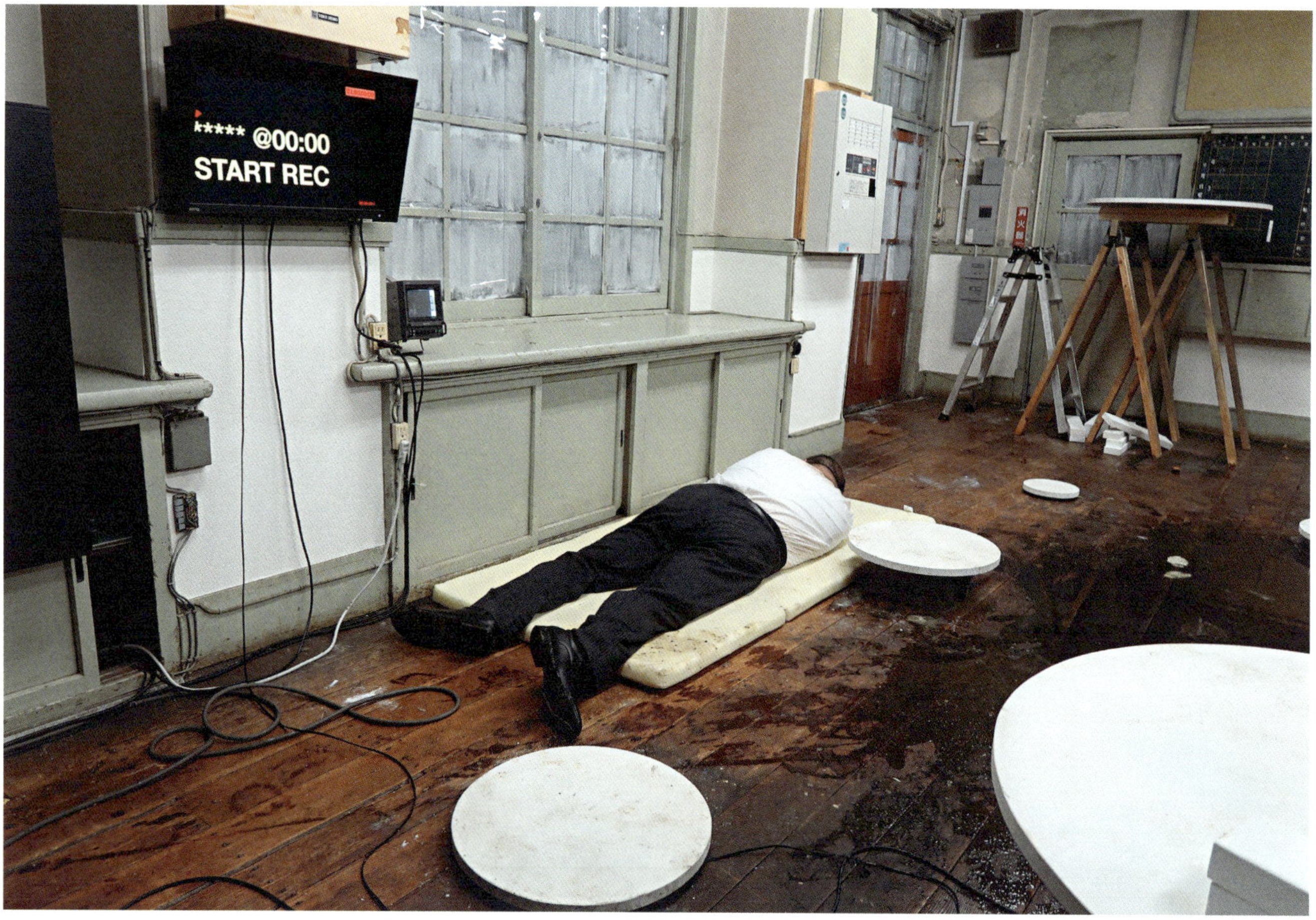

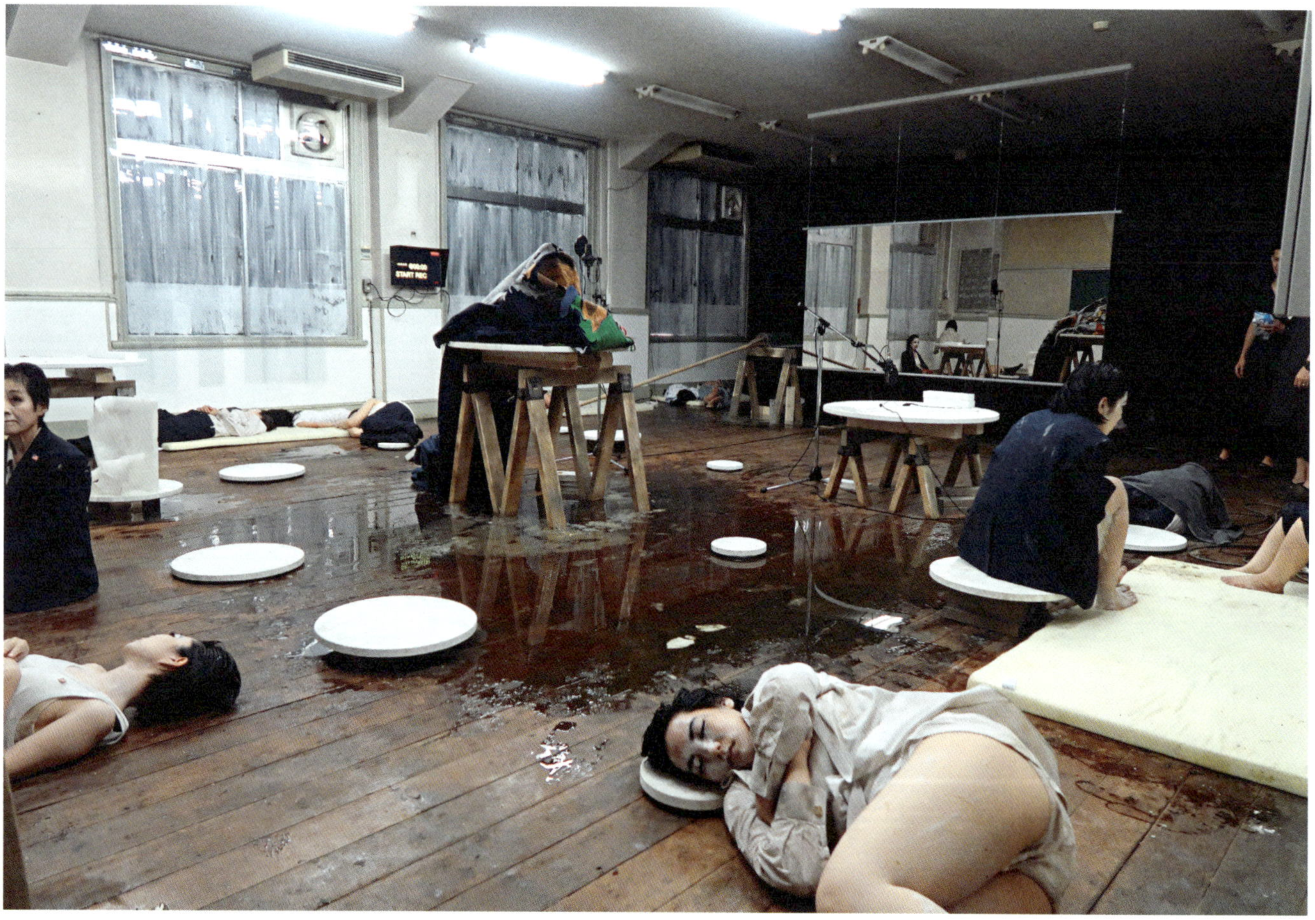

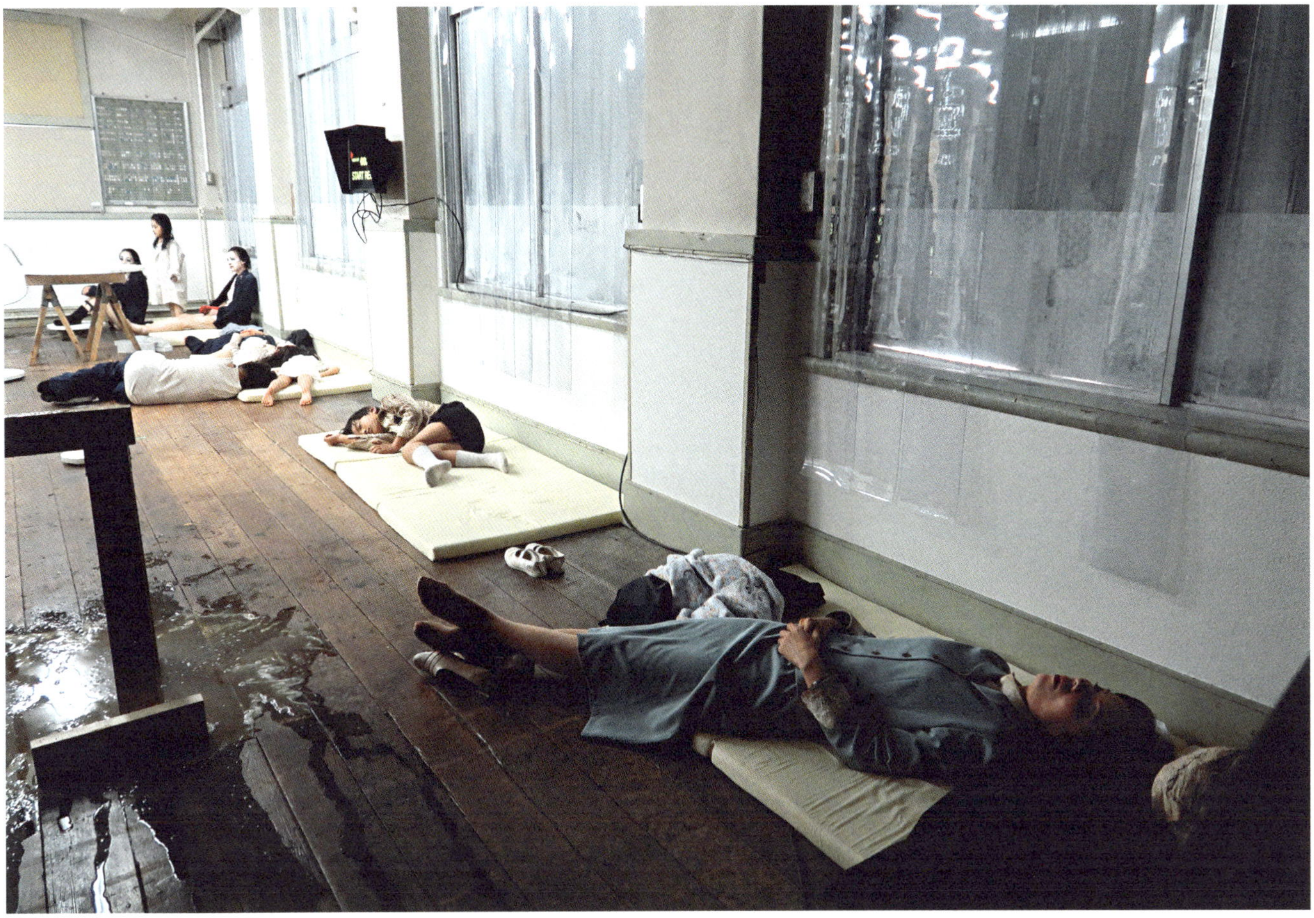

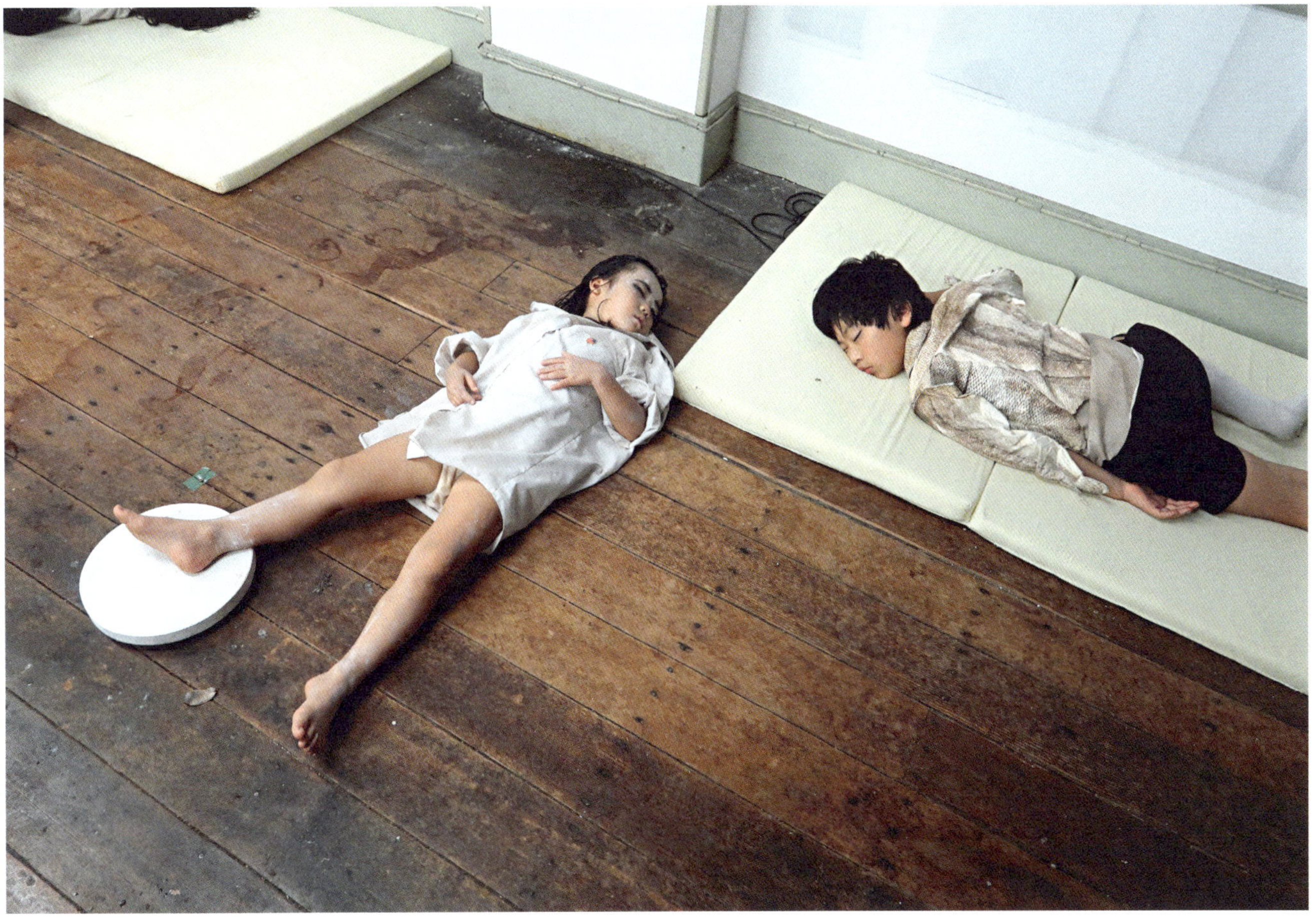

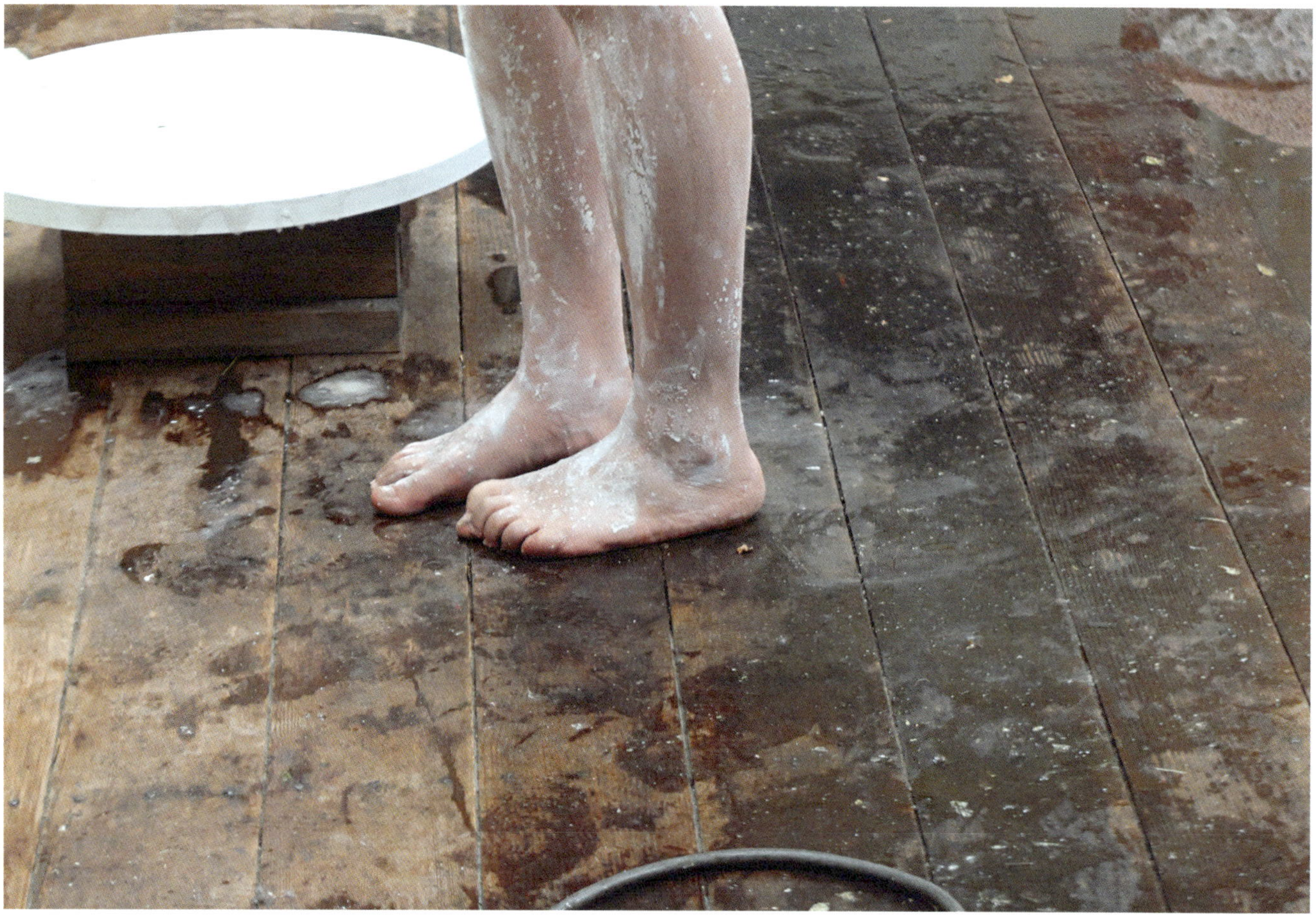

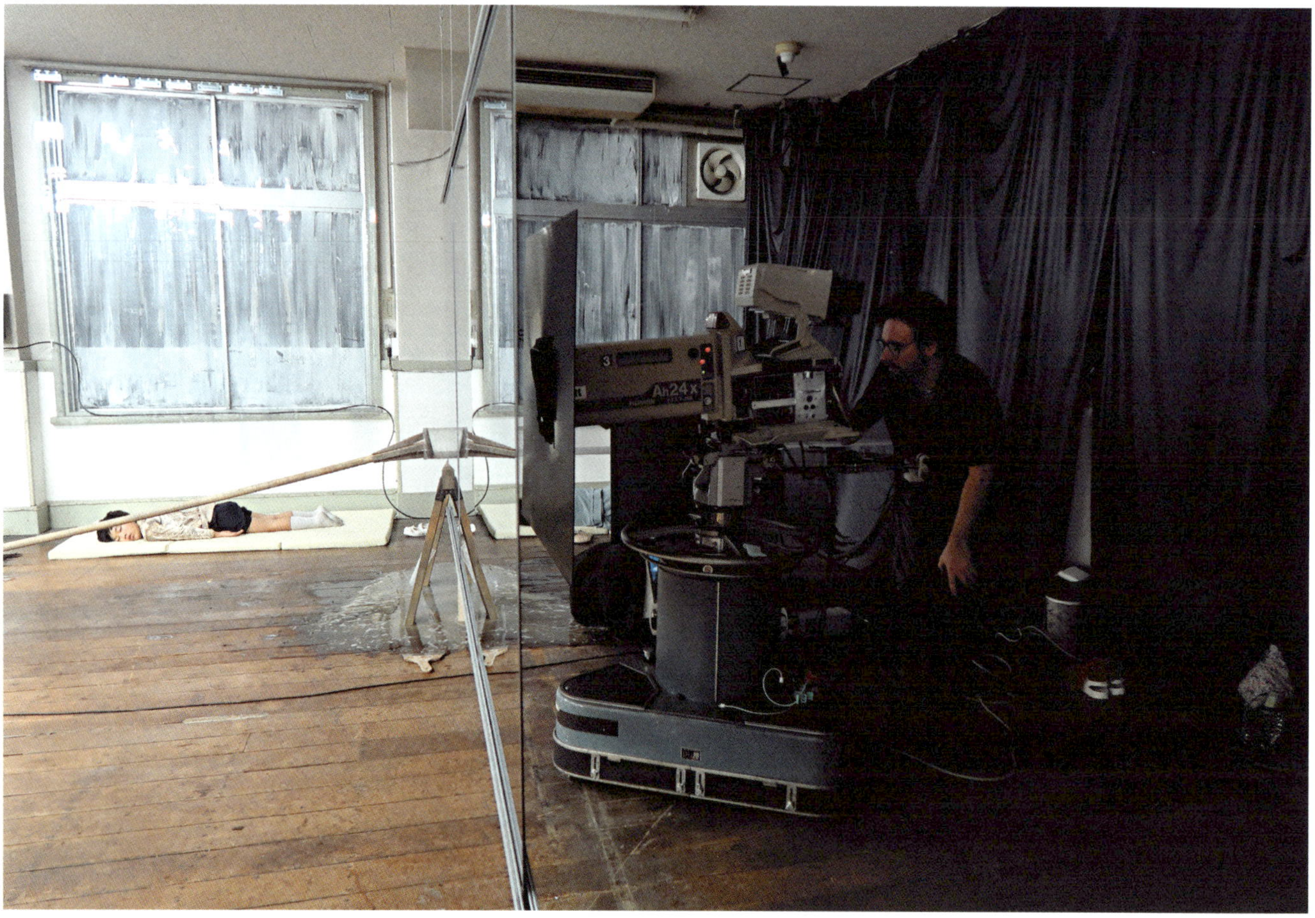

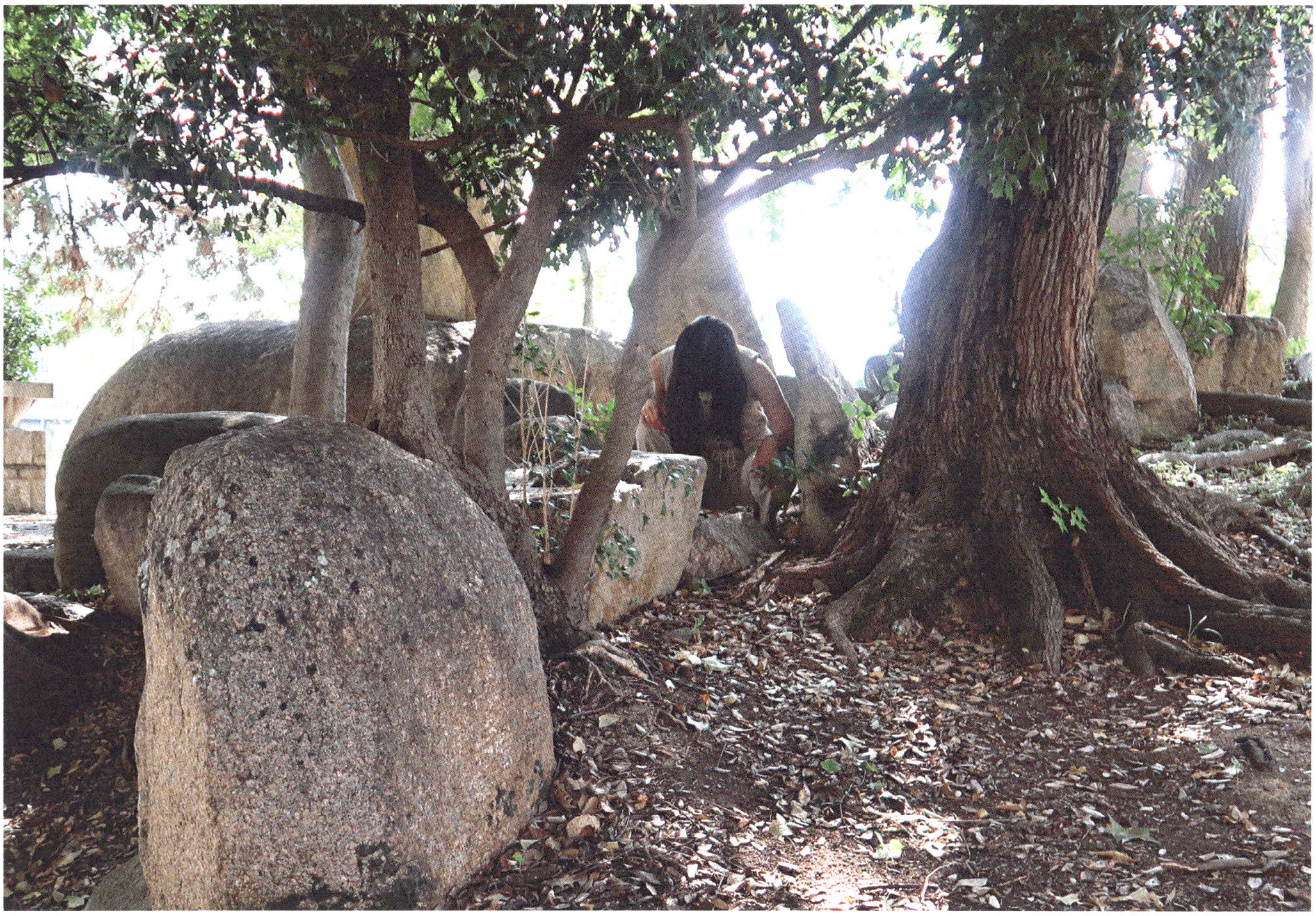

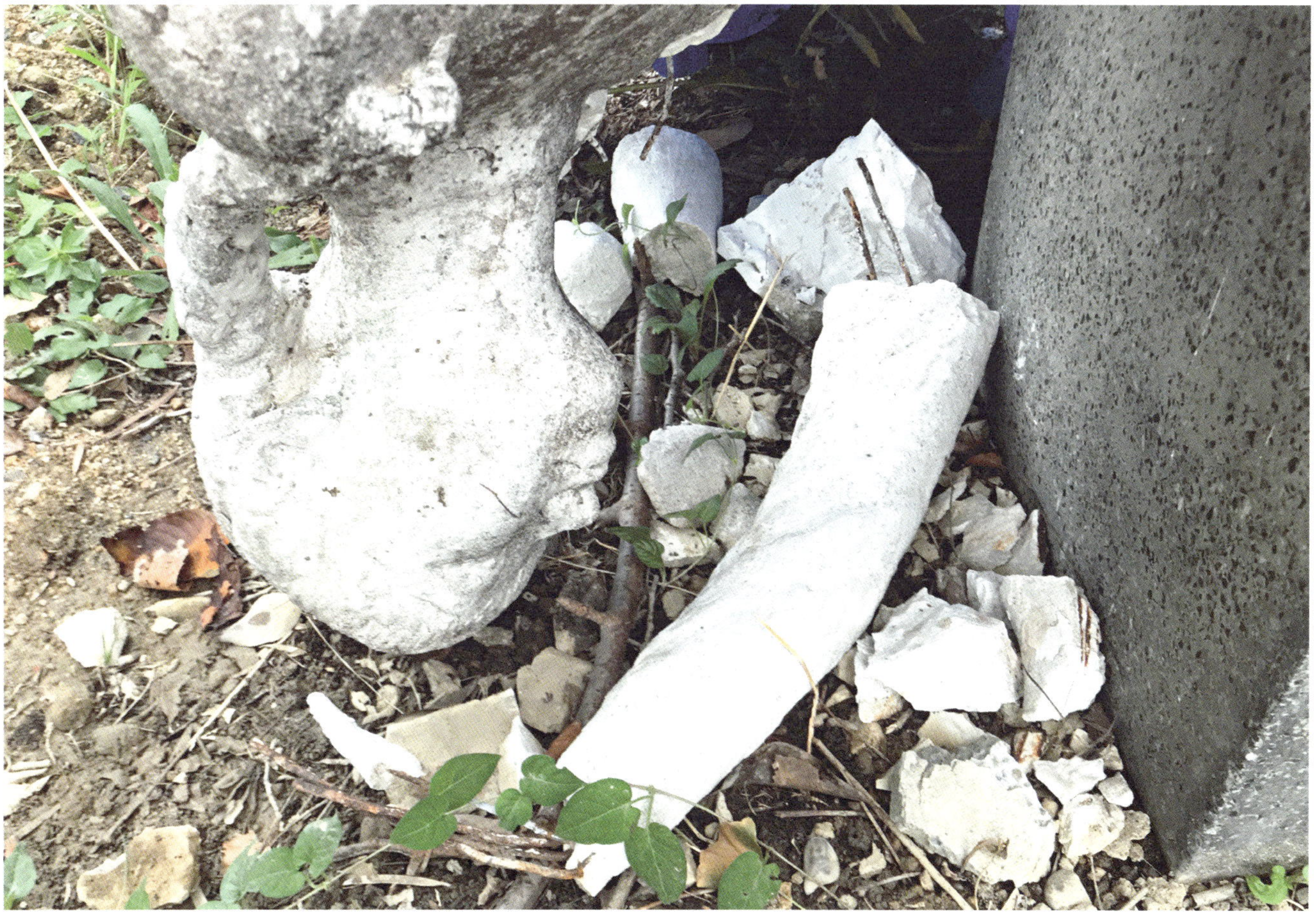

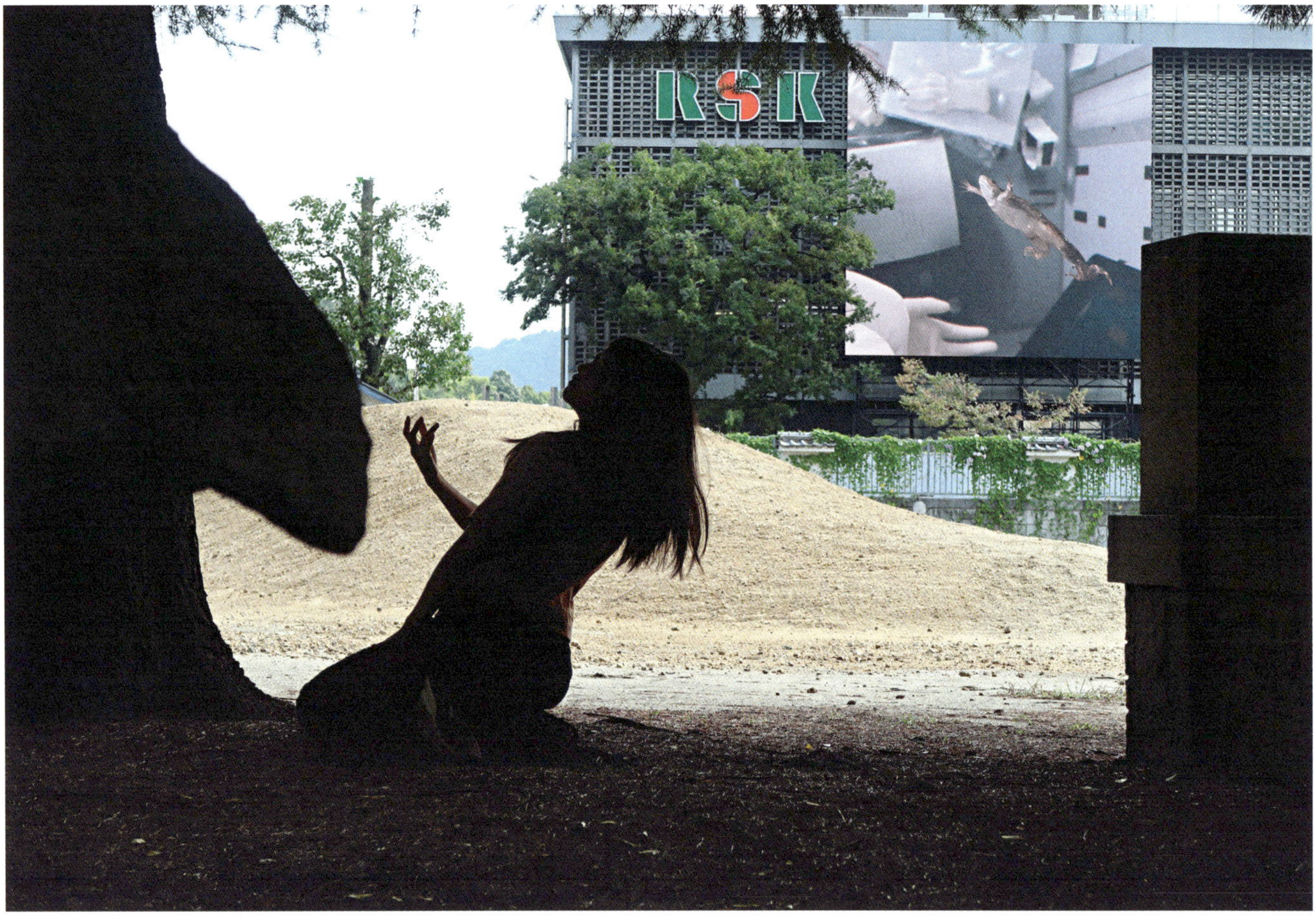

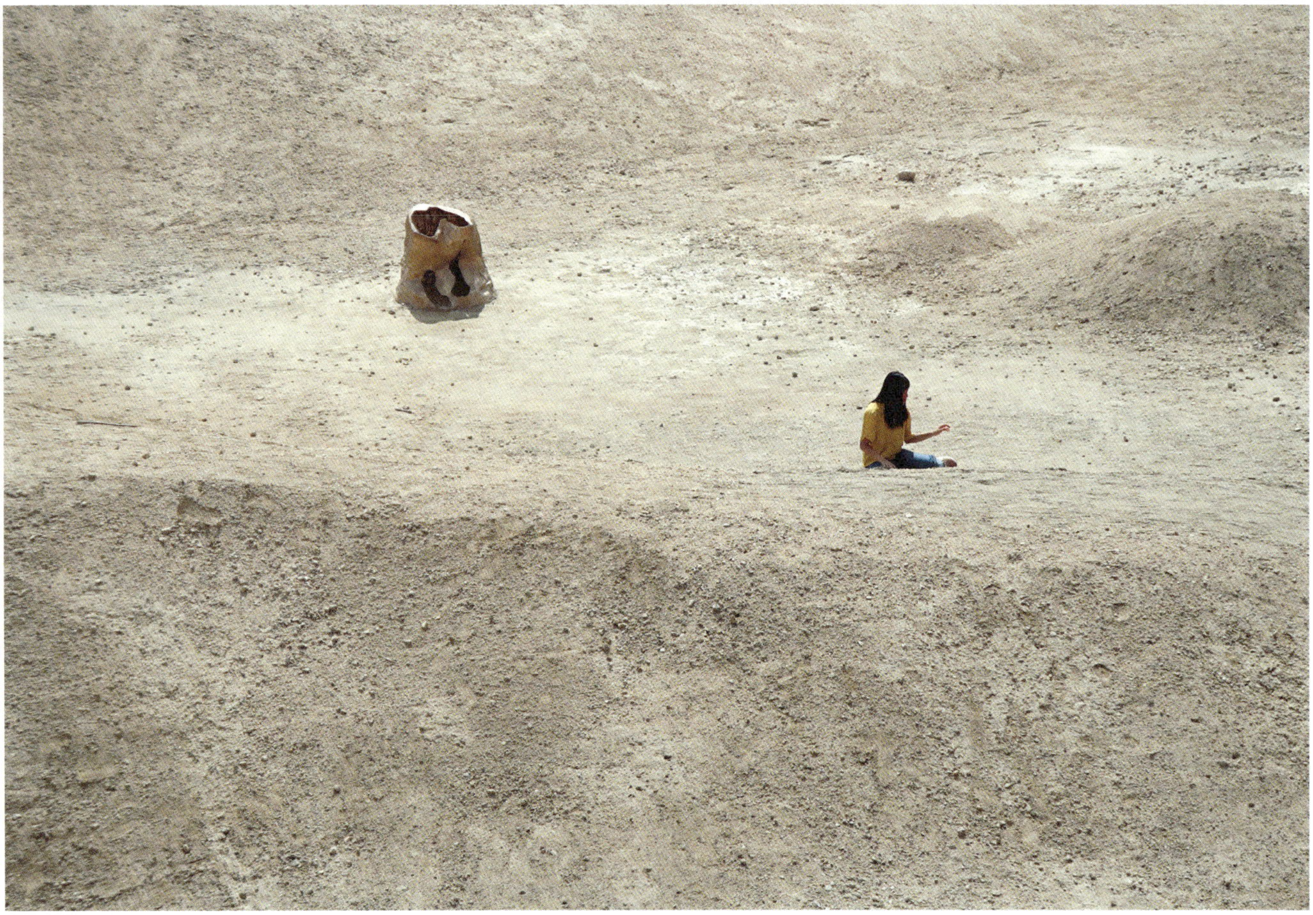

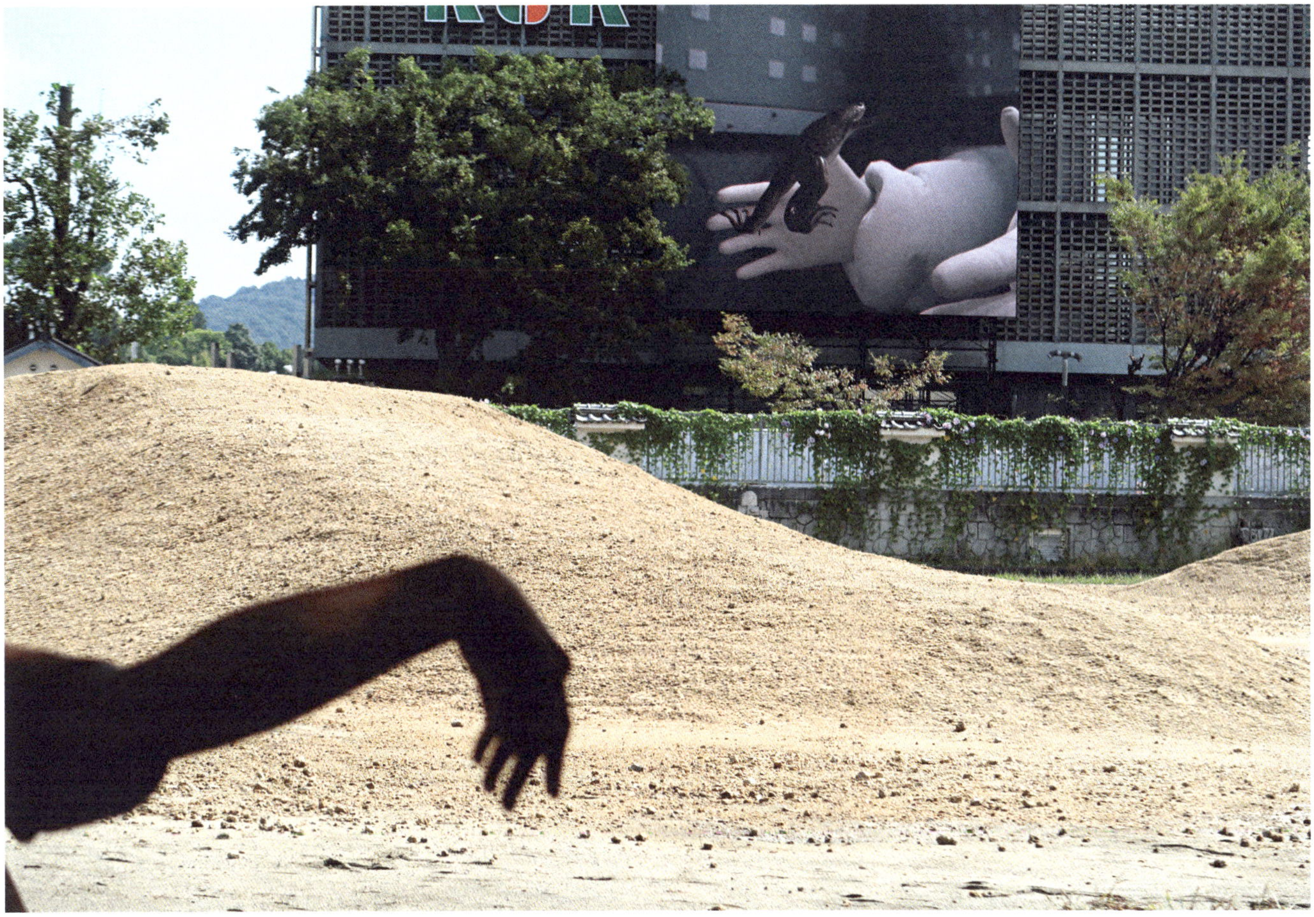

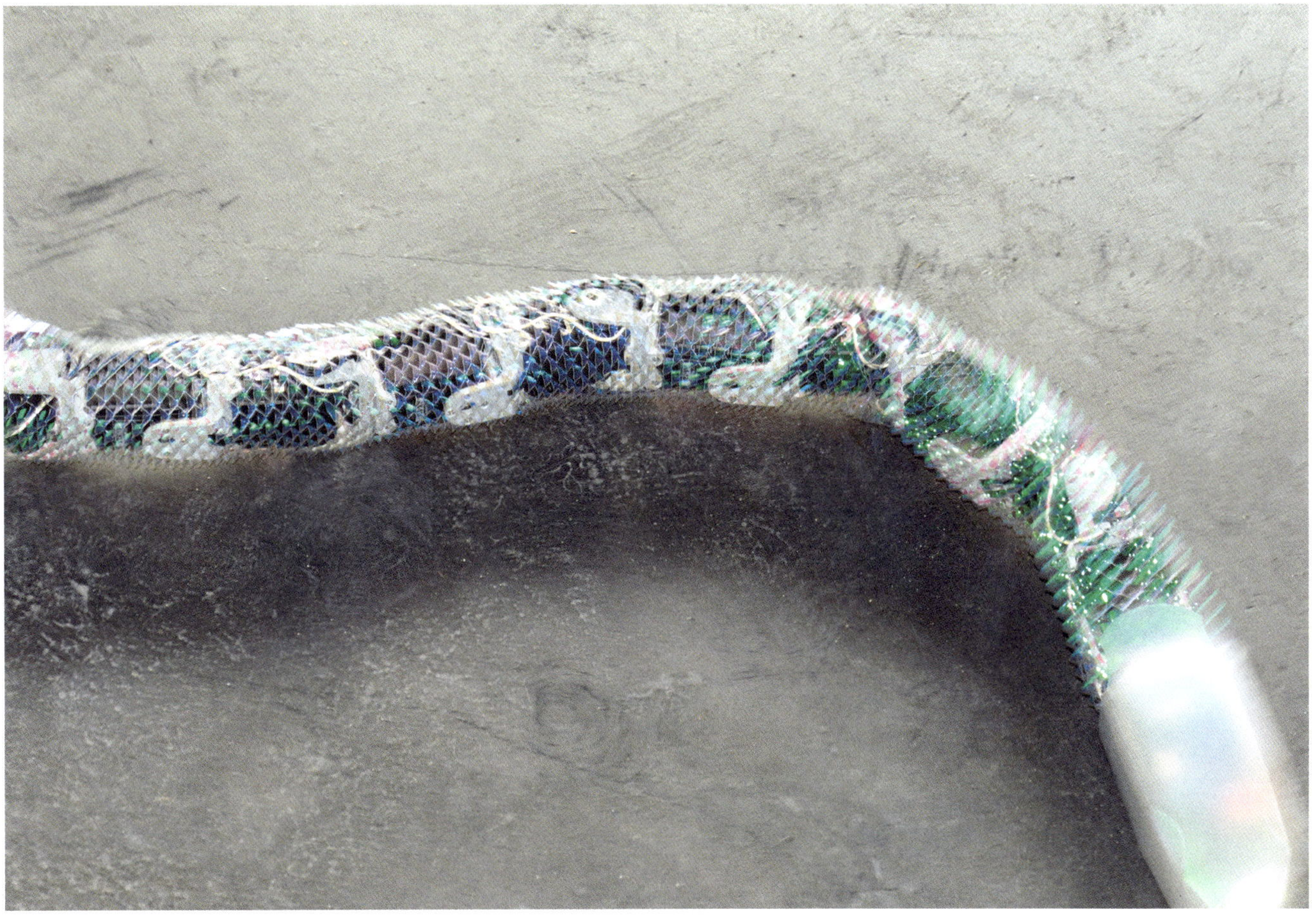

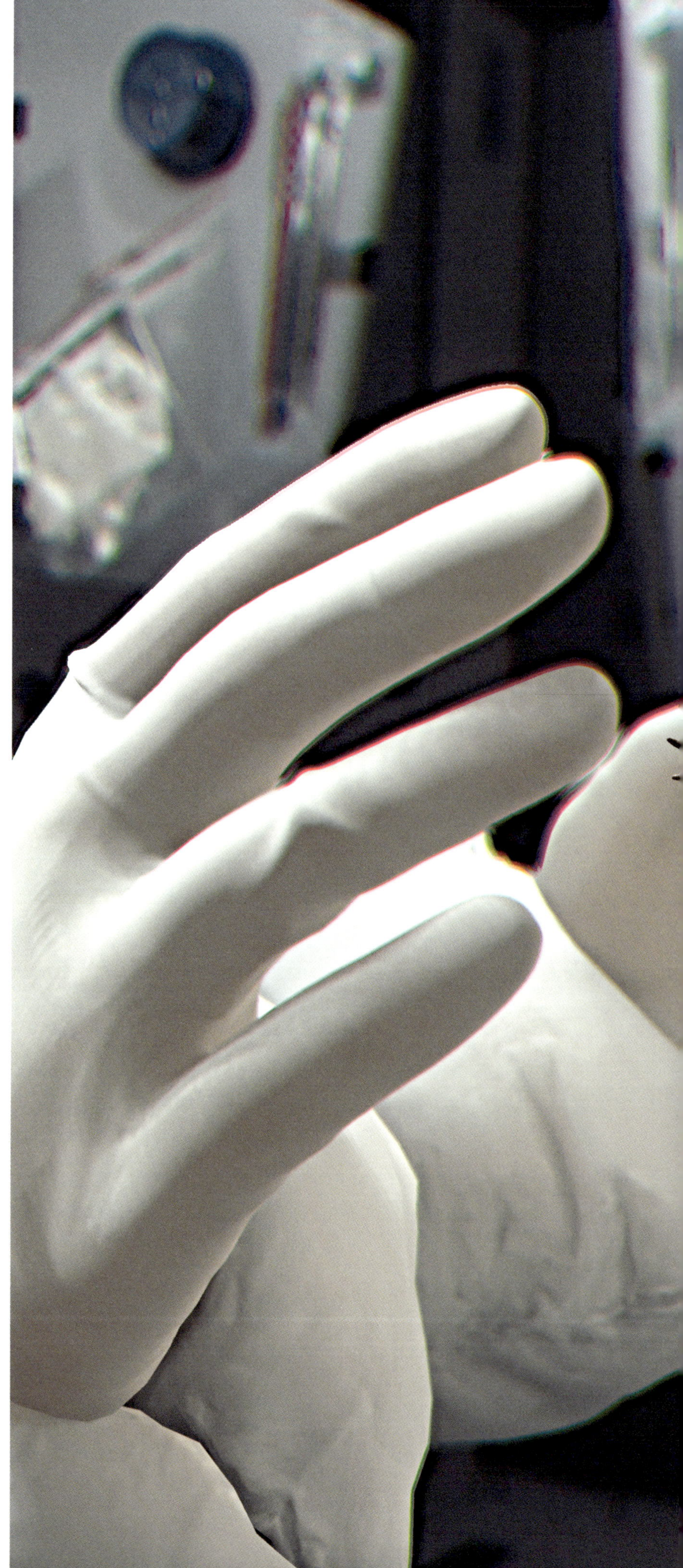

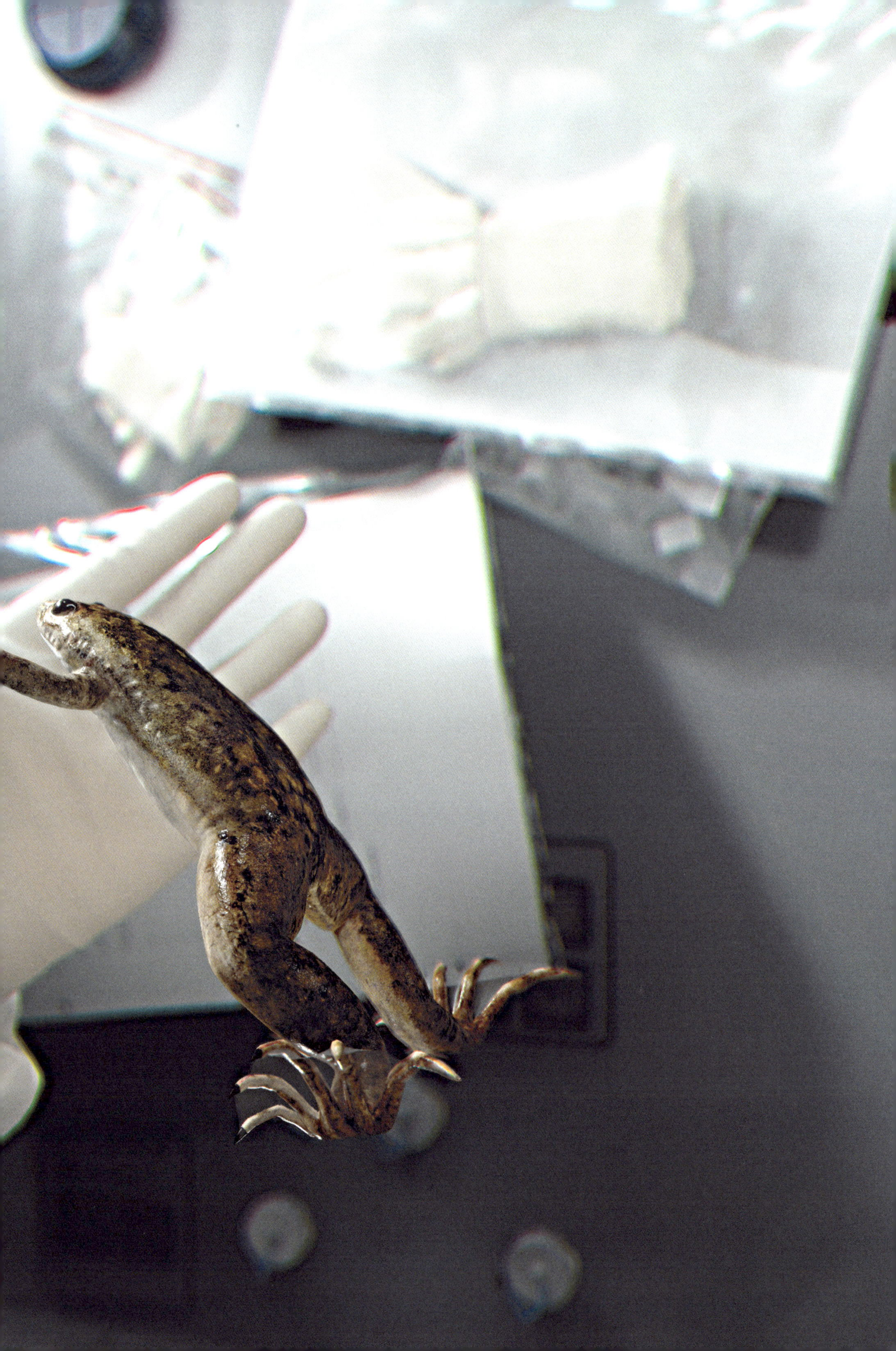

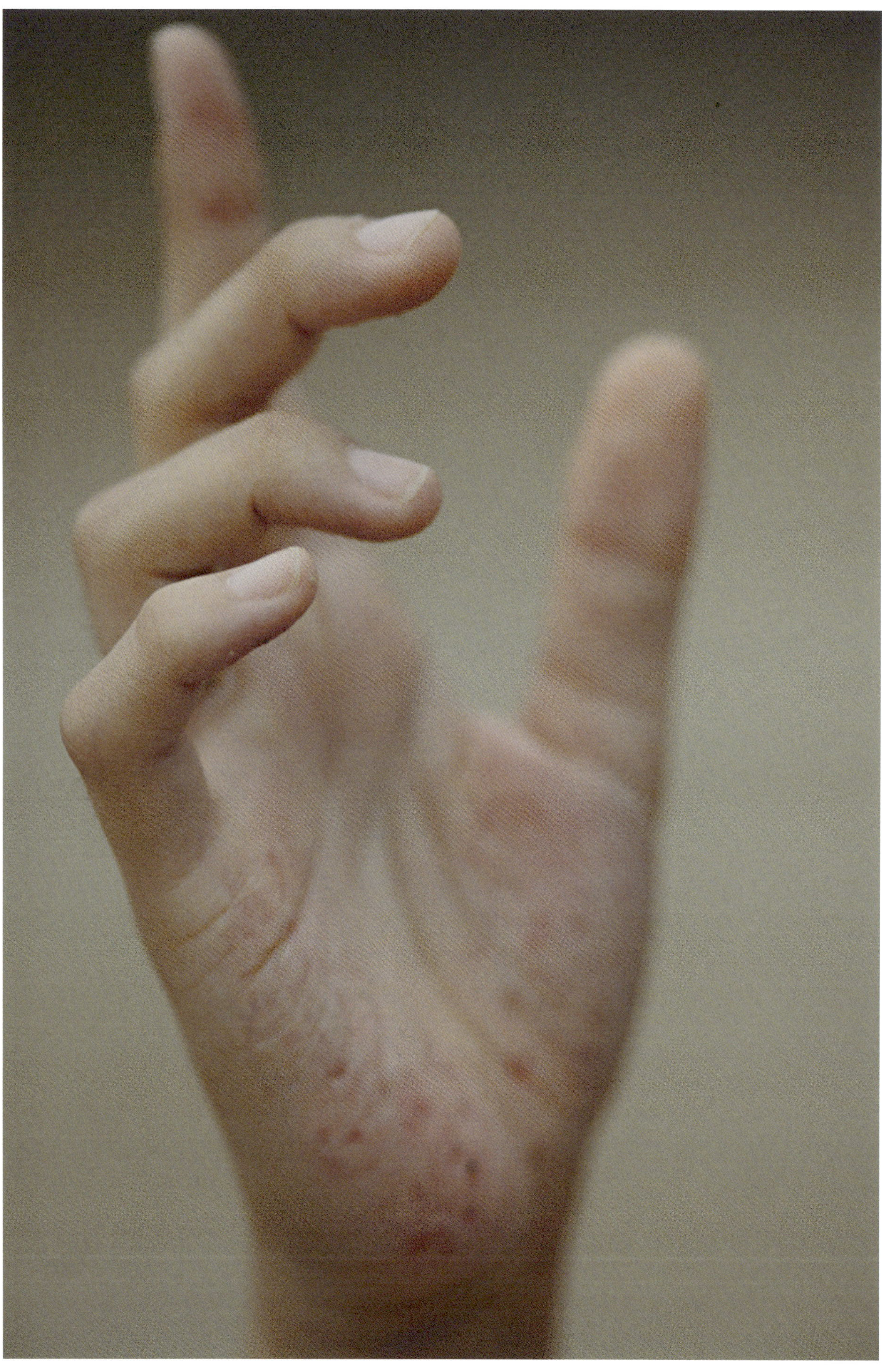

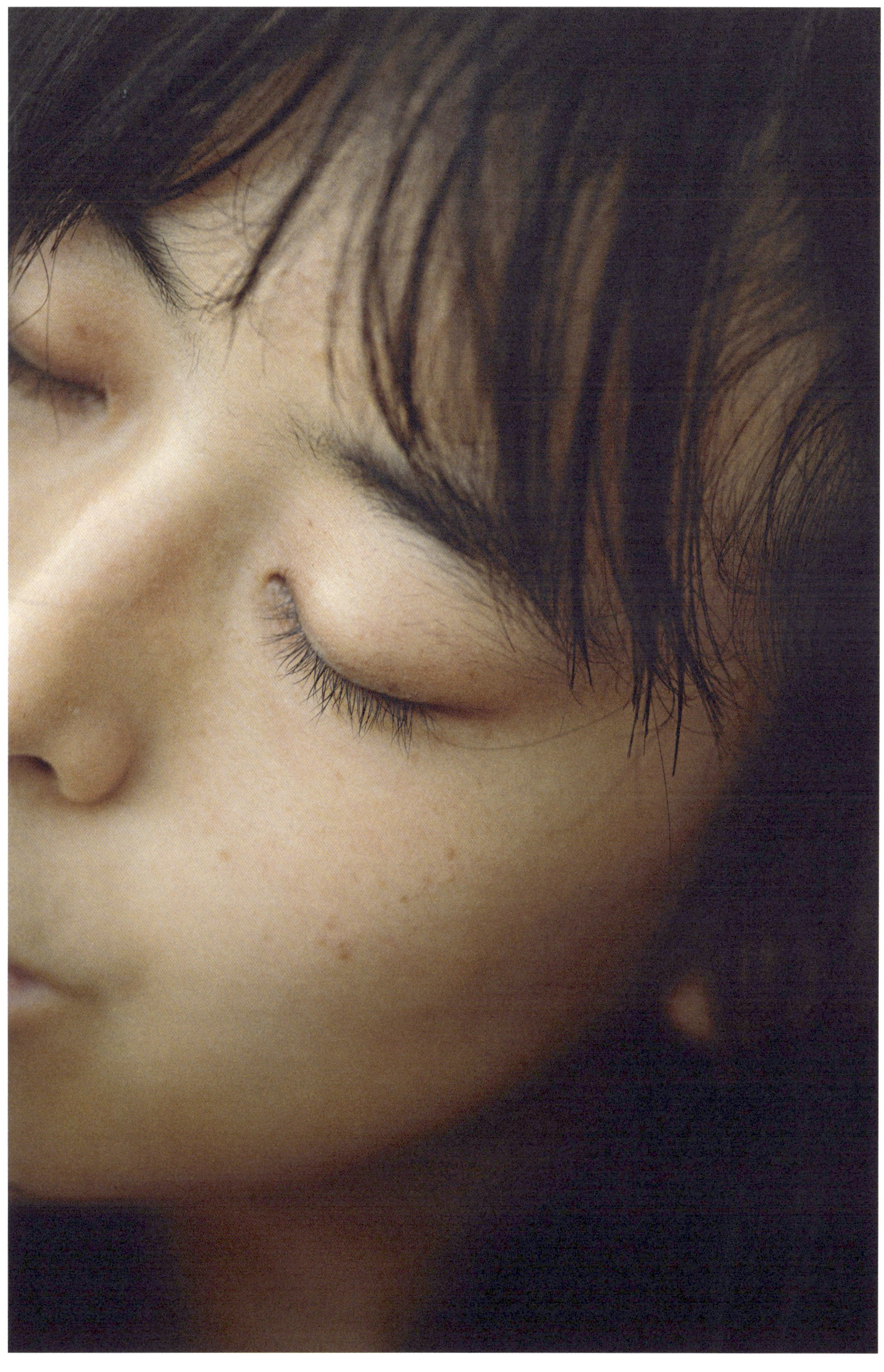

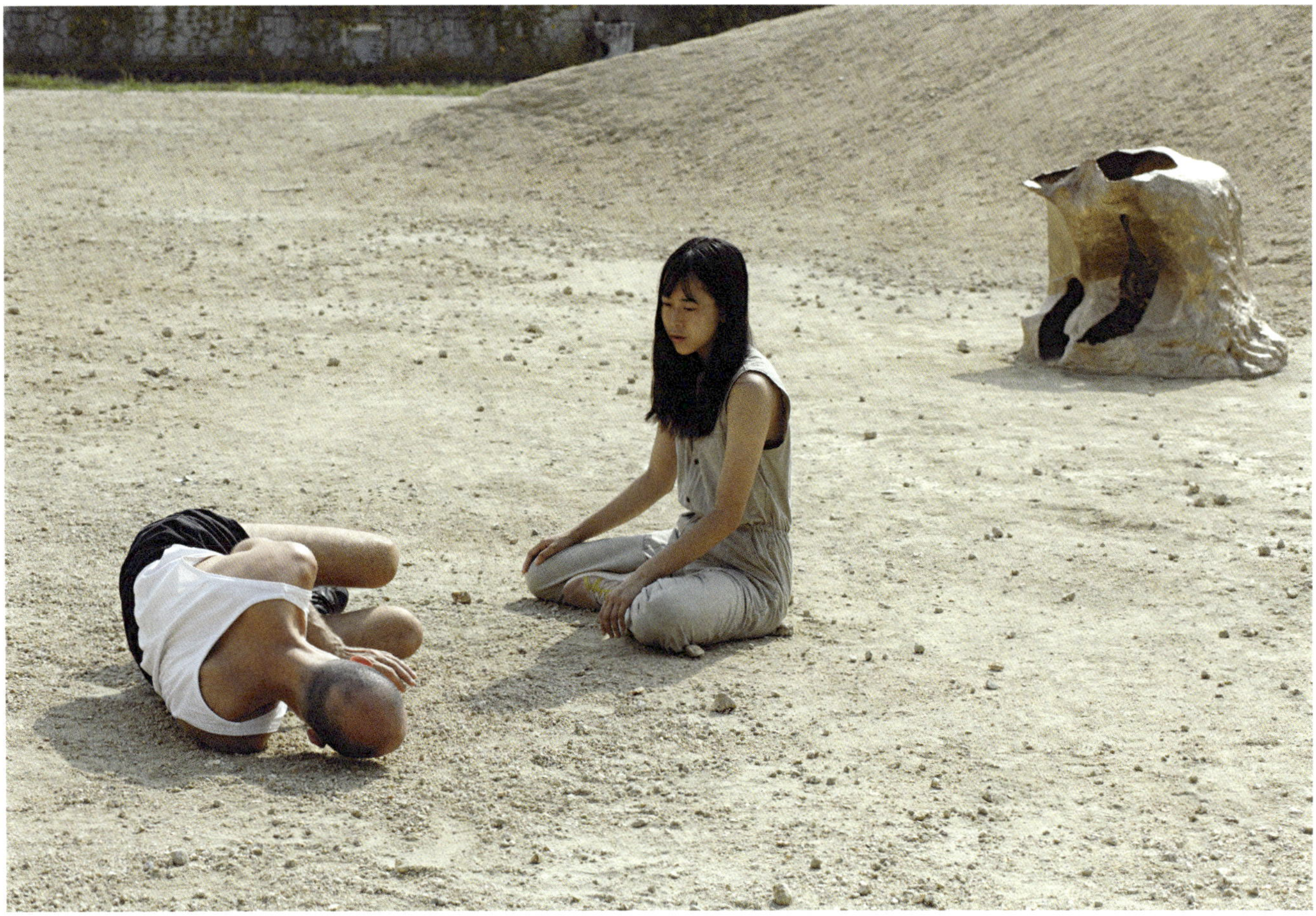

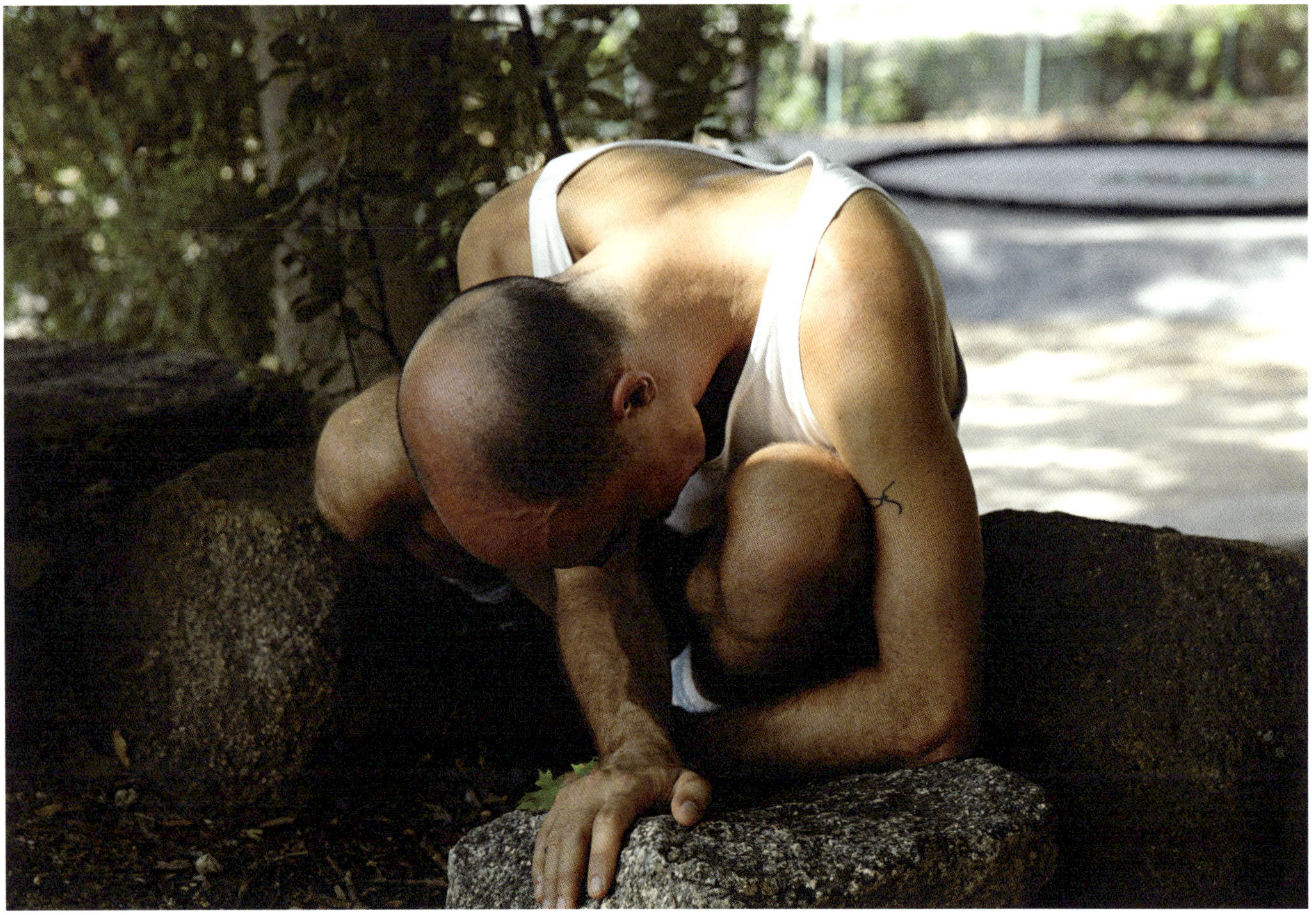

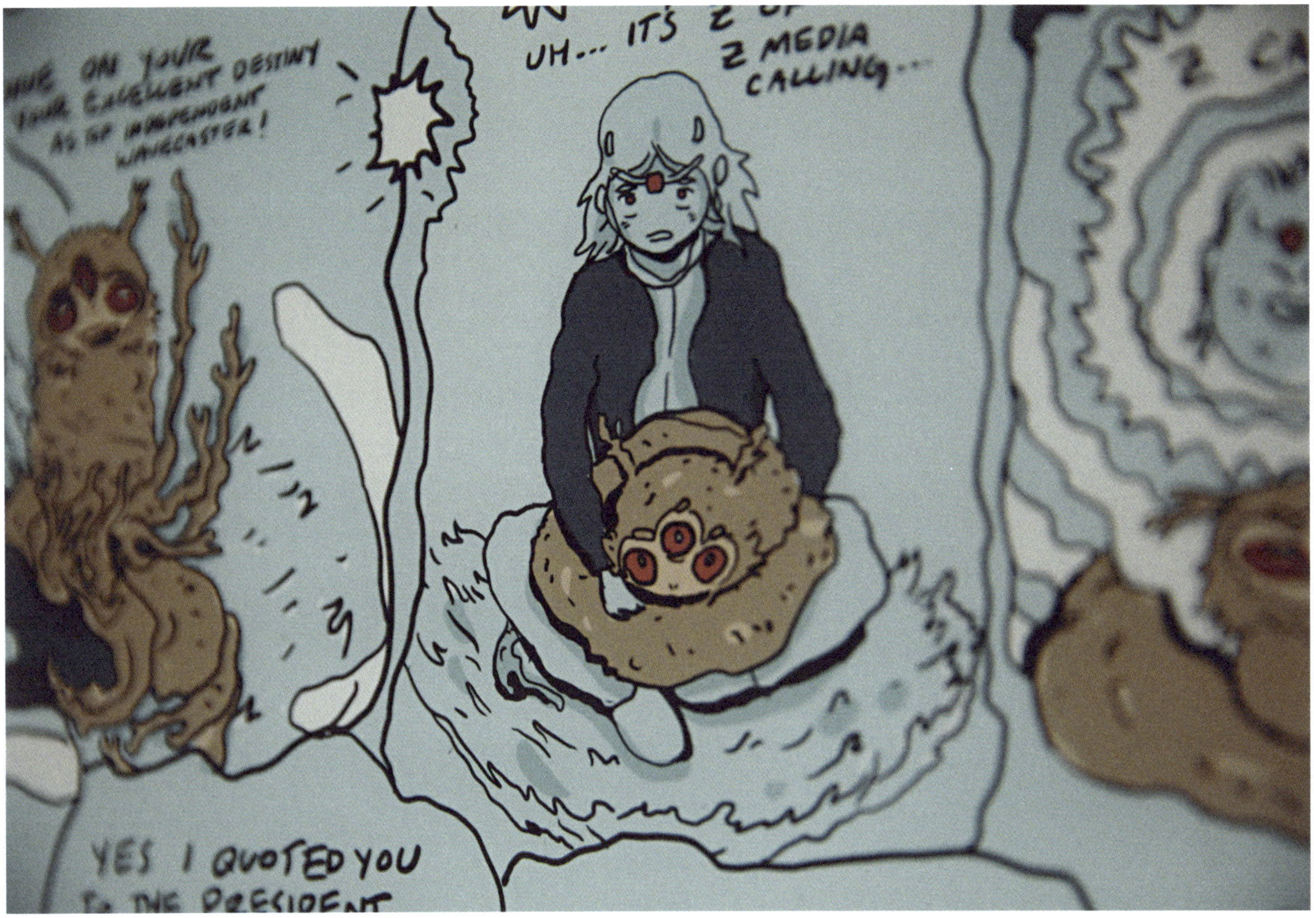

Z MEDIA
CALLING...
YES I QUOTED YOU

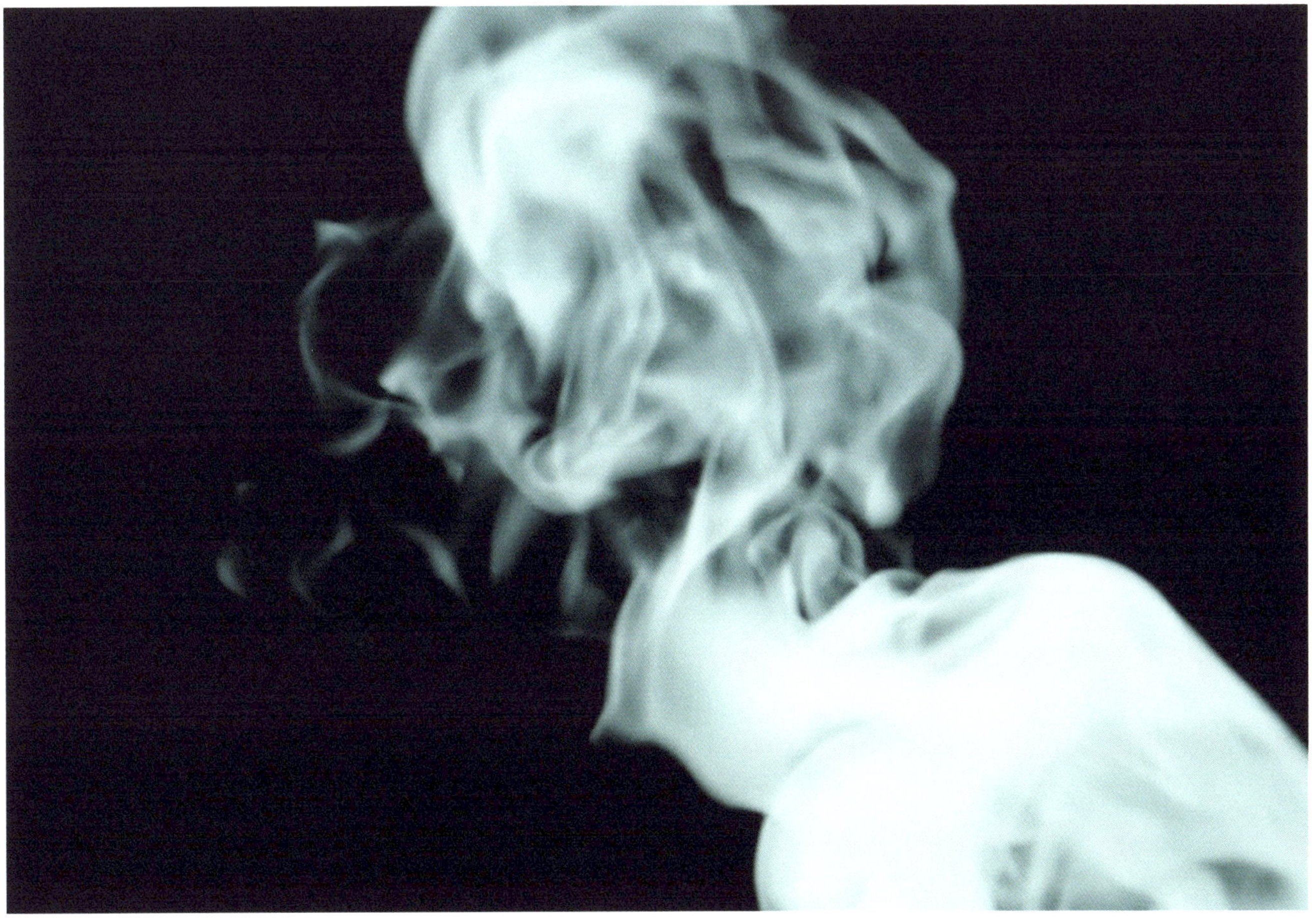

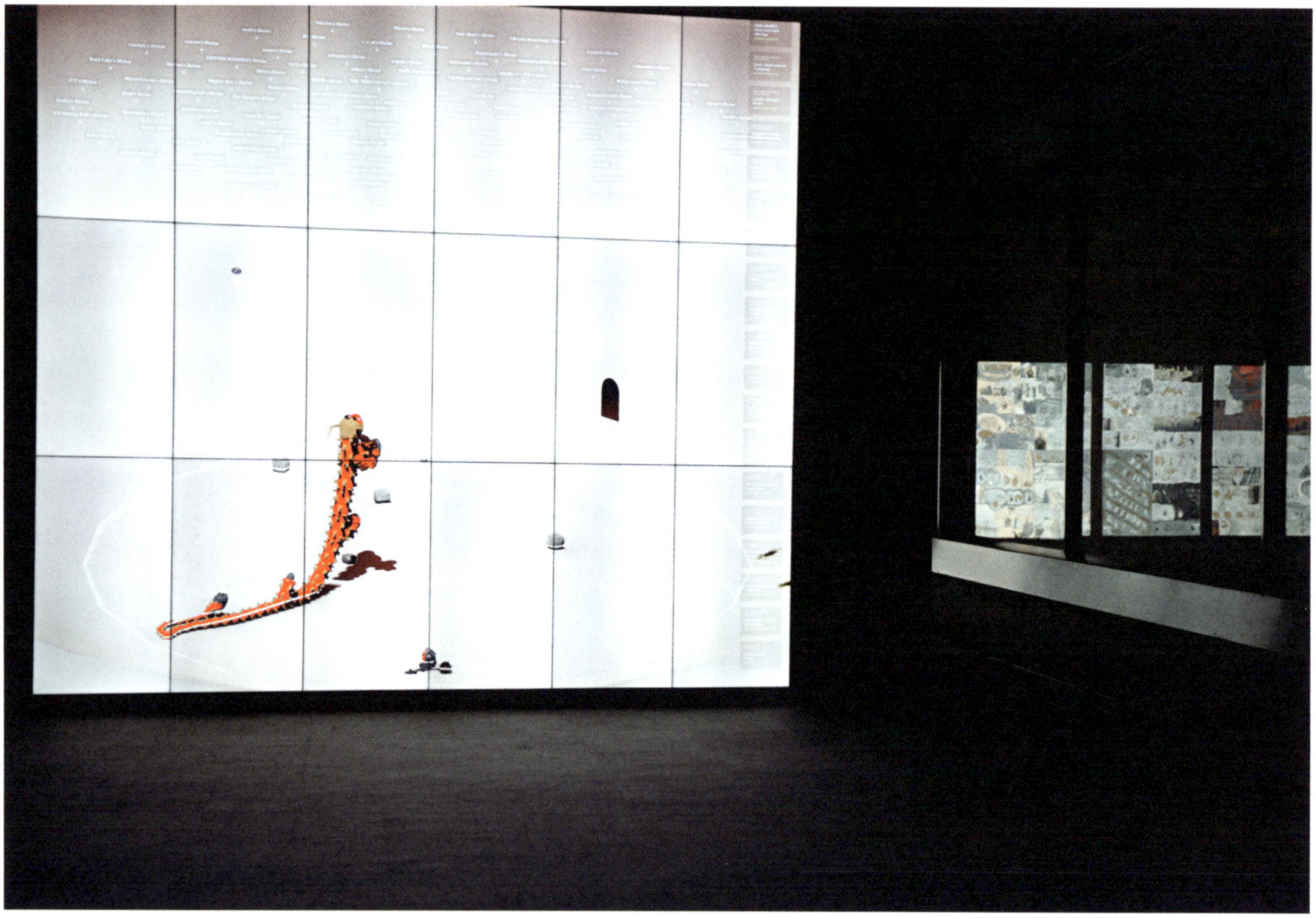

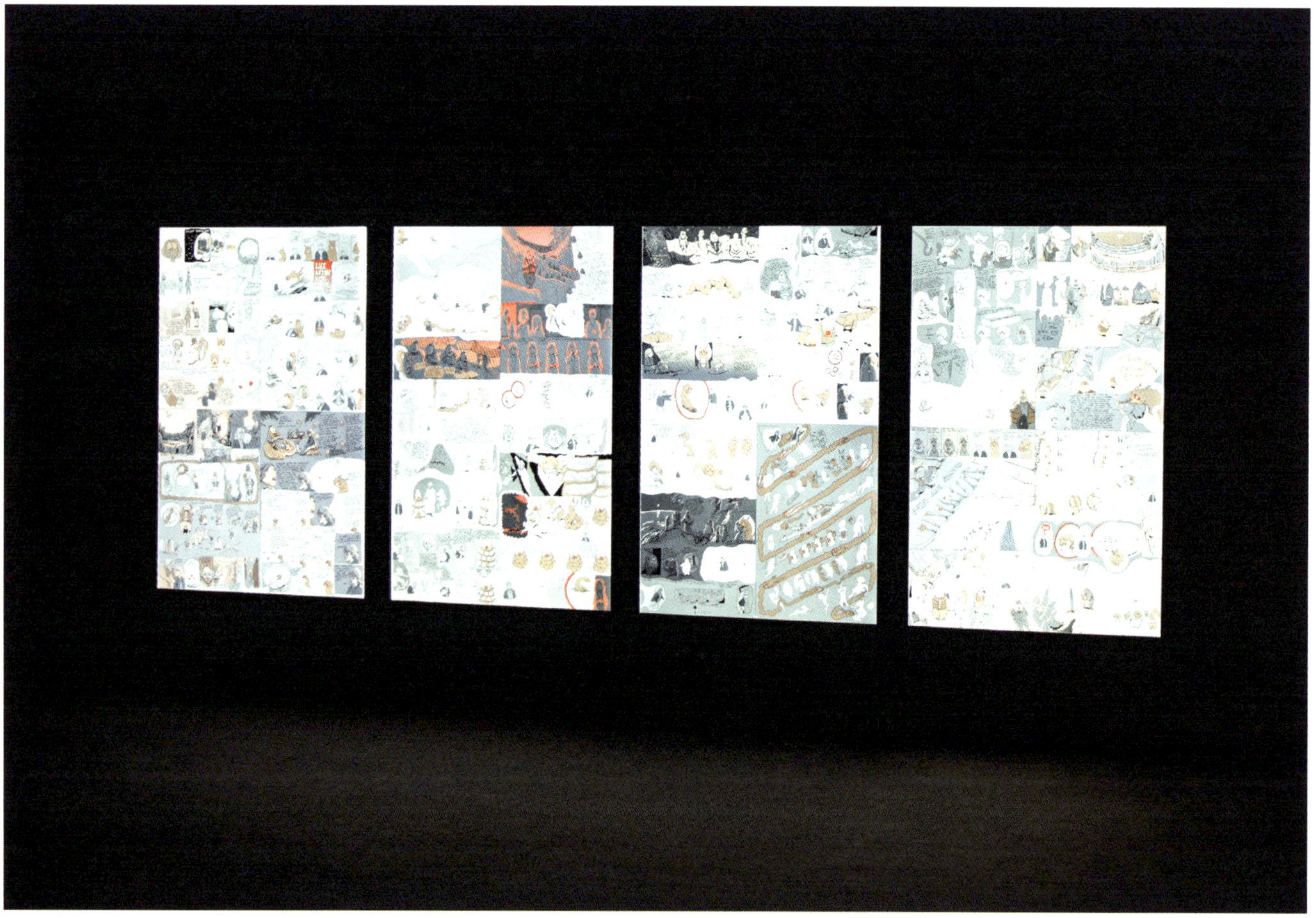

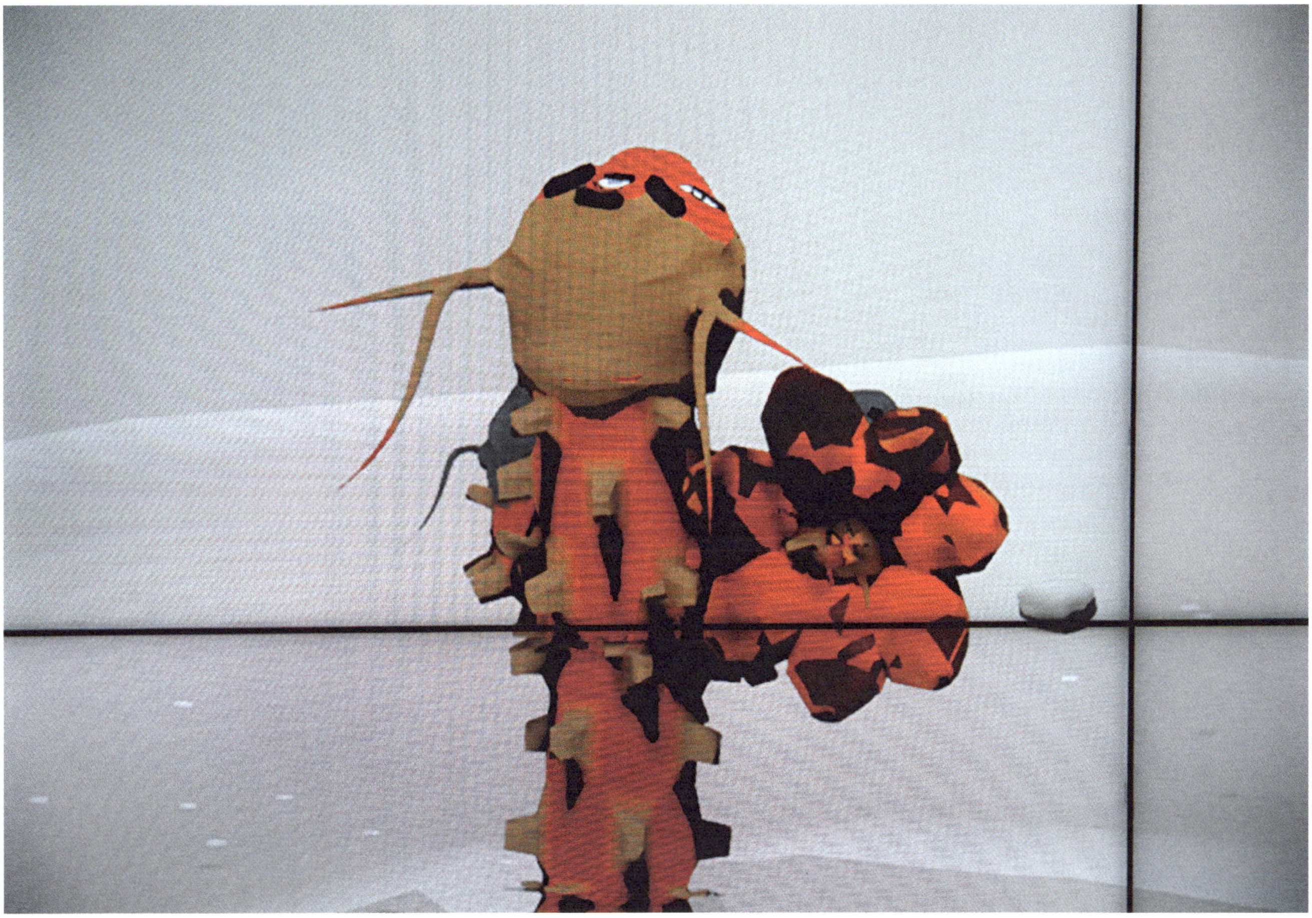

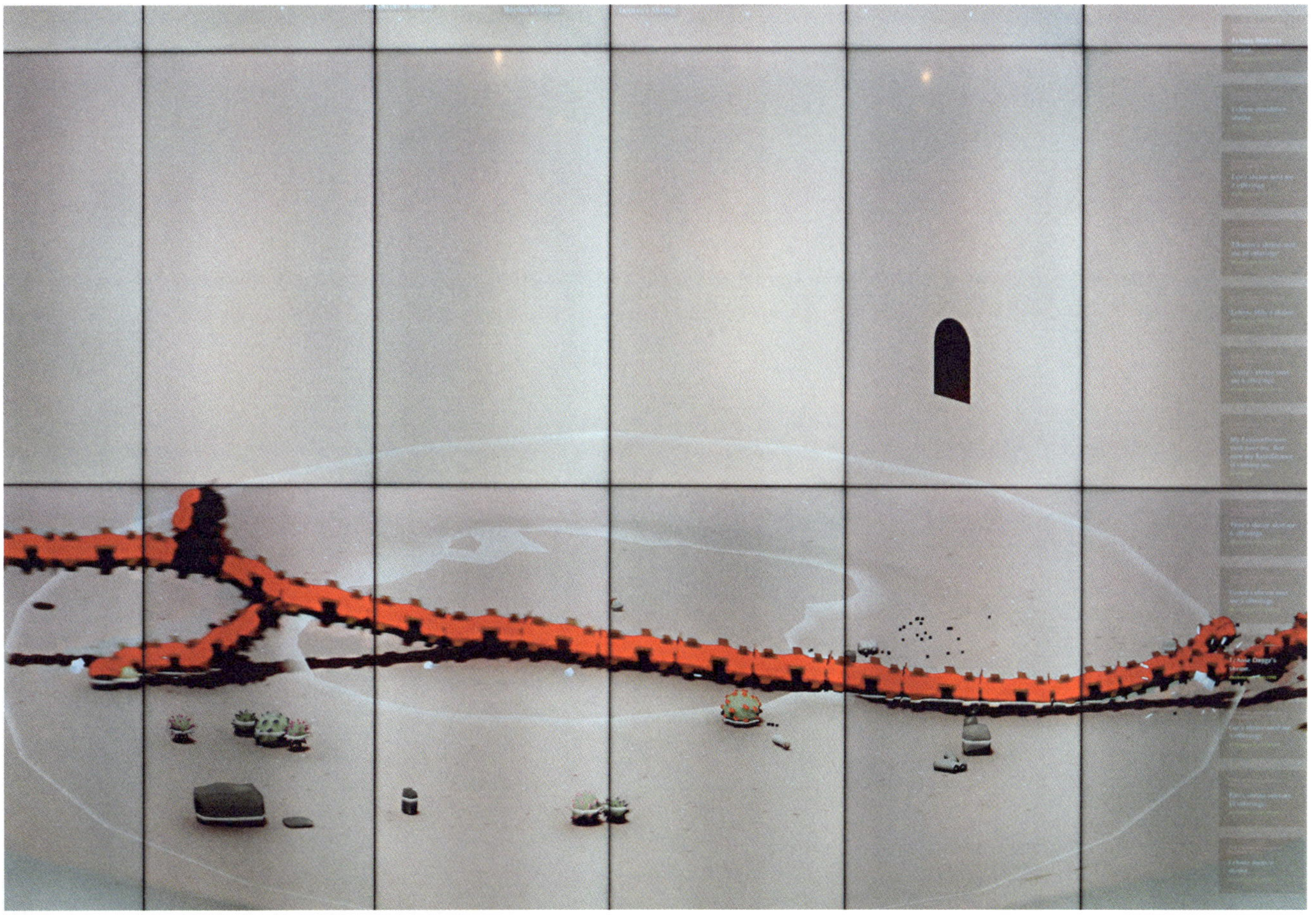

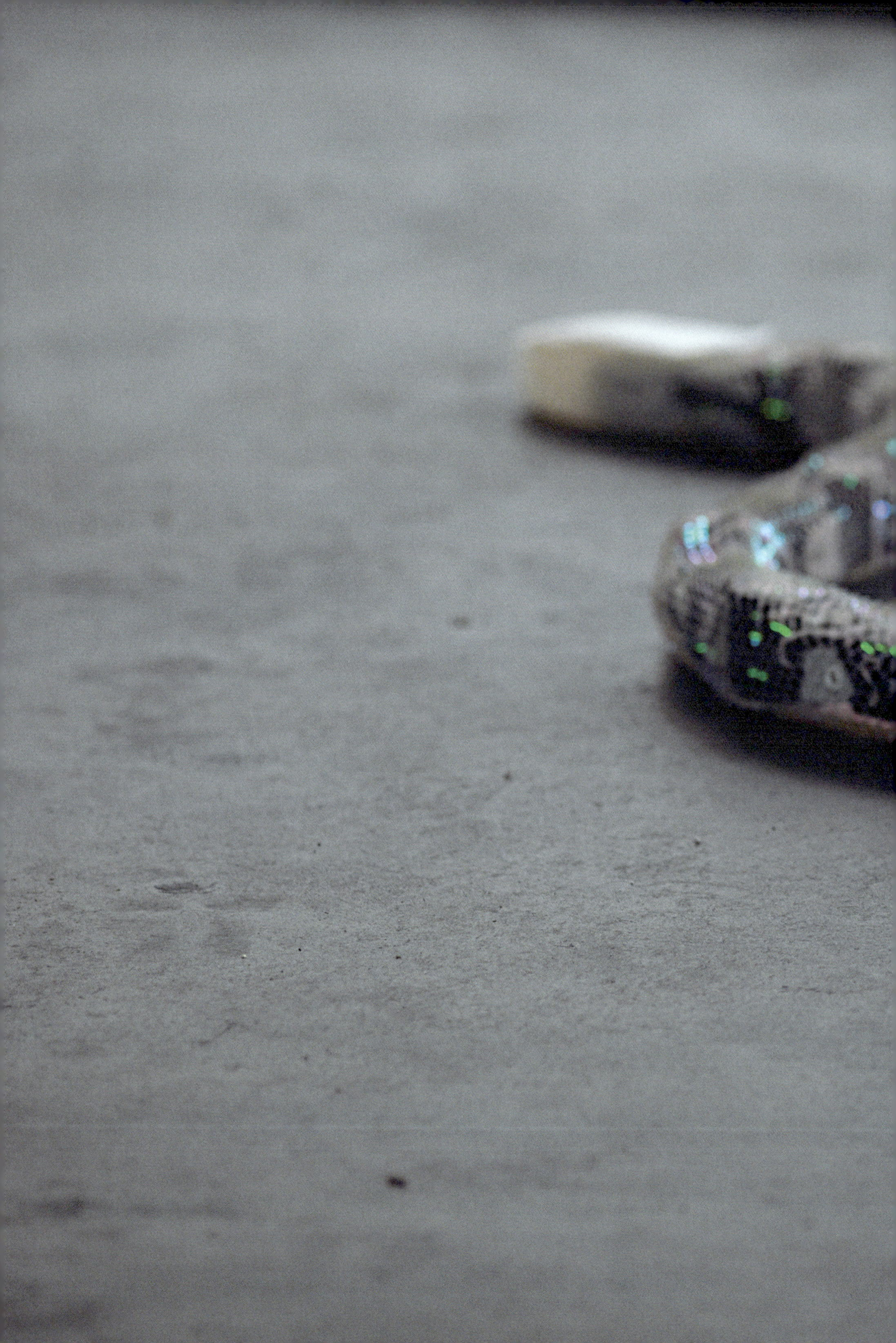

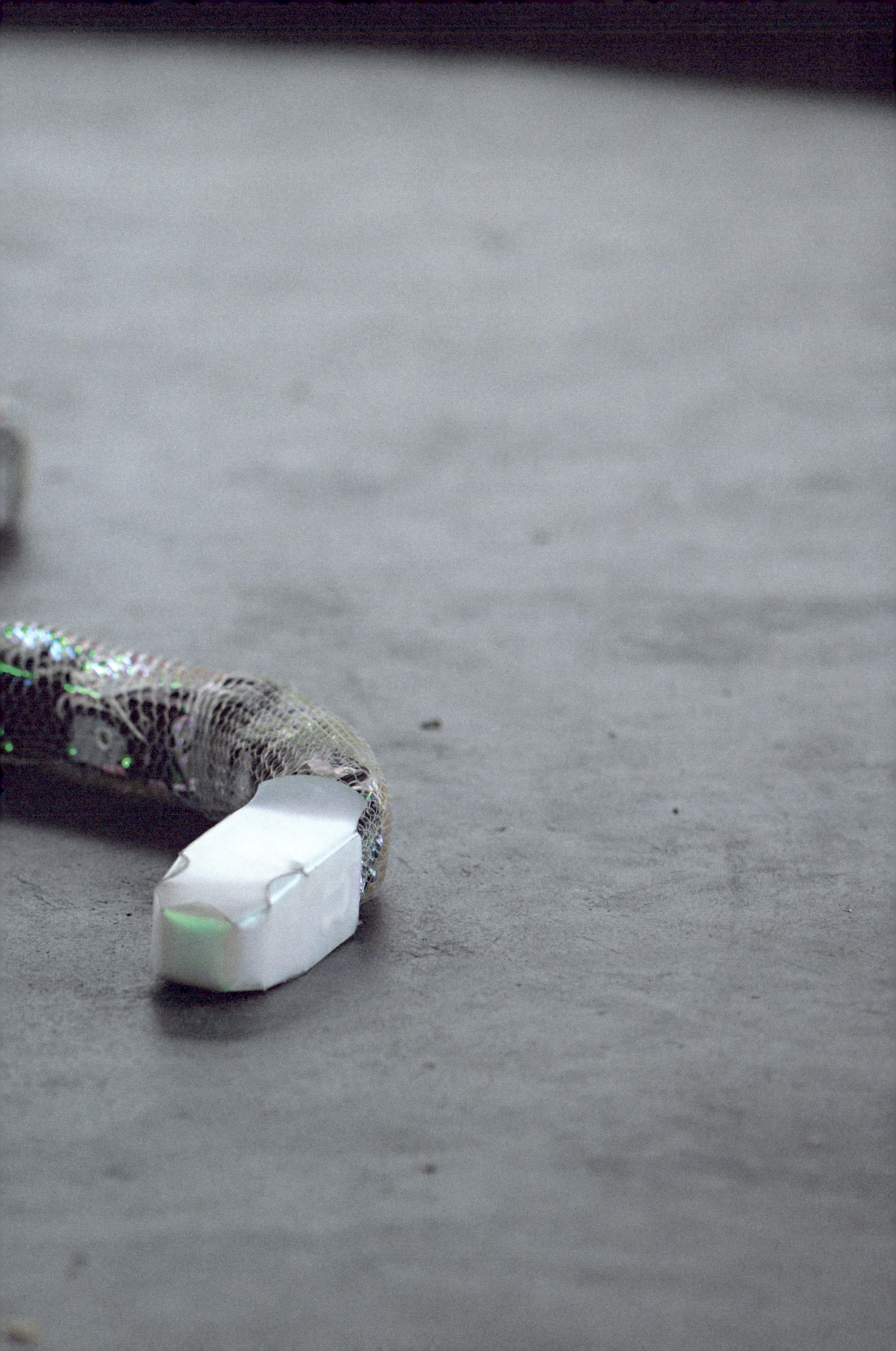

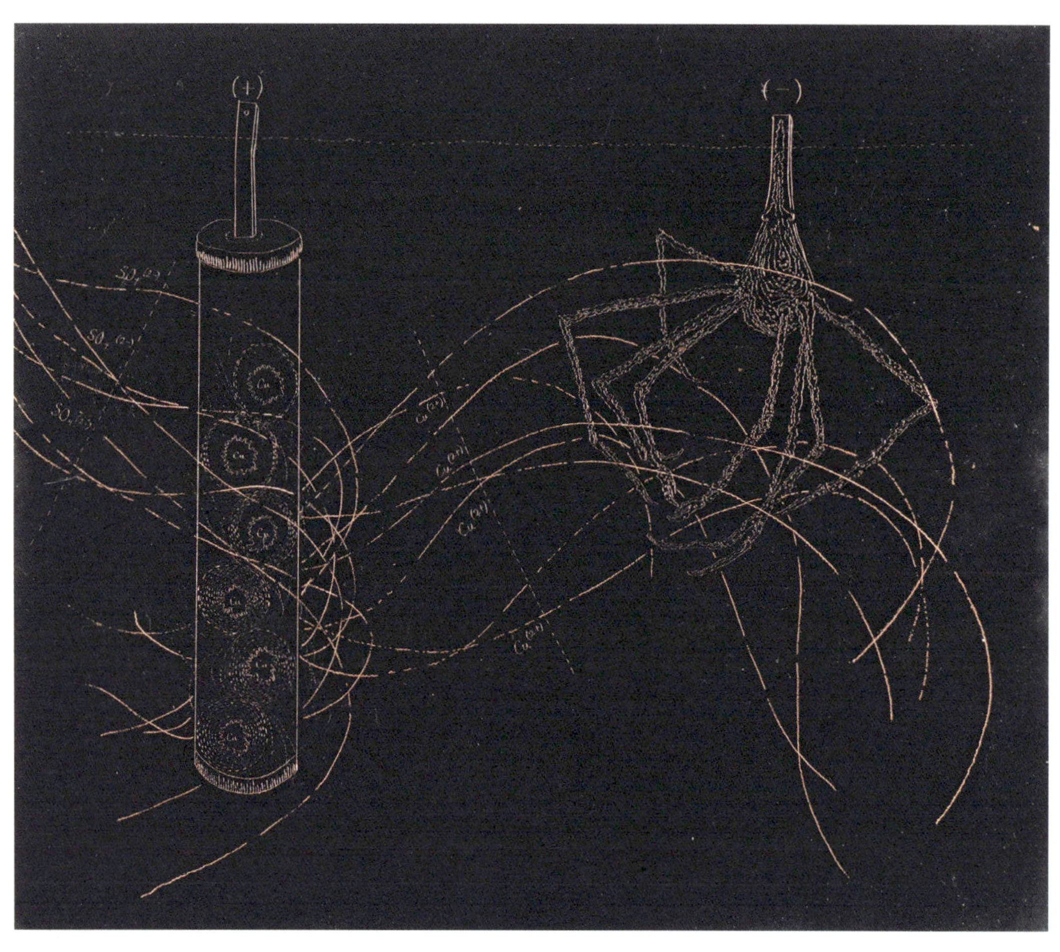

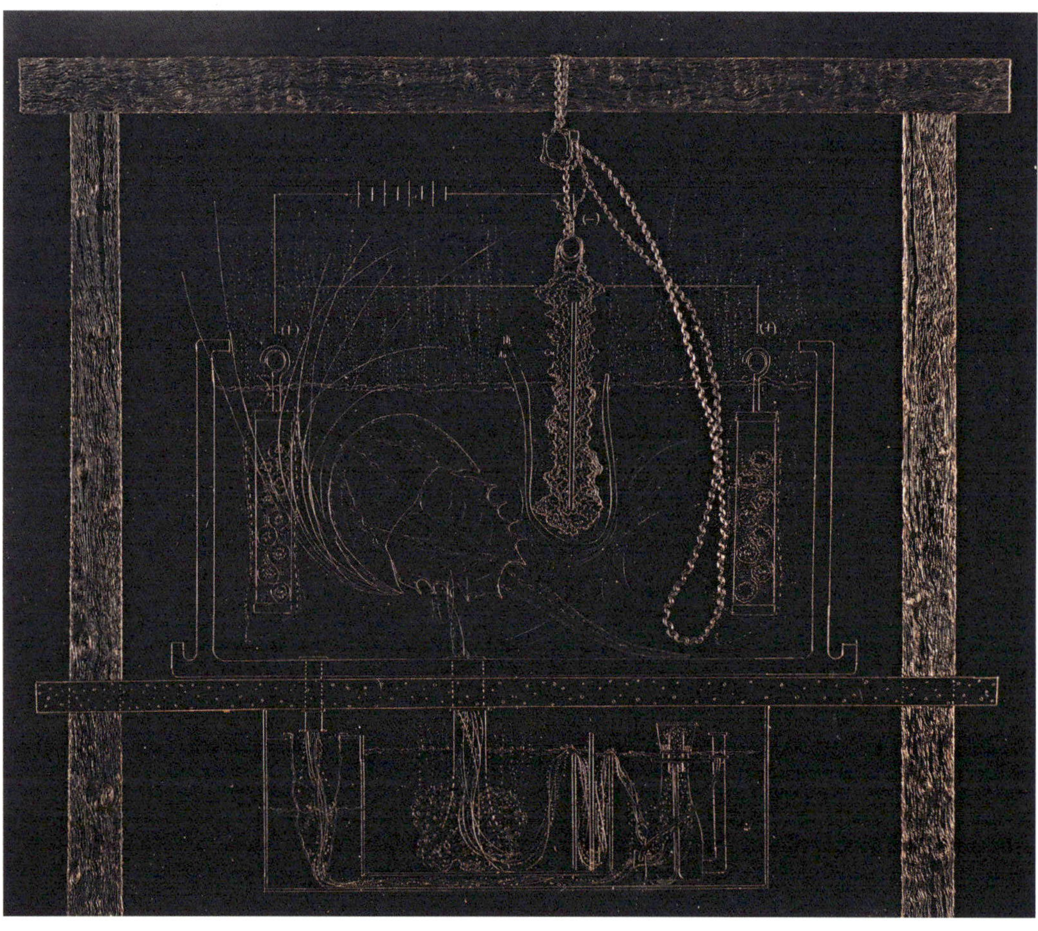

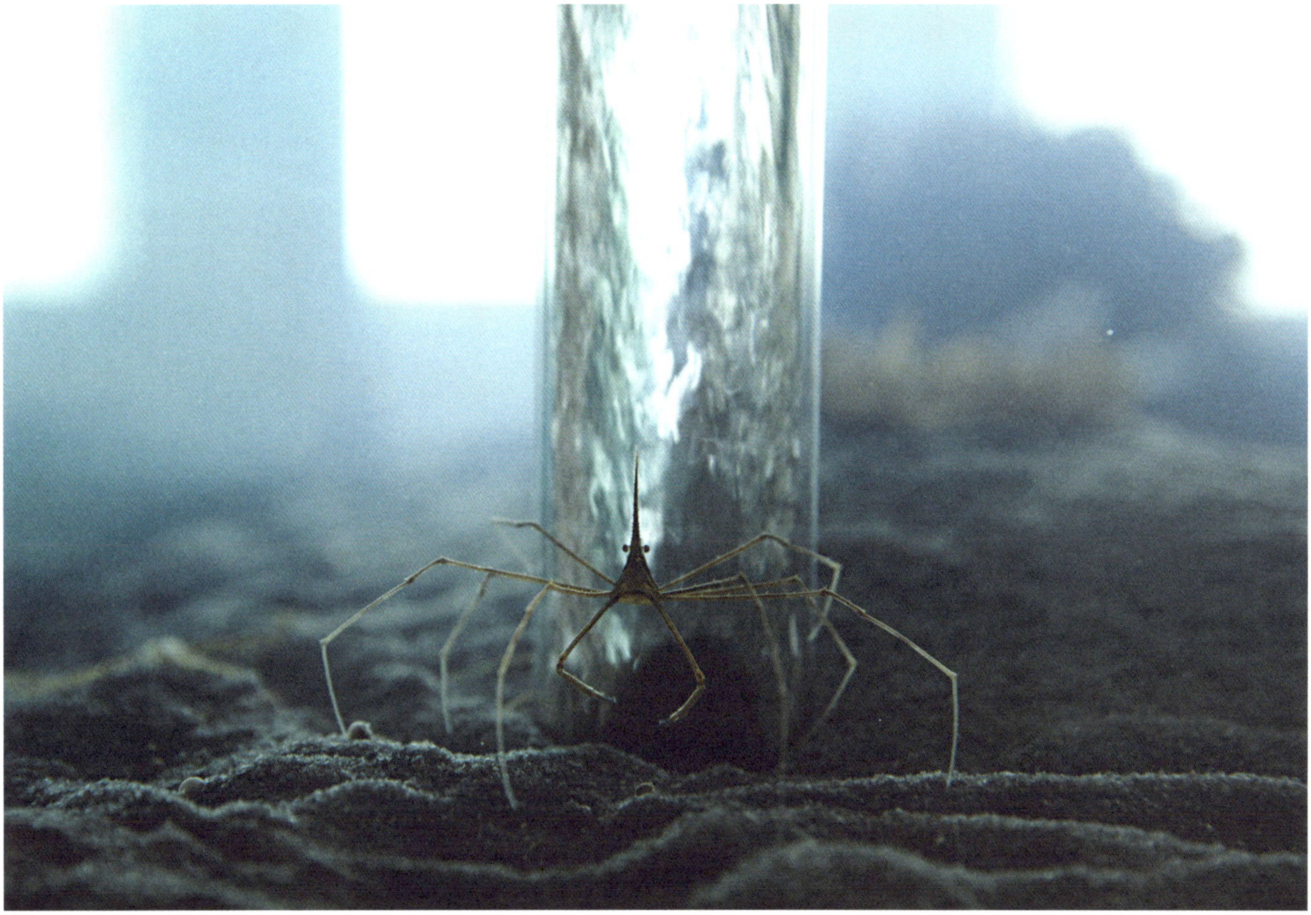

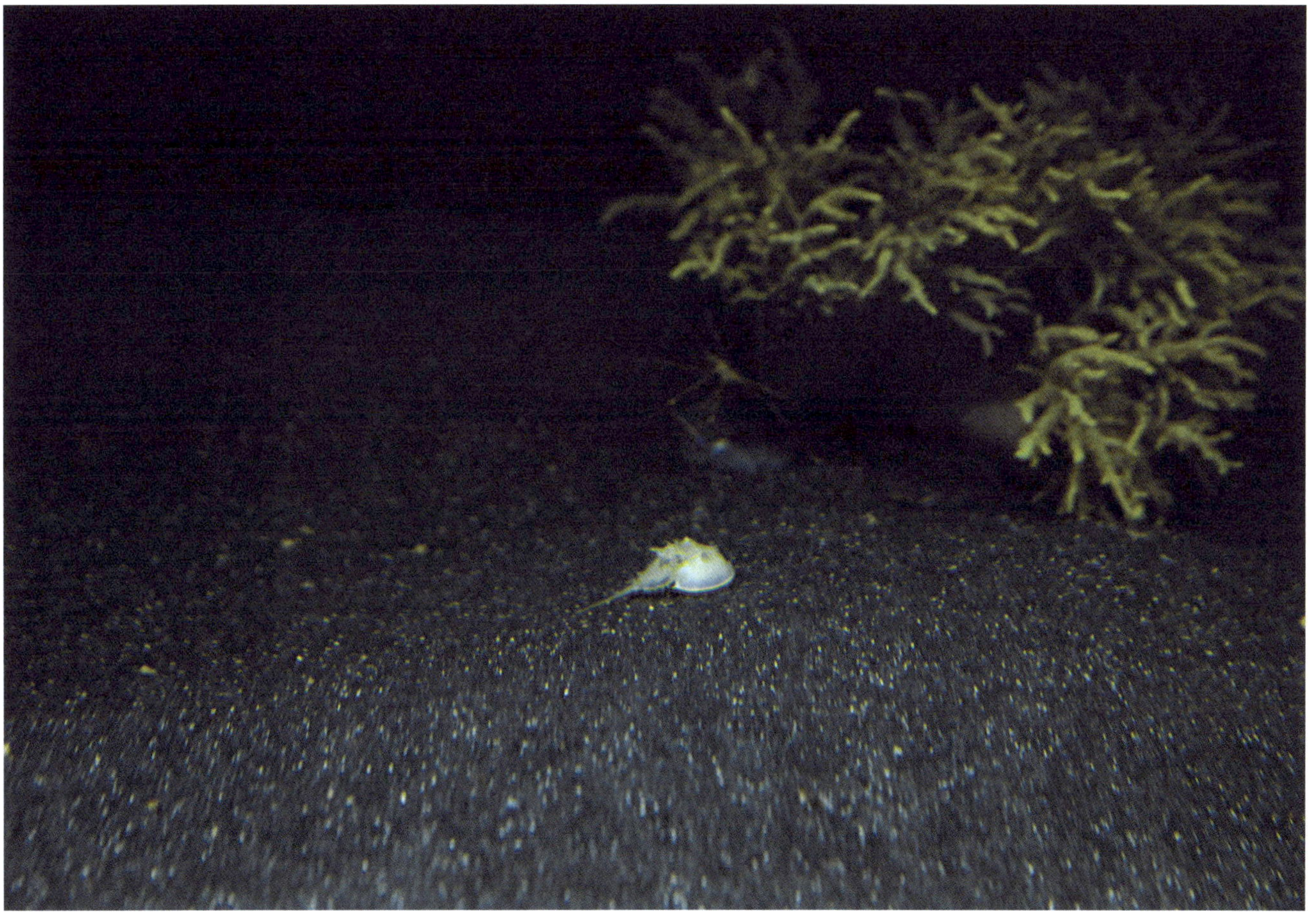

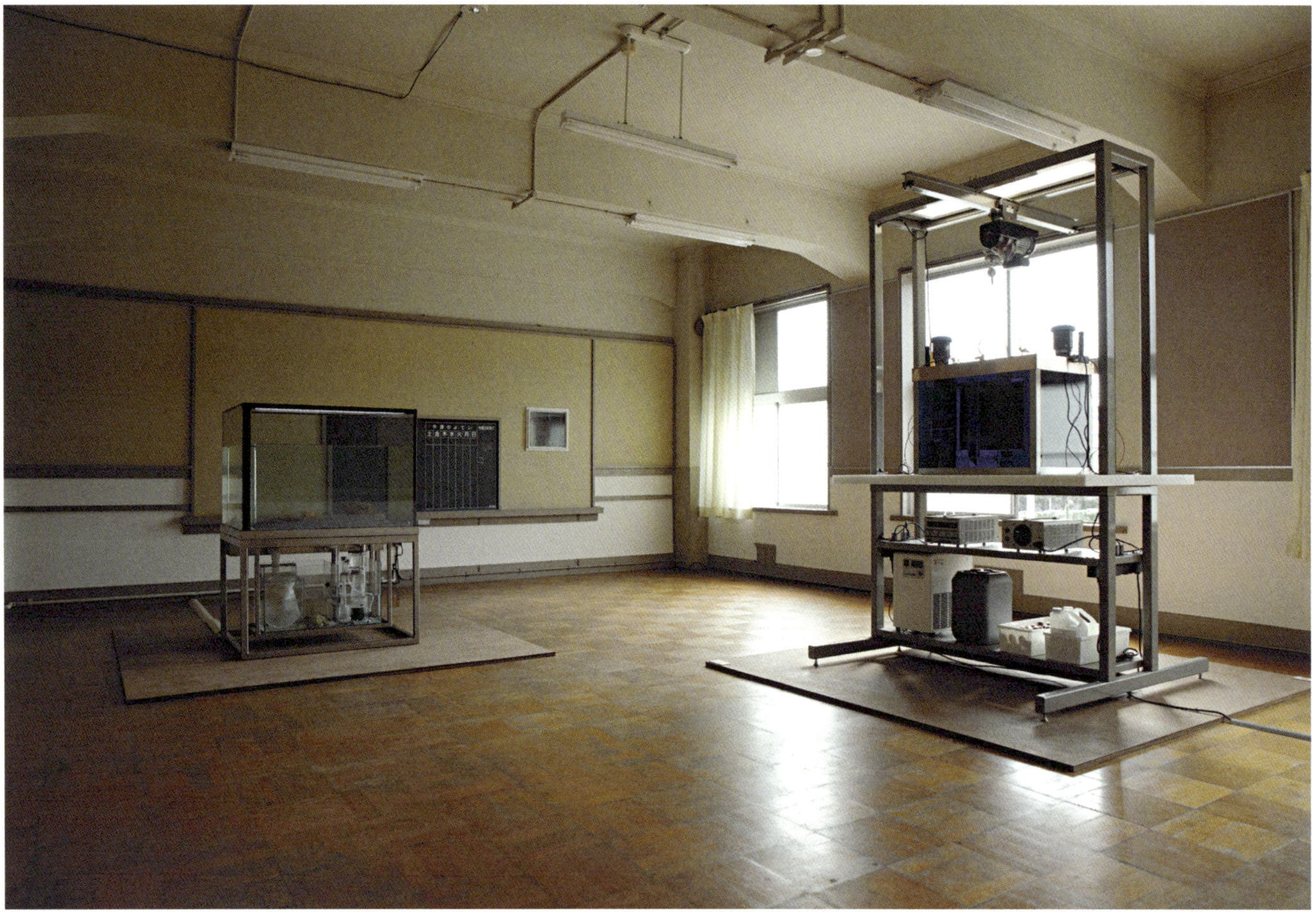

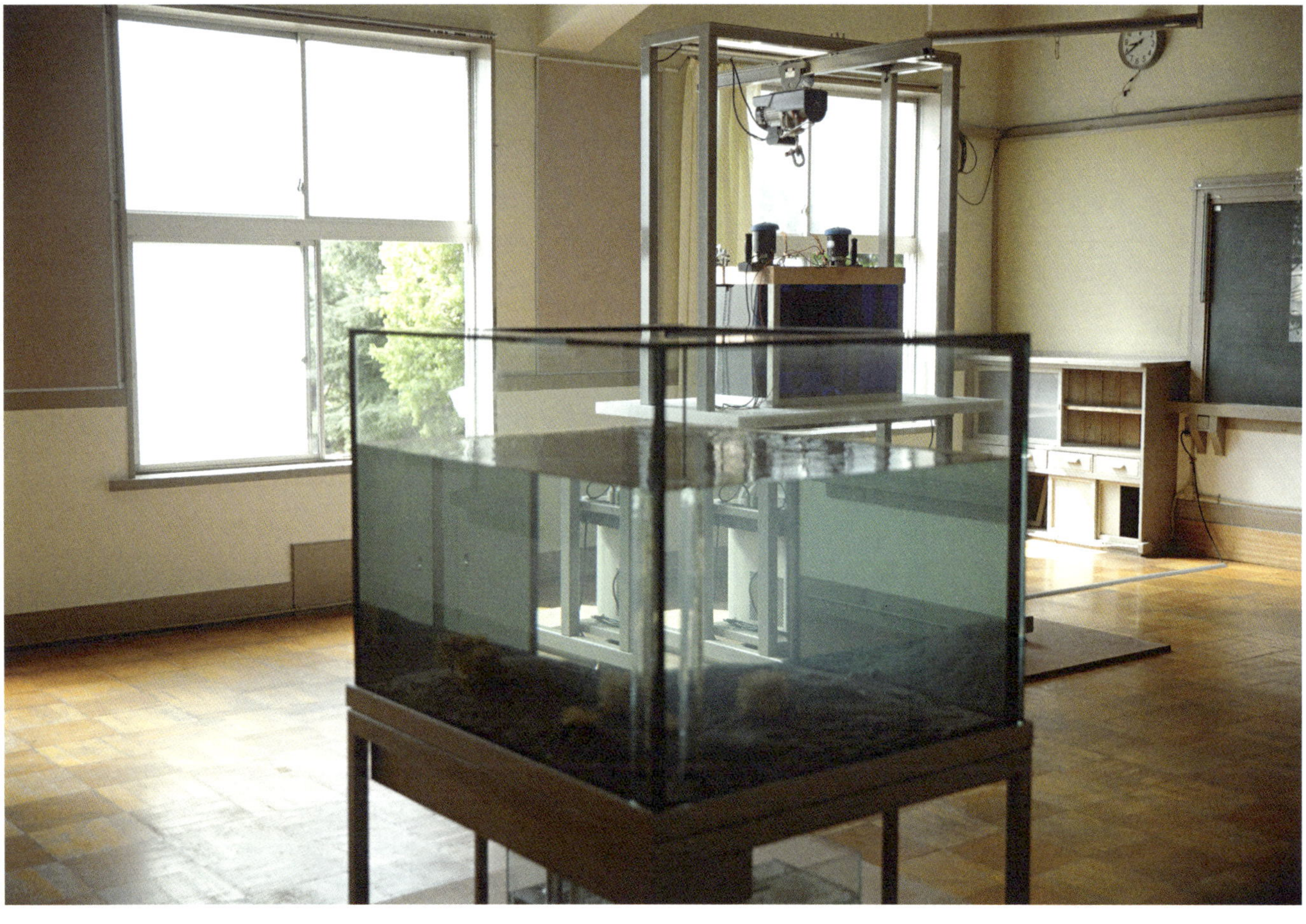

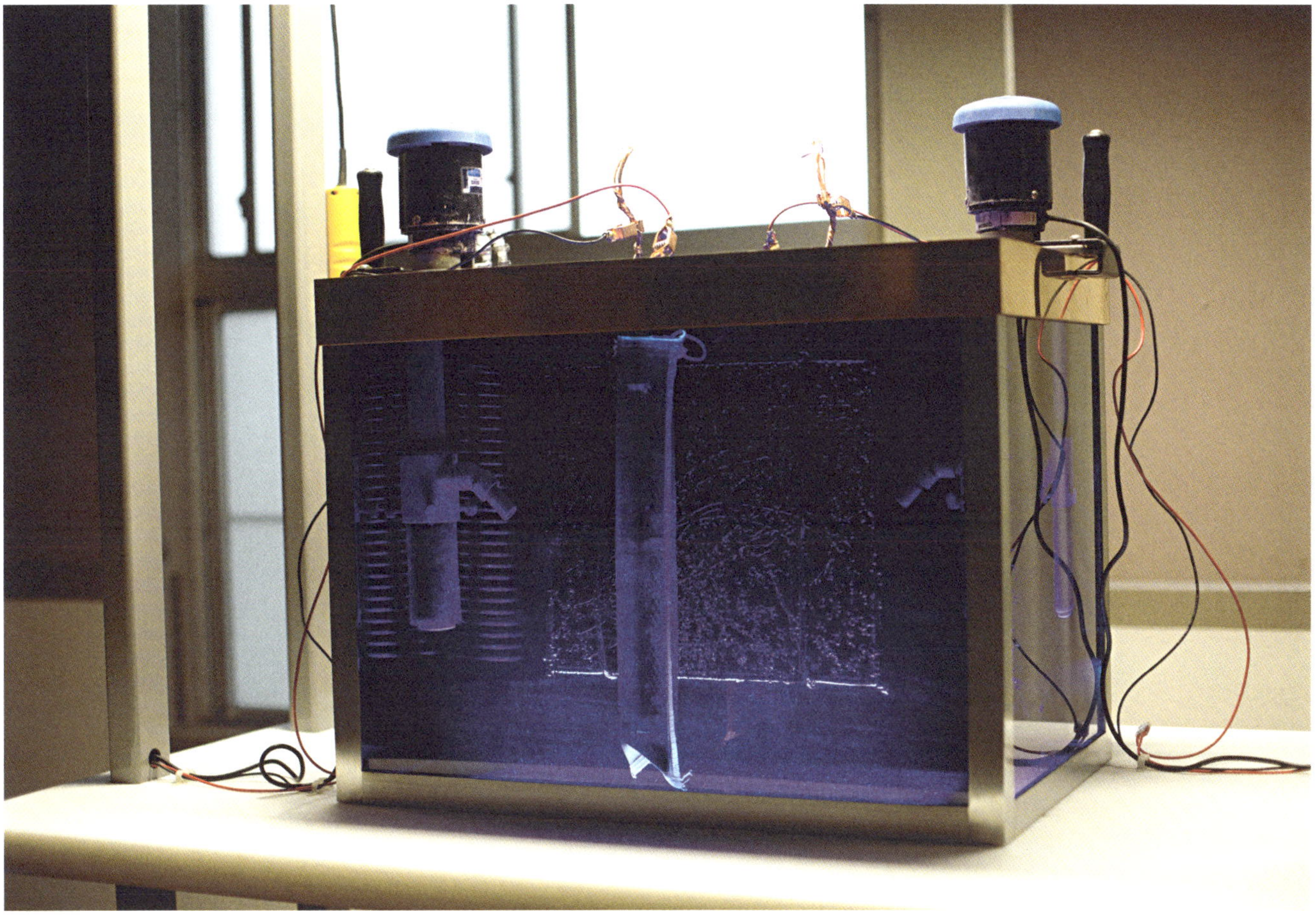

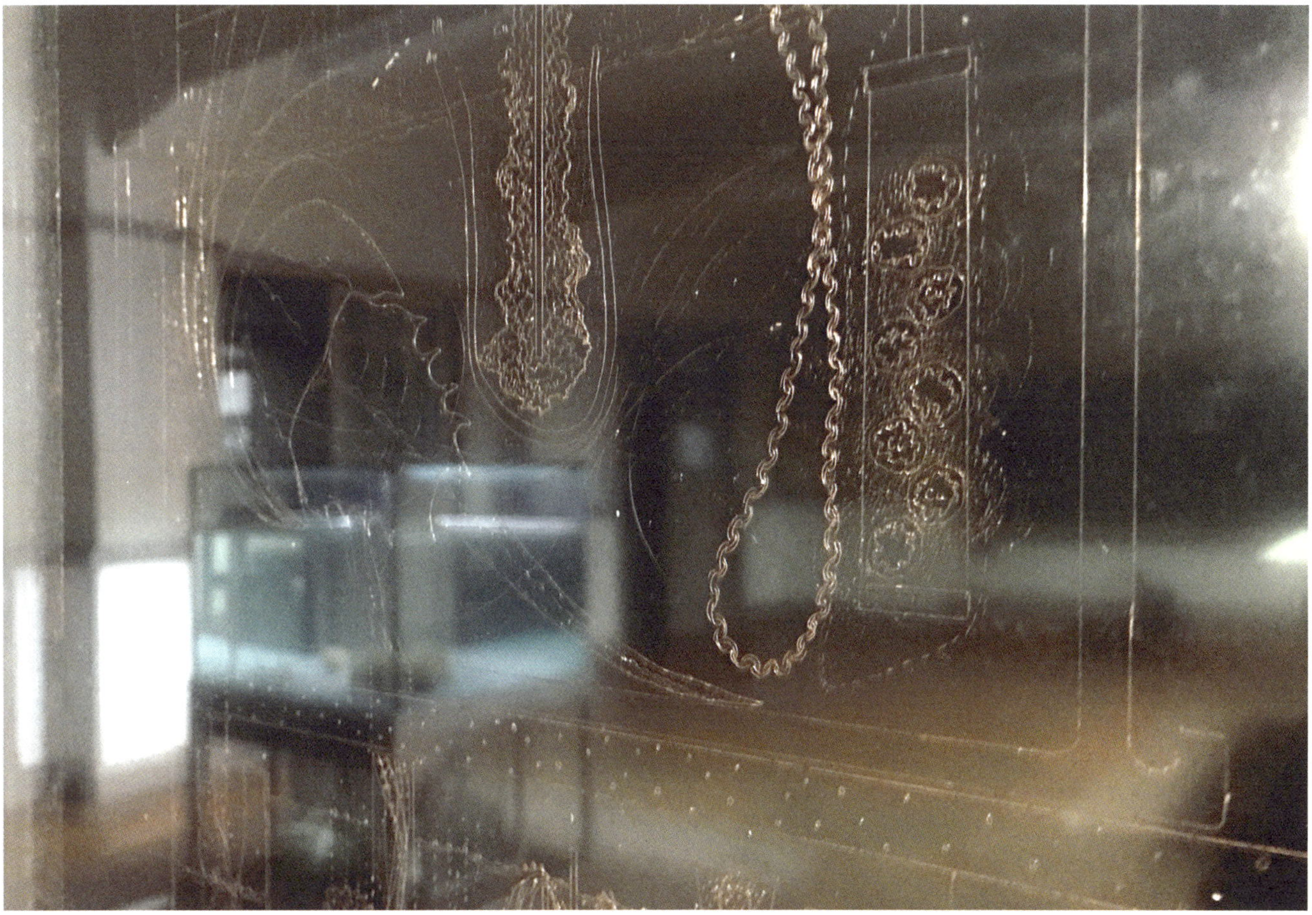

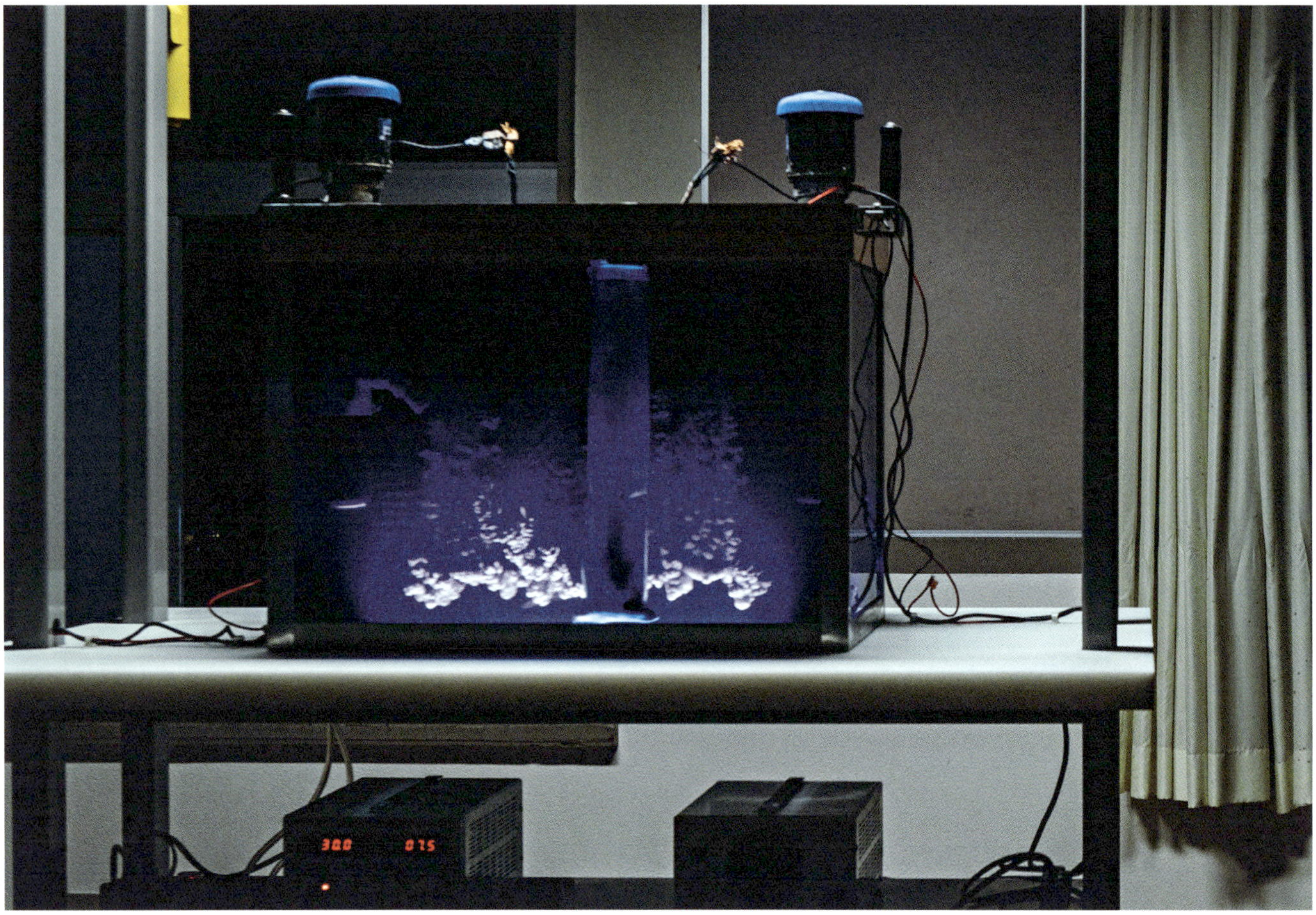

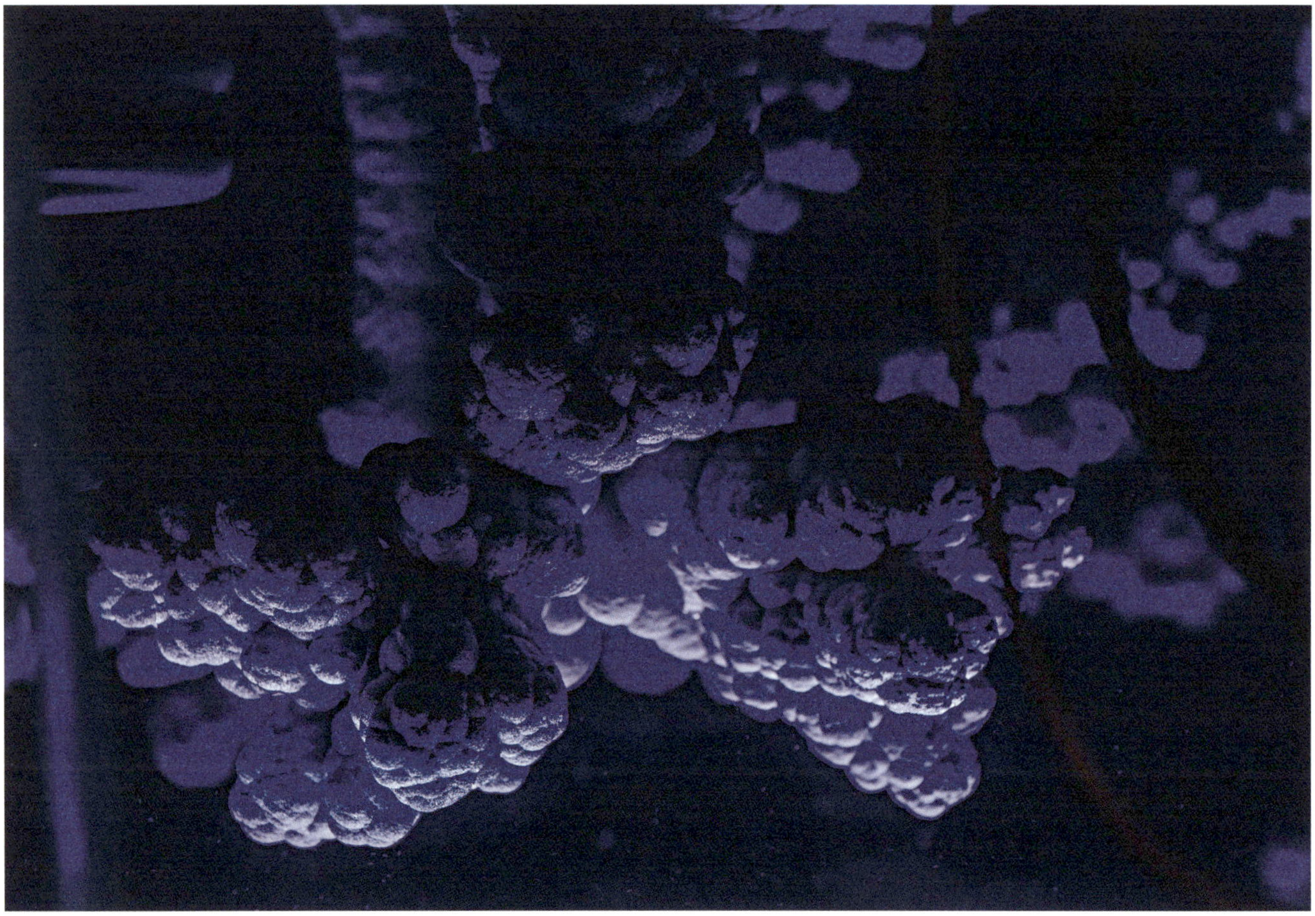

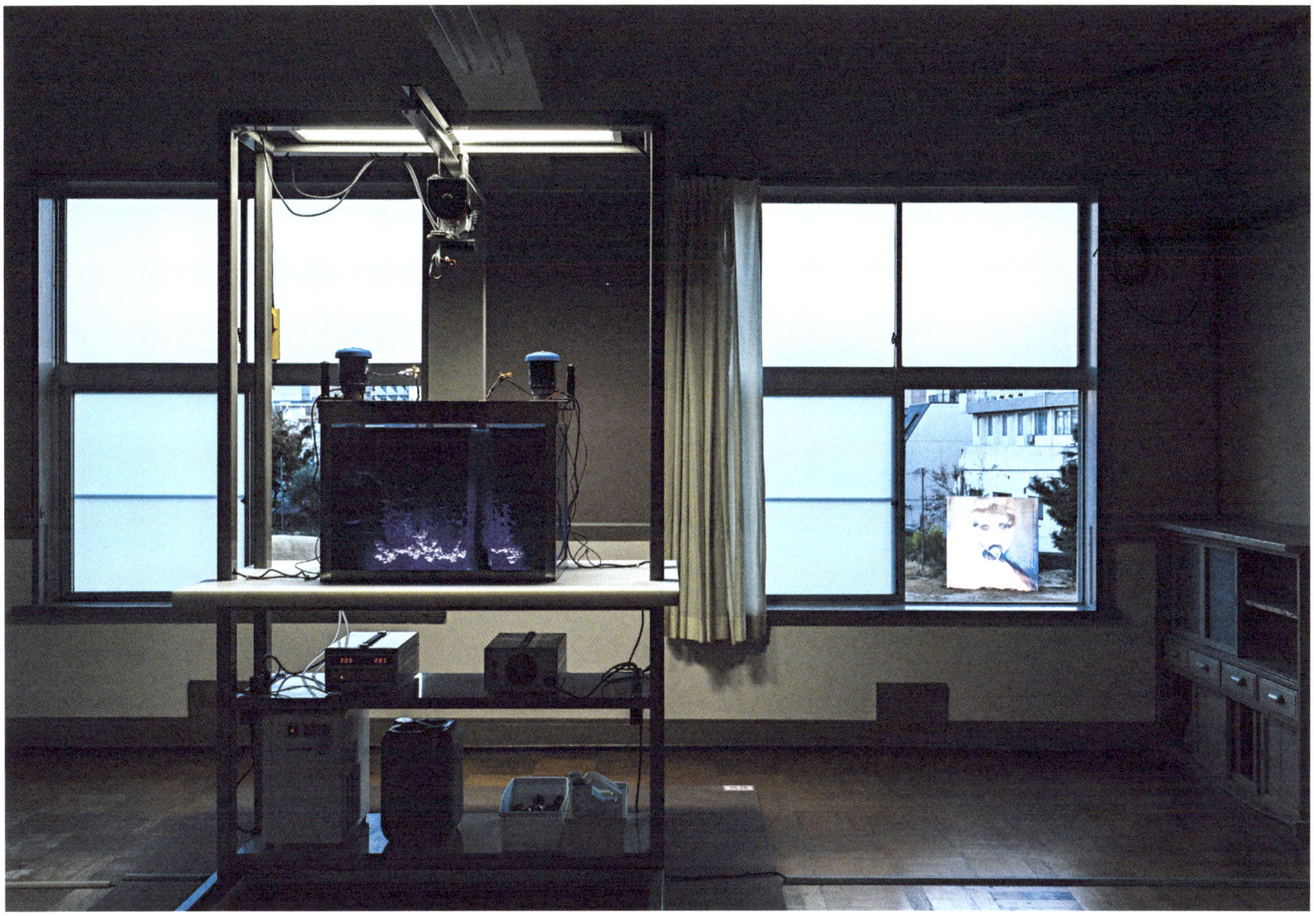

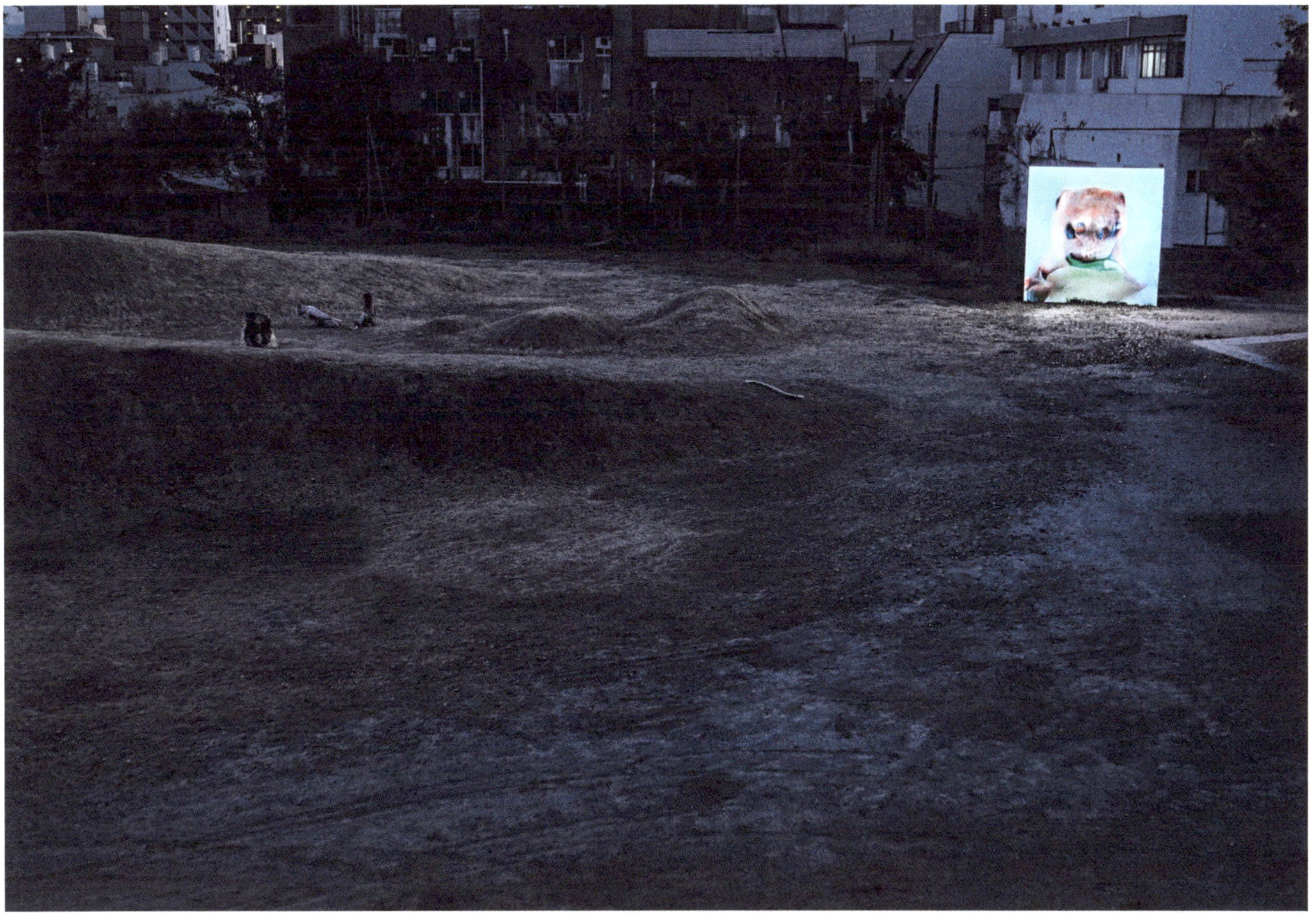

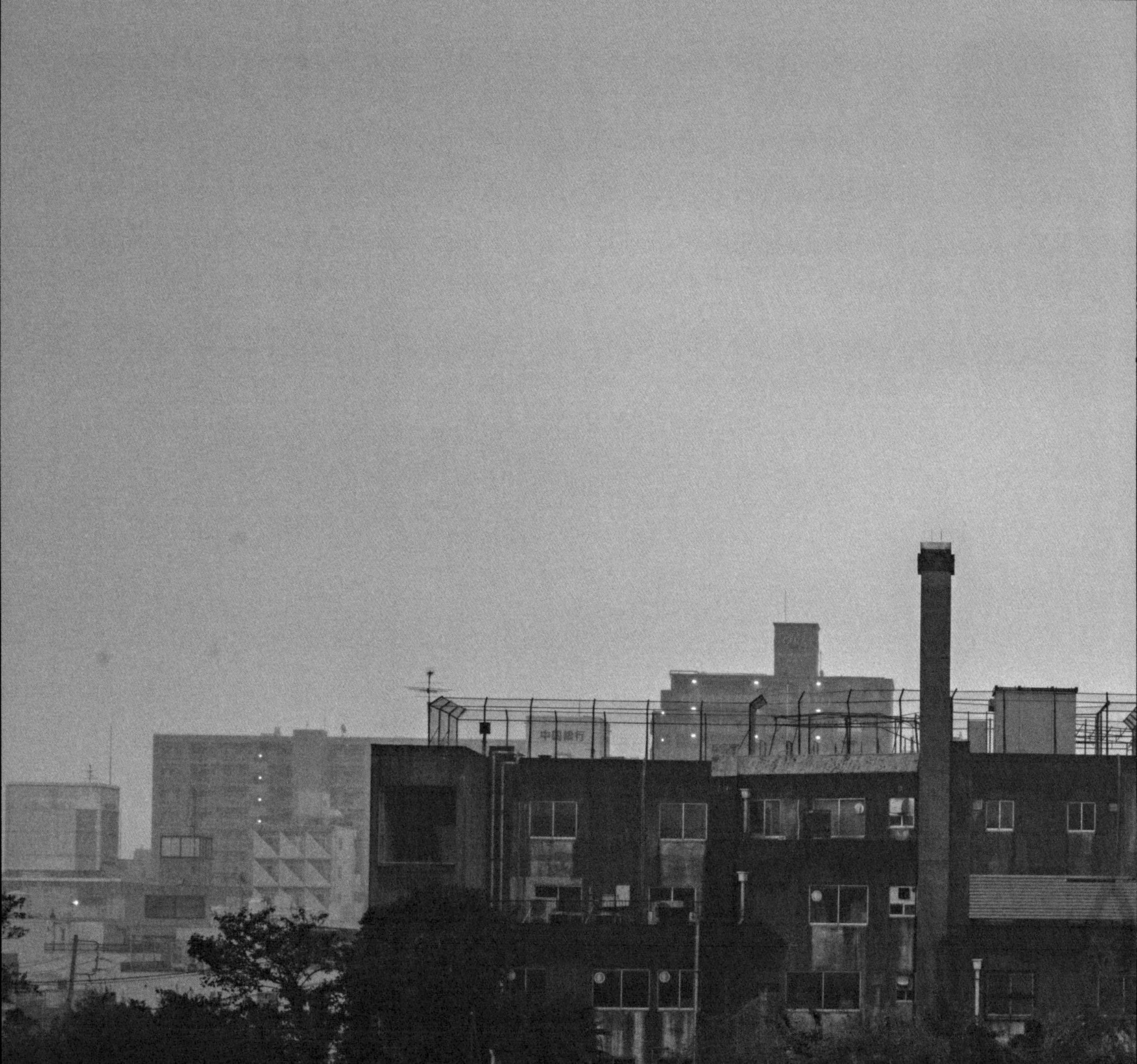

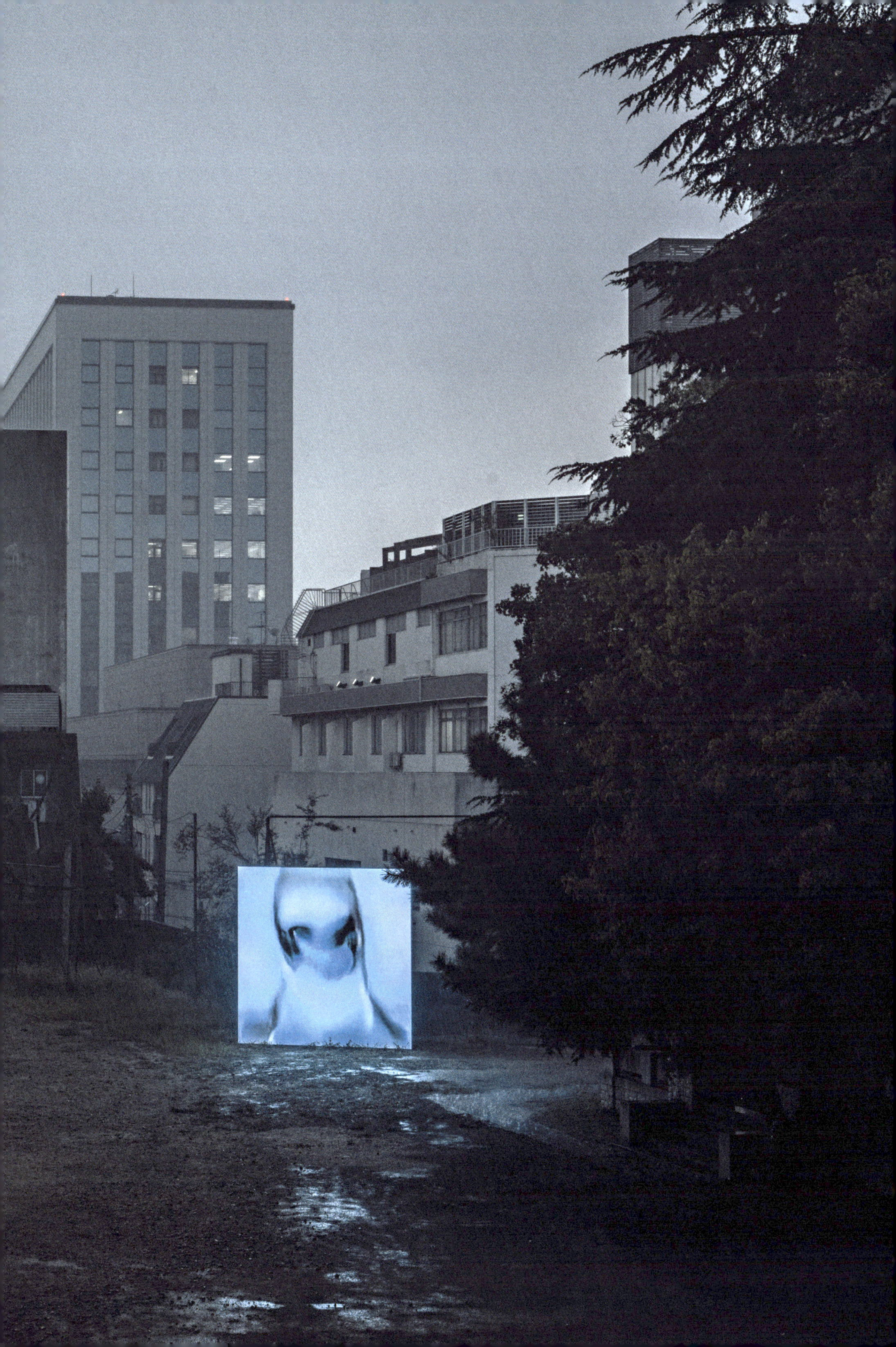

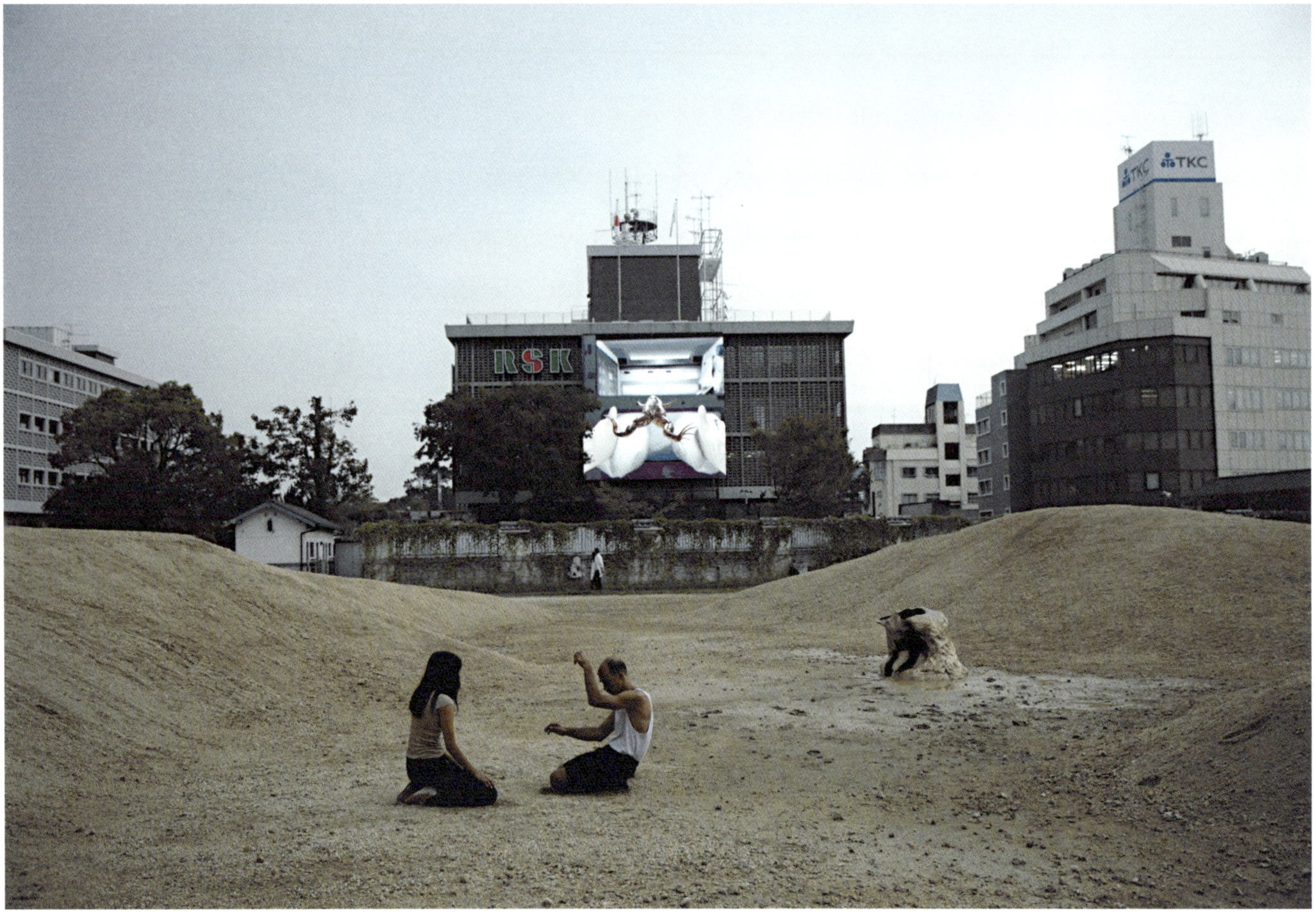

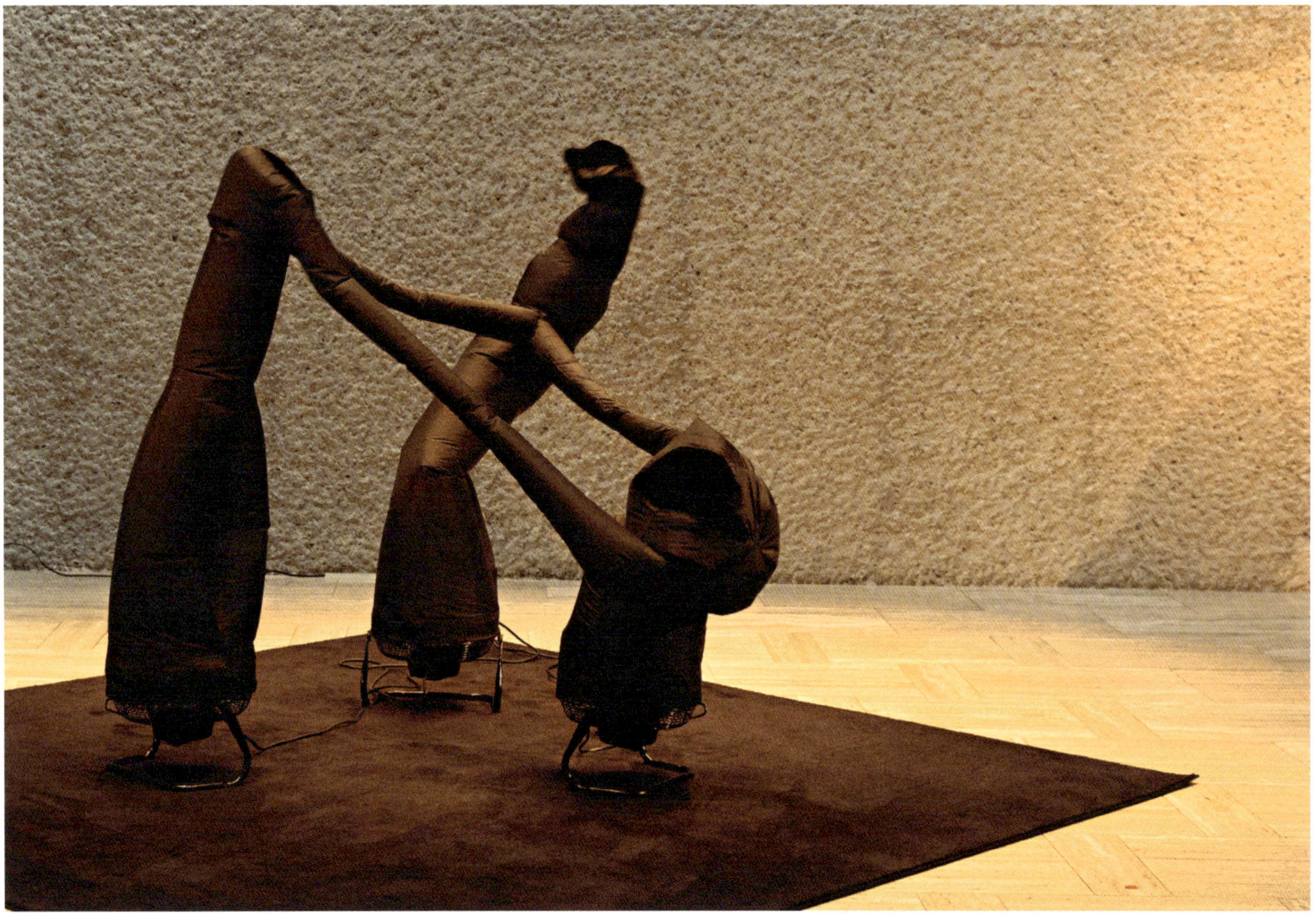

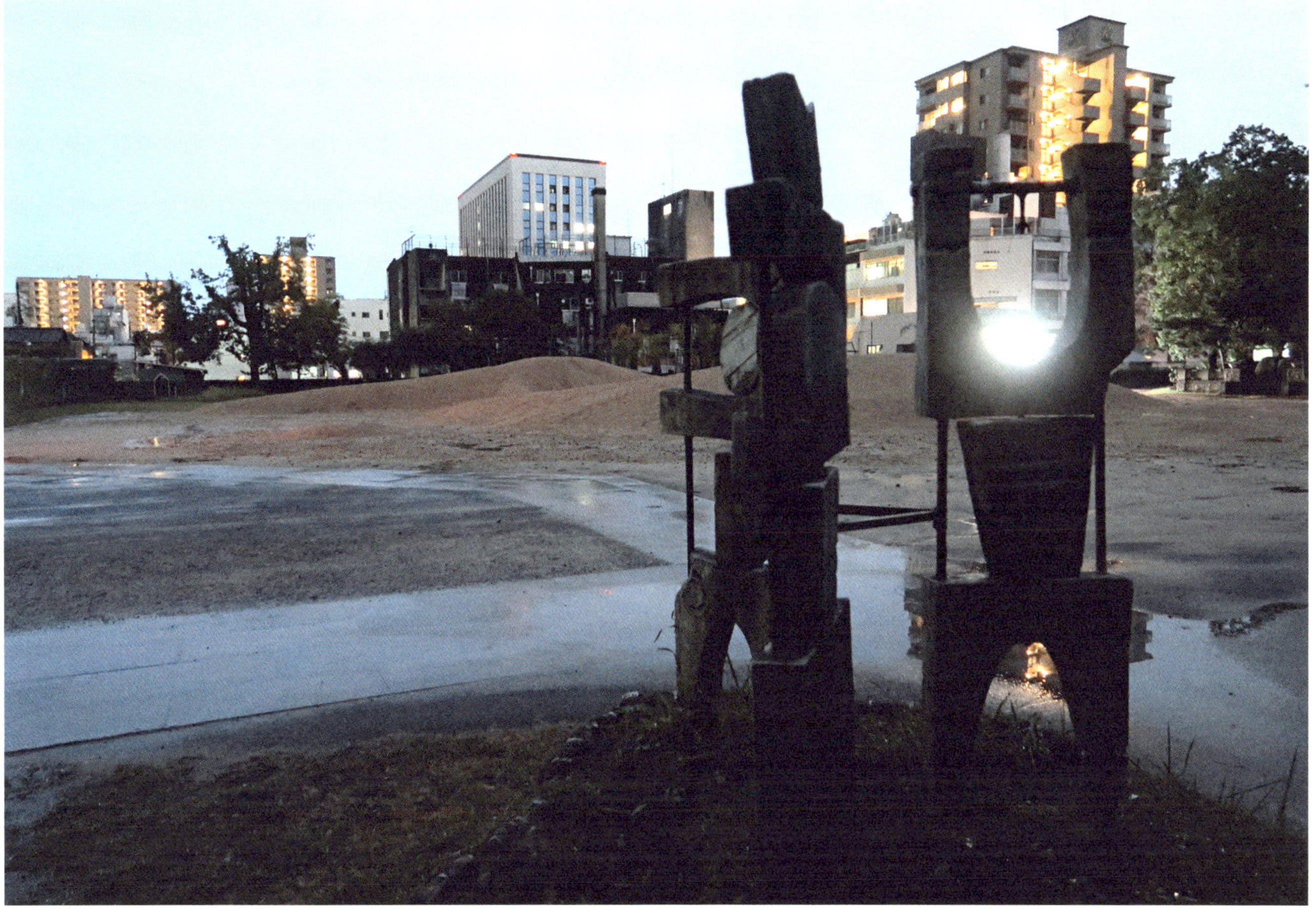

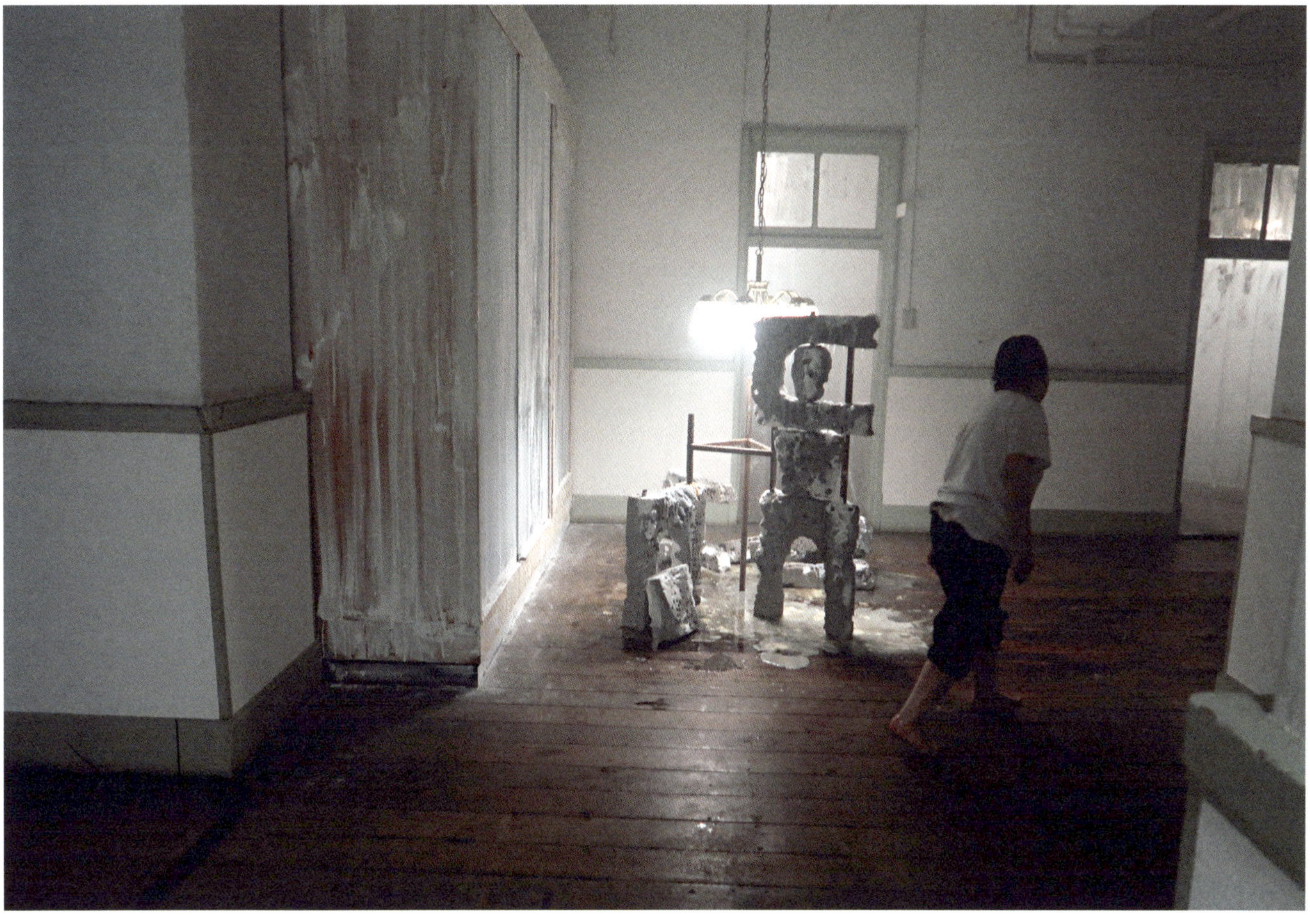

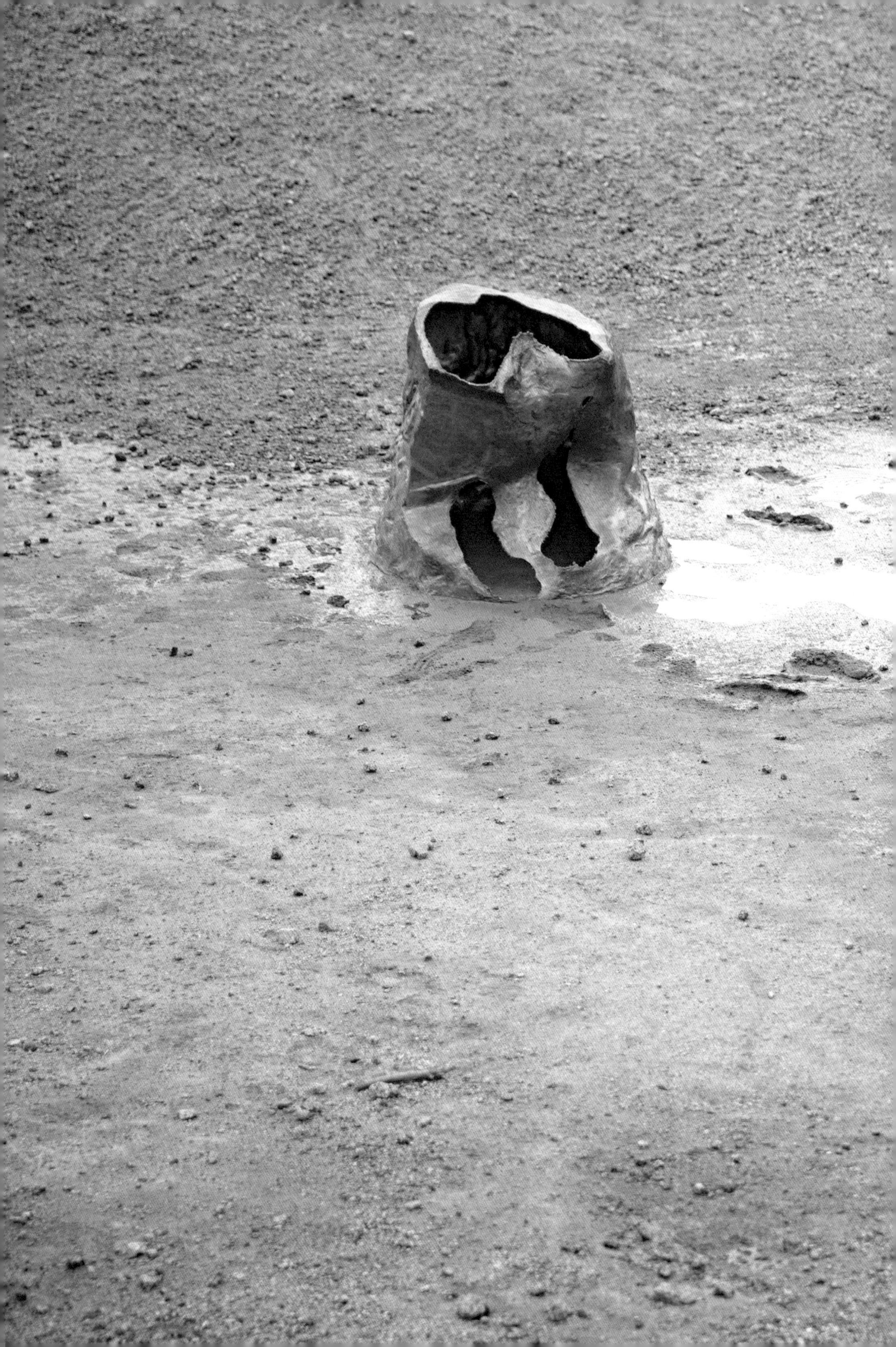

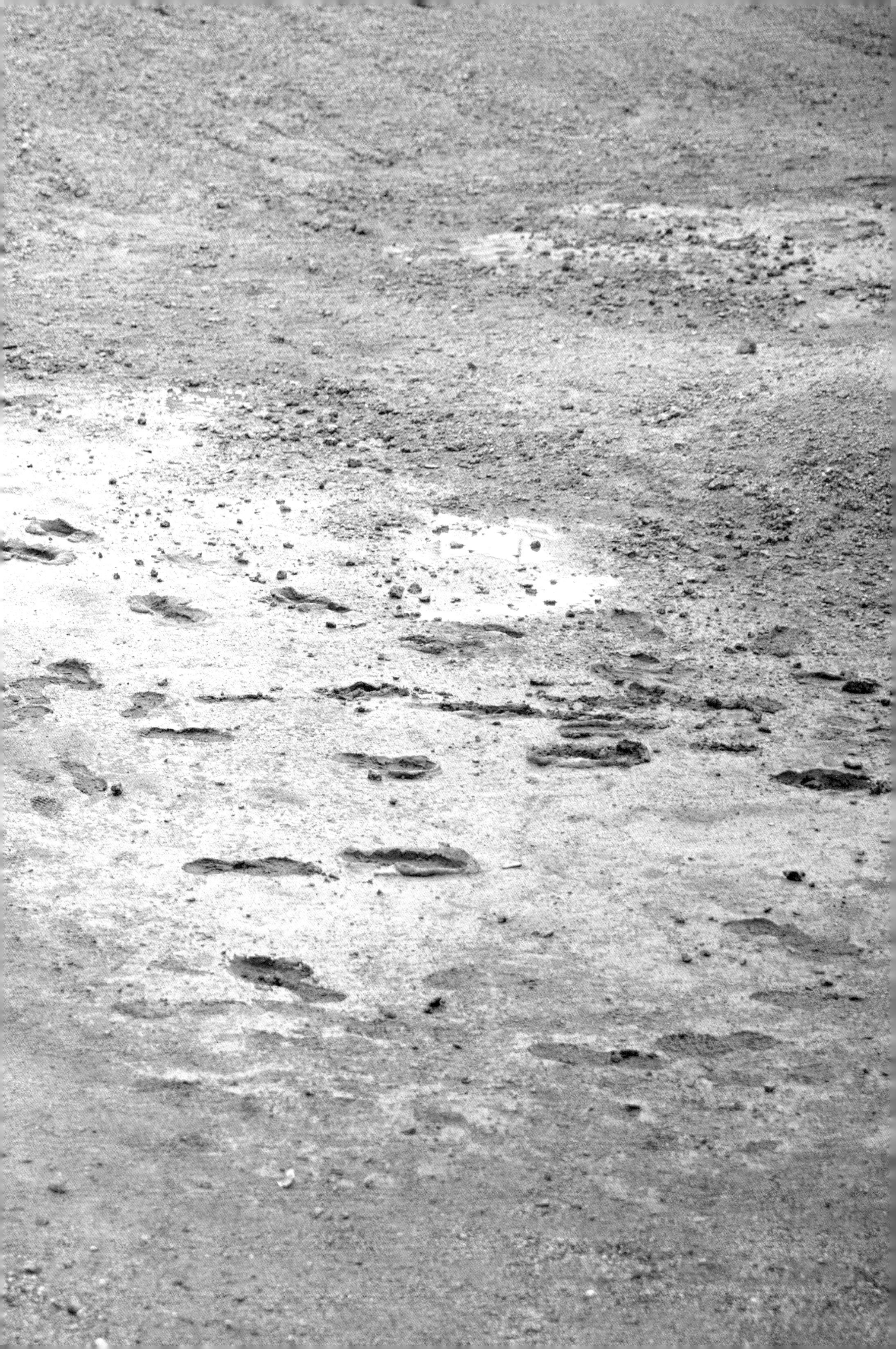

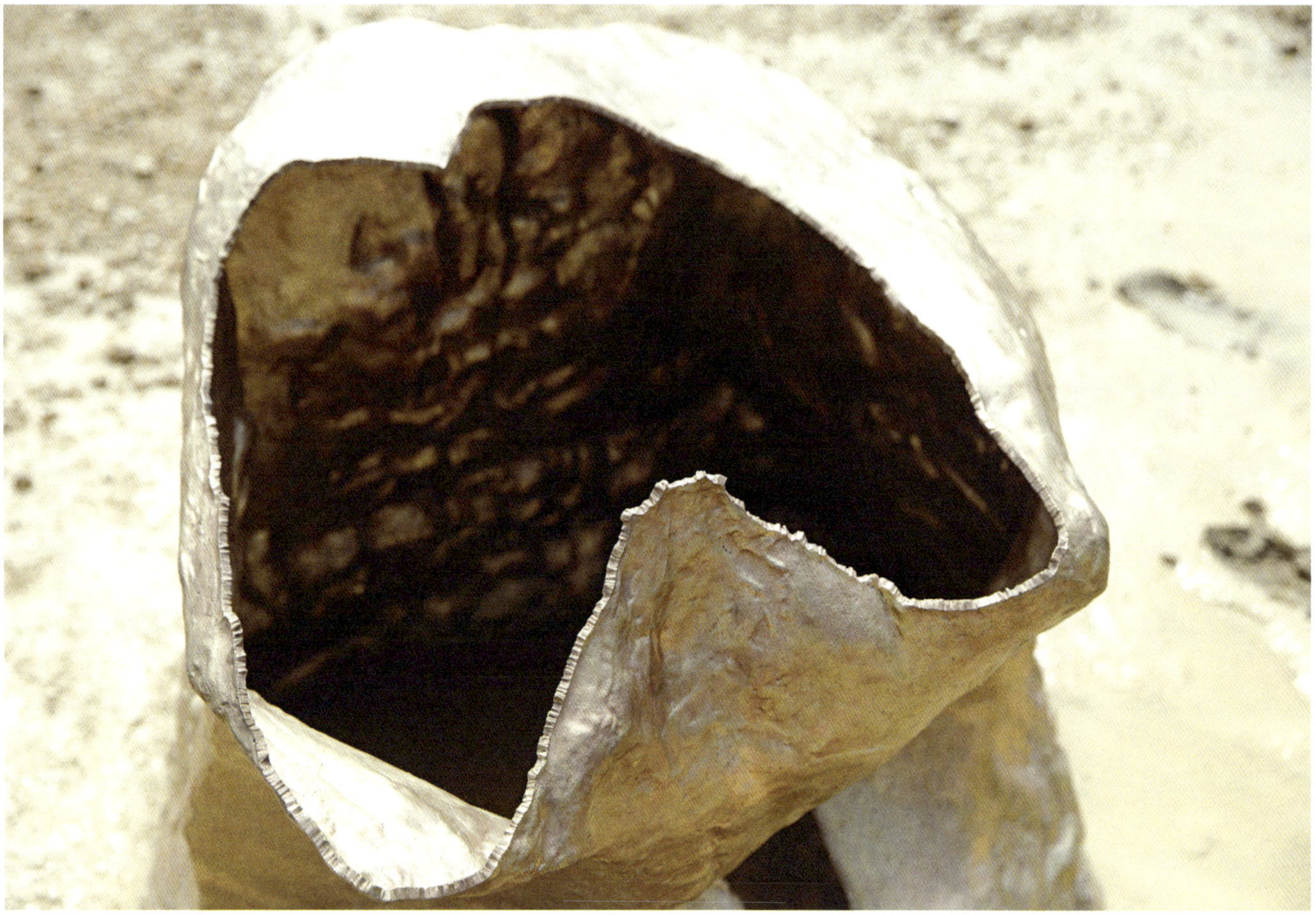

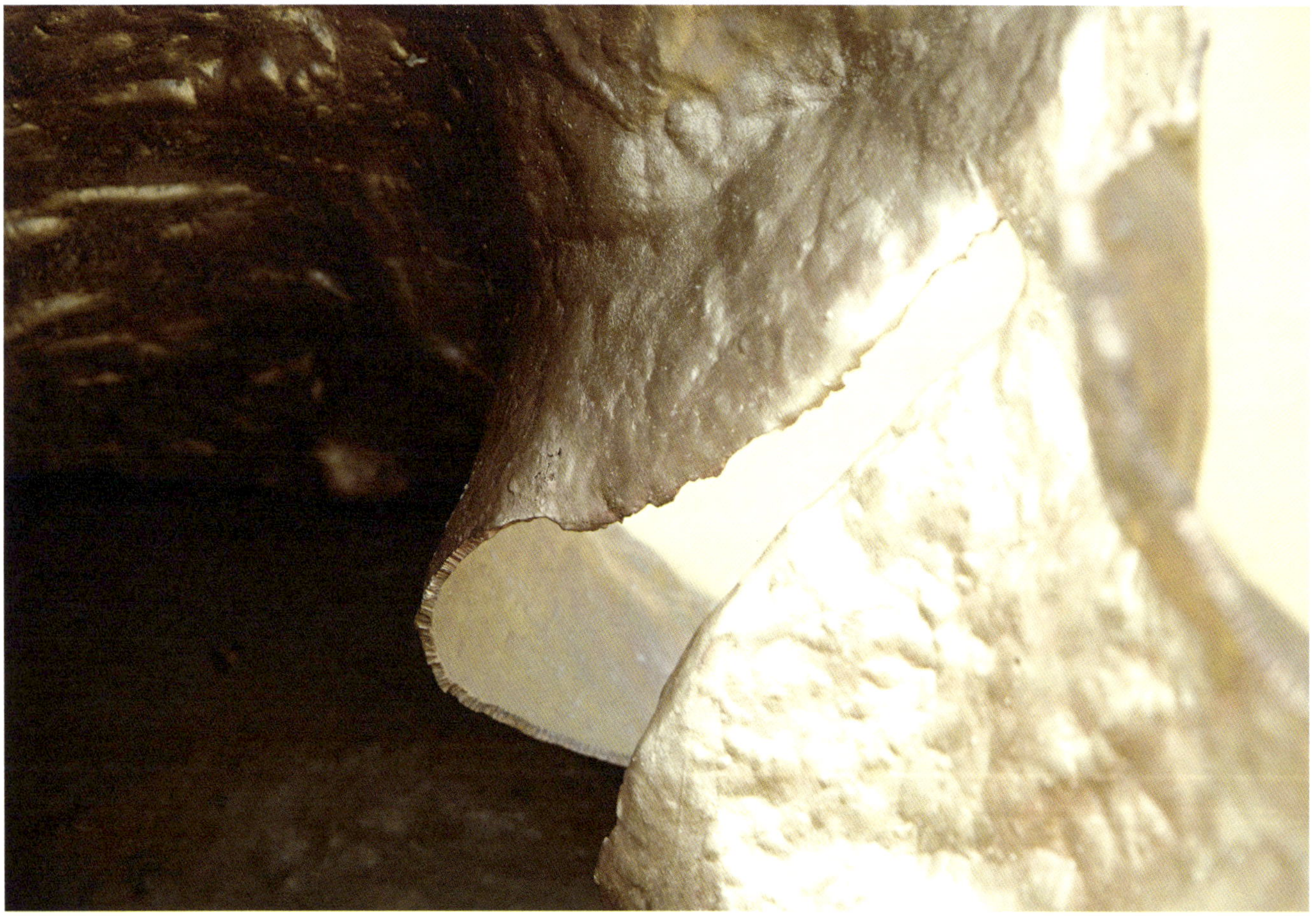

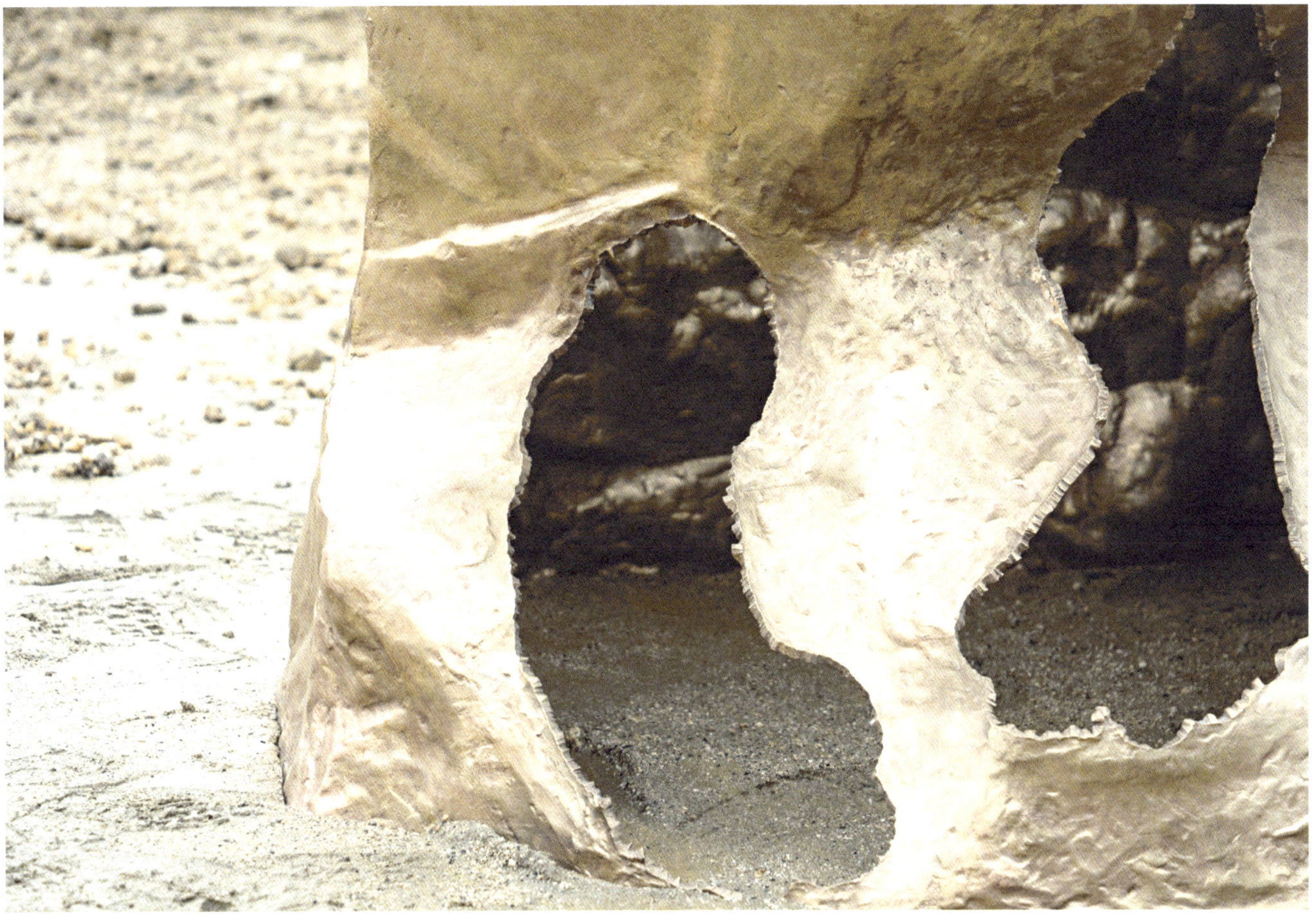

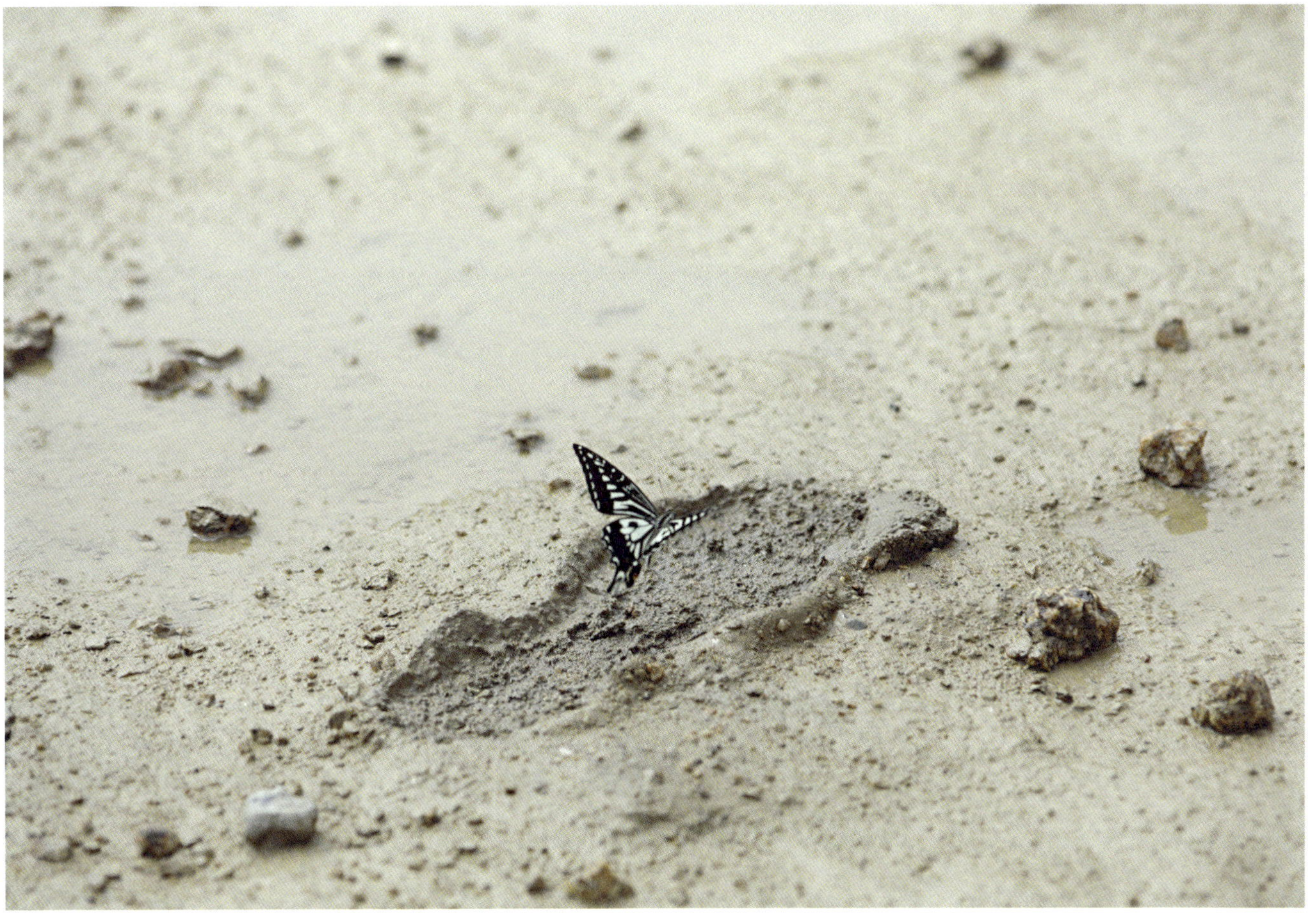

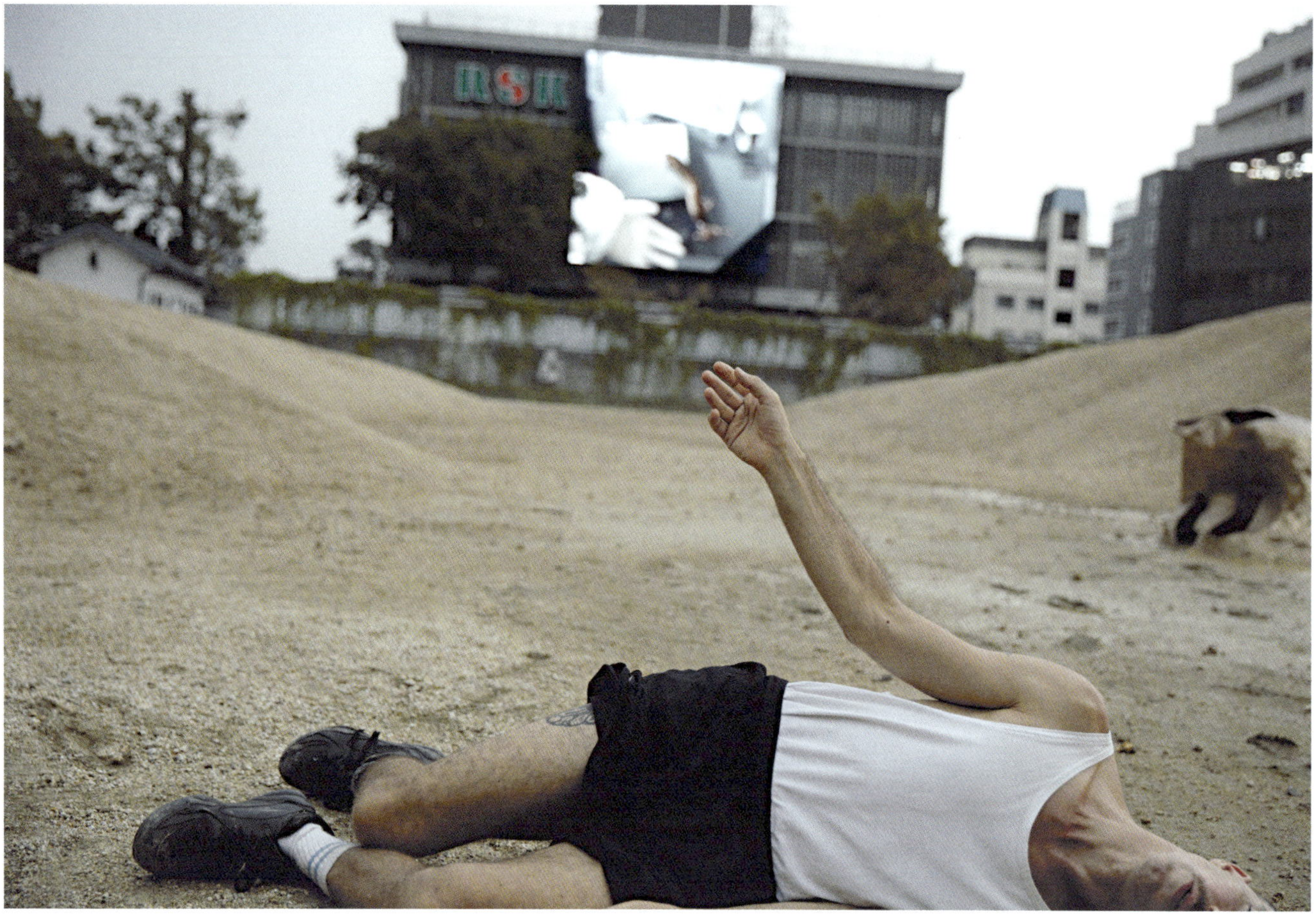

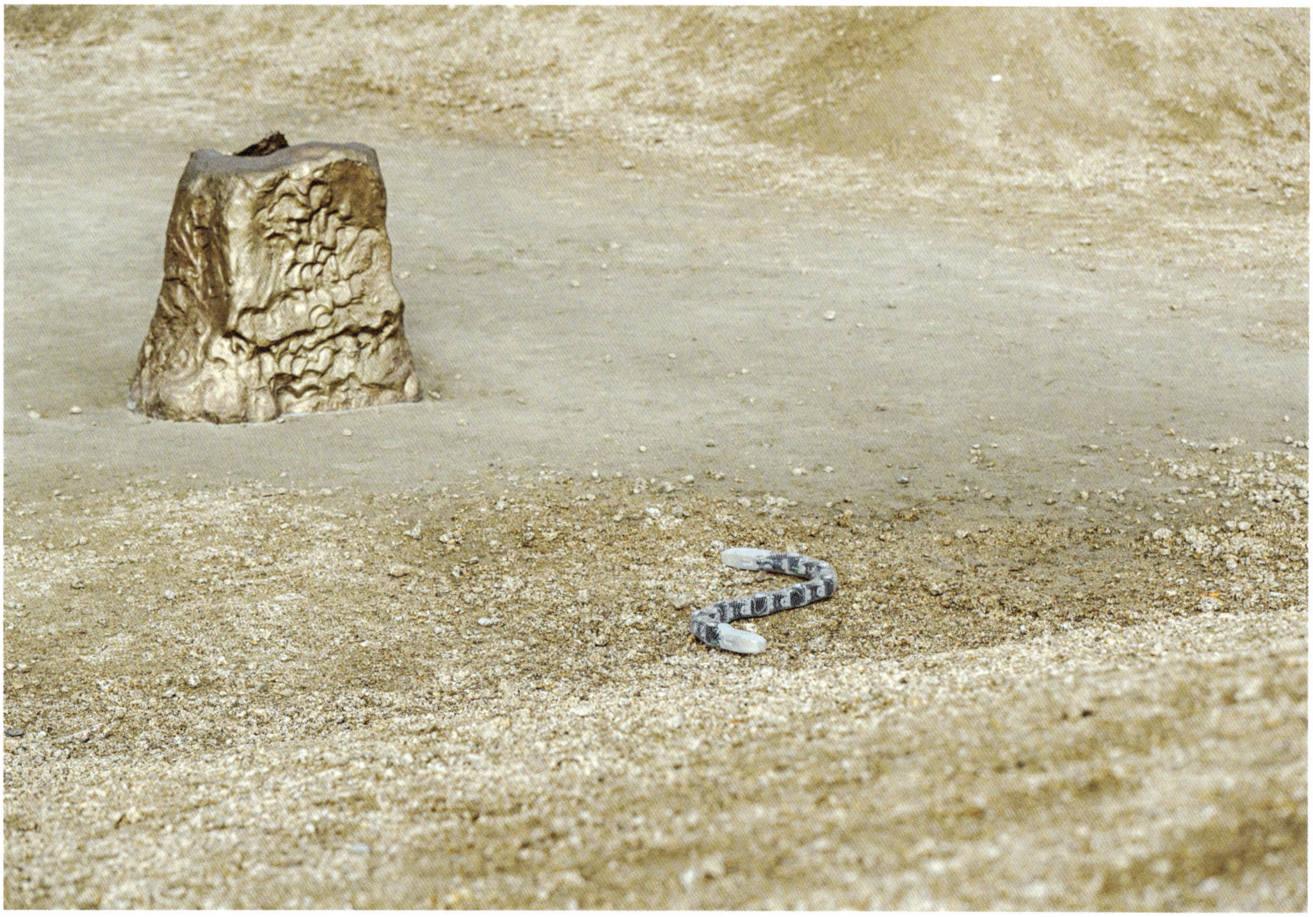

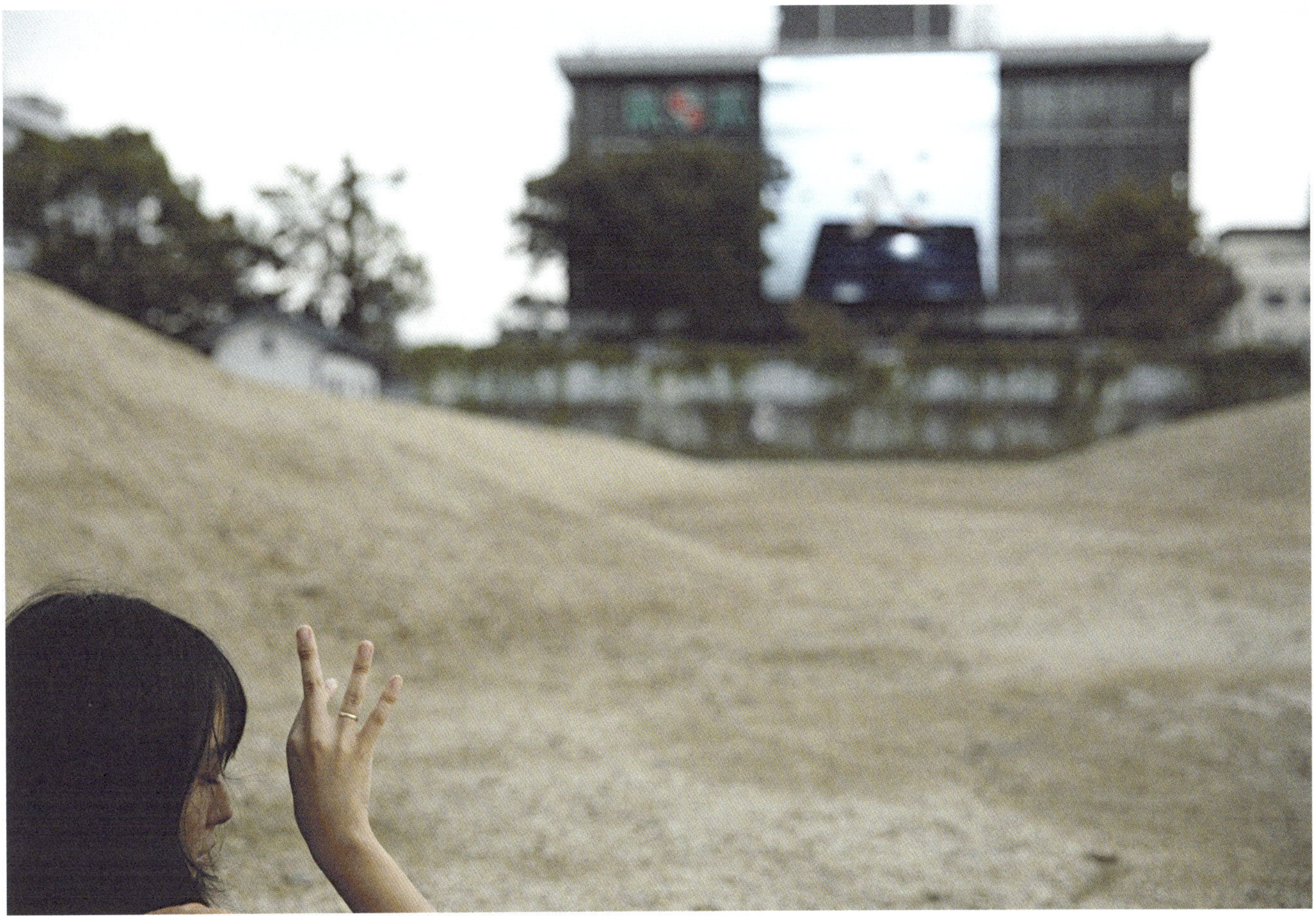

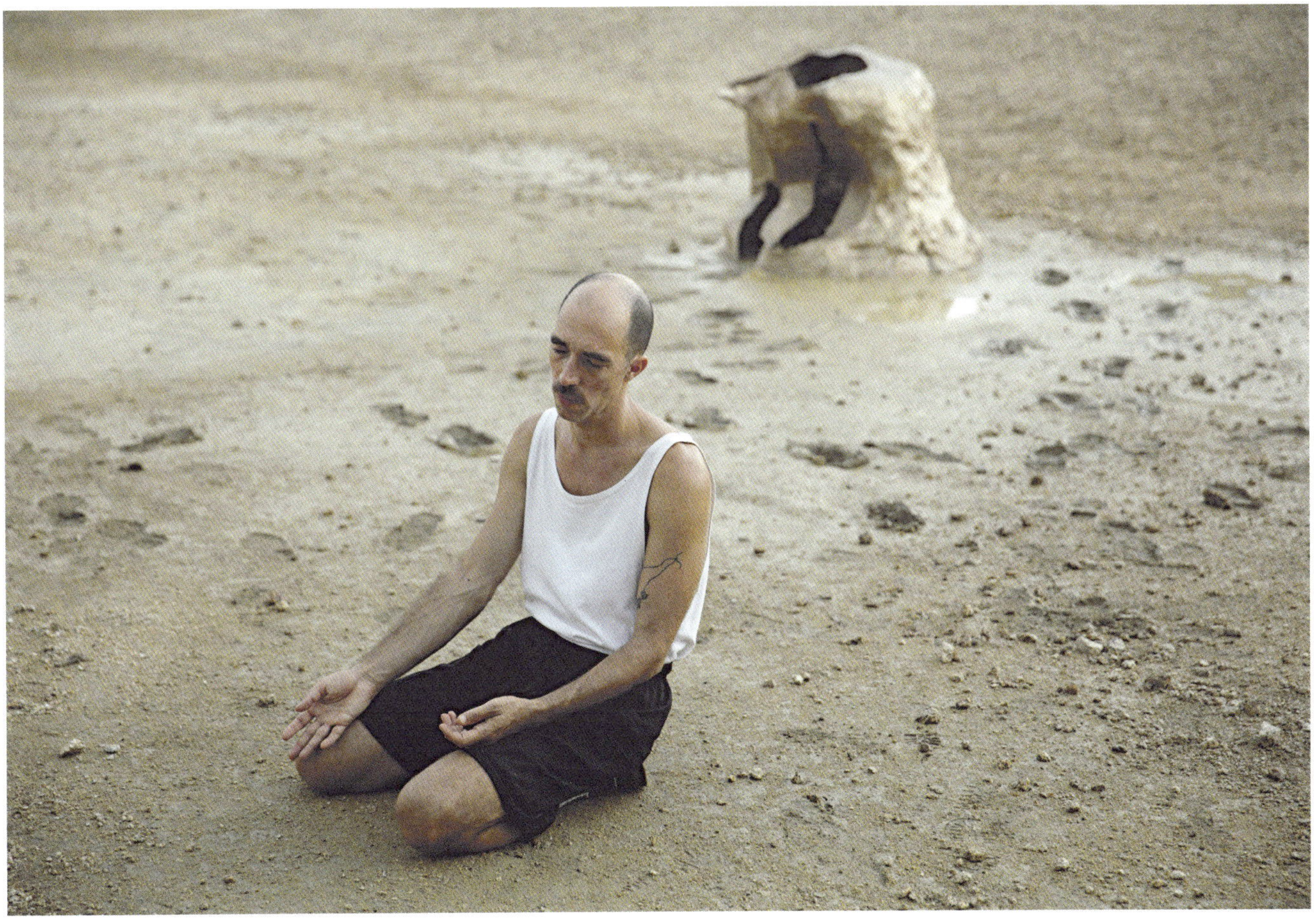

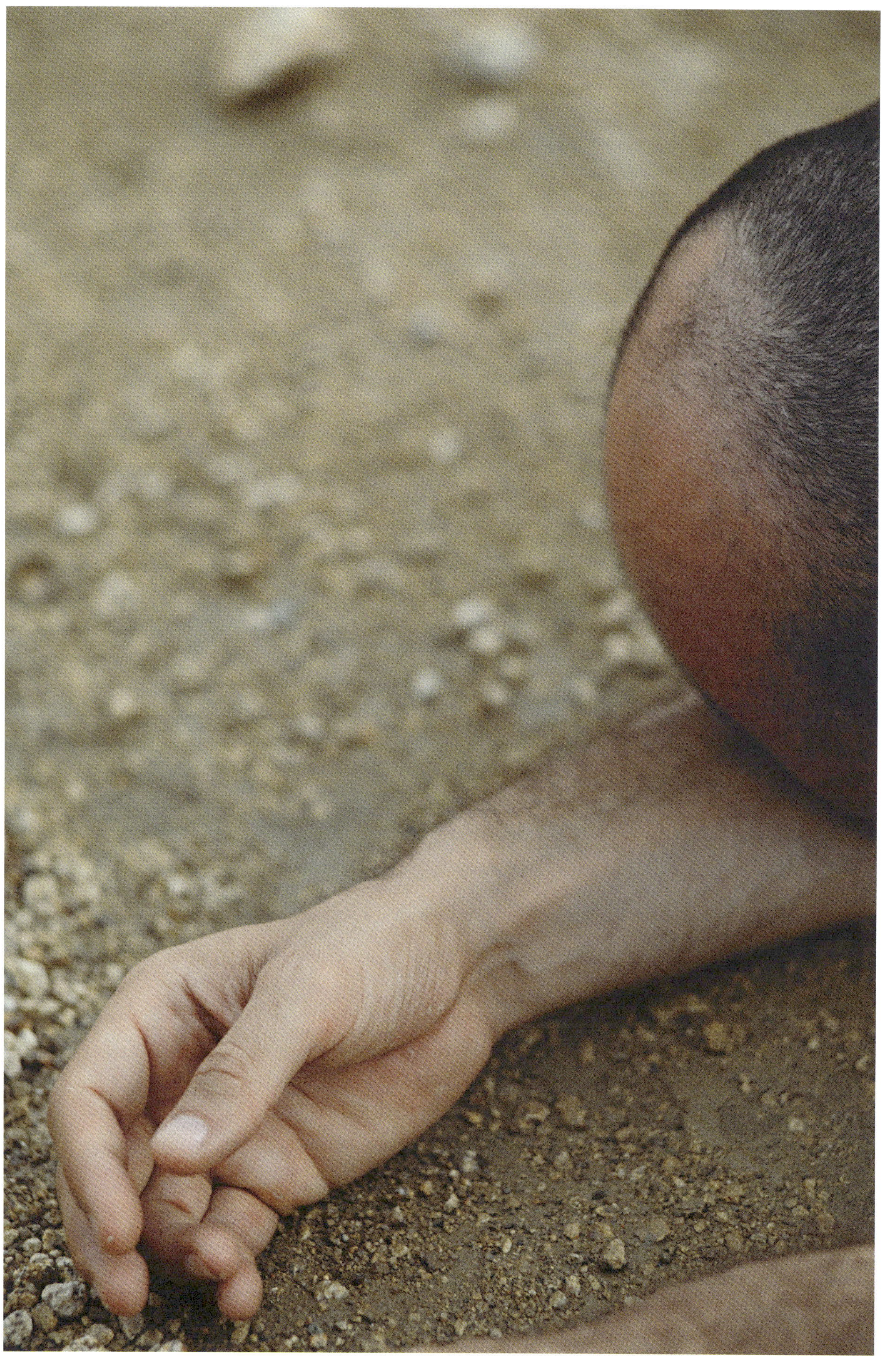

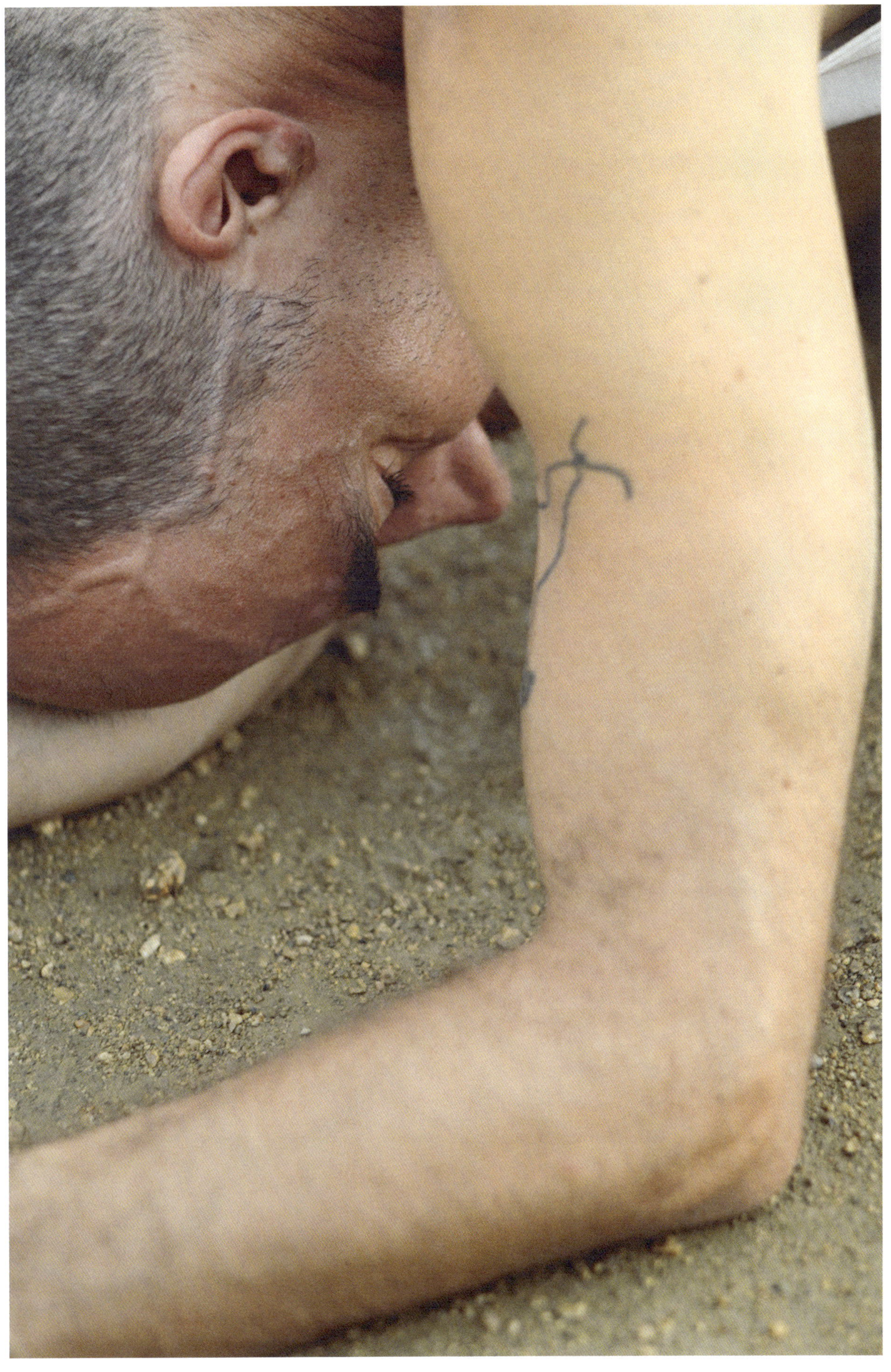

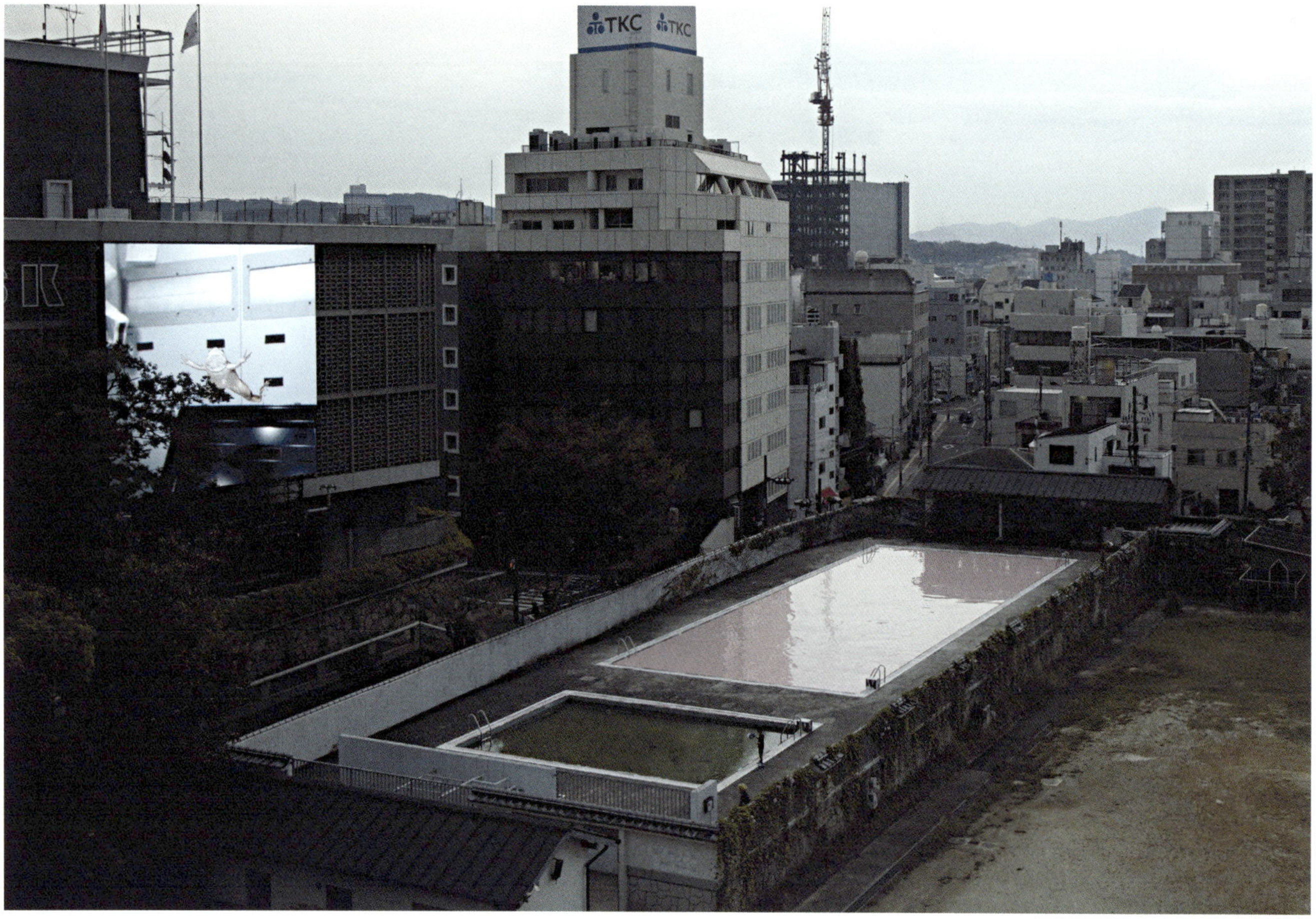

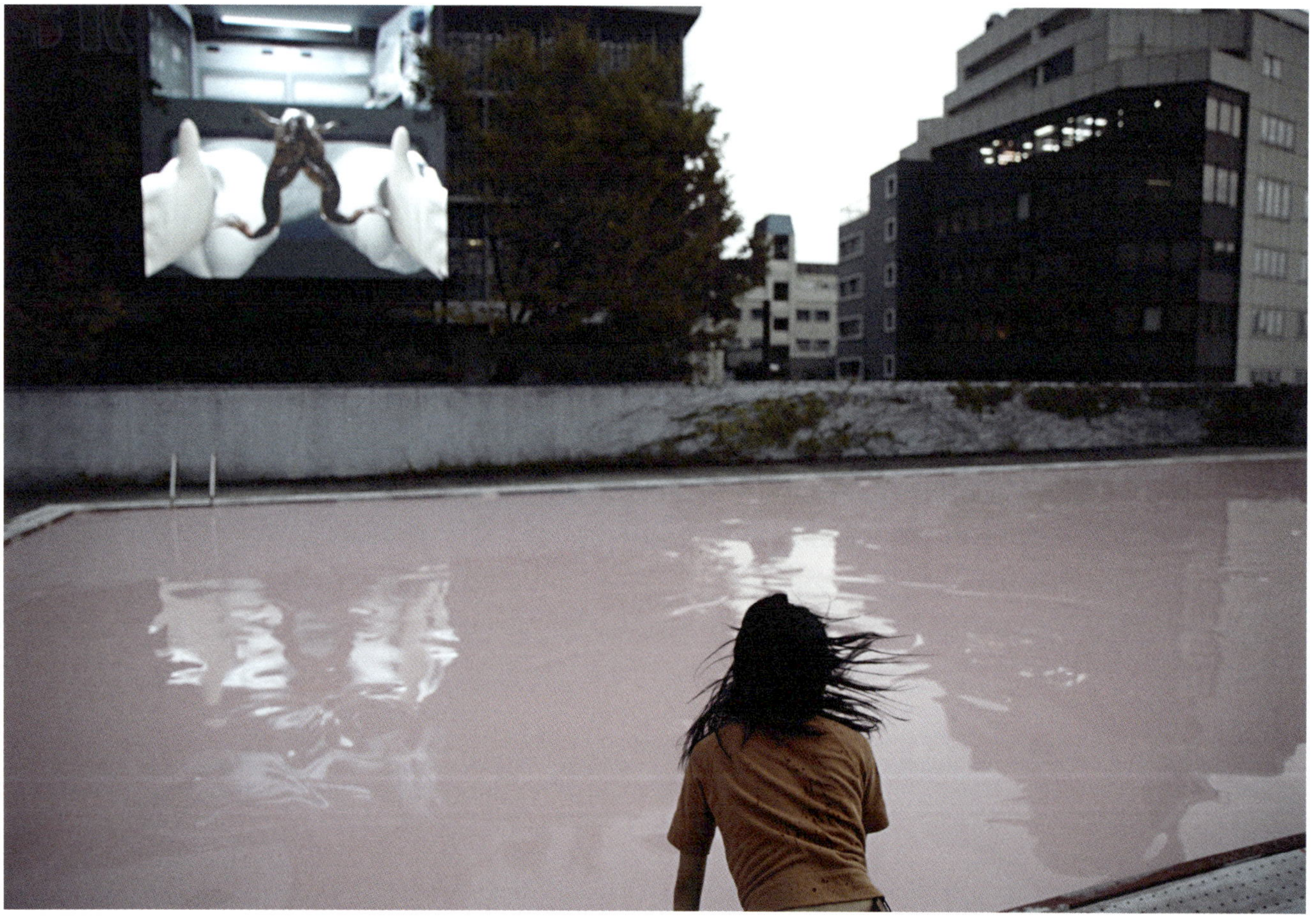

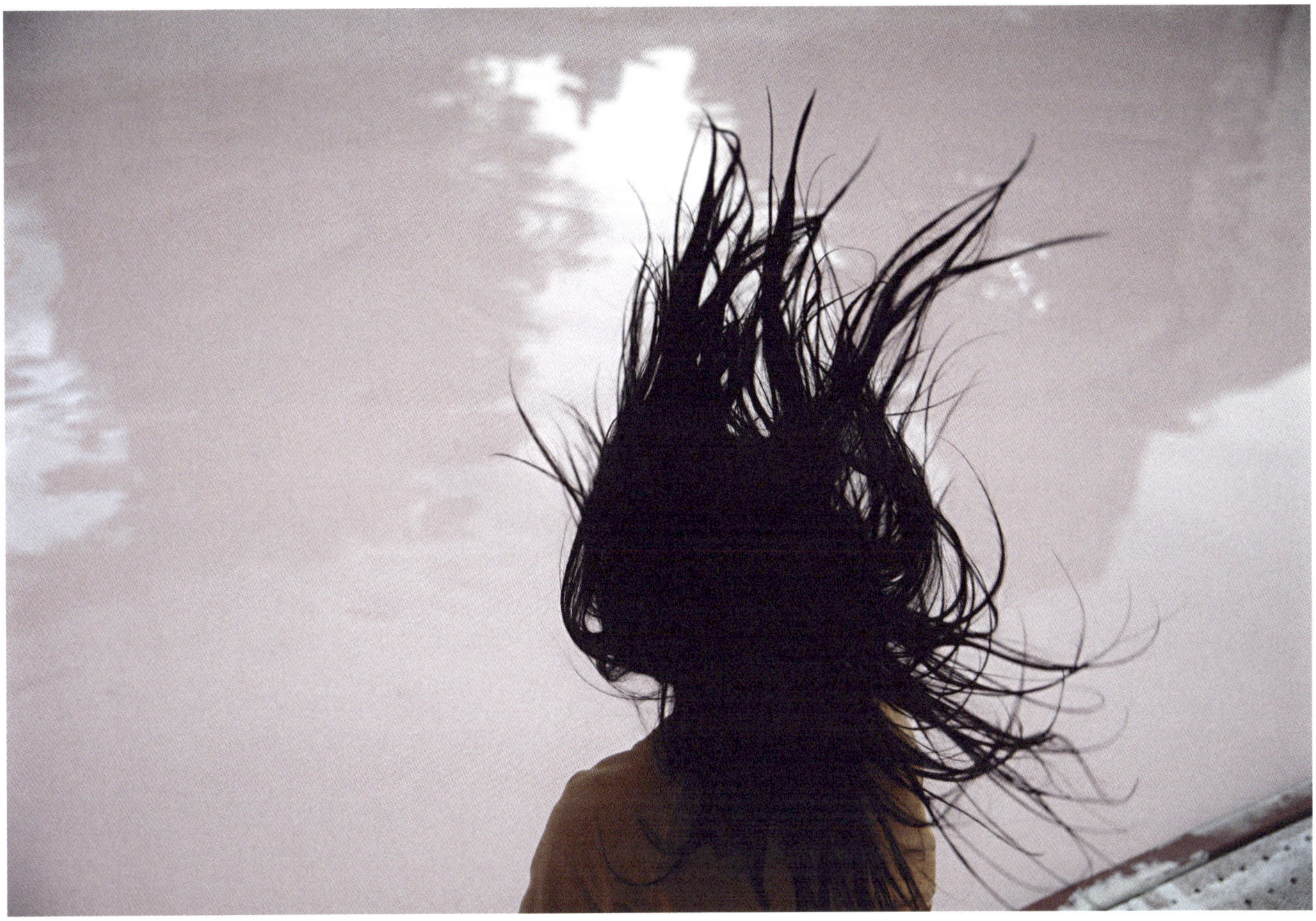

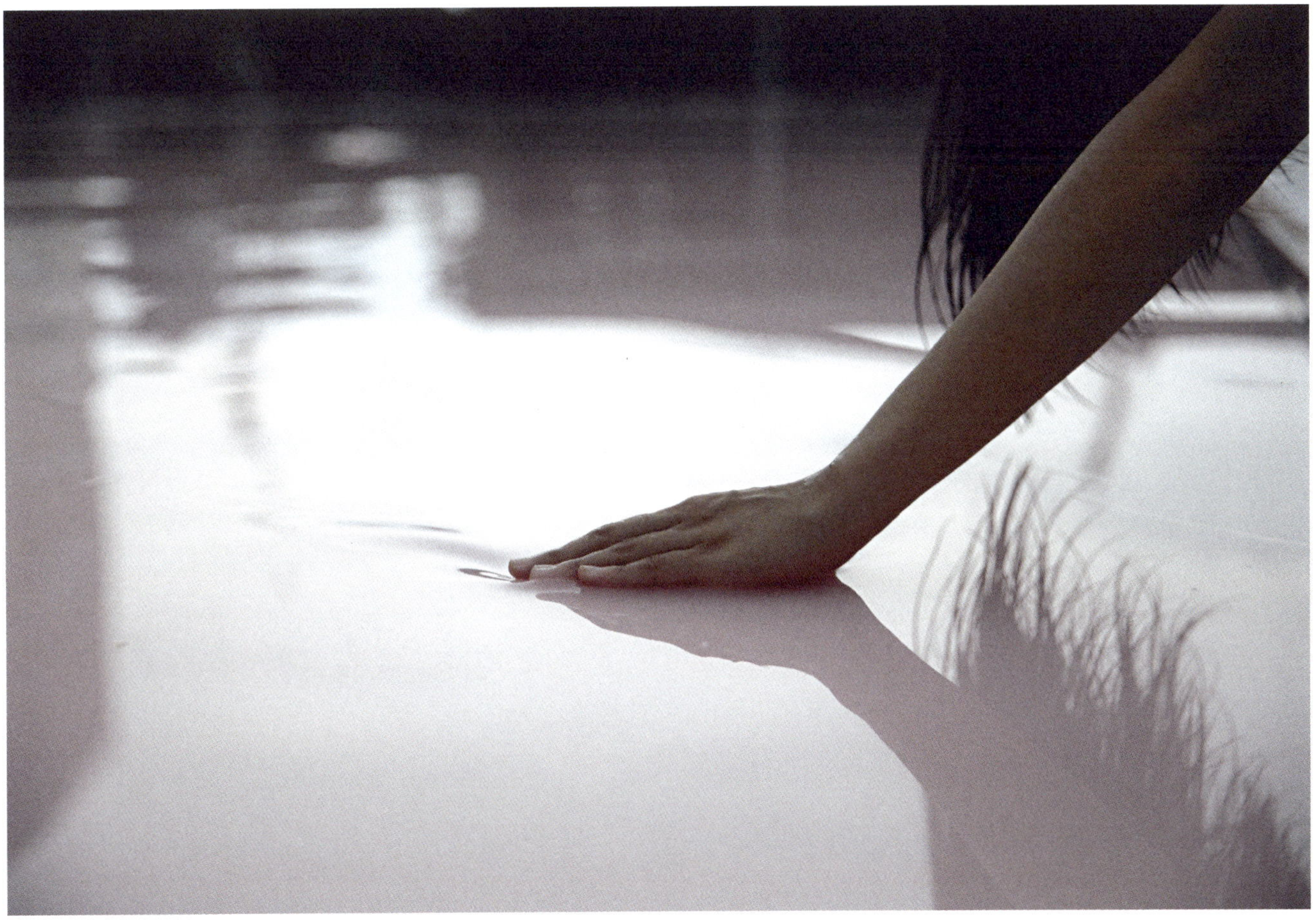

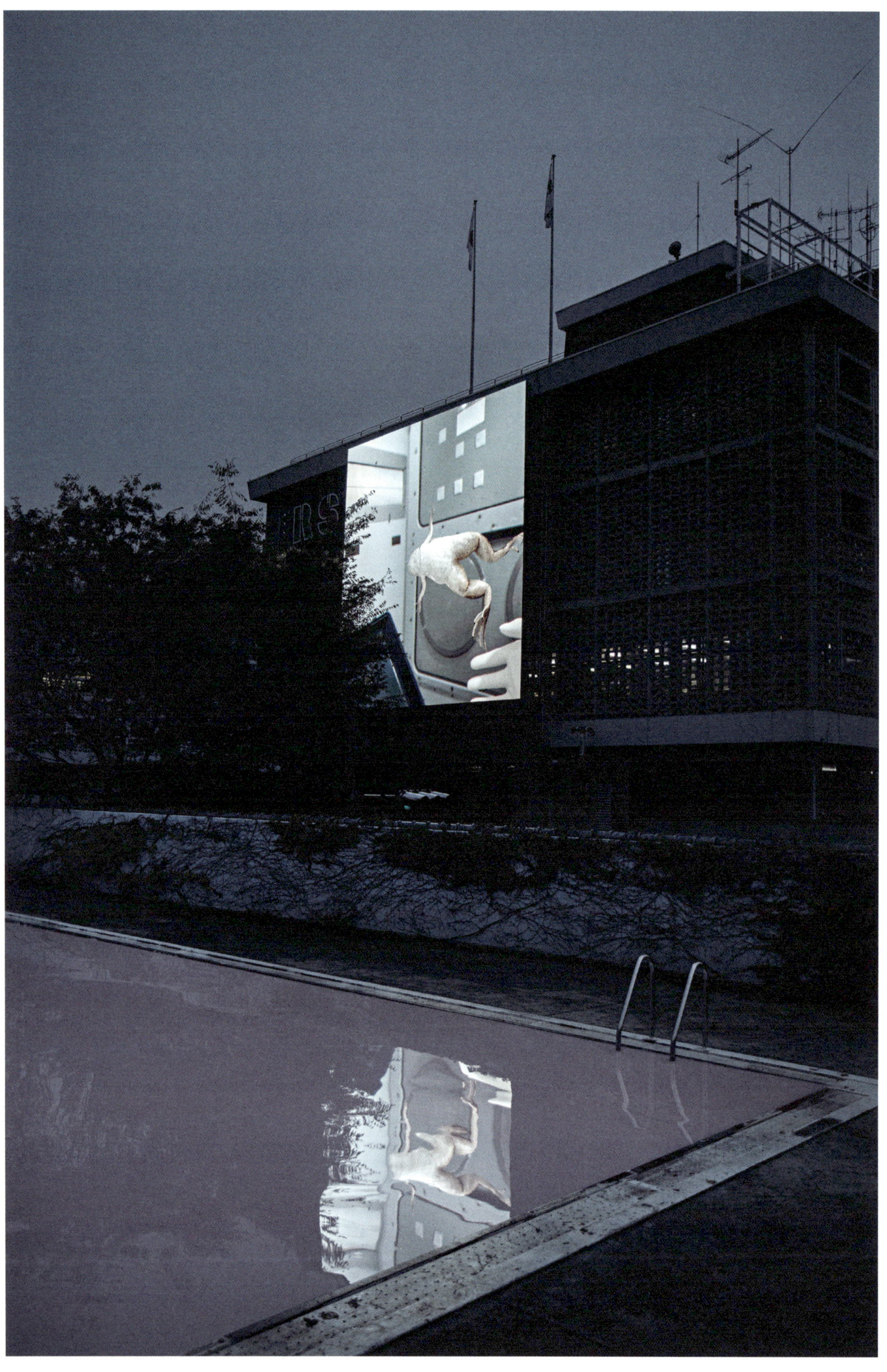

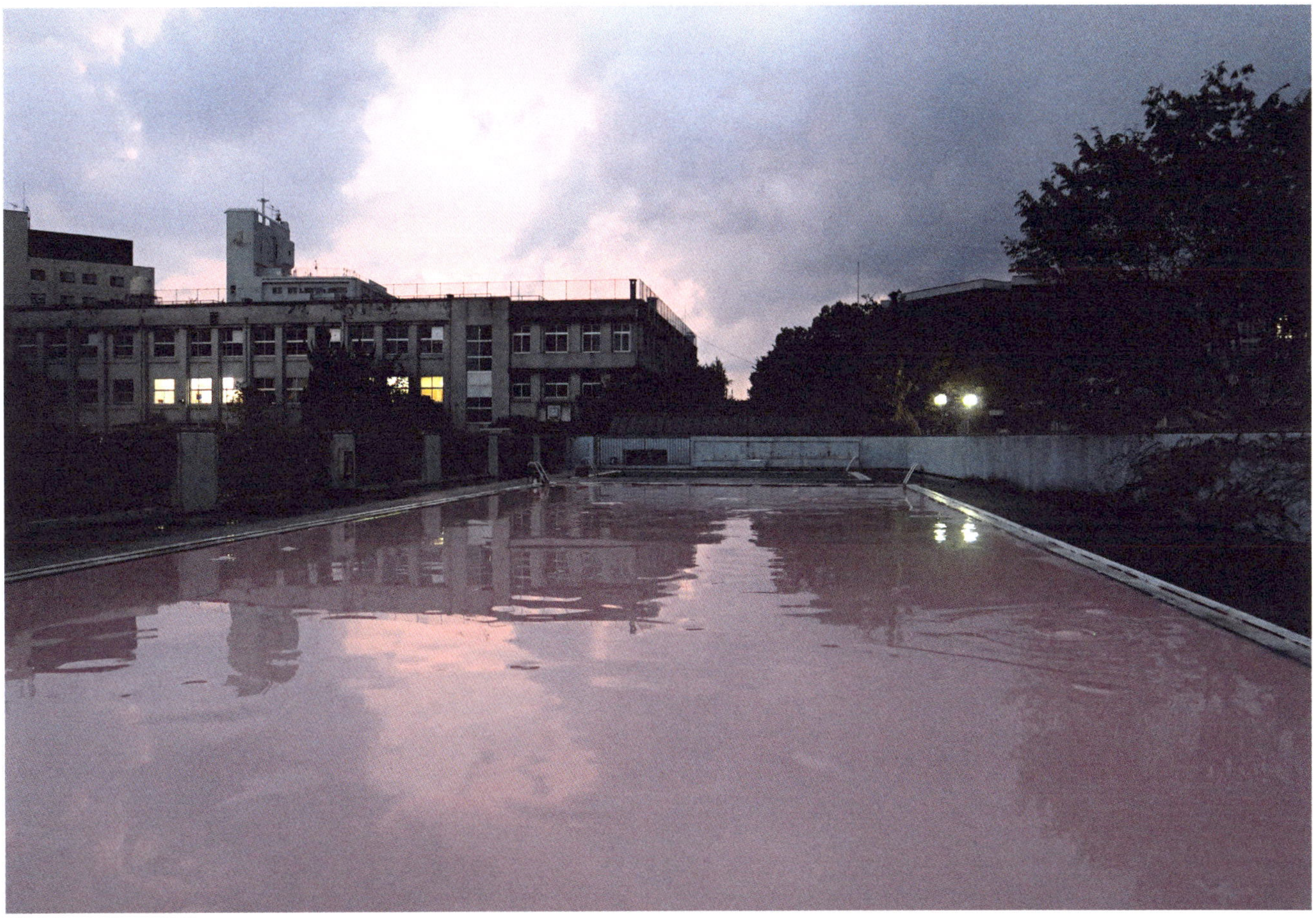

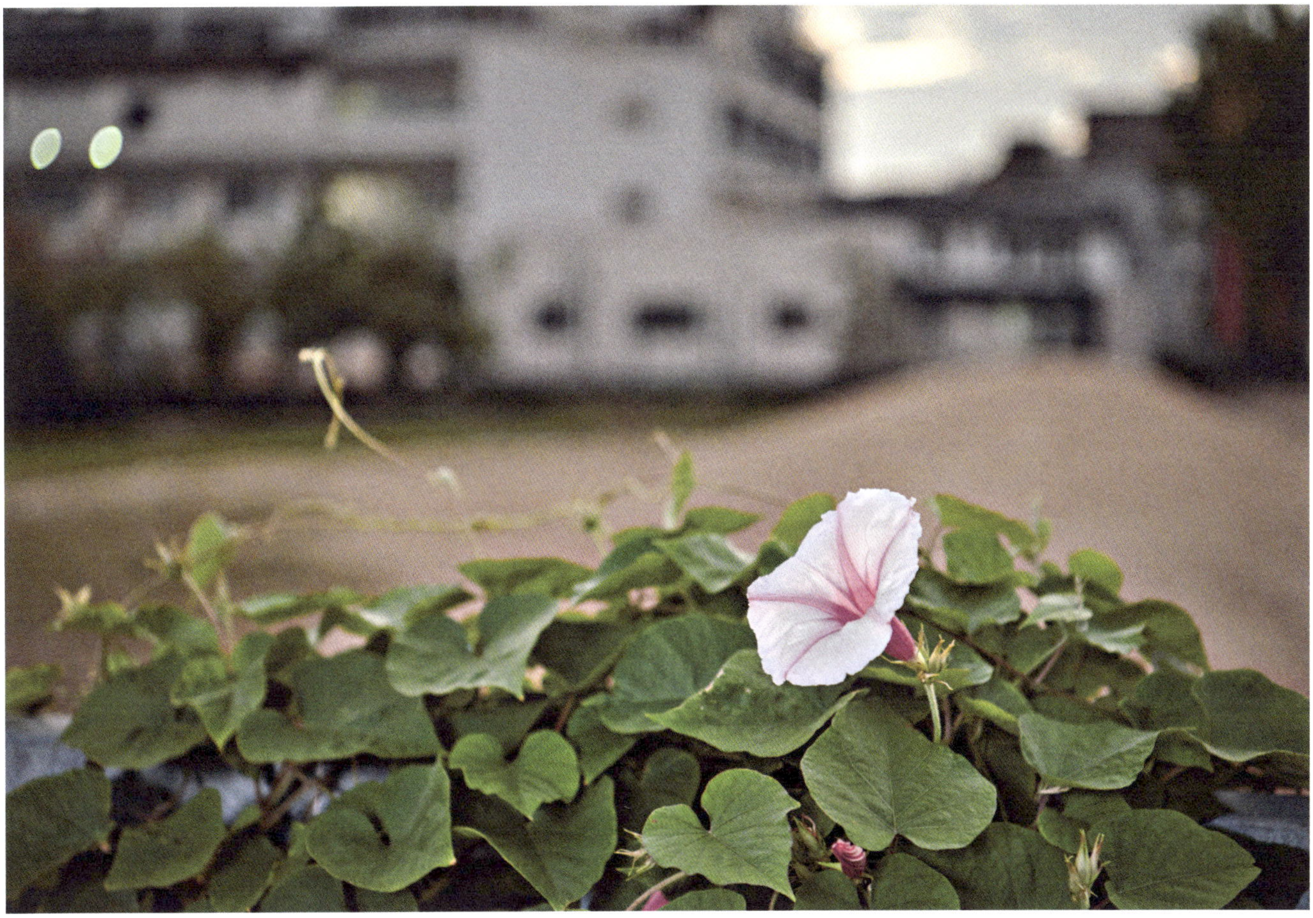

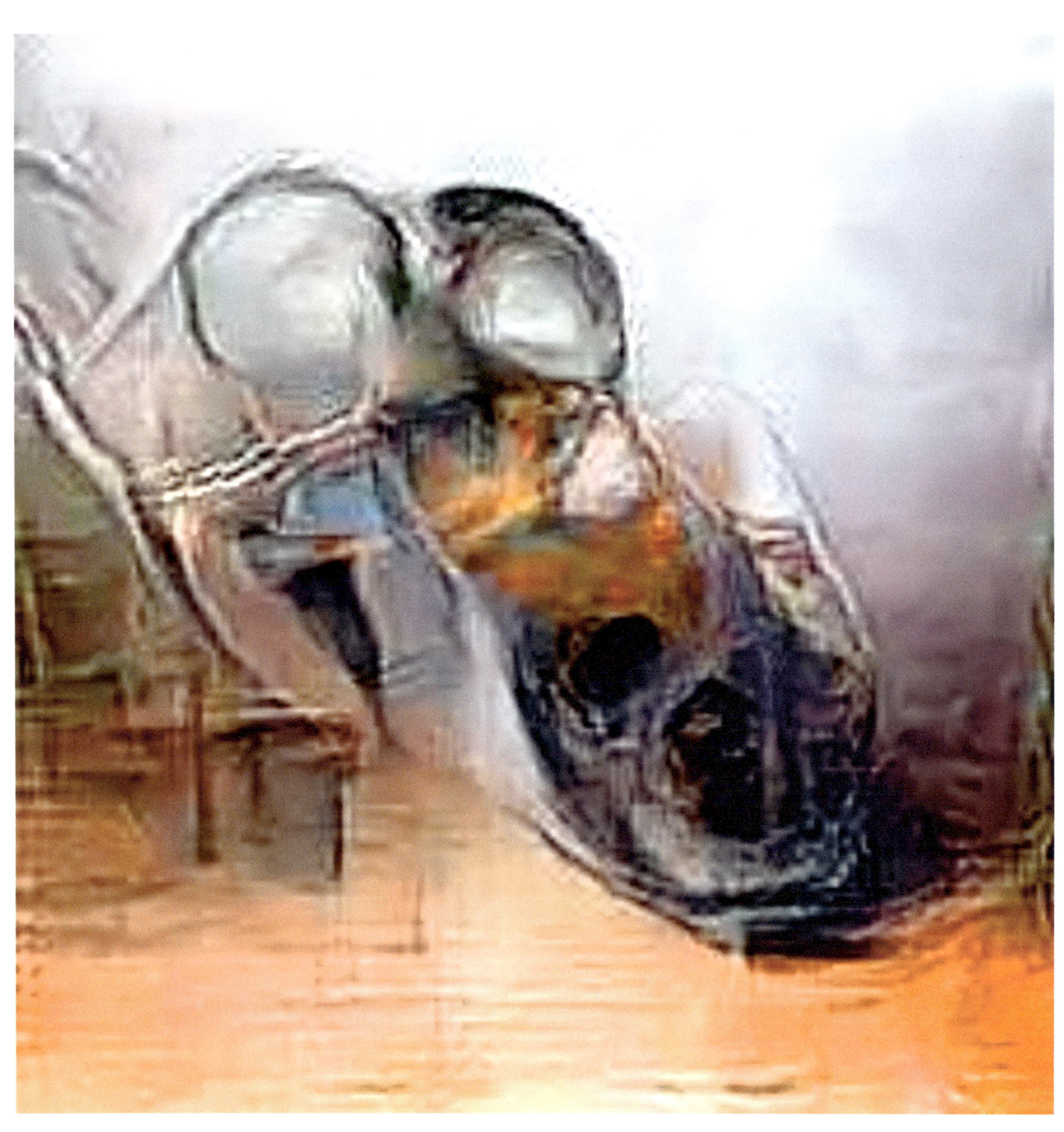

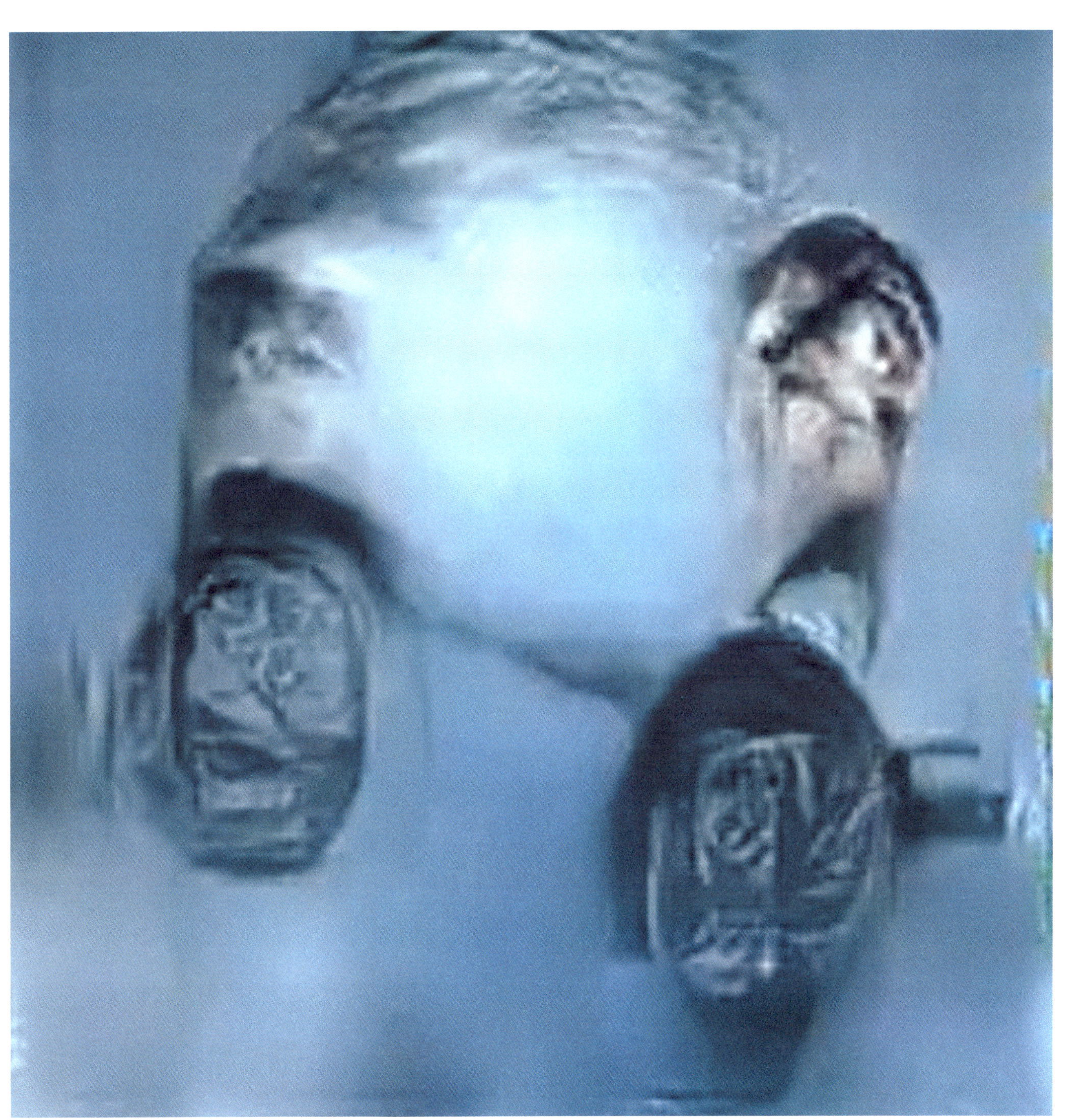

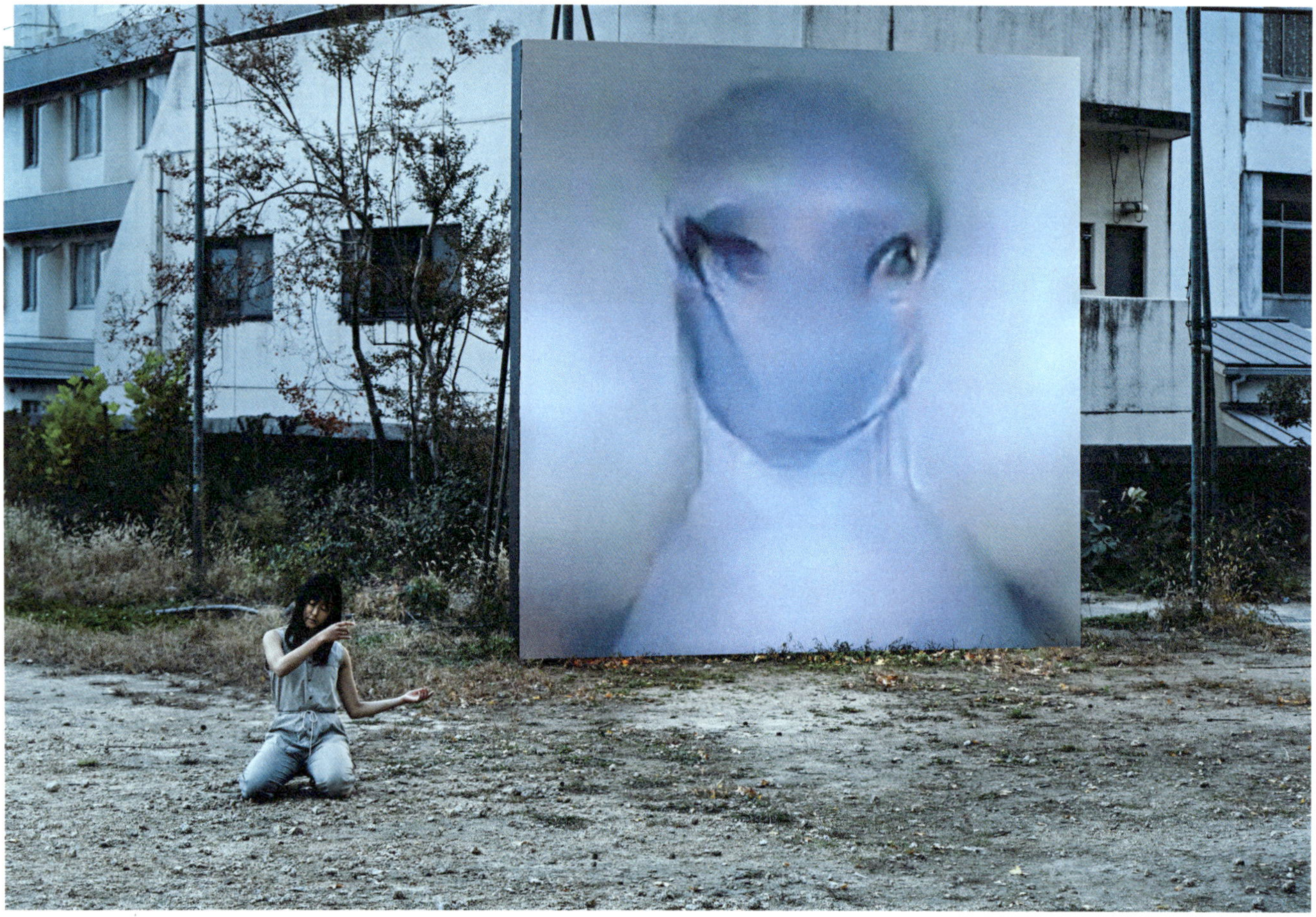

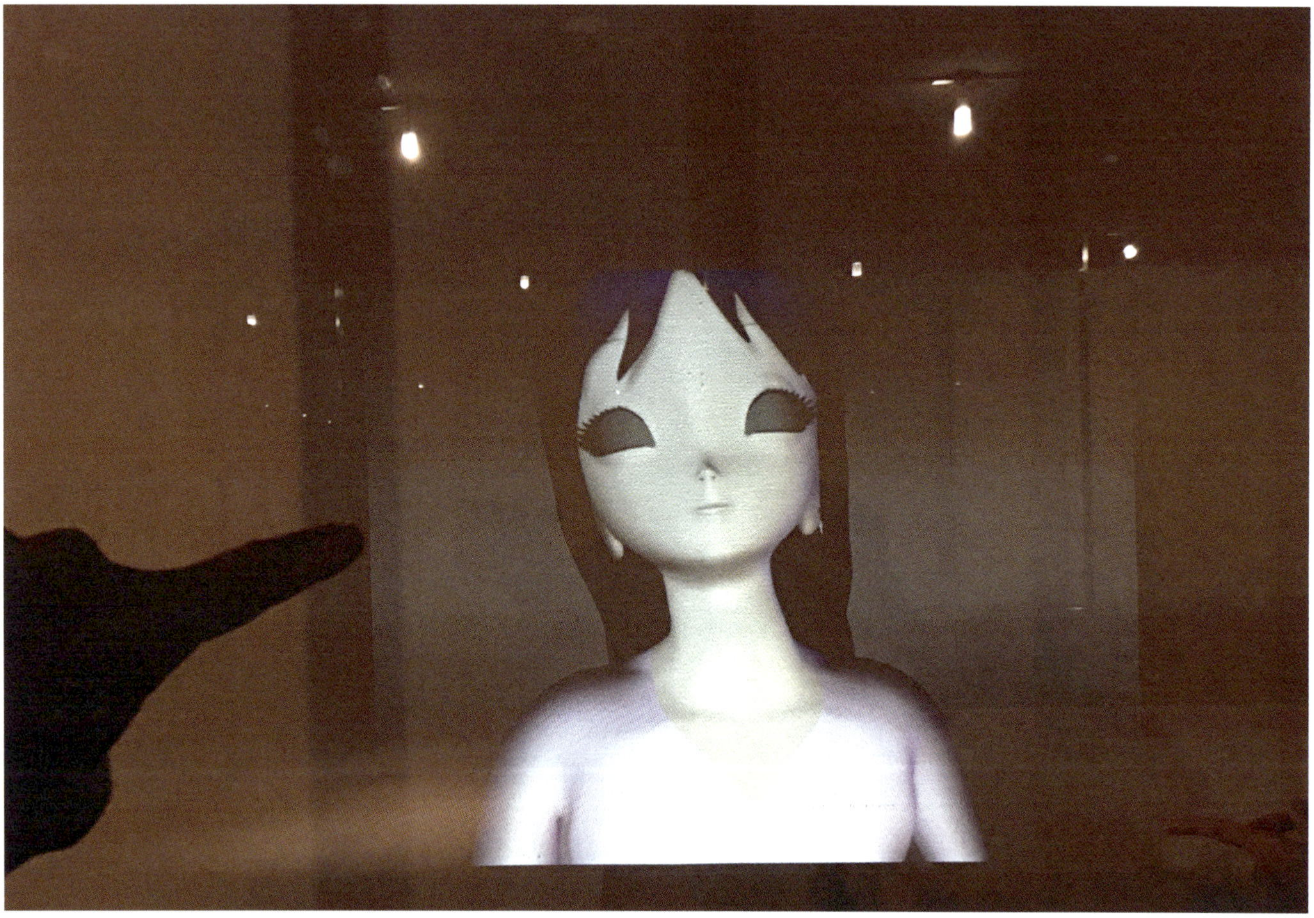

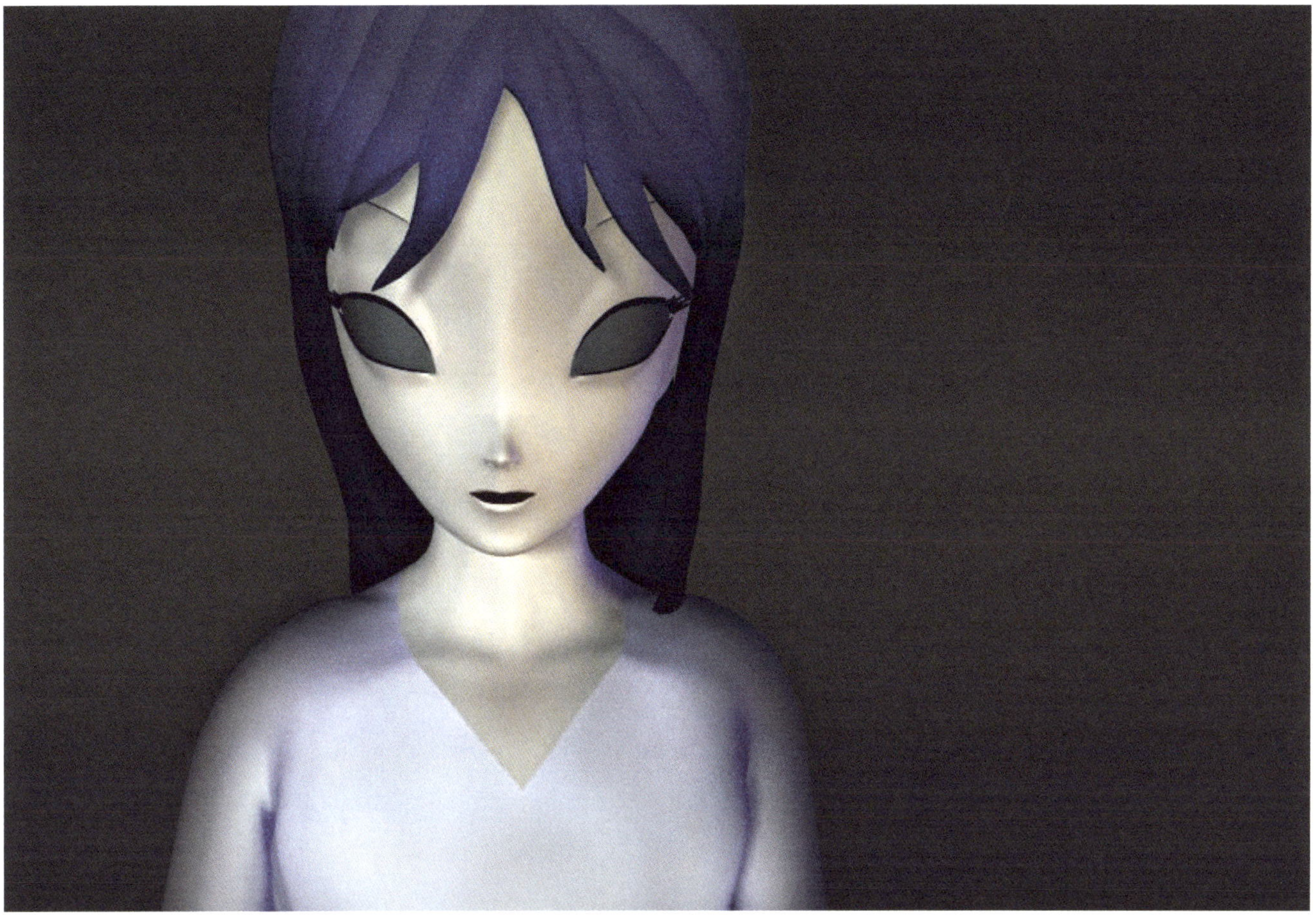

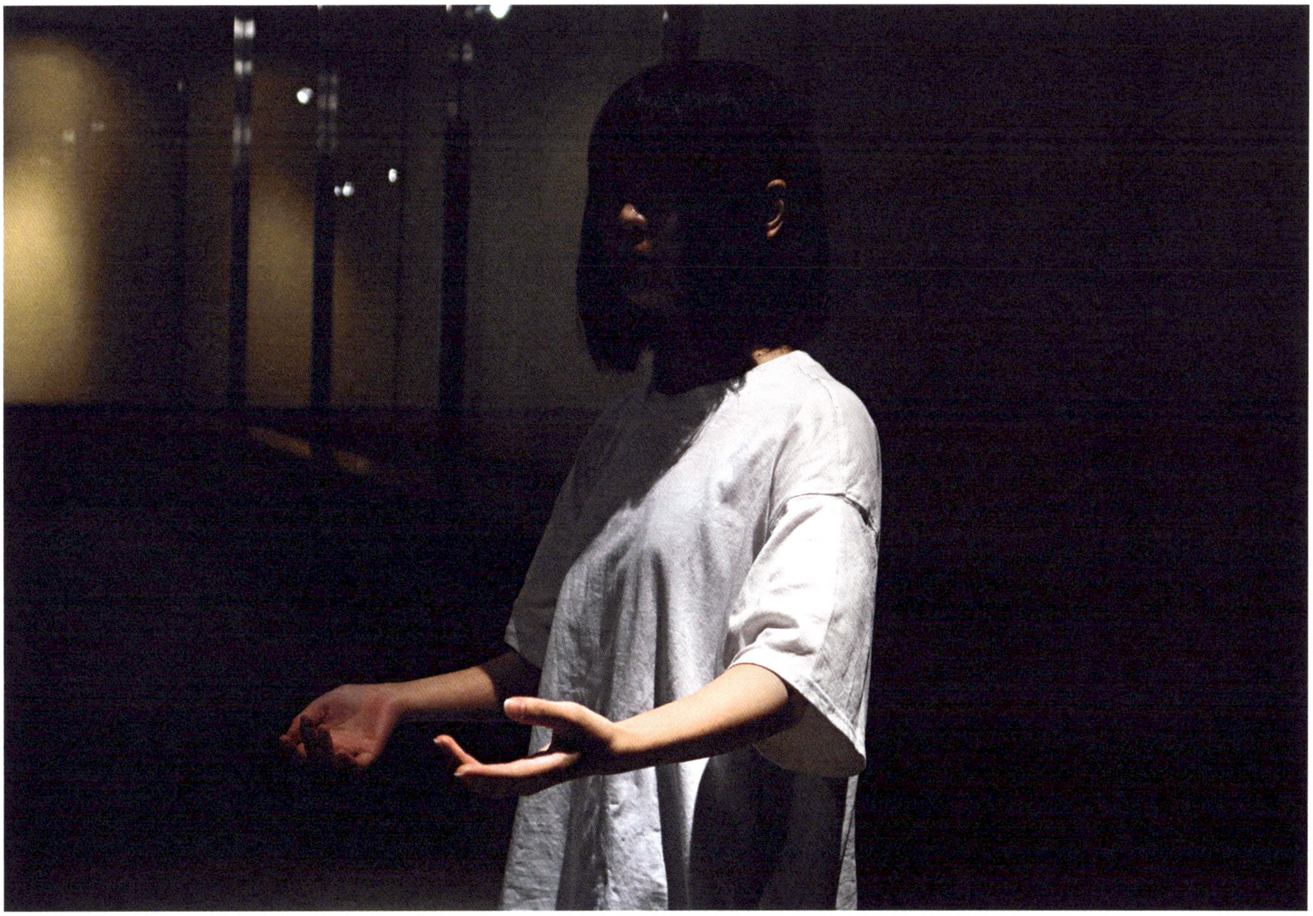

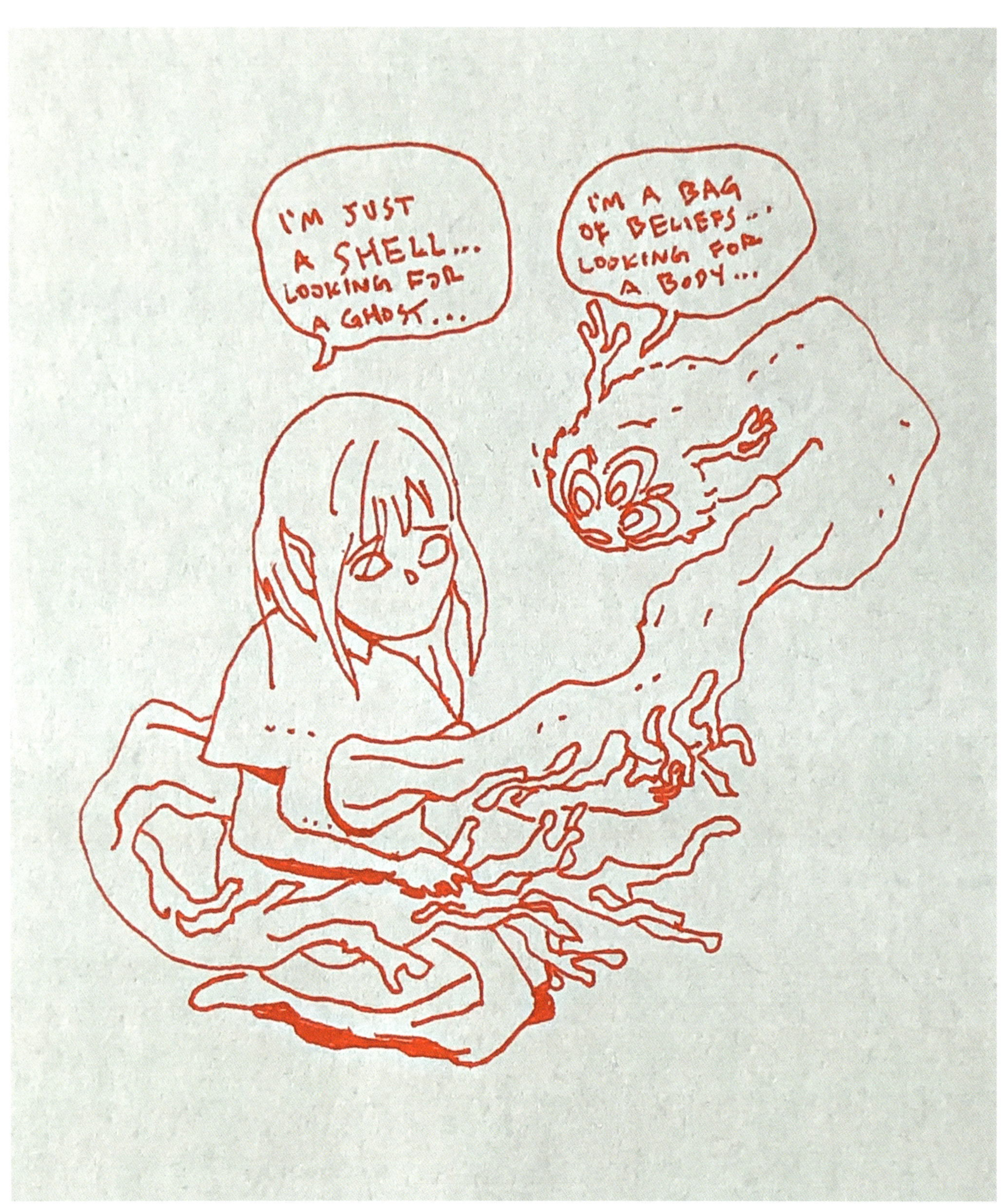
I'M JUST A SHELL... LOOKING FOR A GHOST...
I'M A BAG OF BELIEFS... LOOKING FOR A BODY...

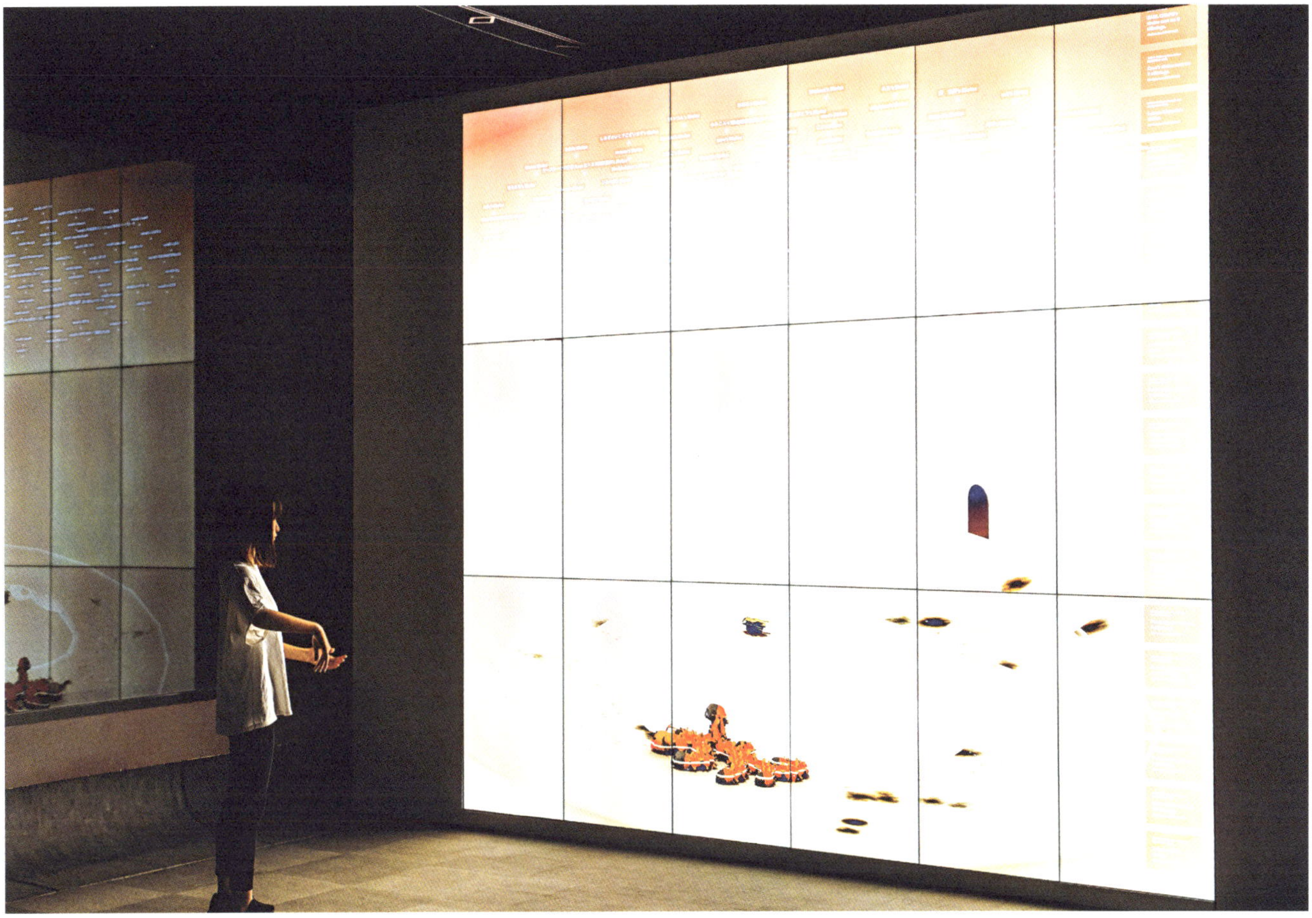

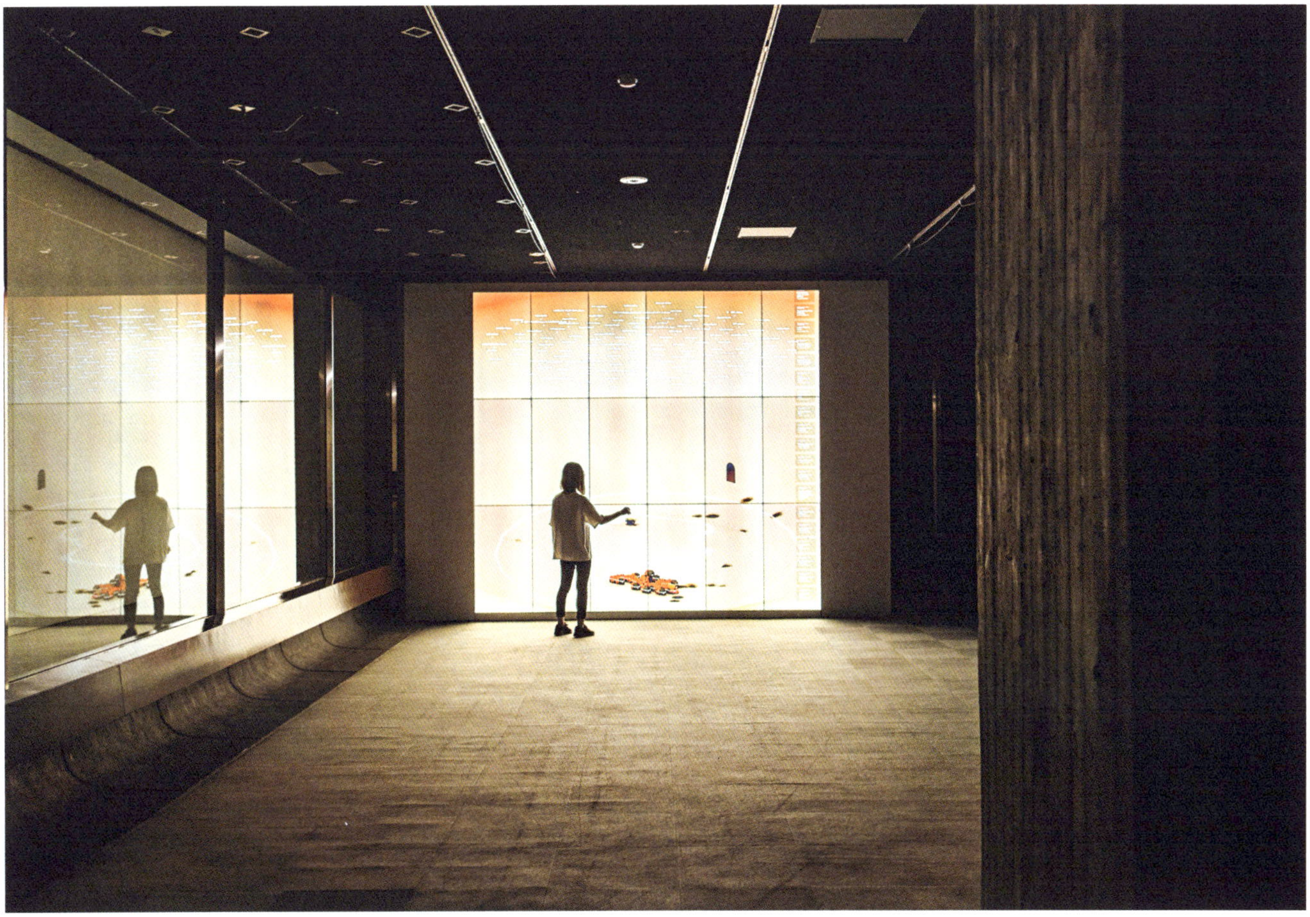

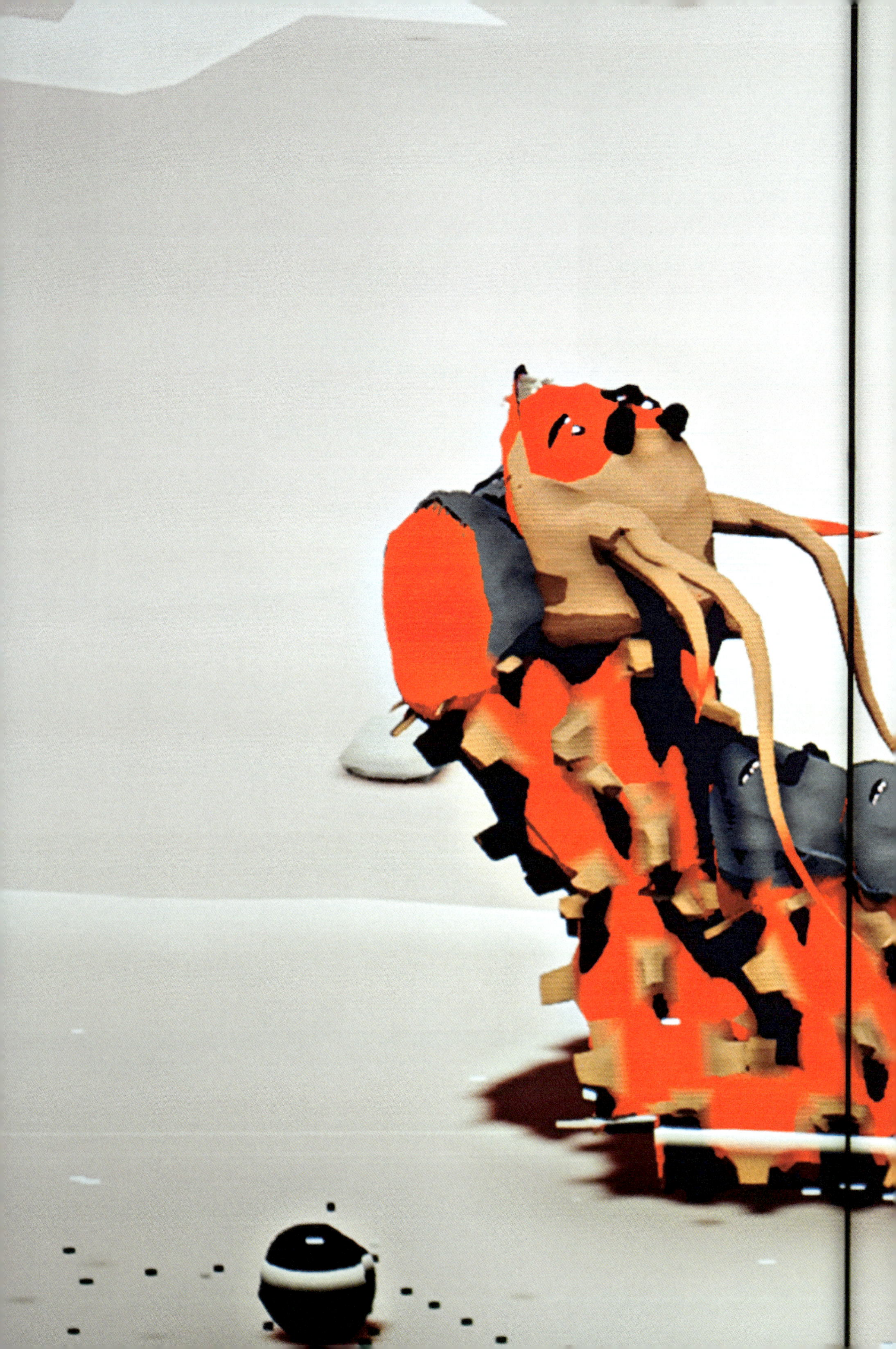

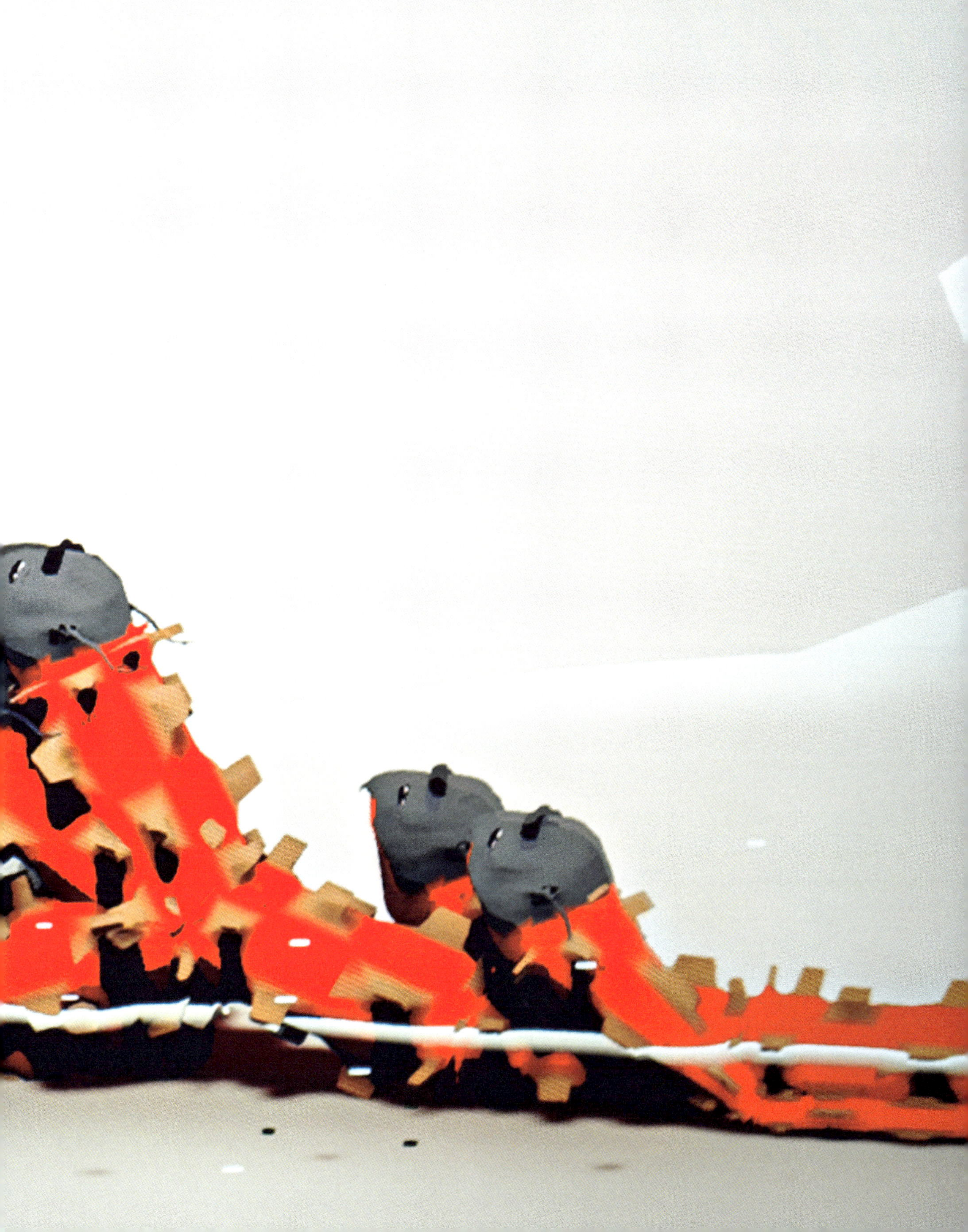

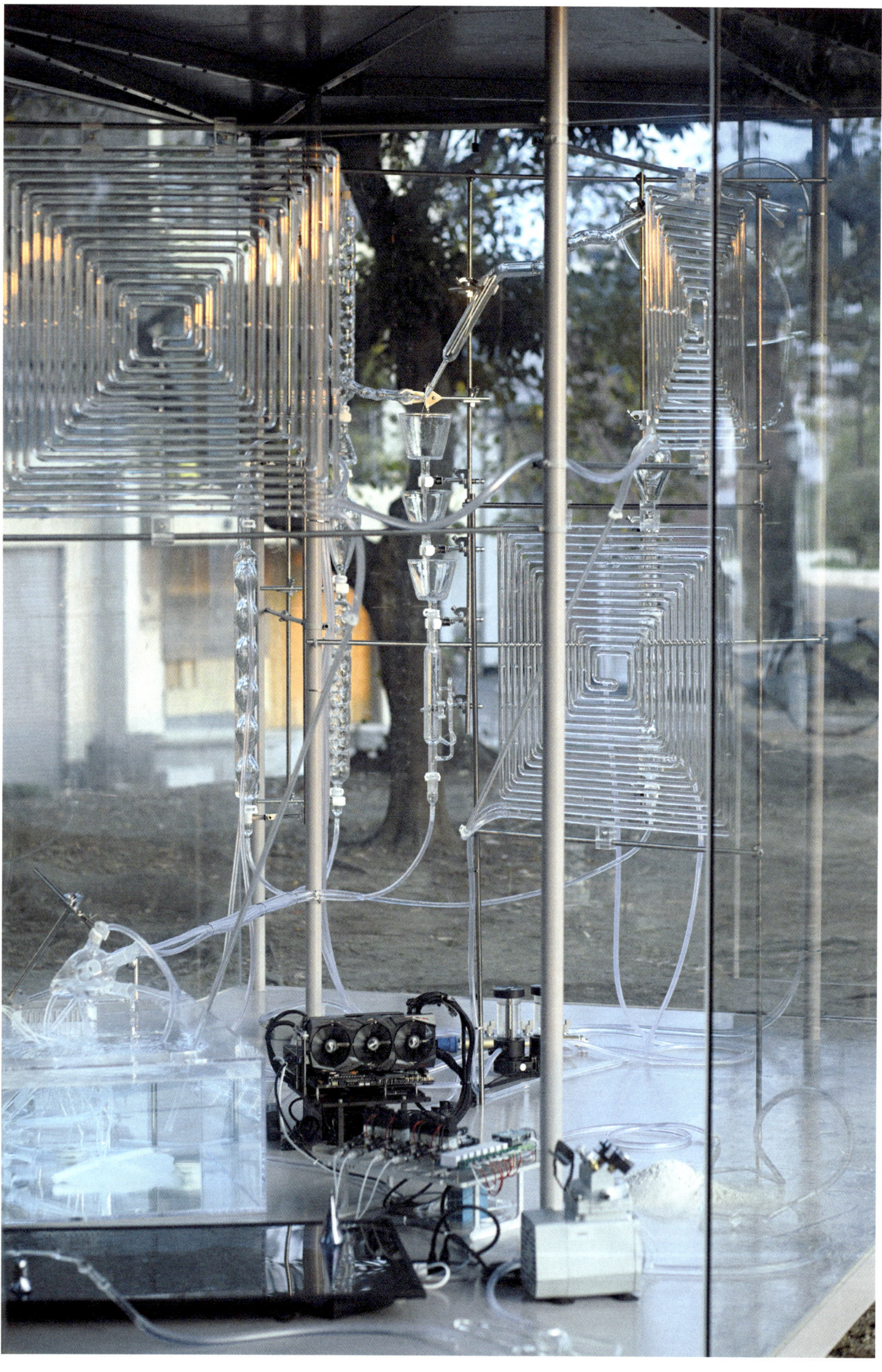

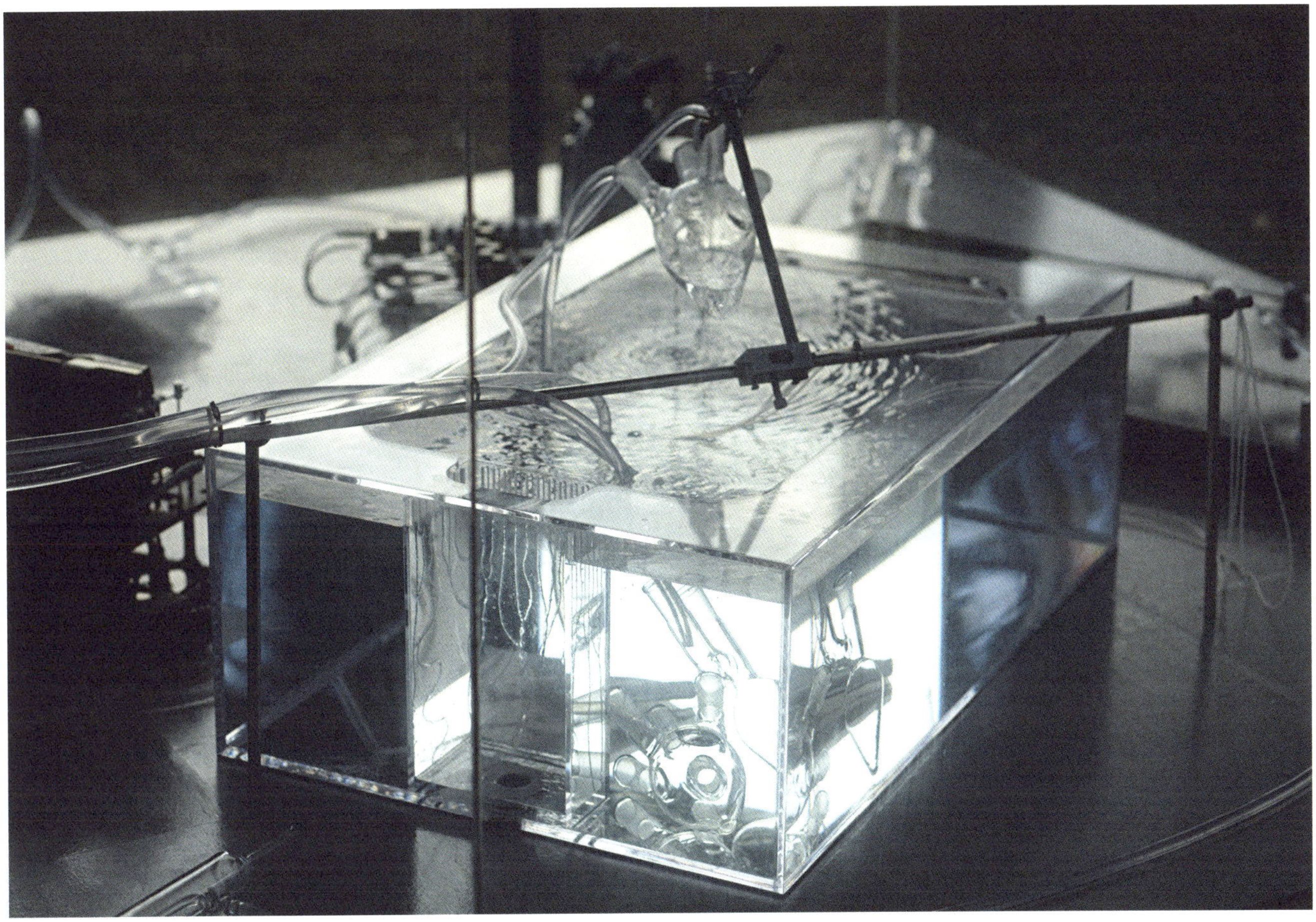

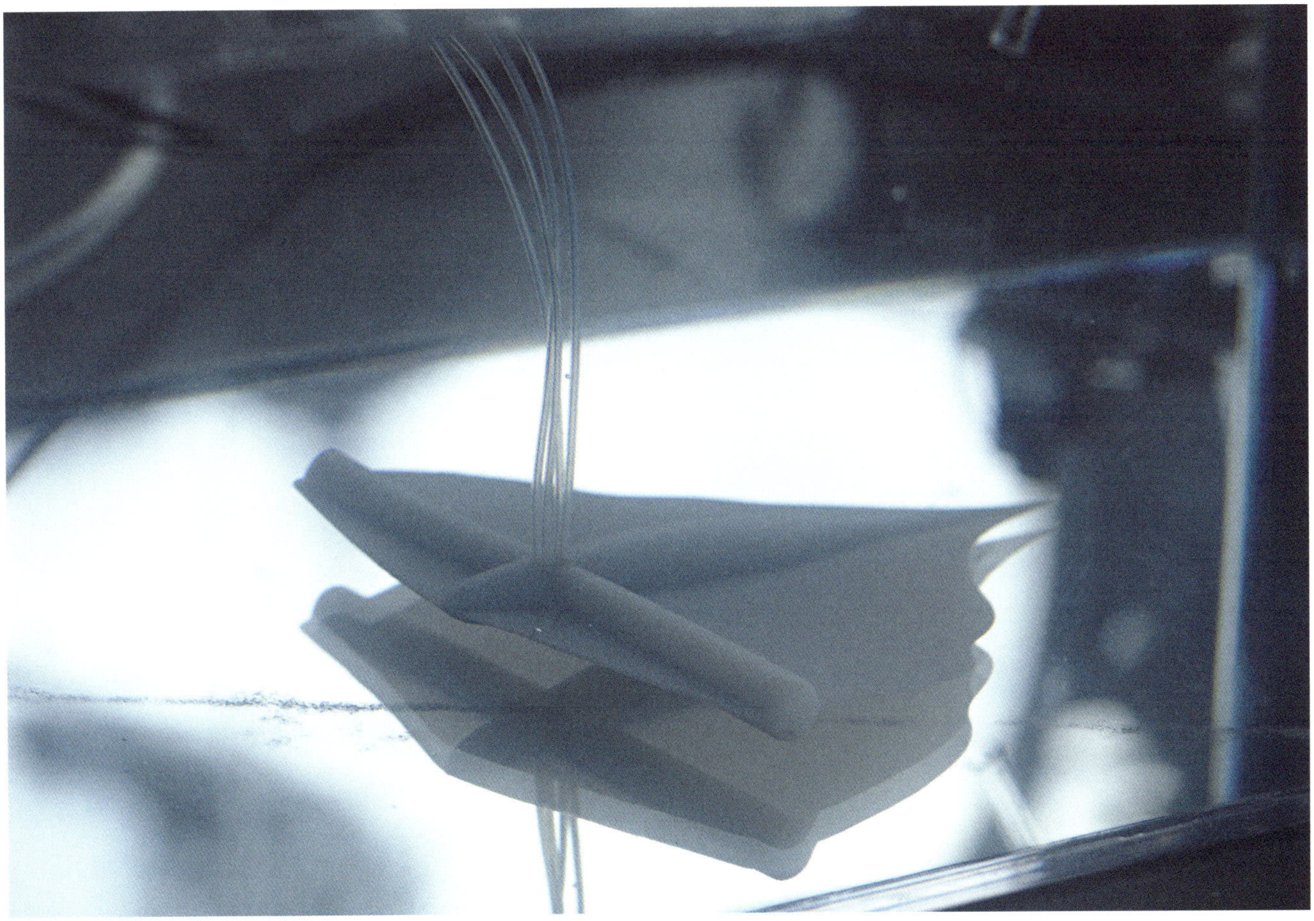

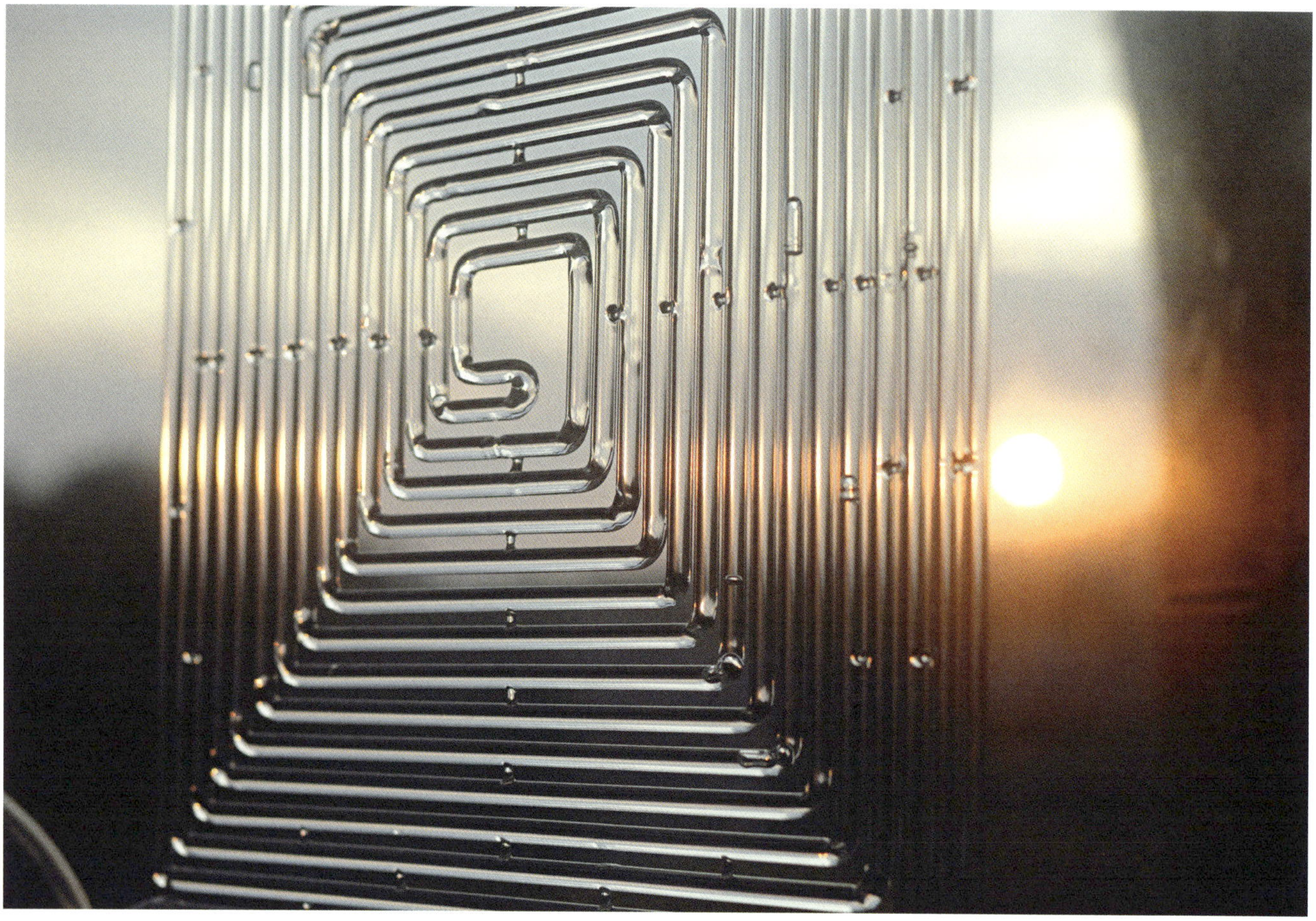

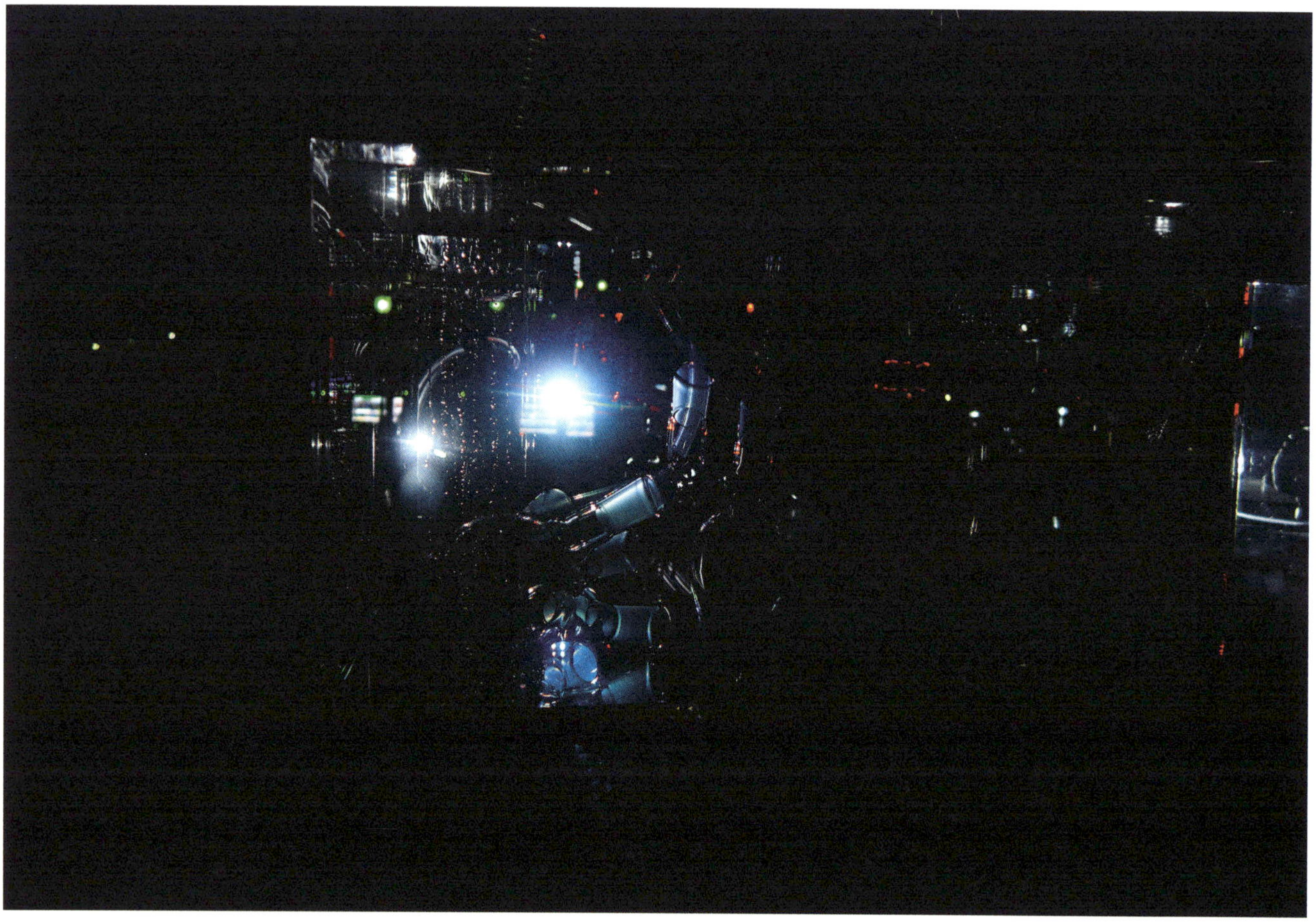

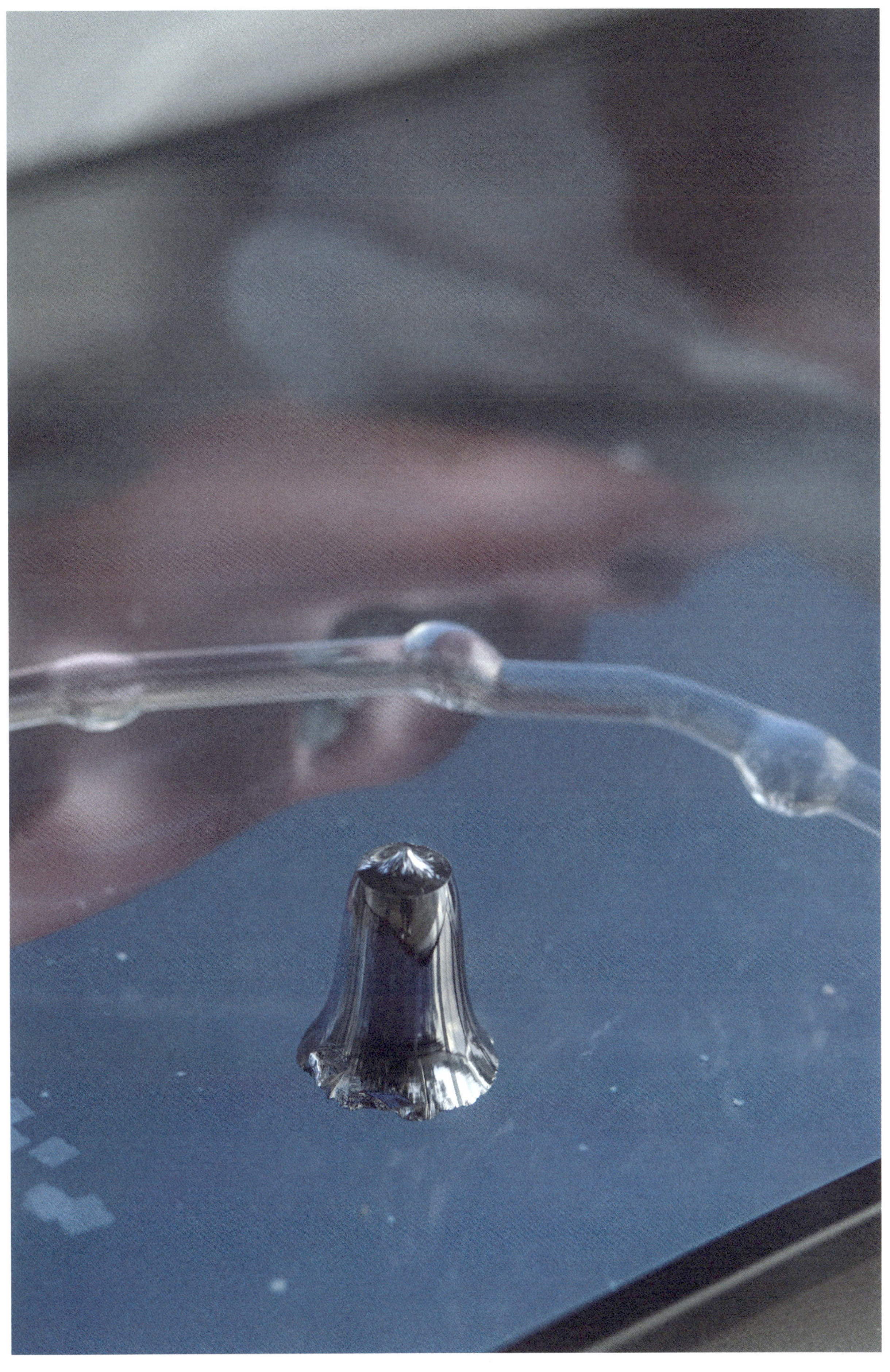

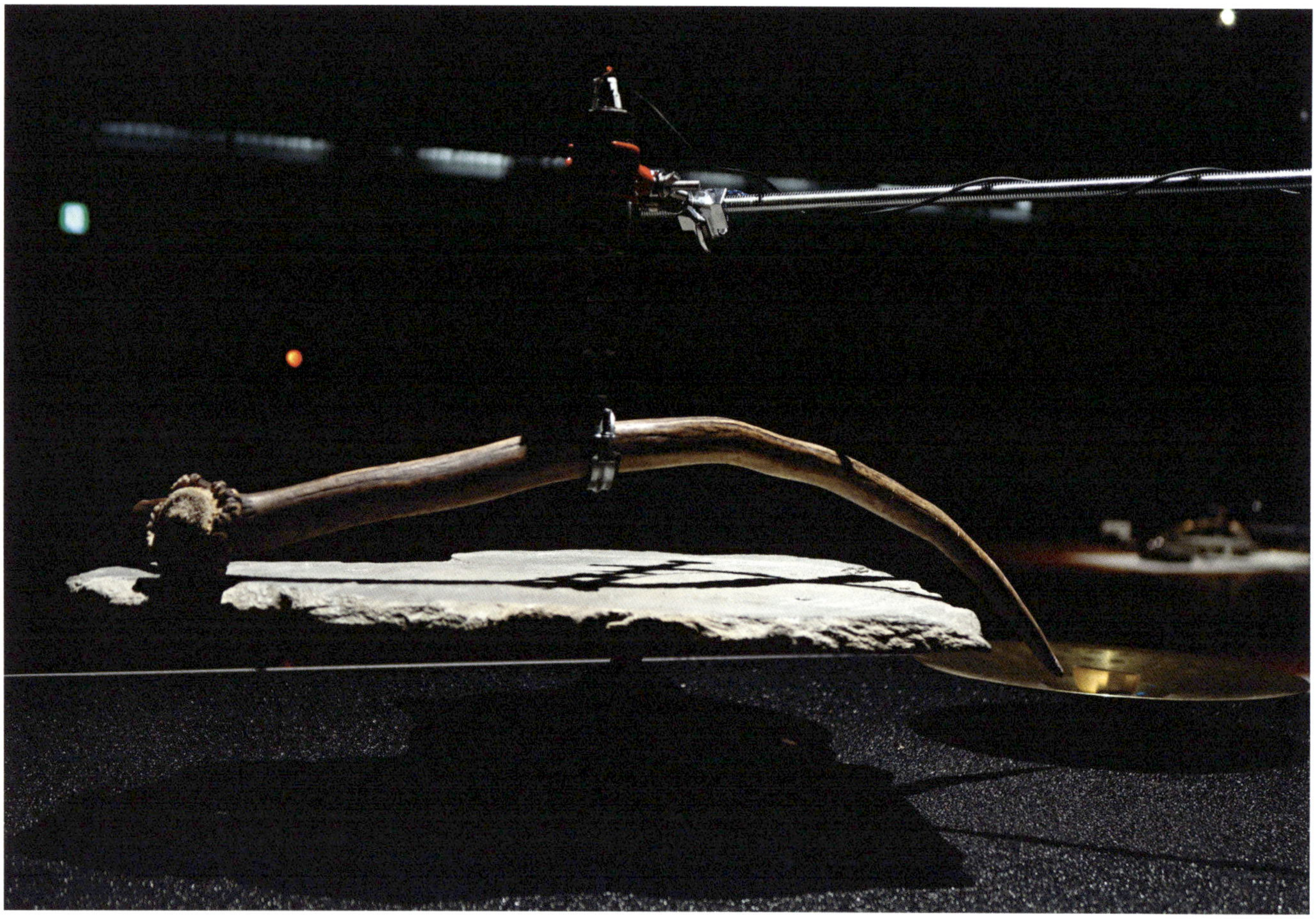

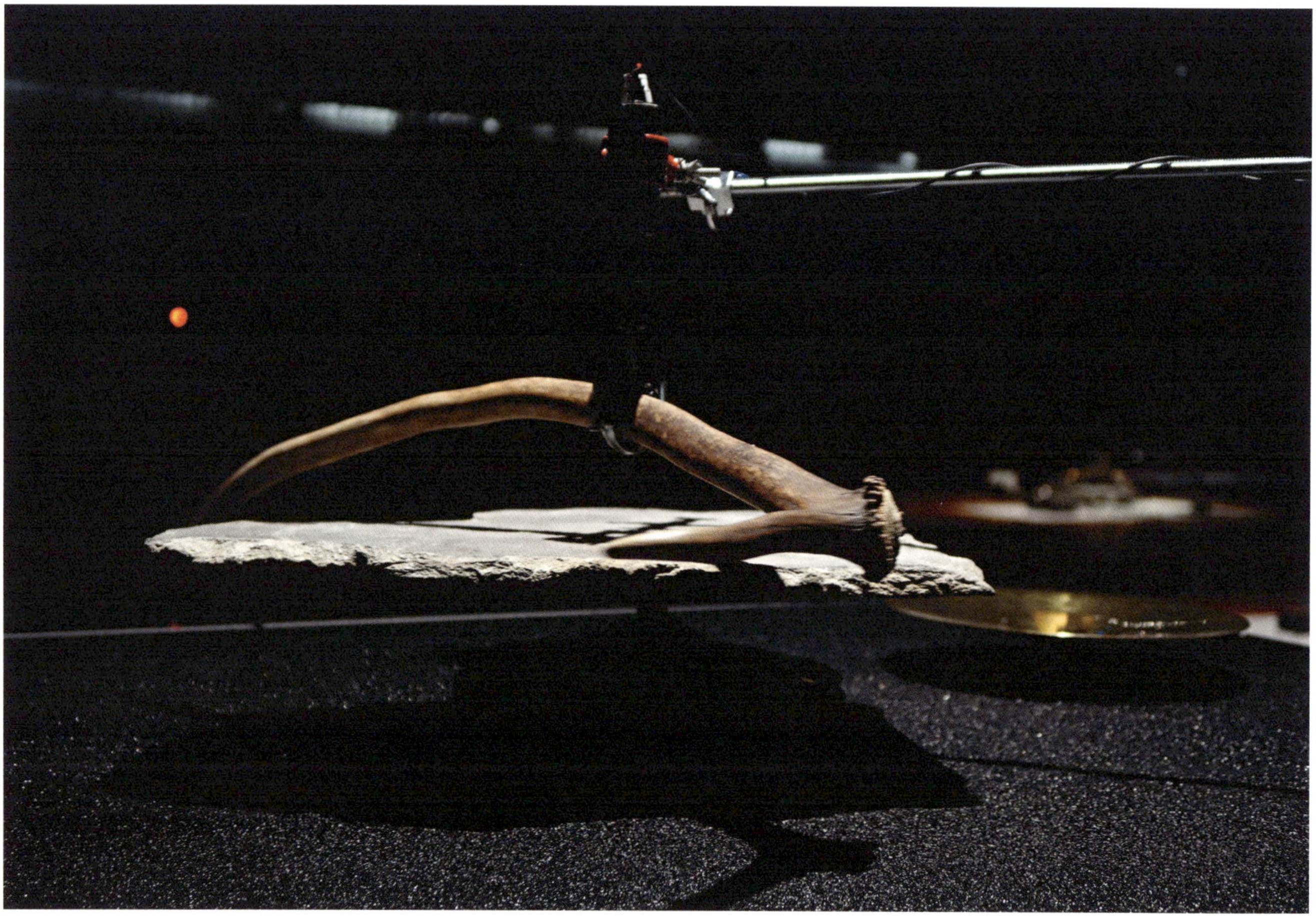

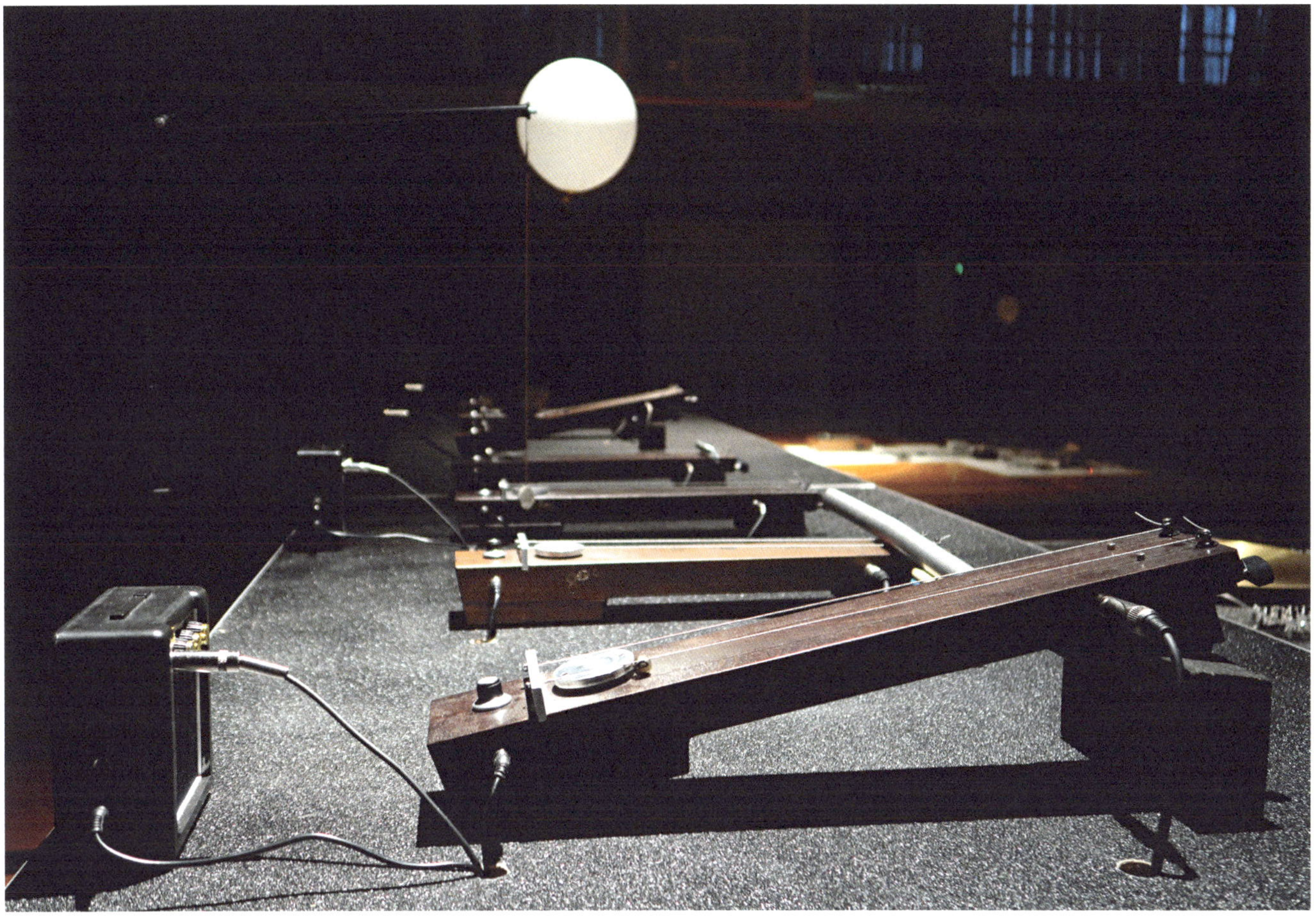

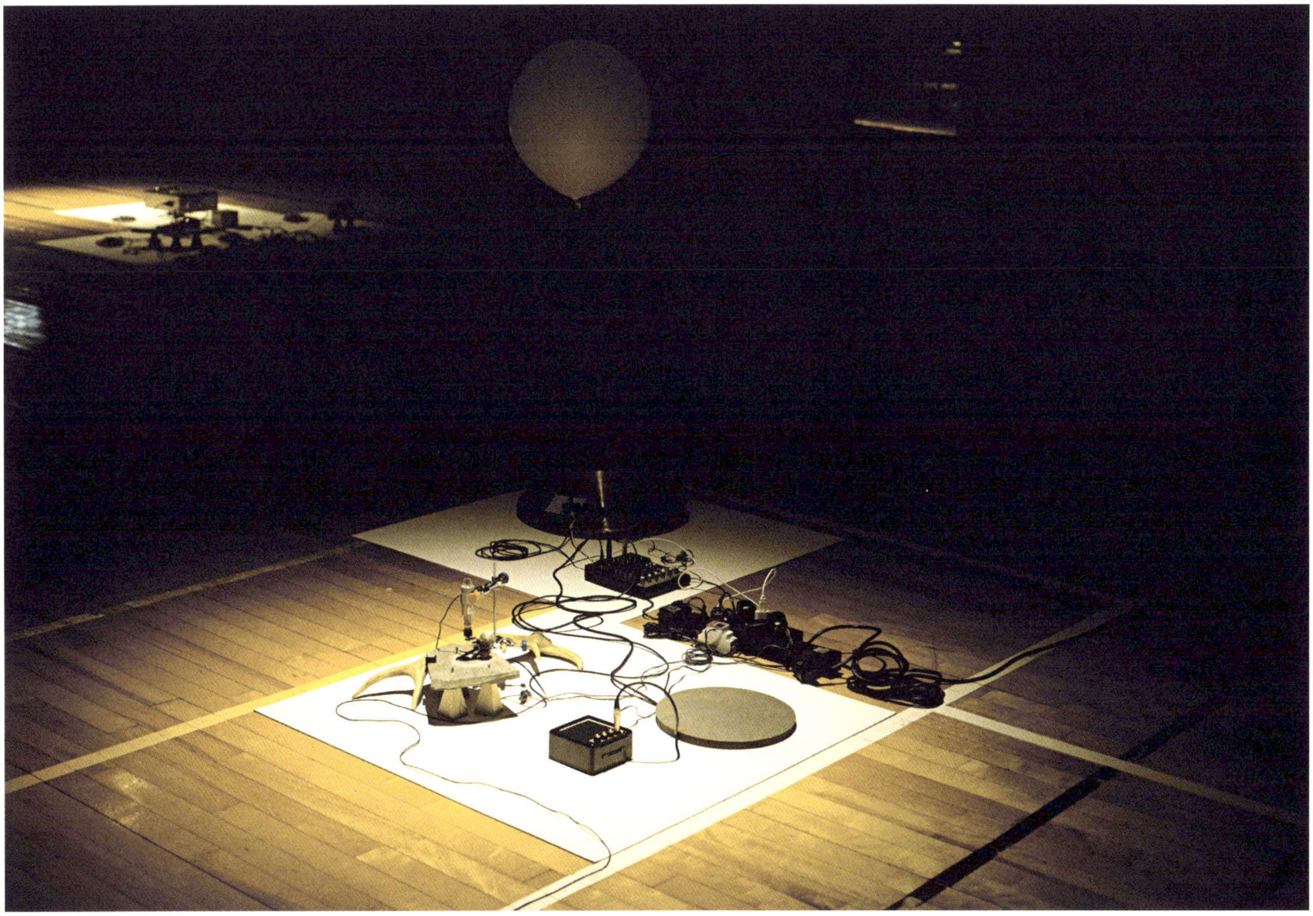

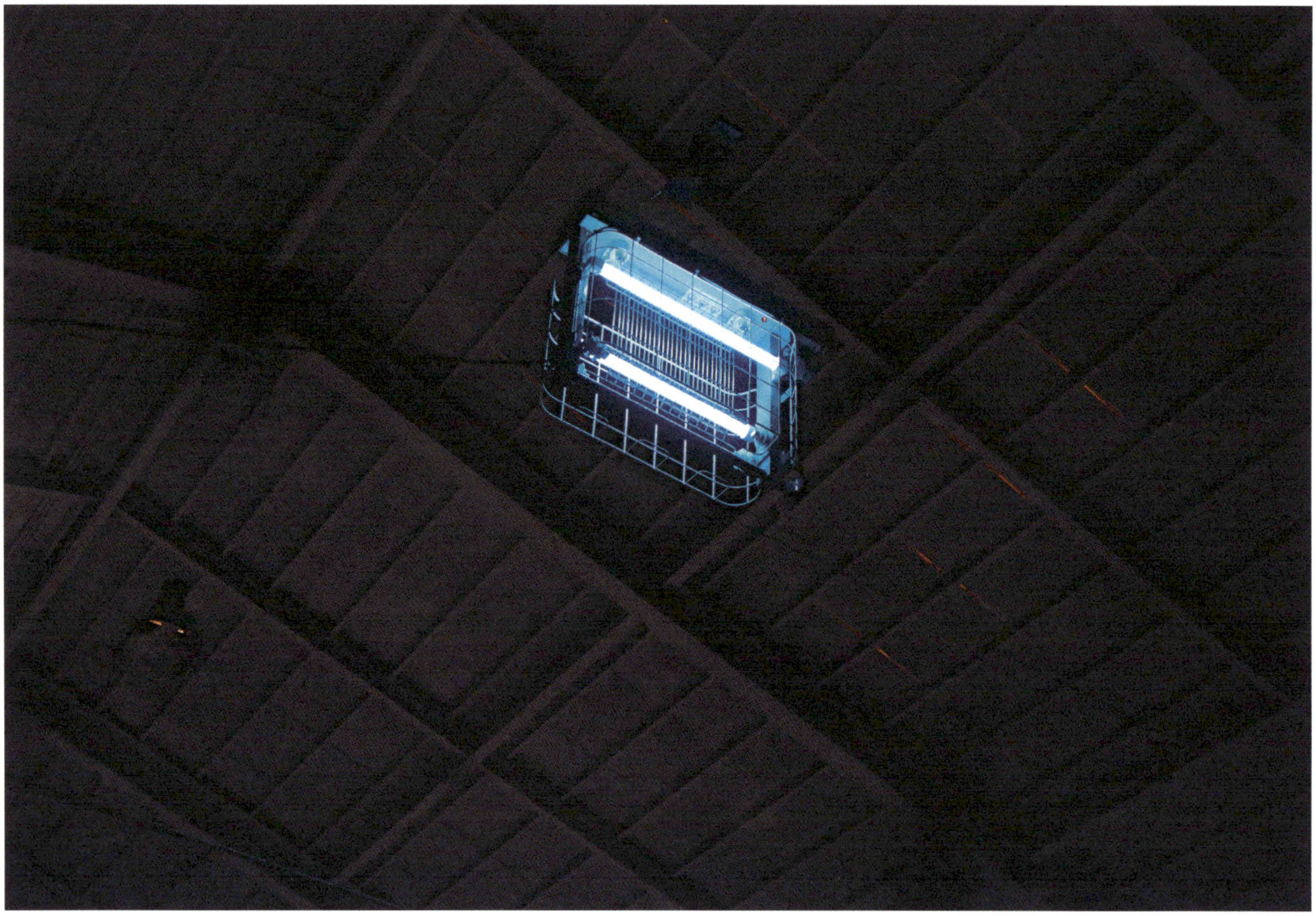

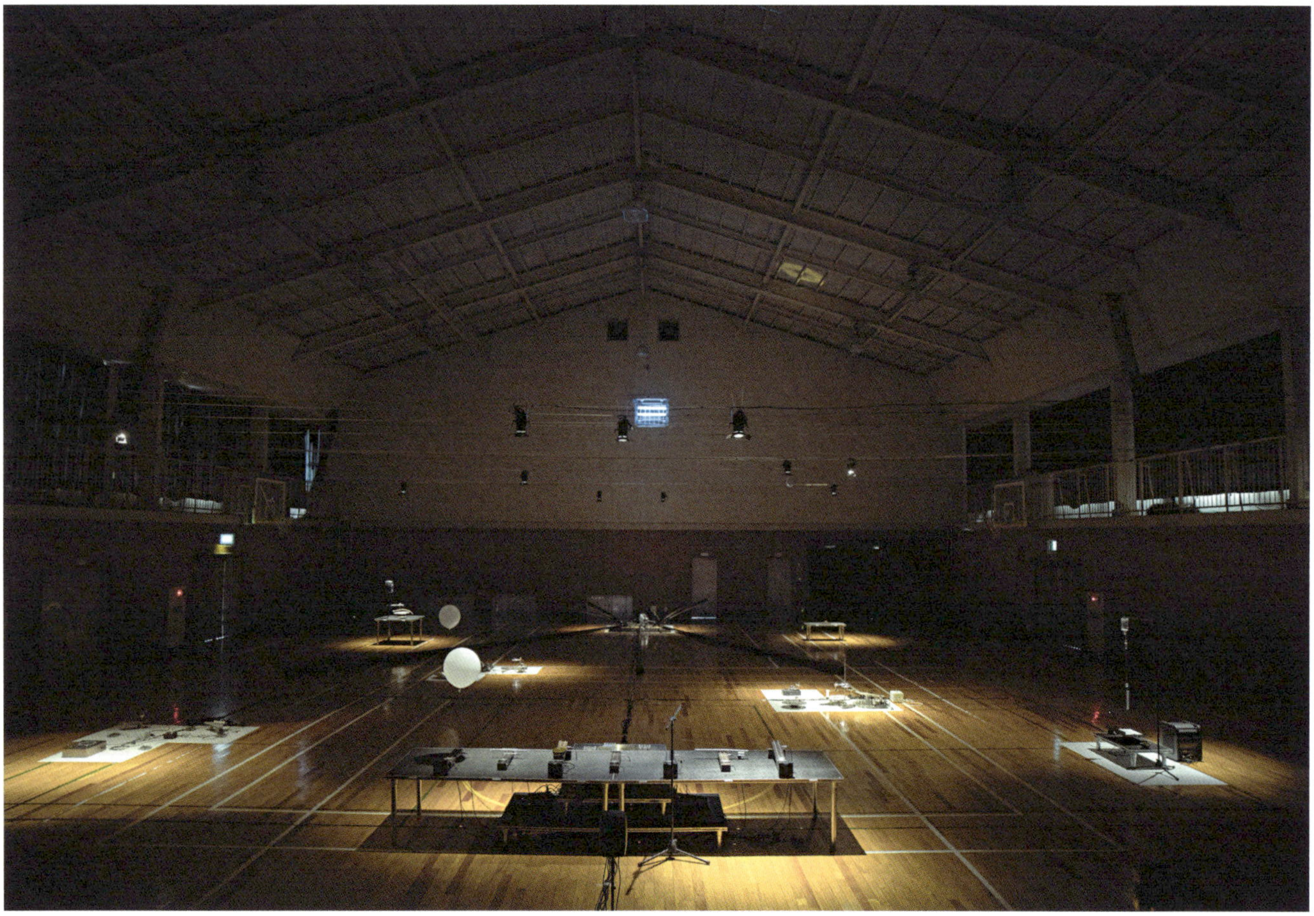

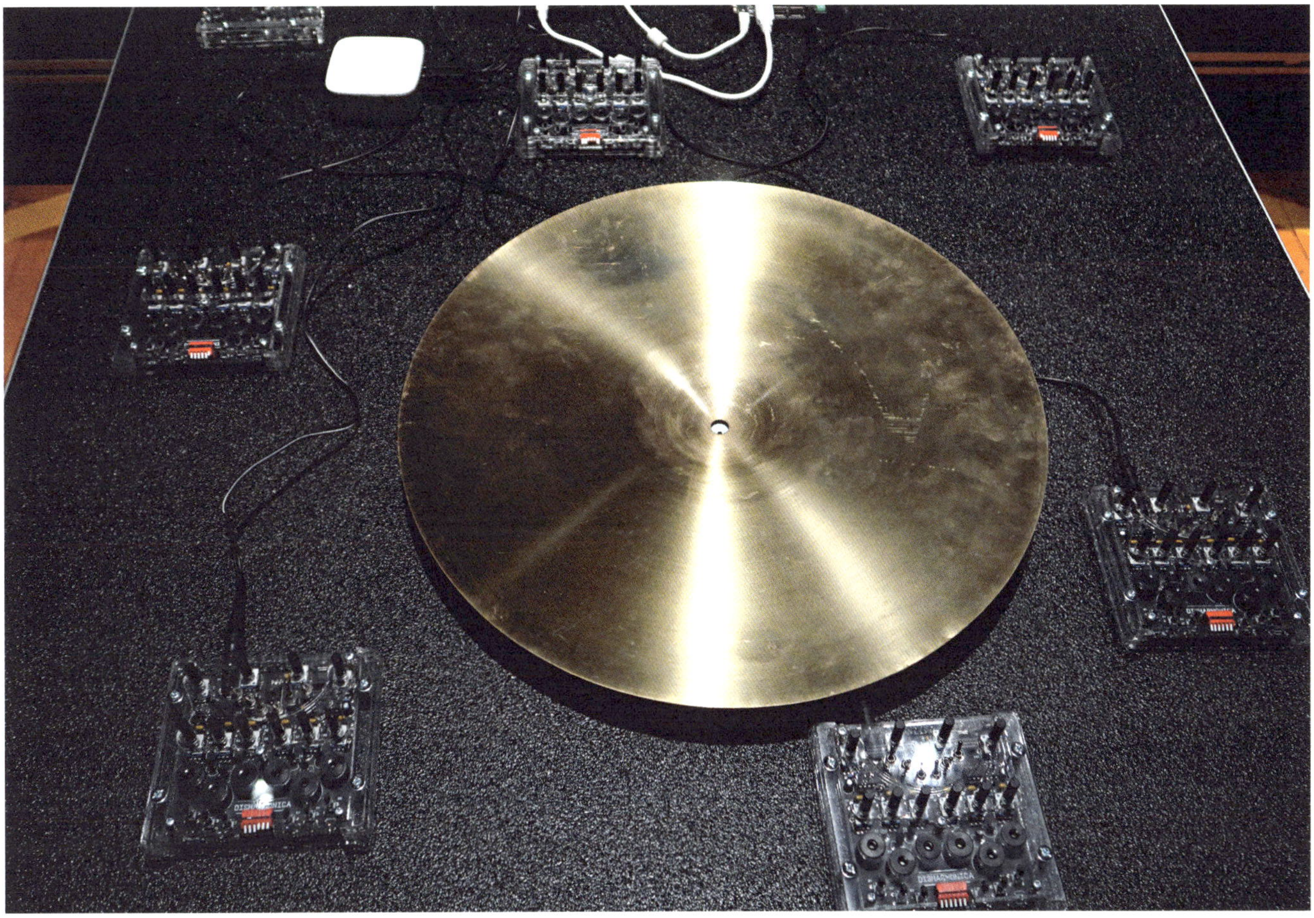

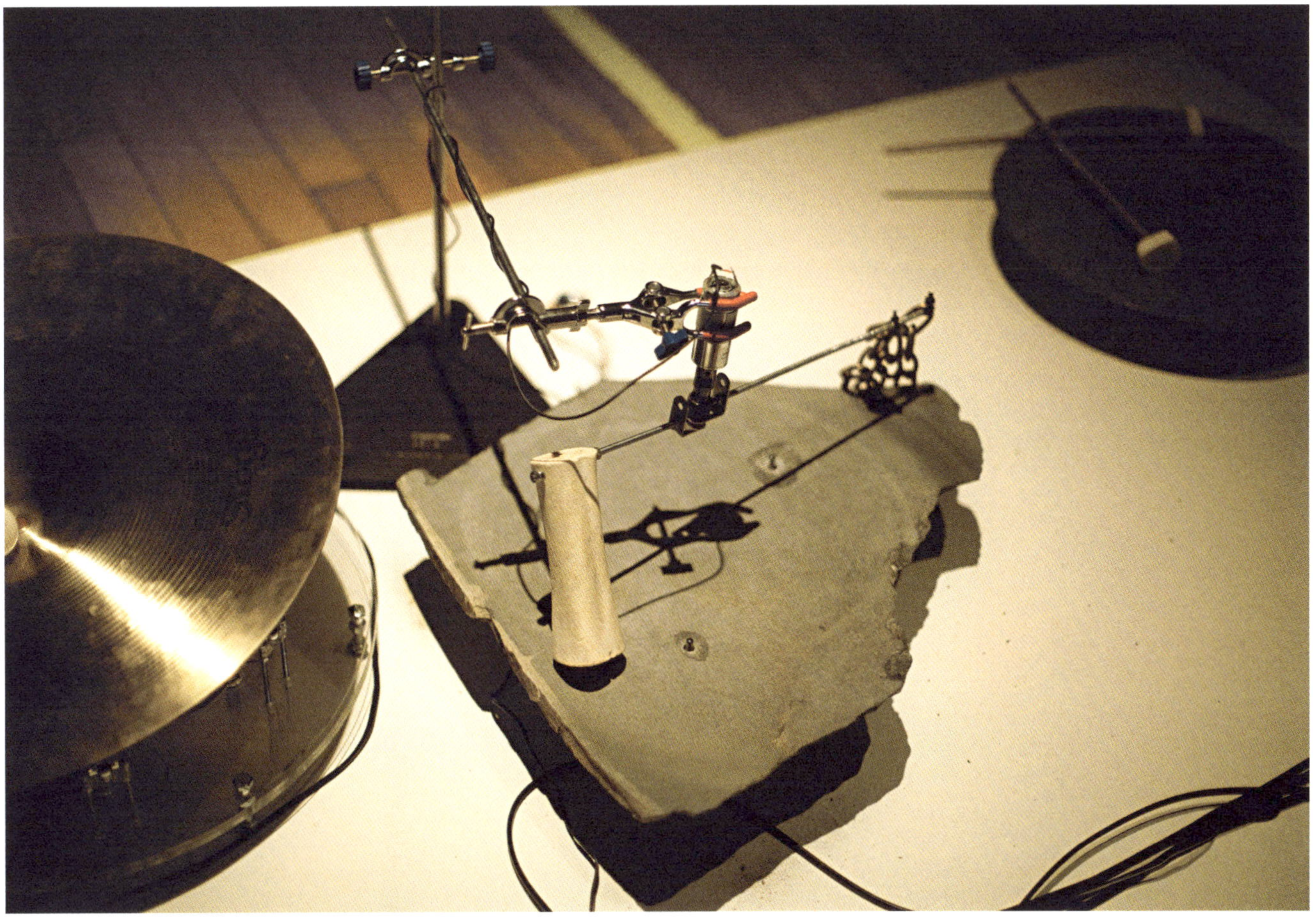

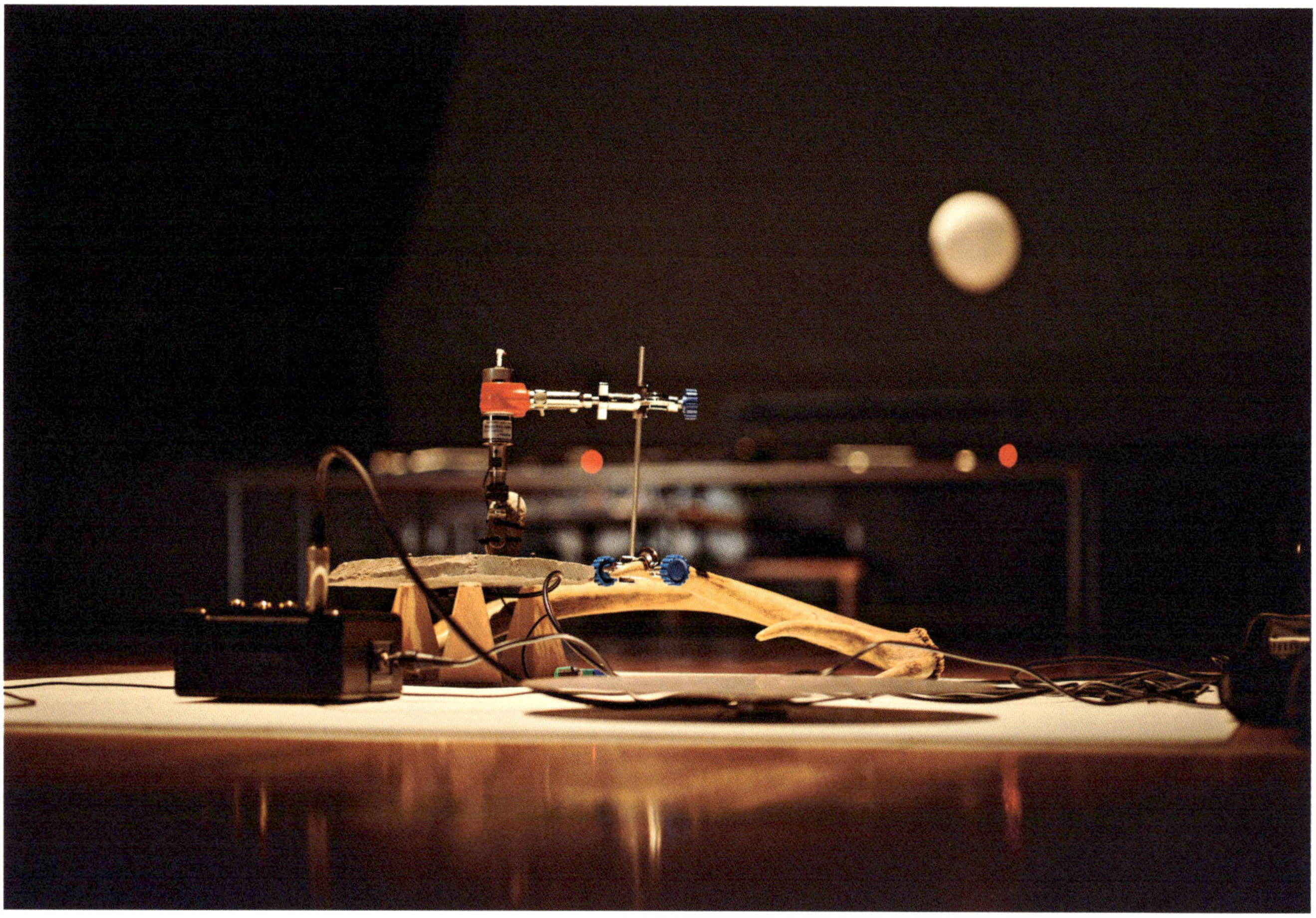

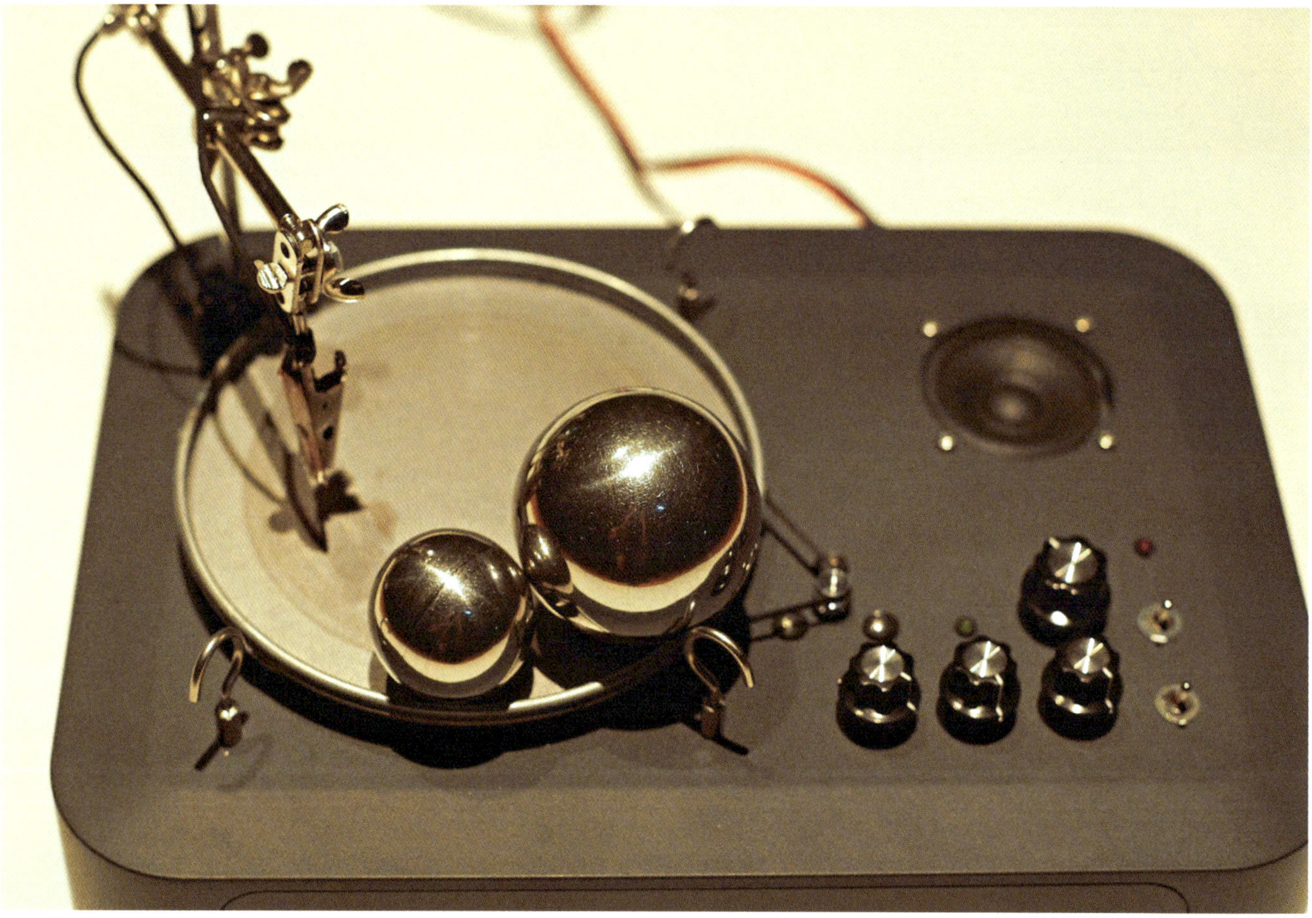

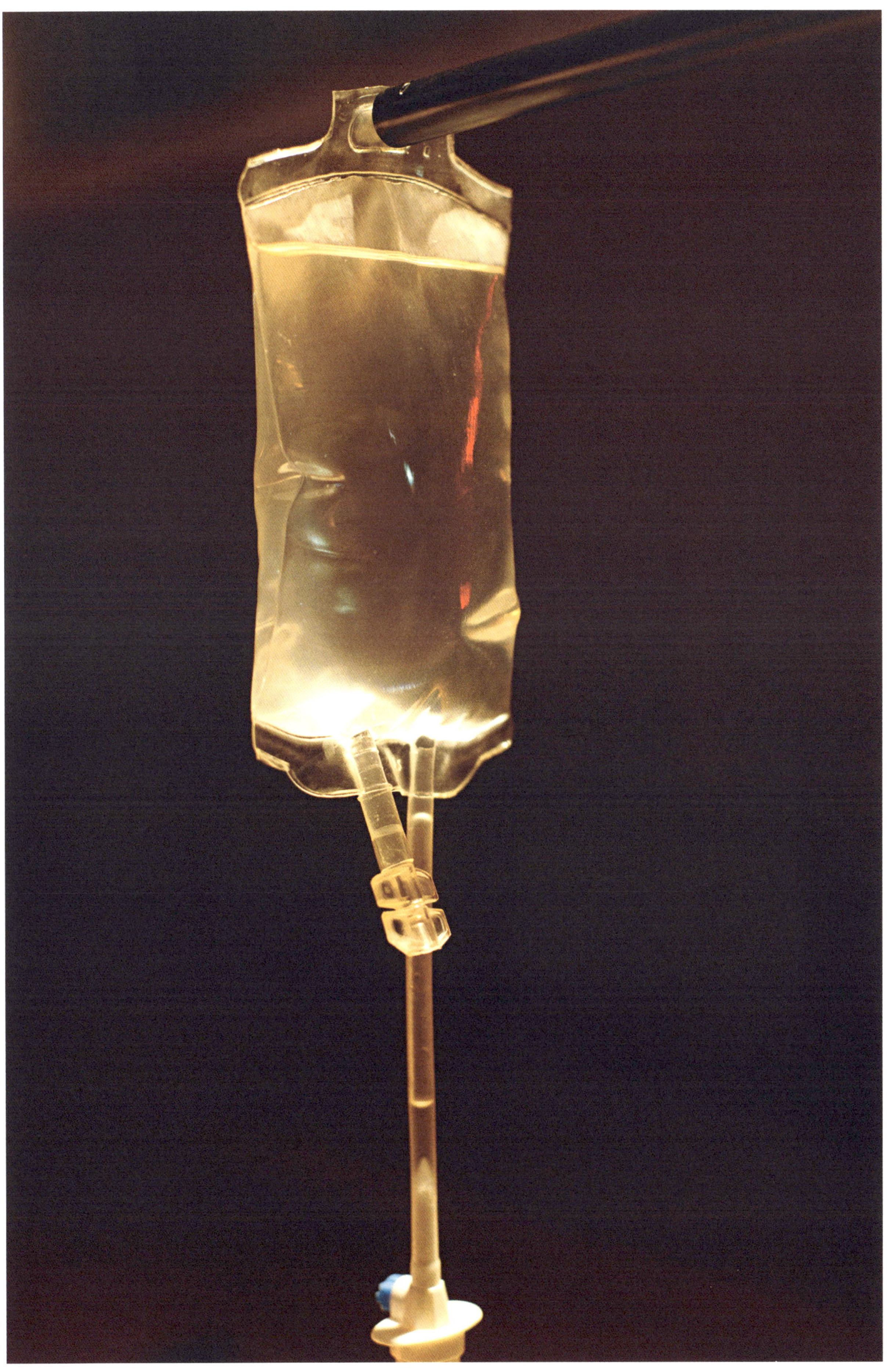

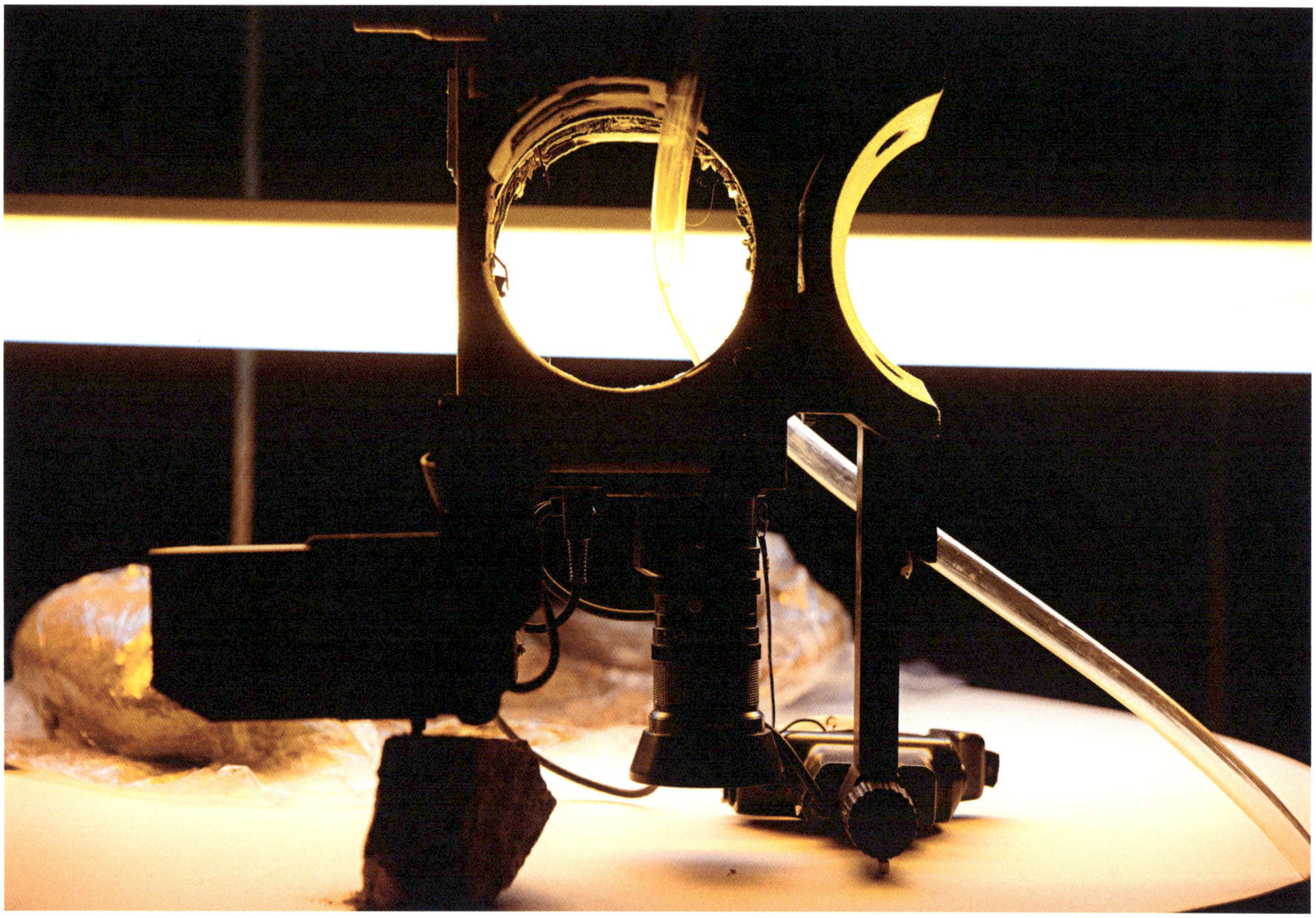

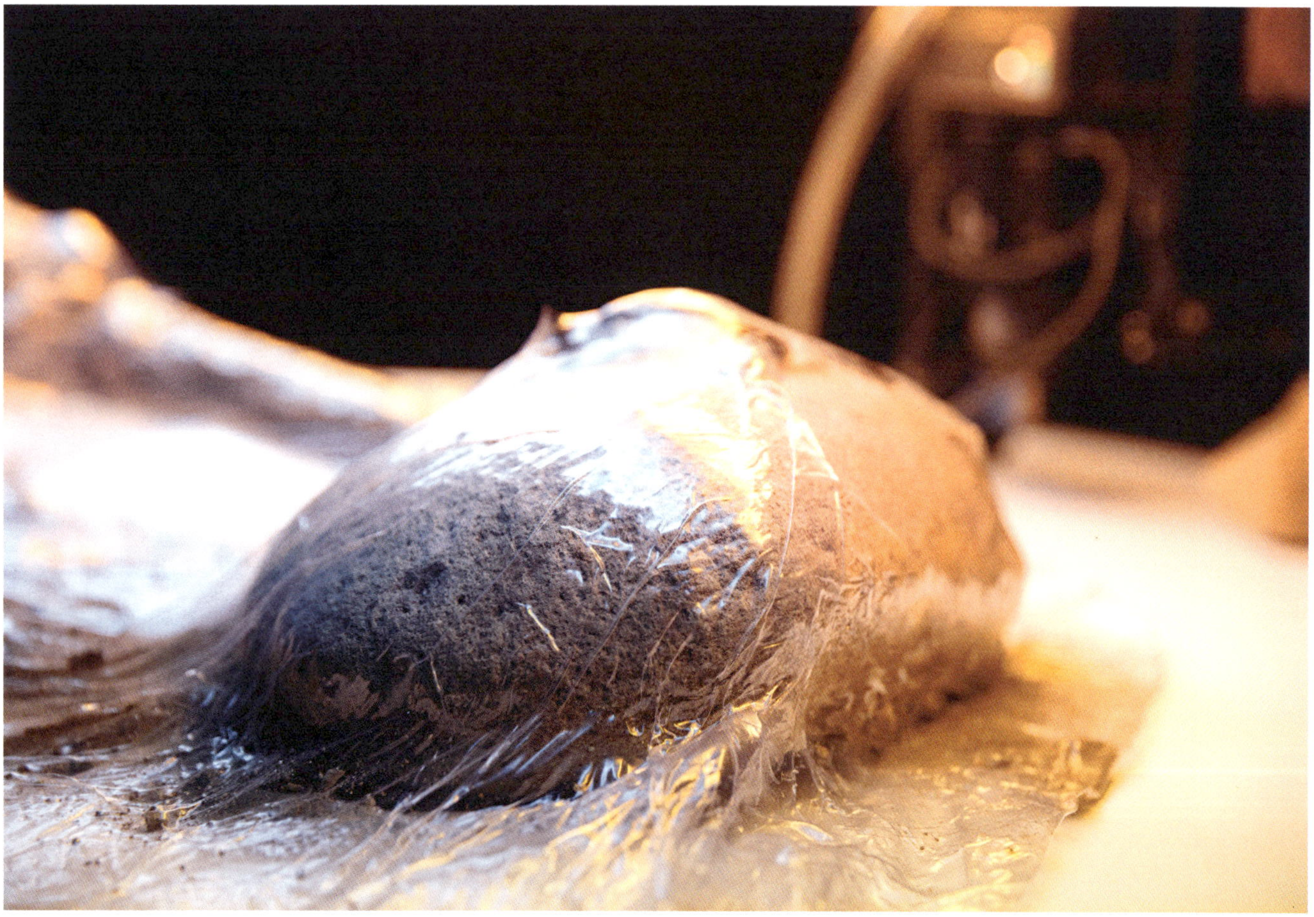

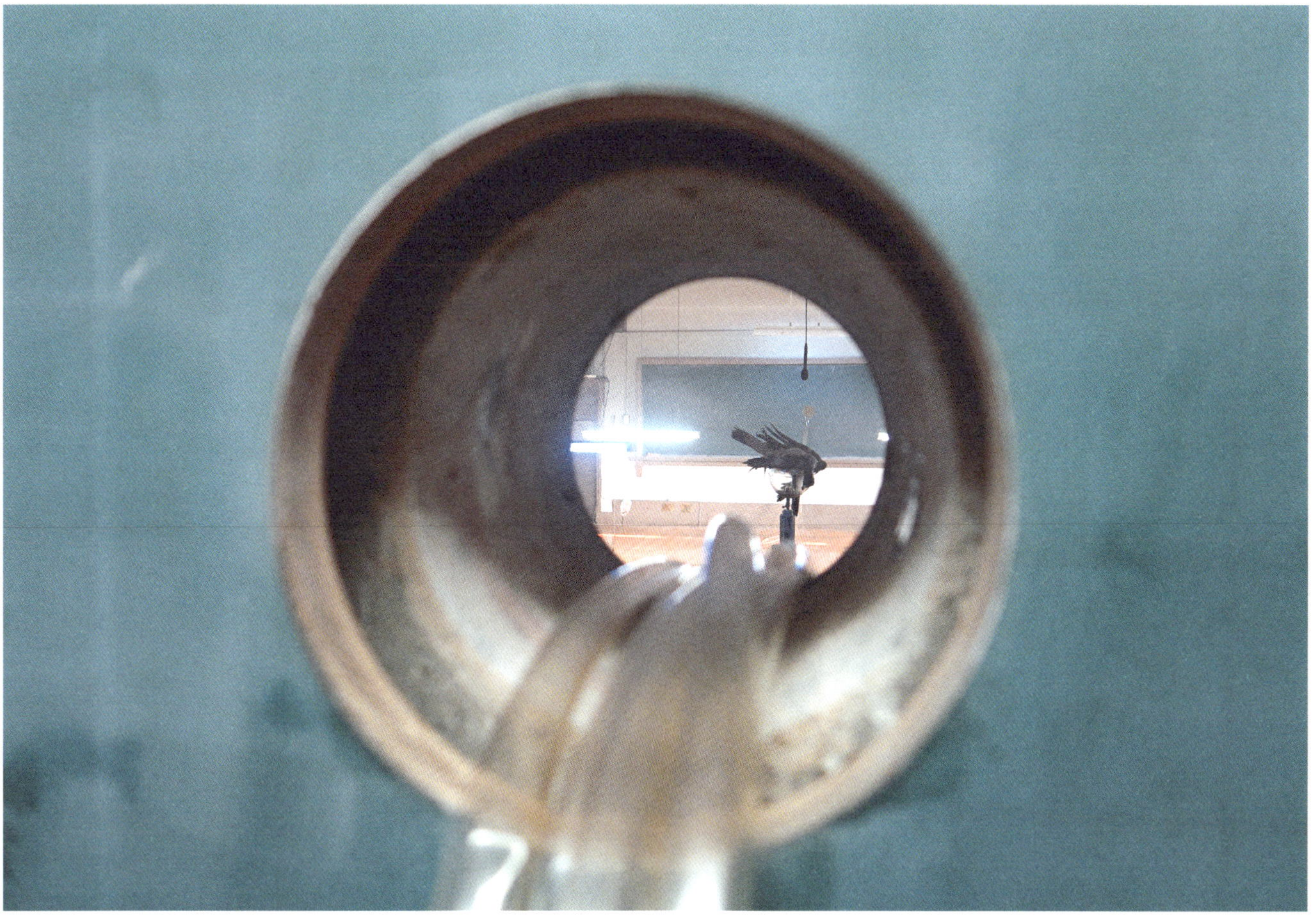

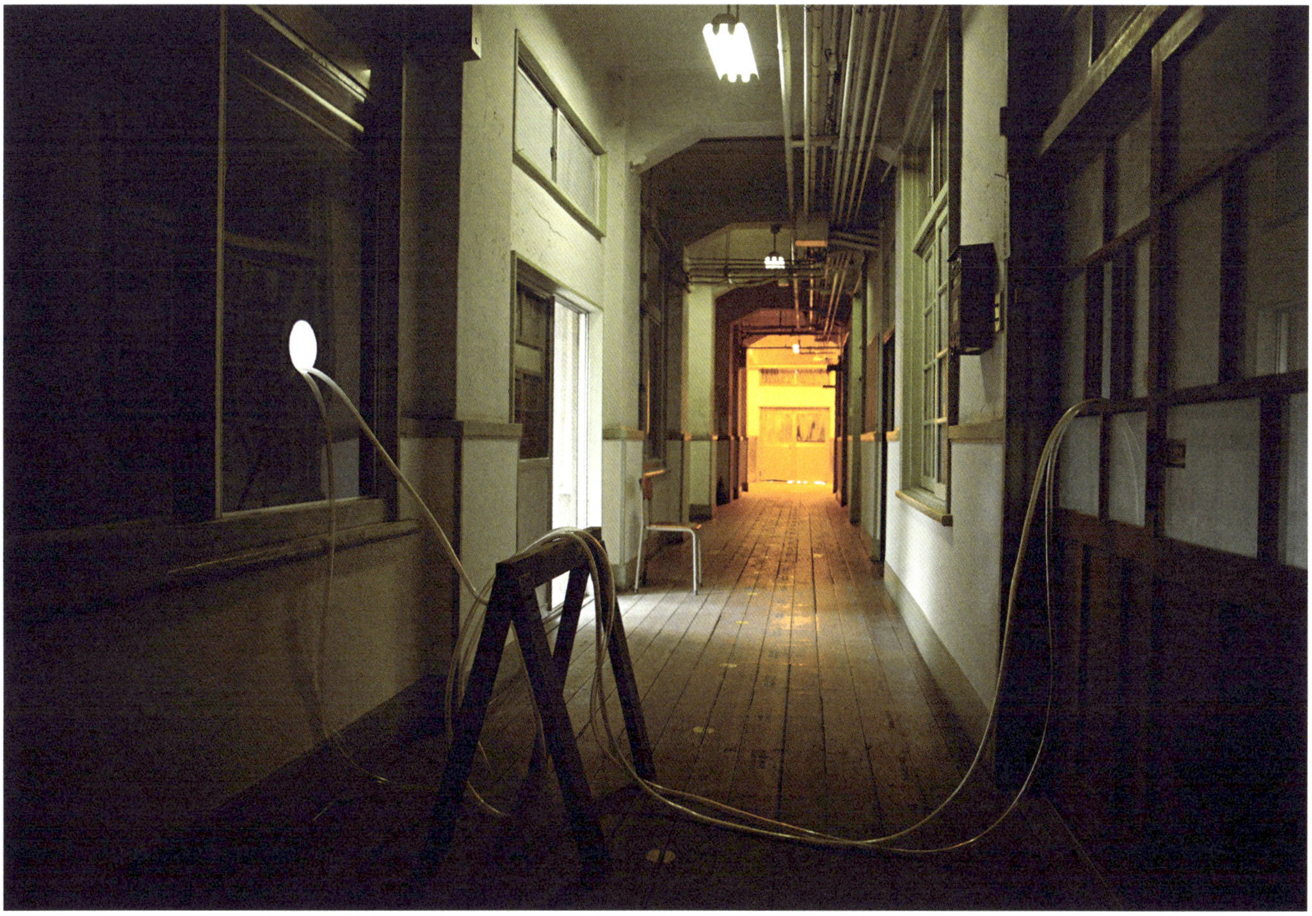

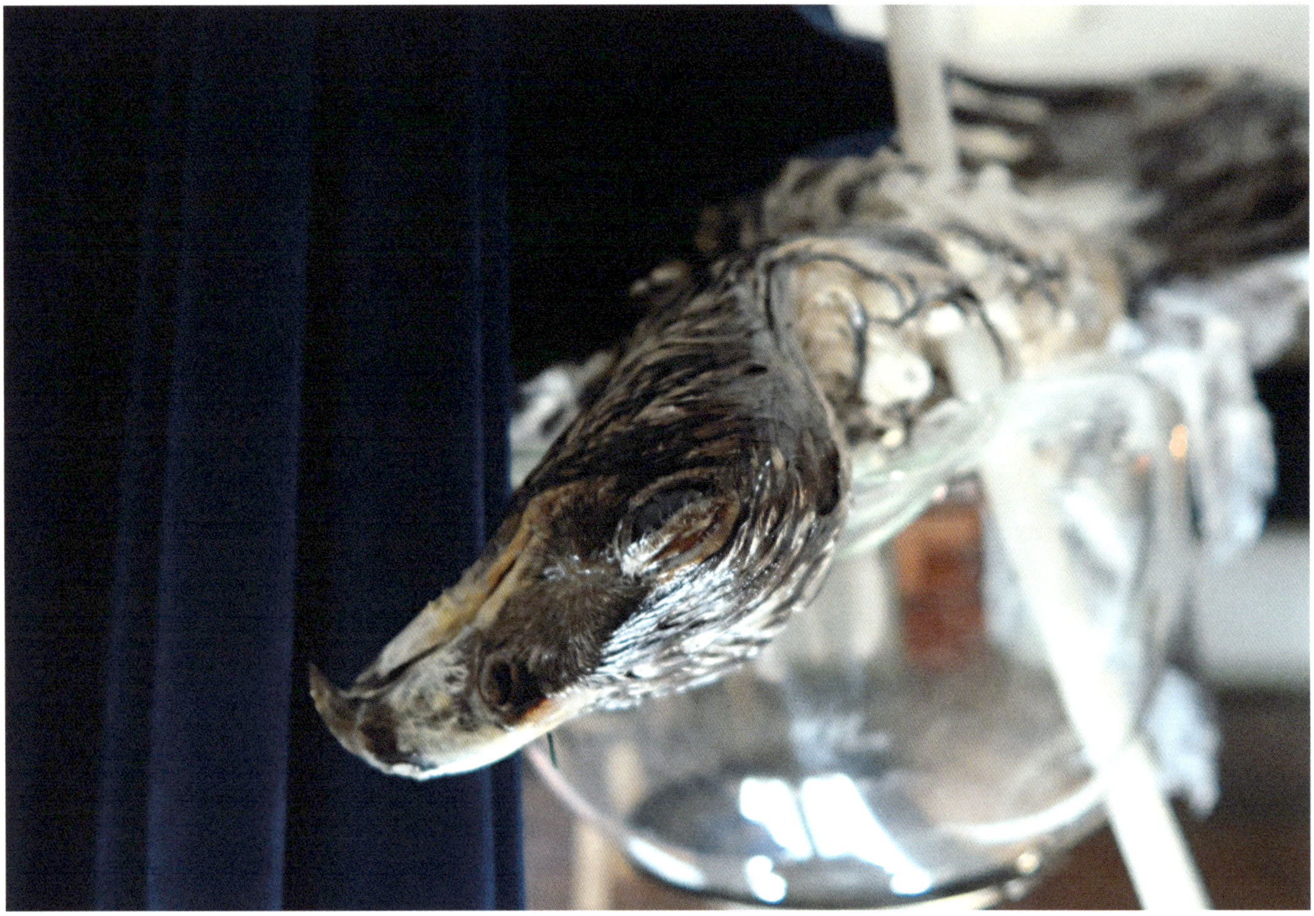

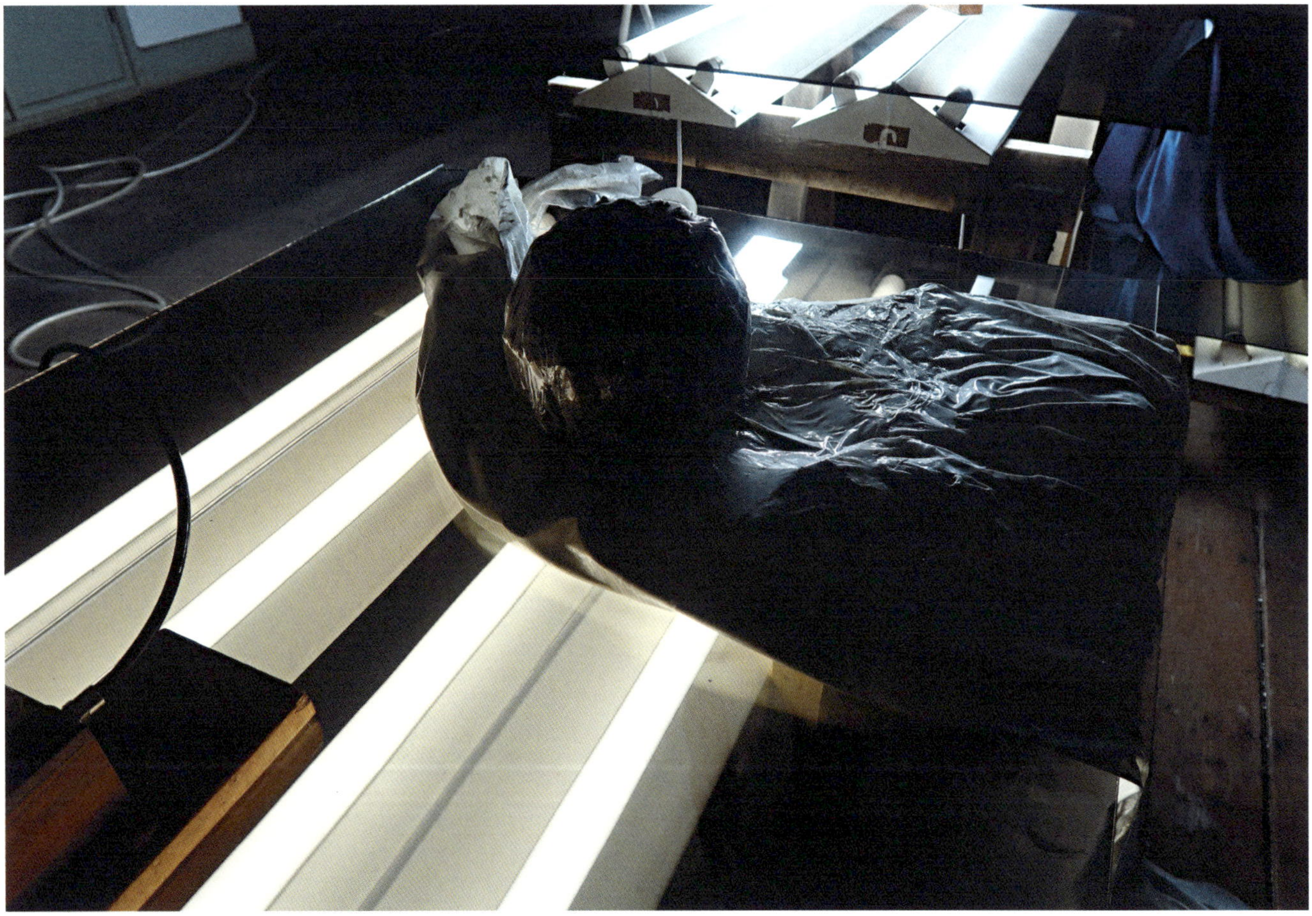

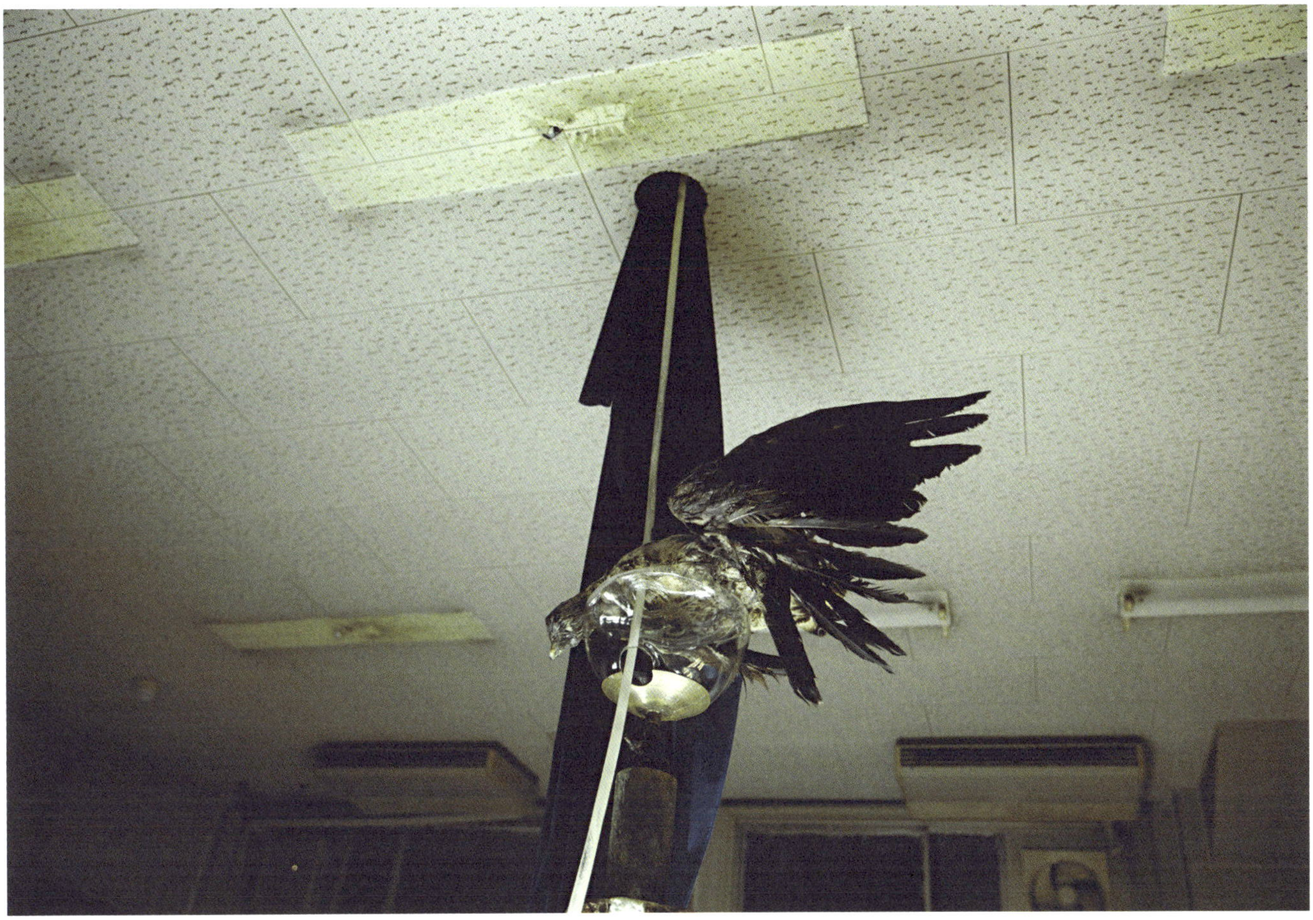

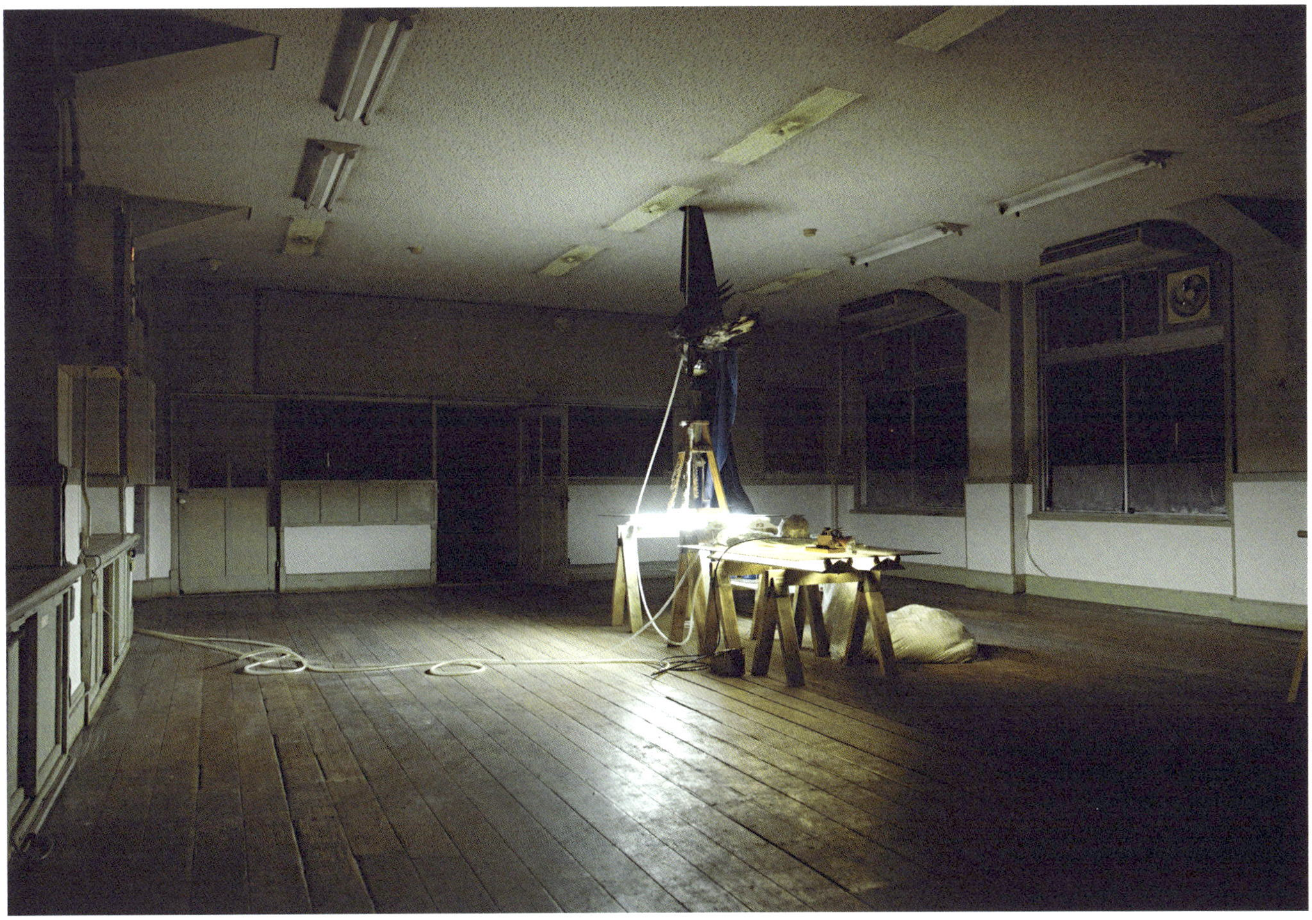

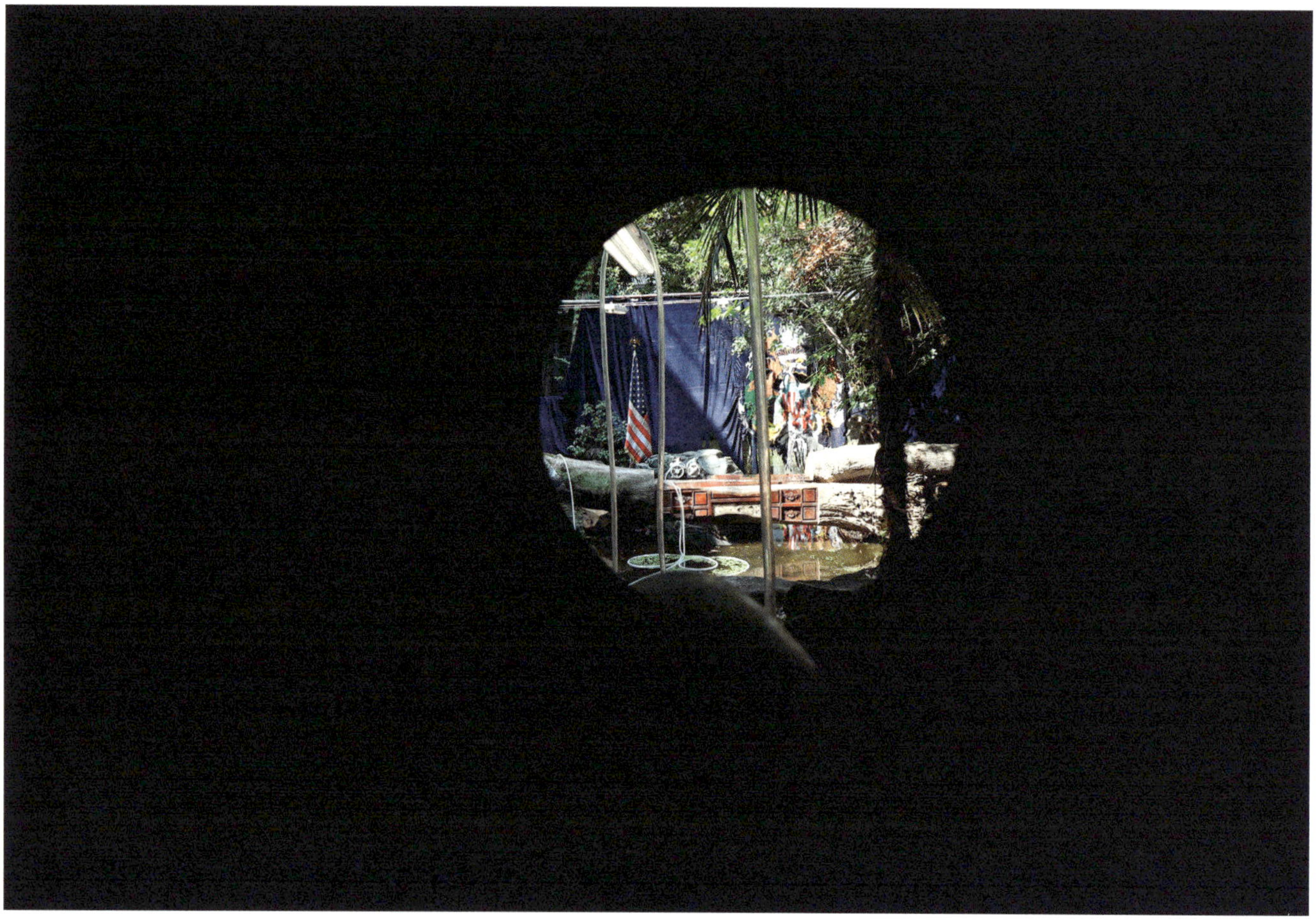

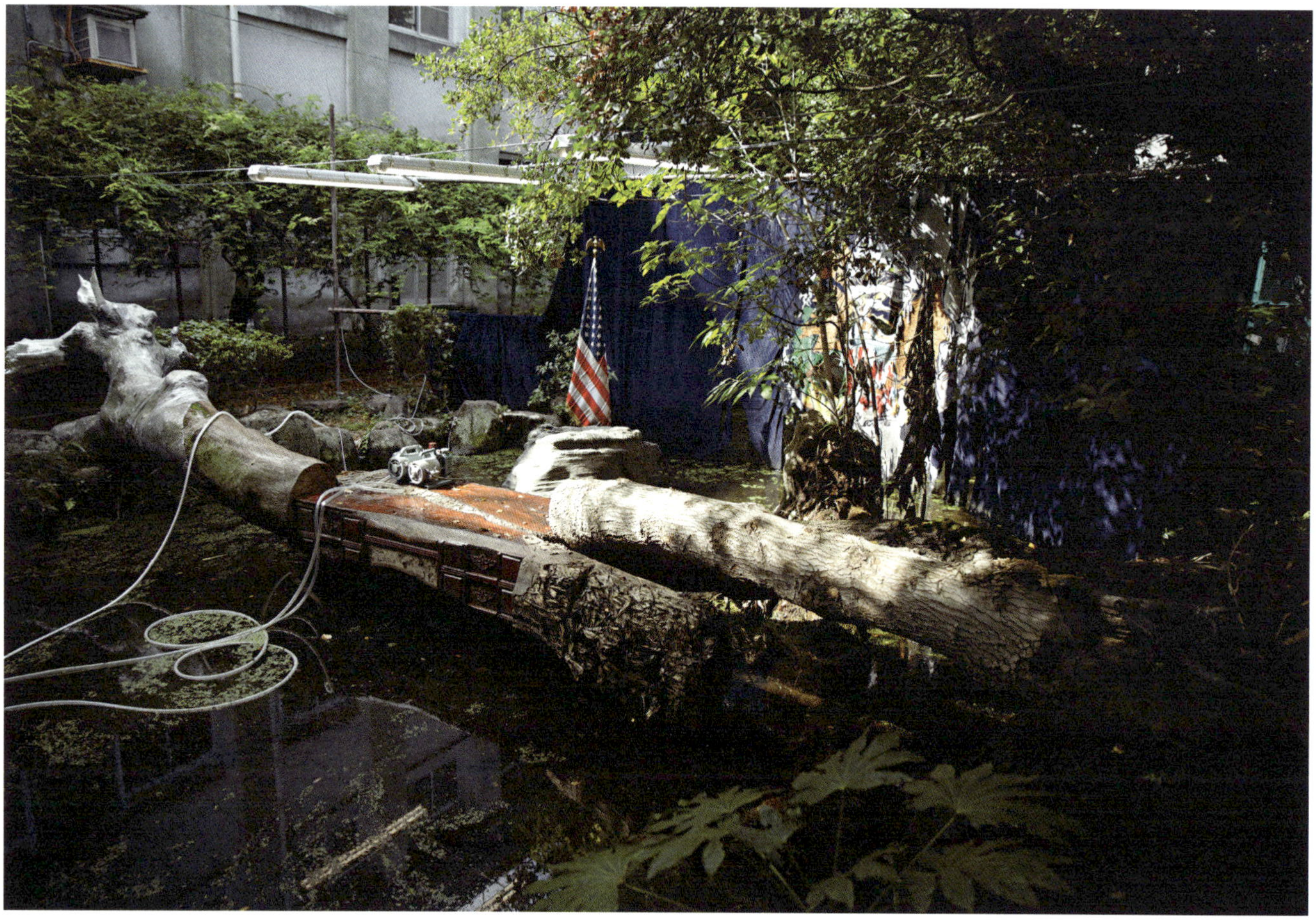

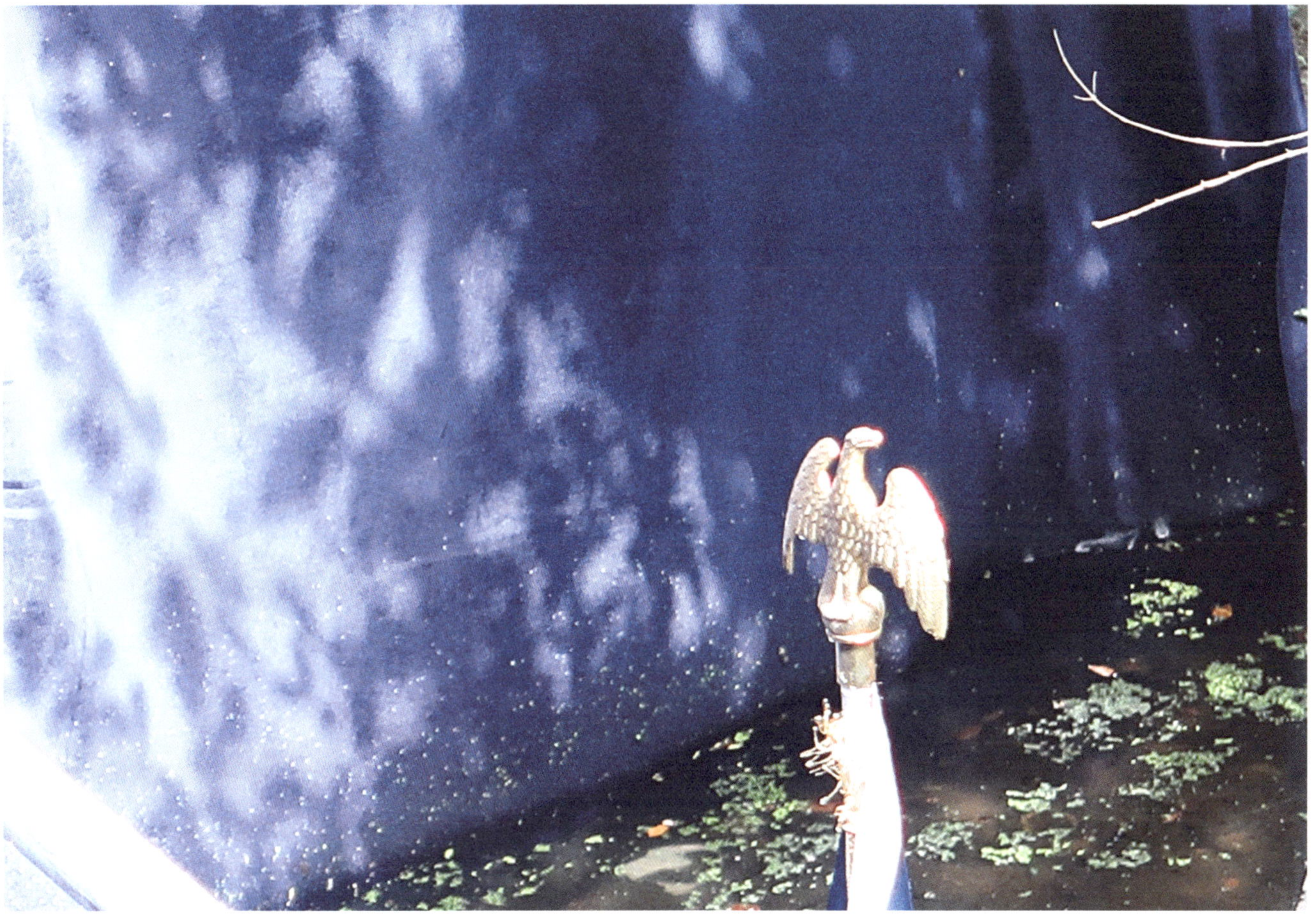

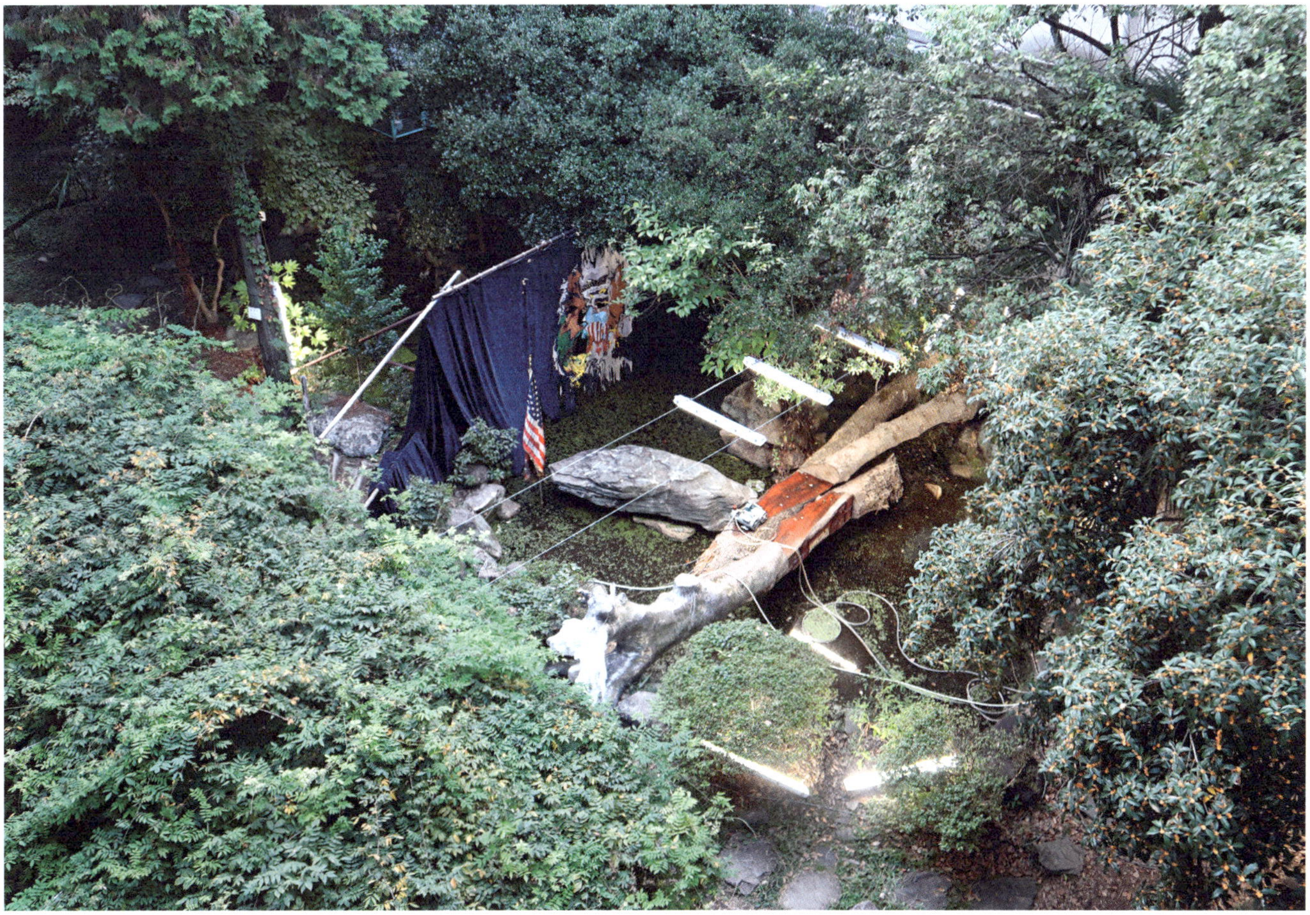

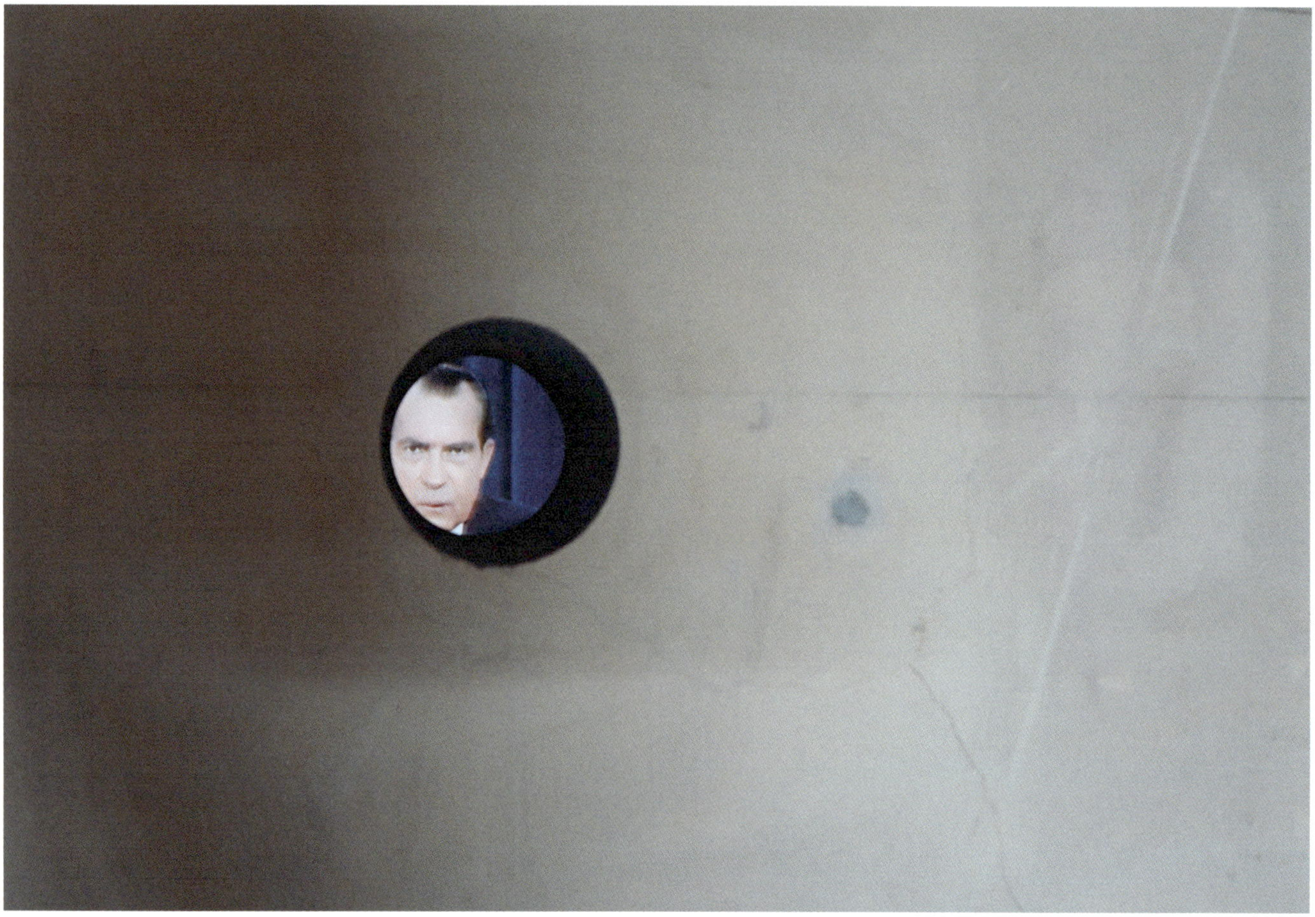

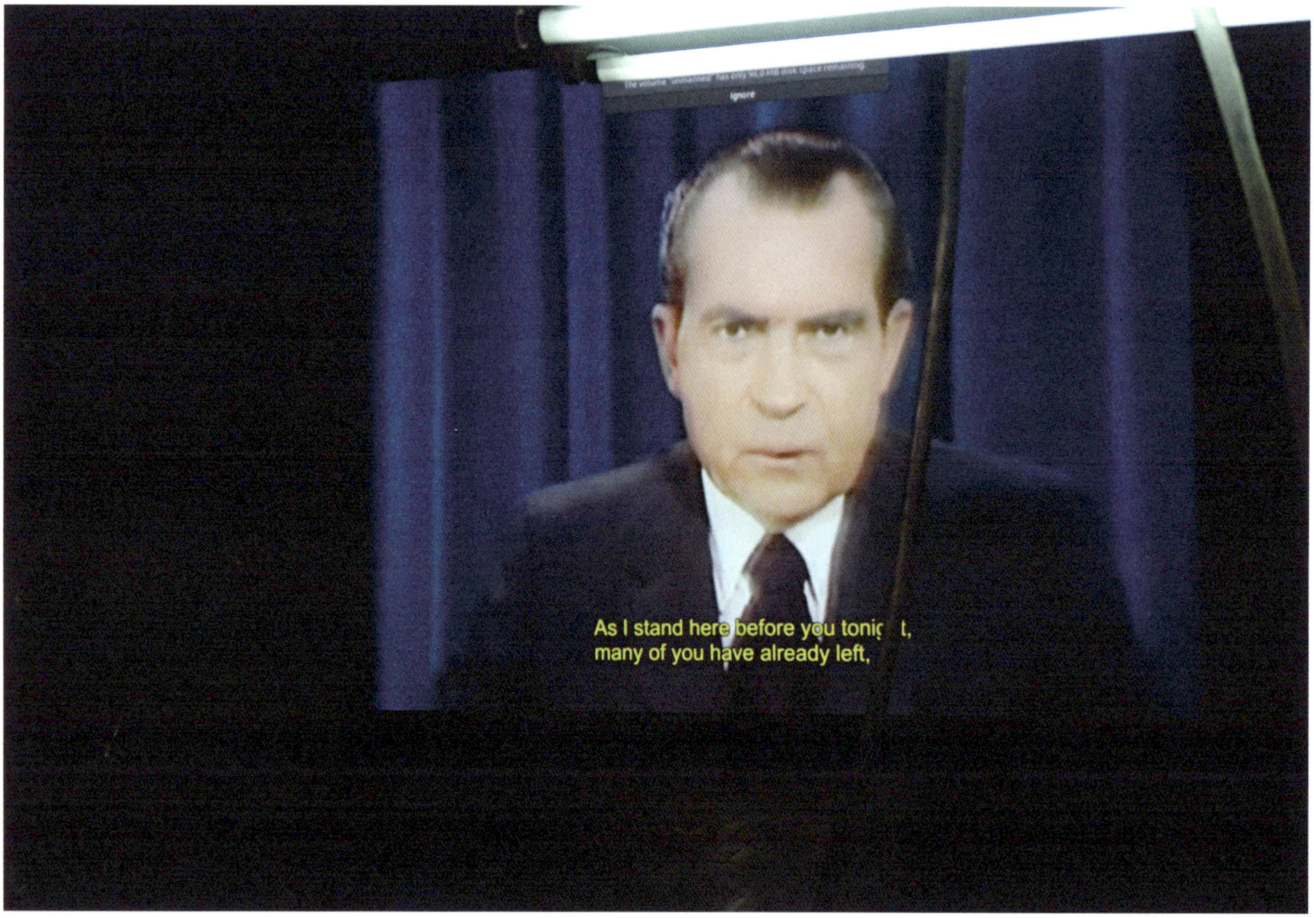

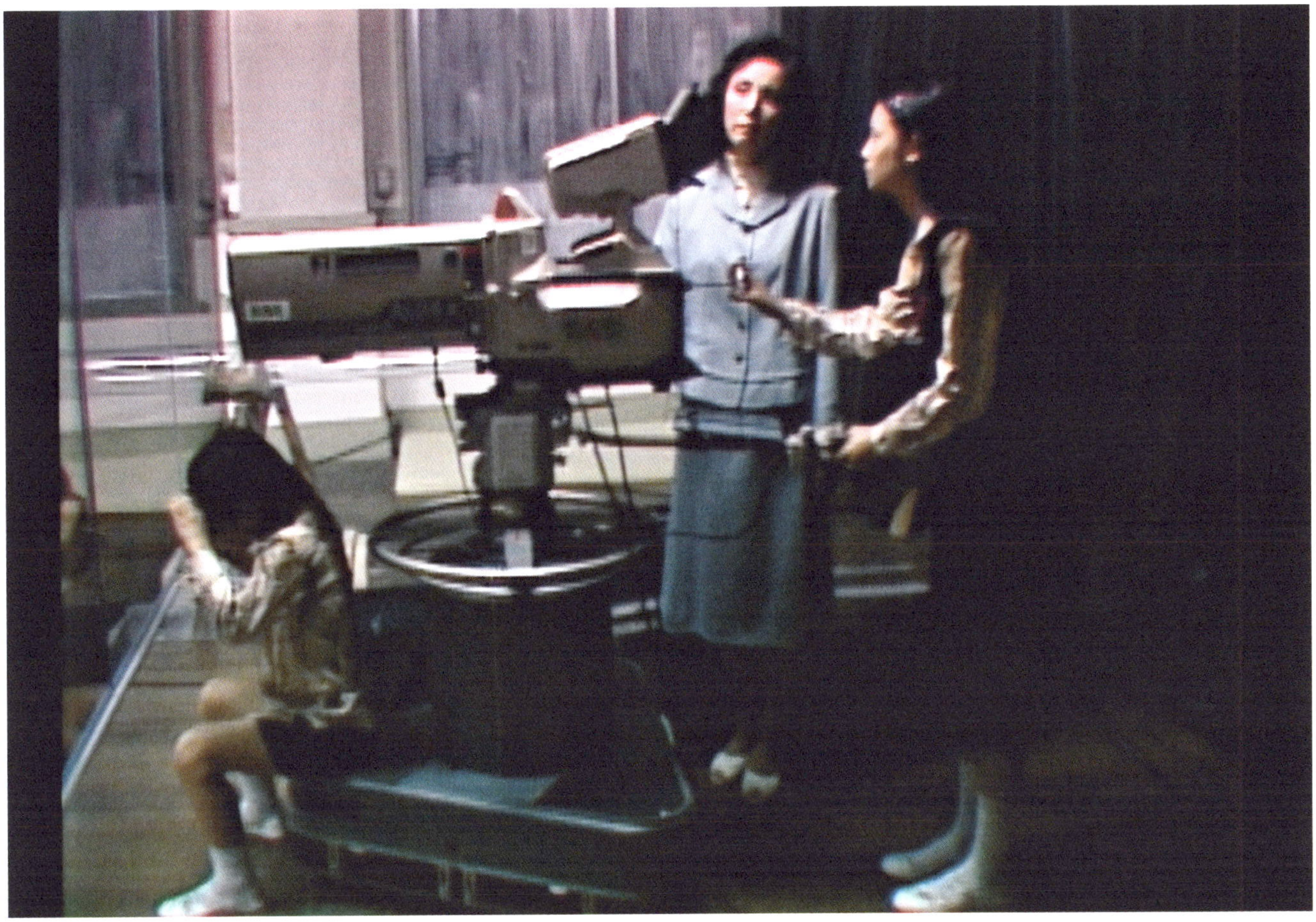

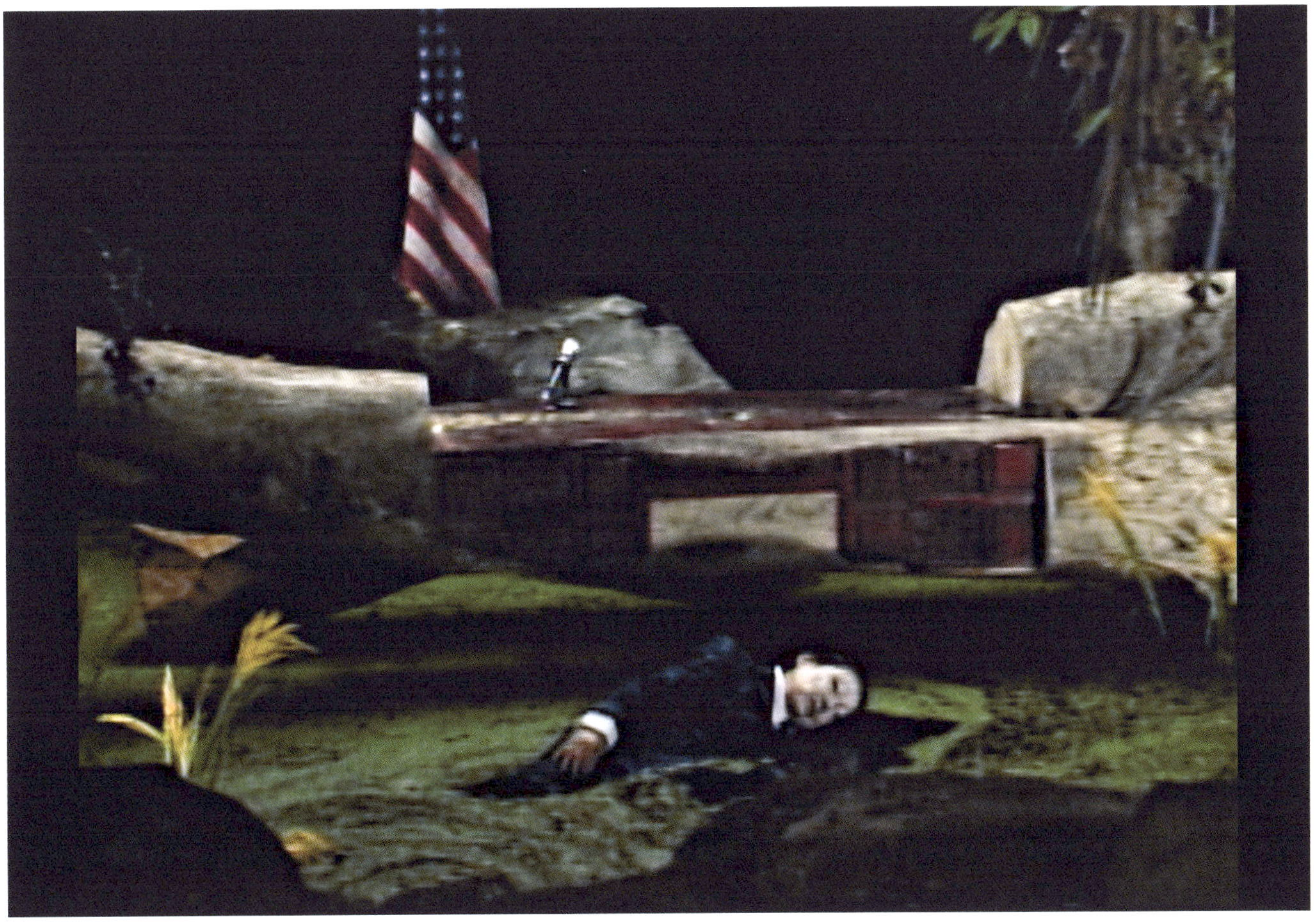

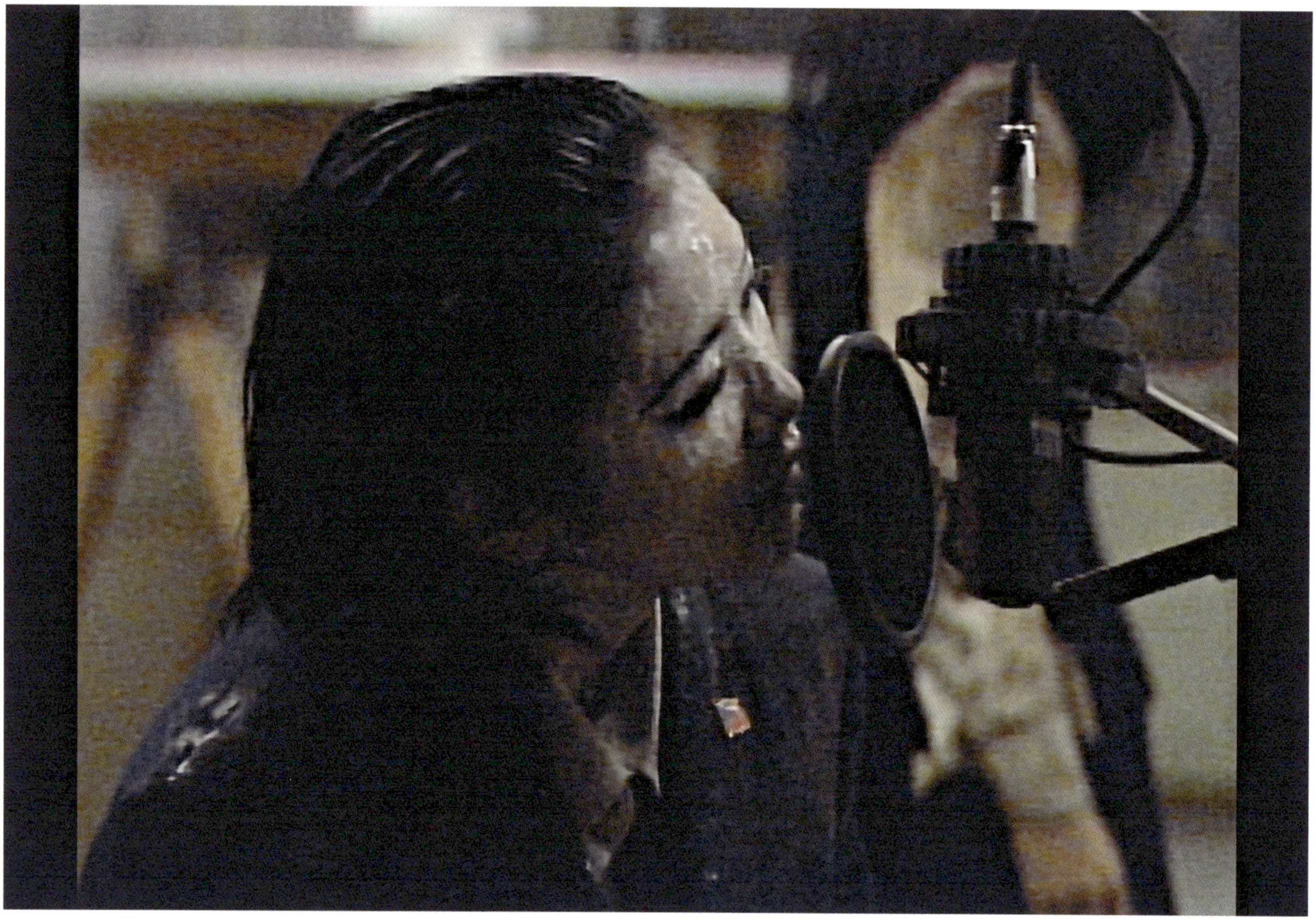

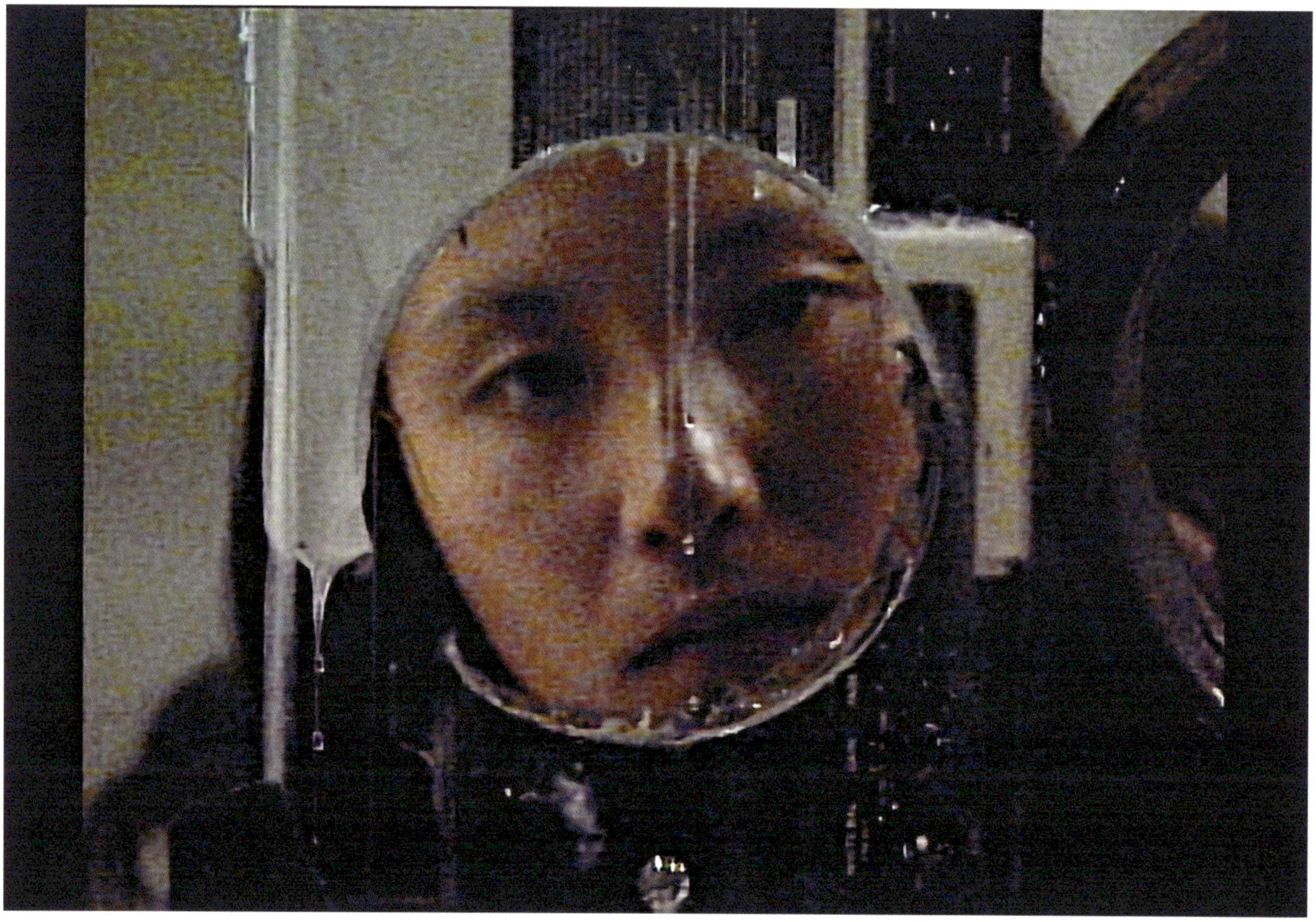

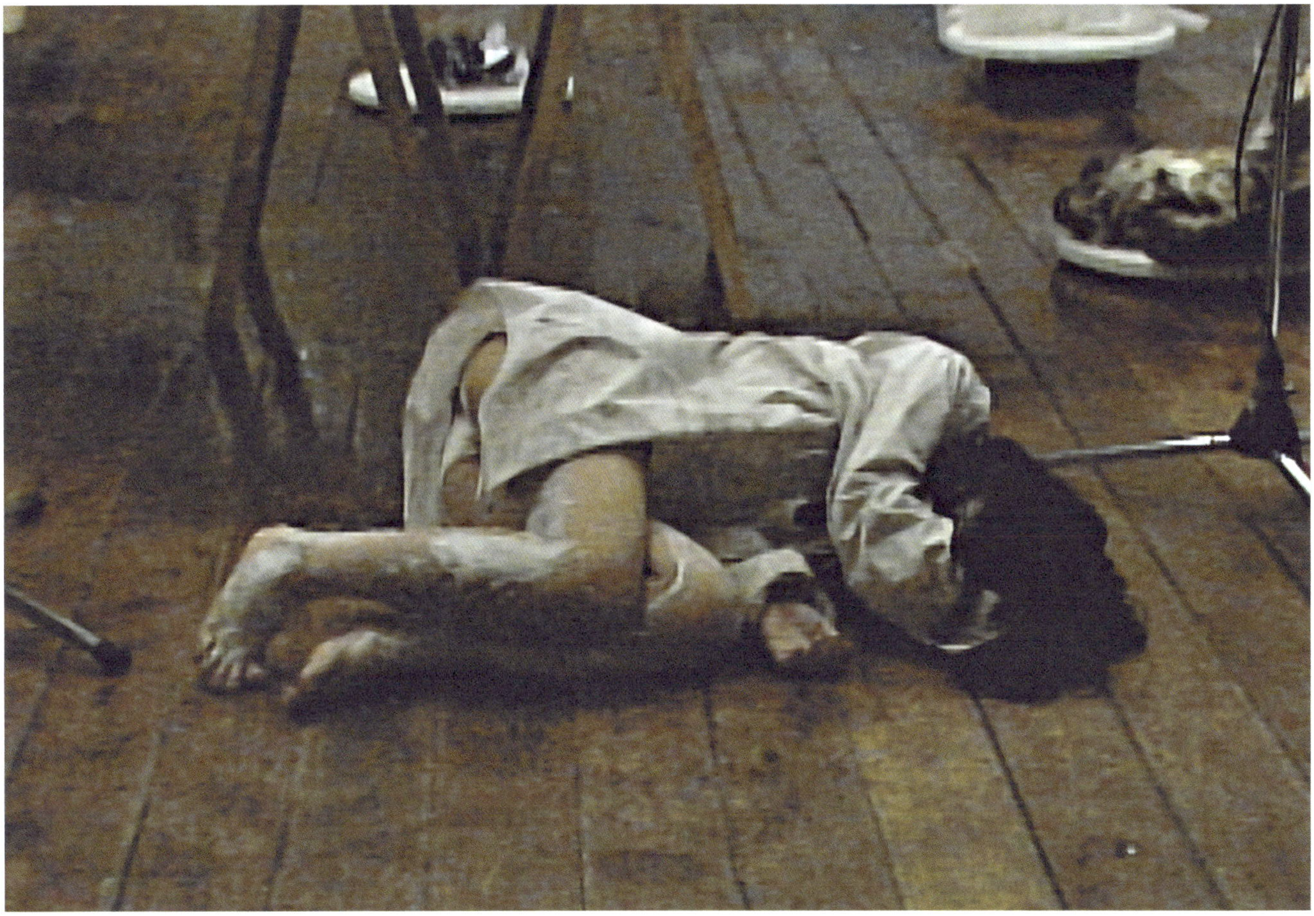

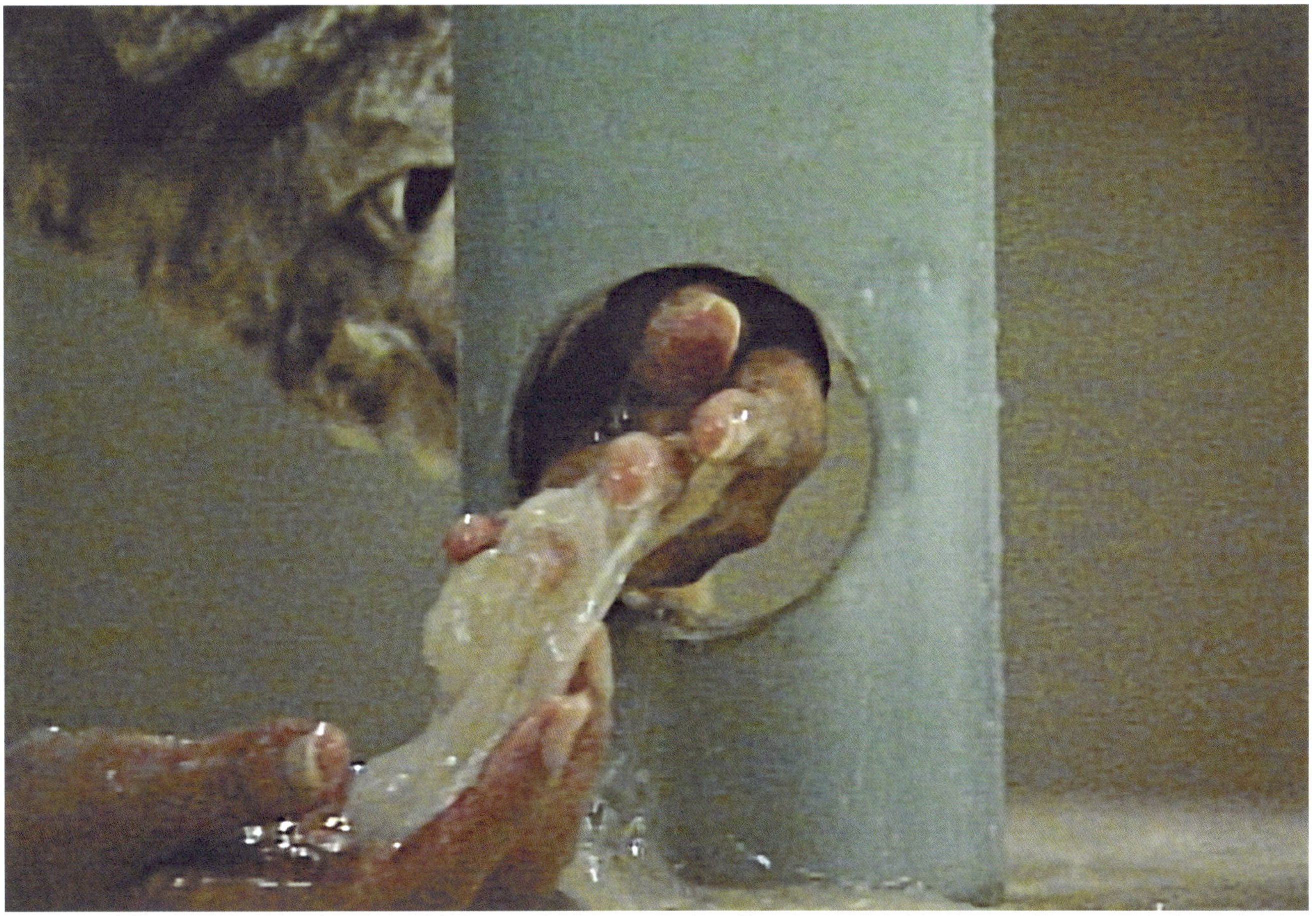

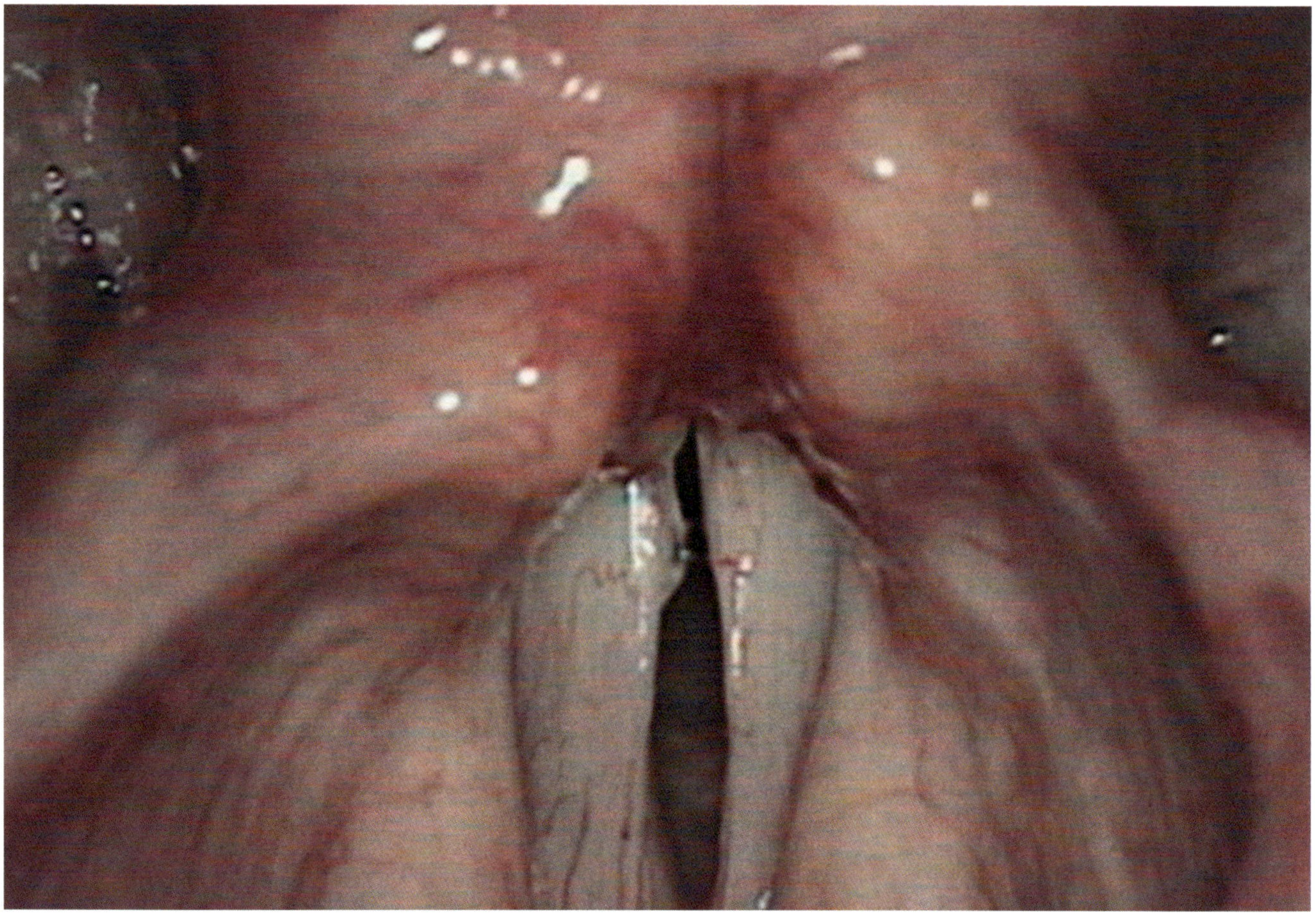

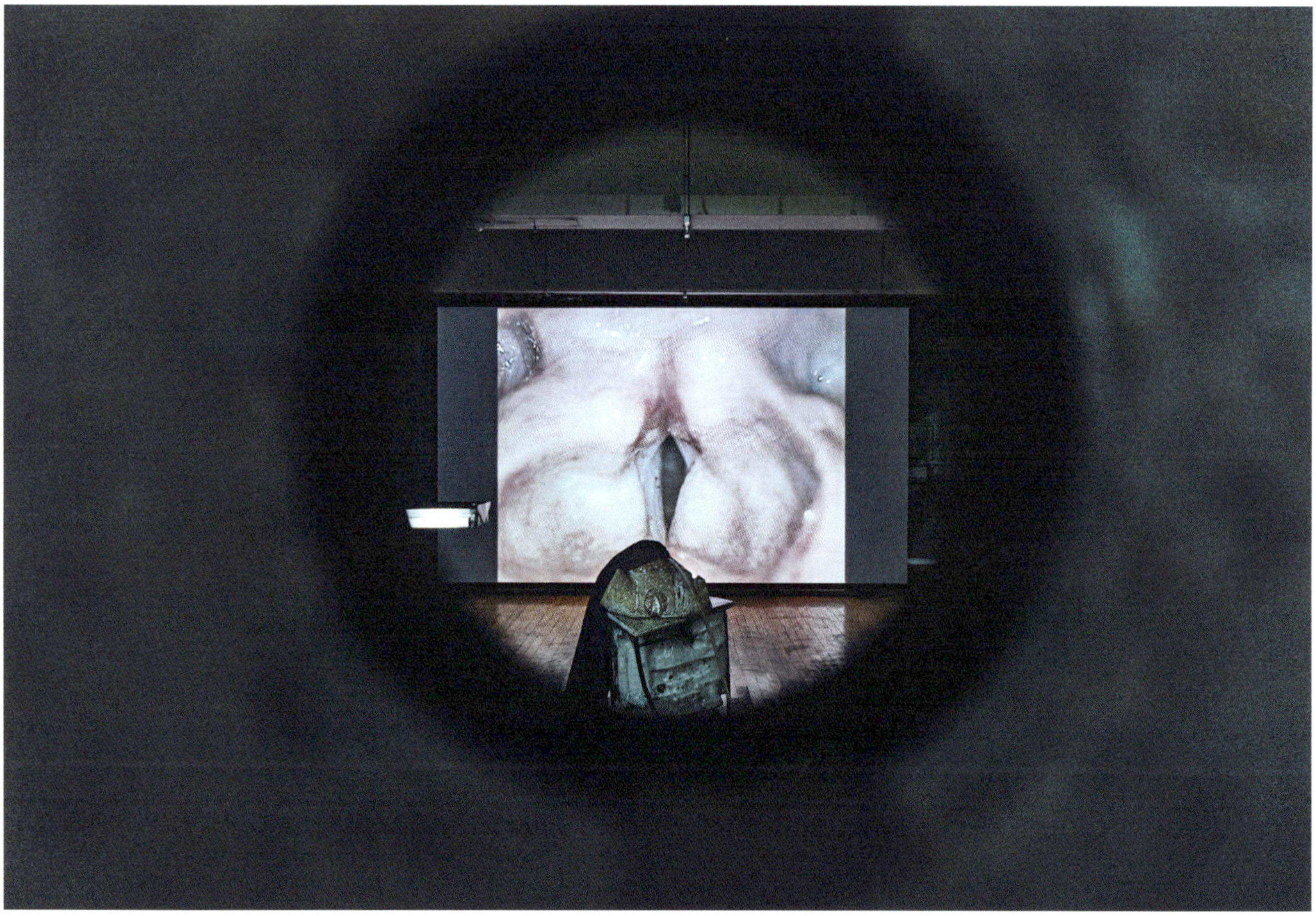

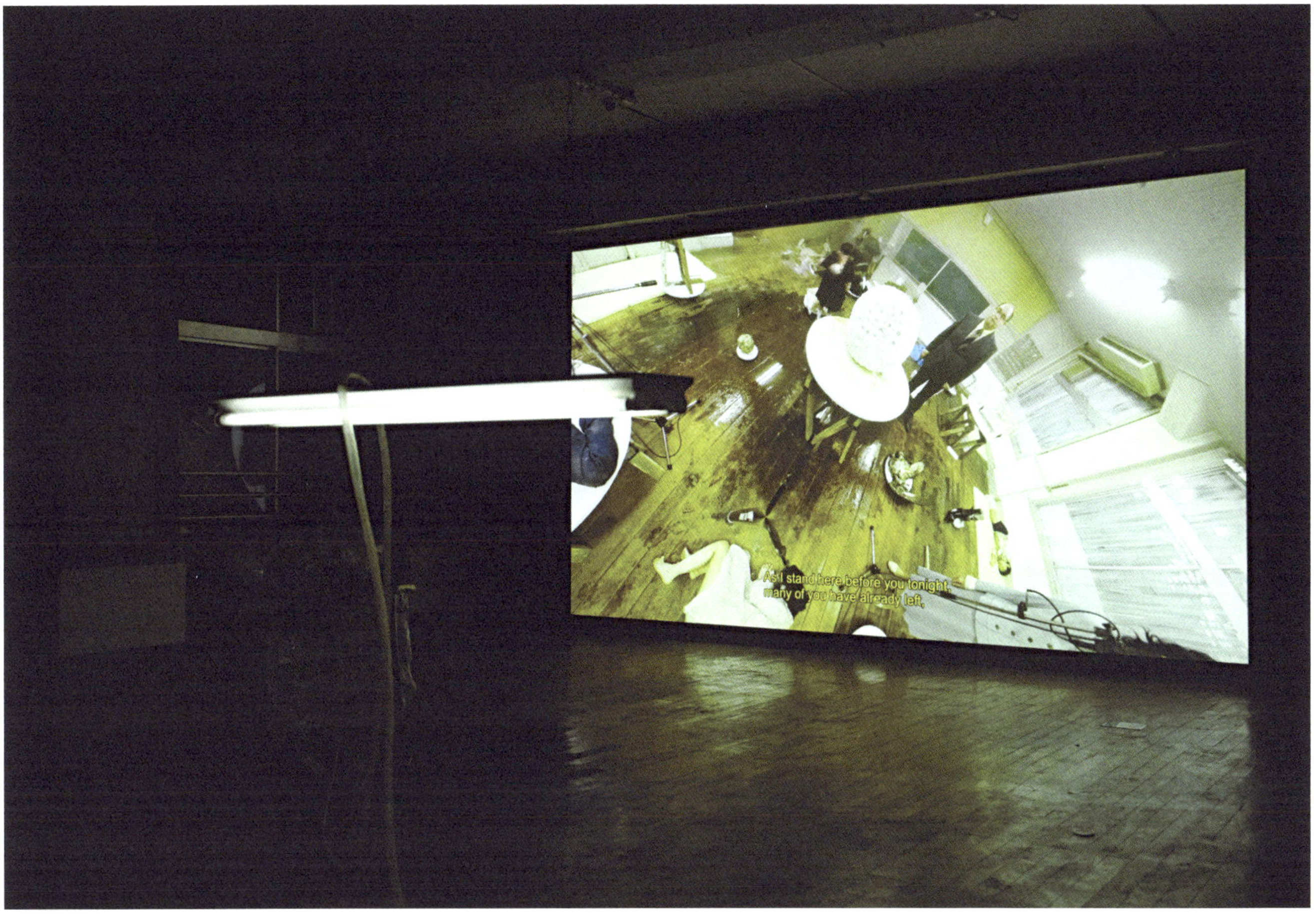

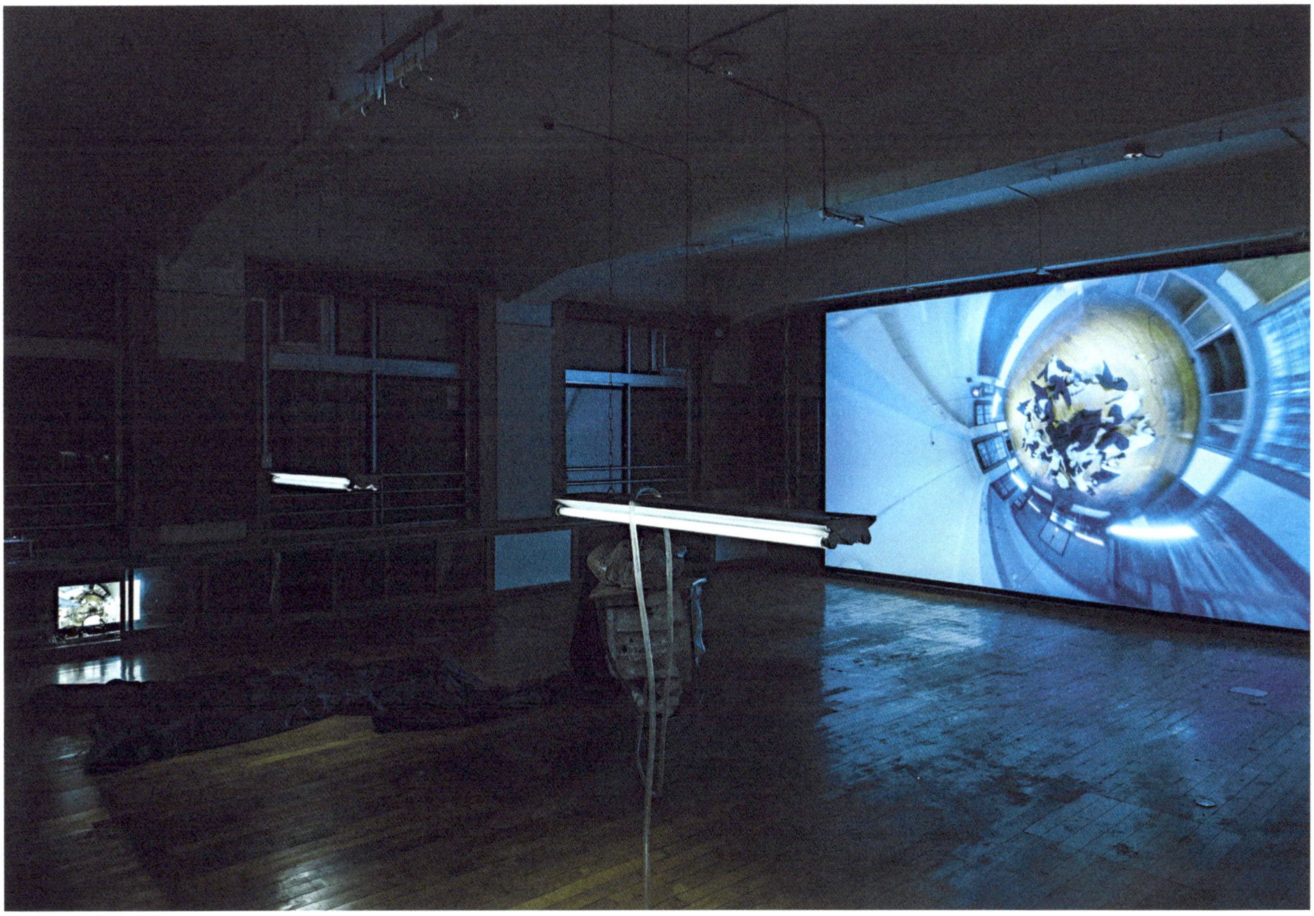

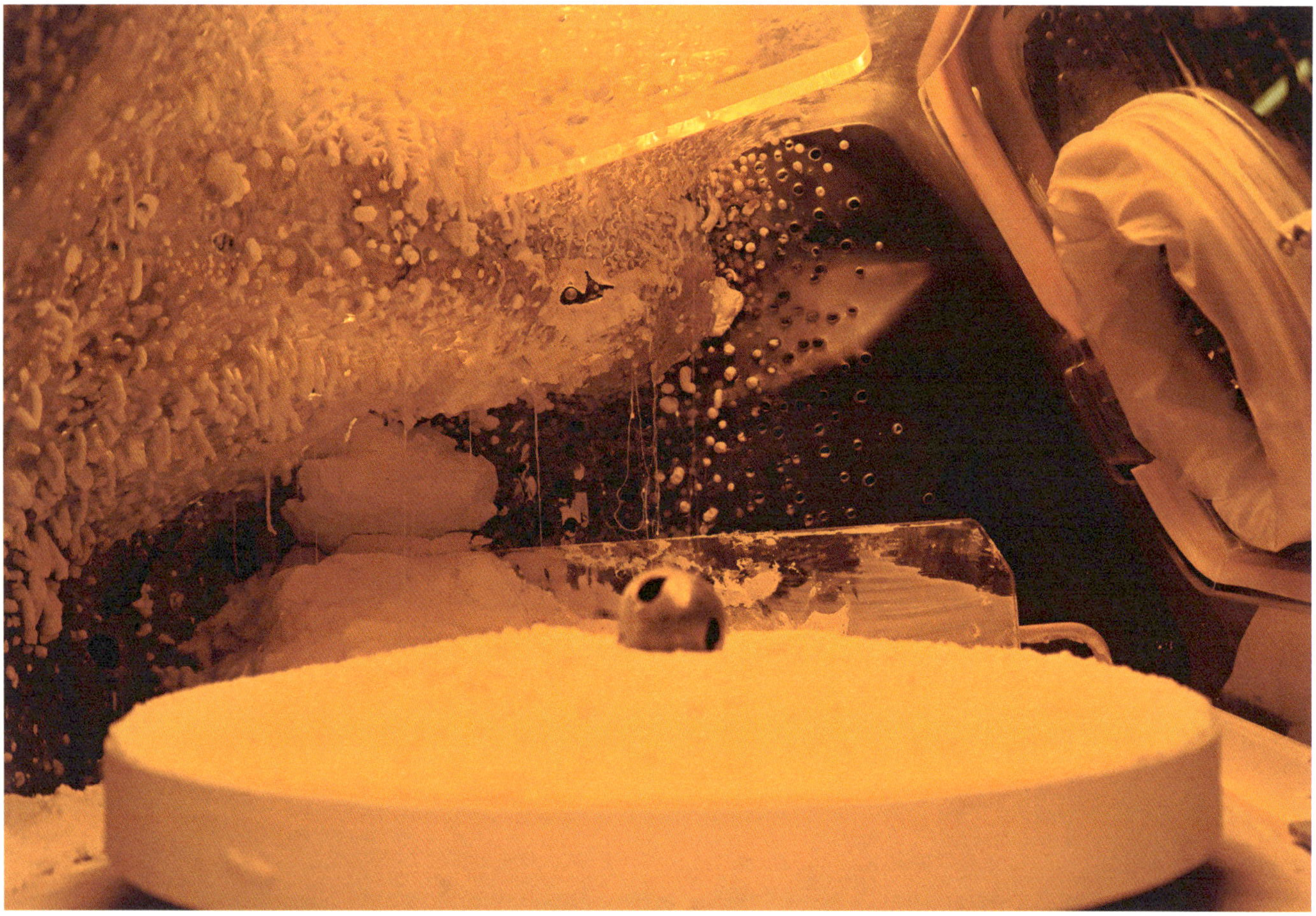

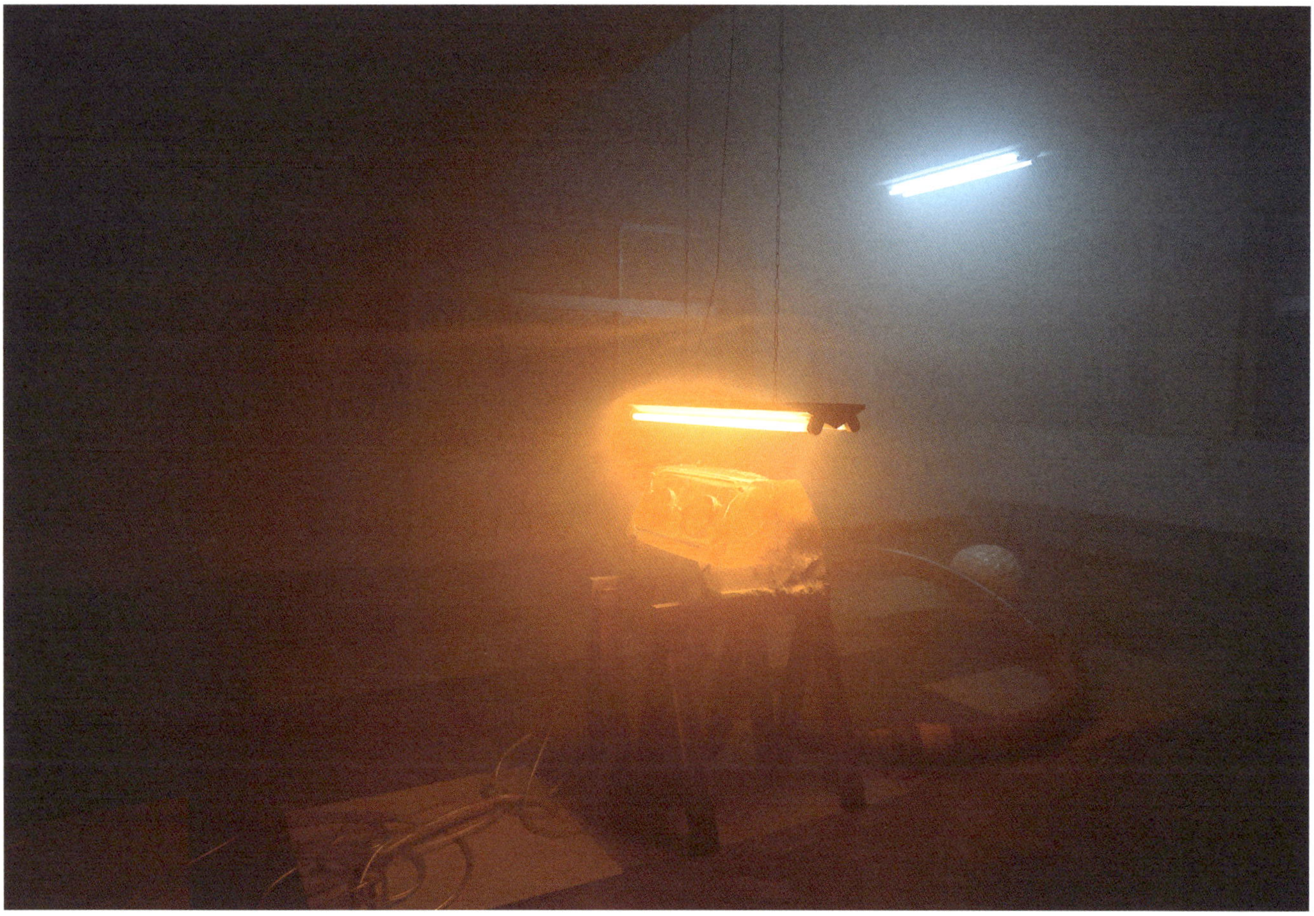

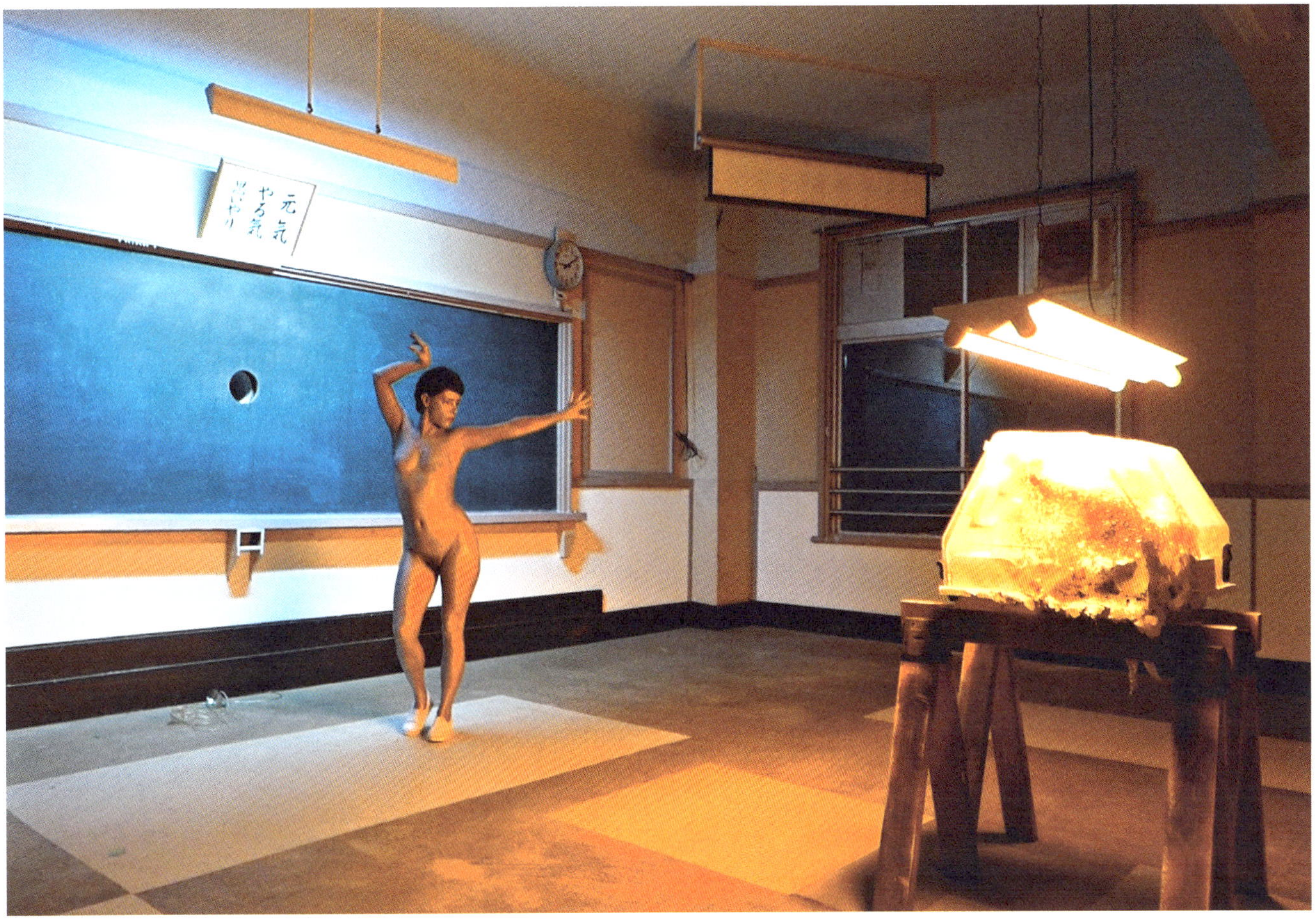

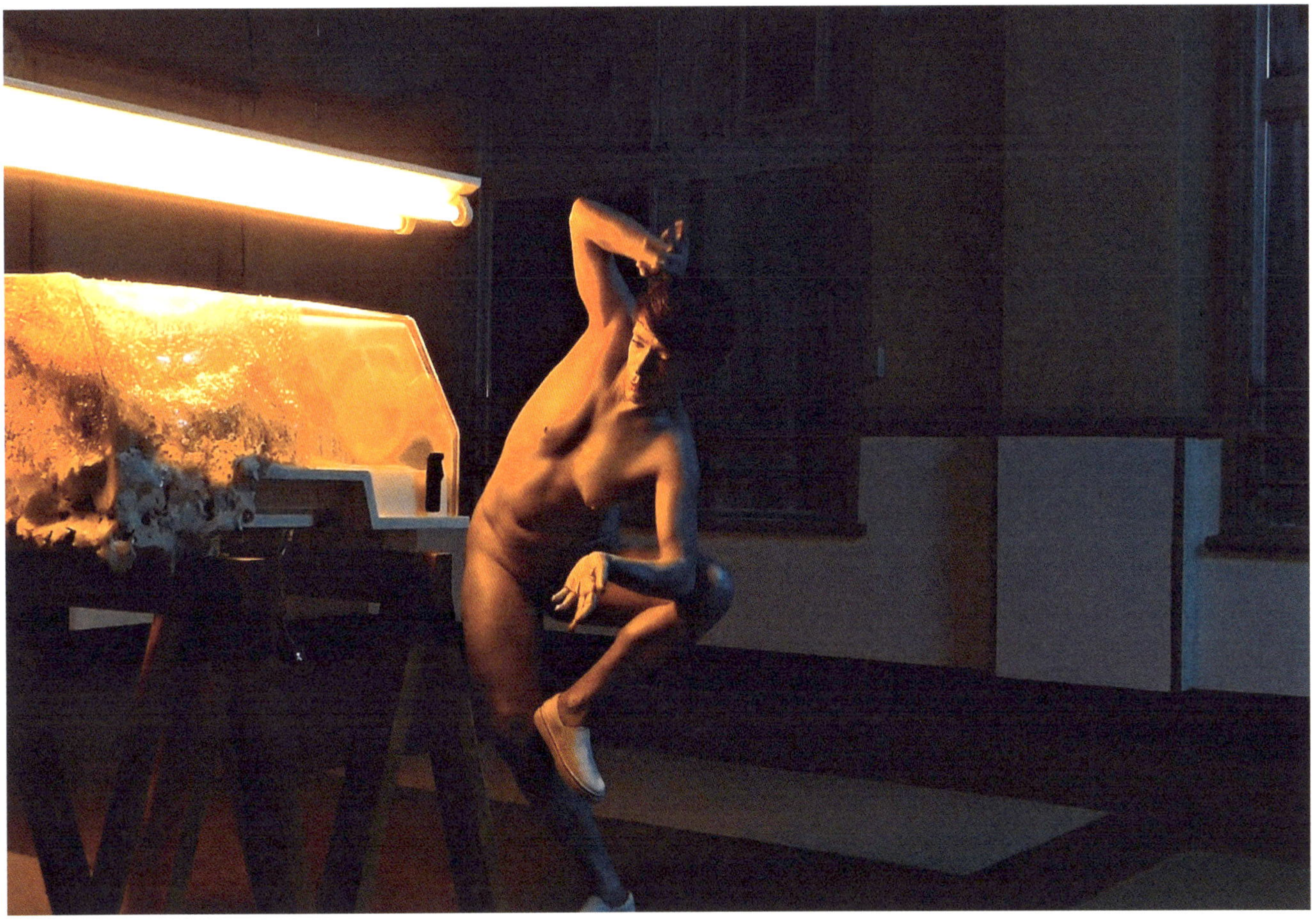

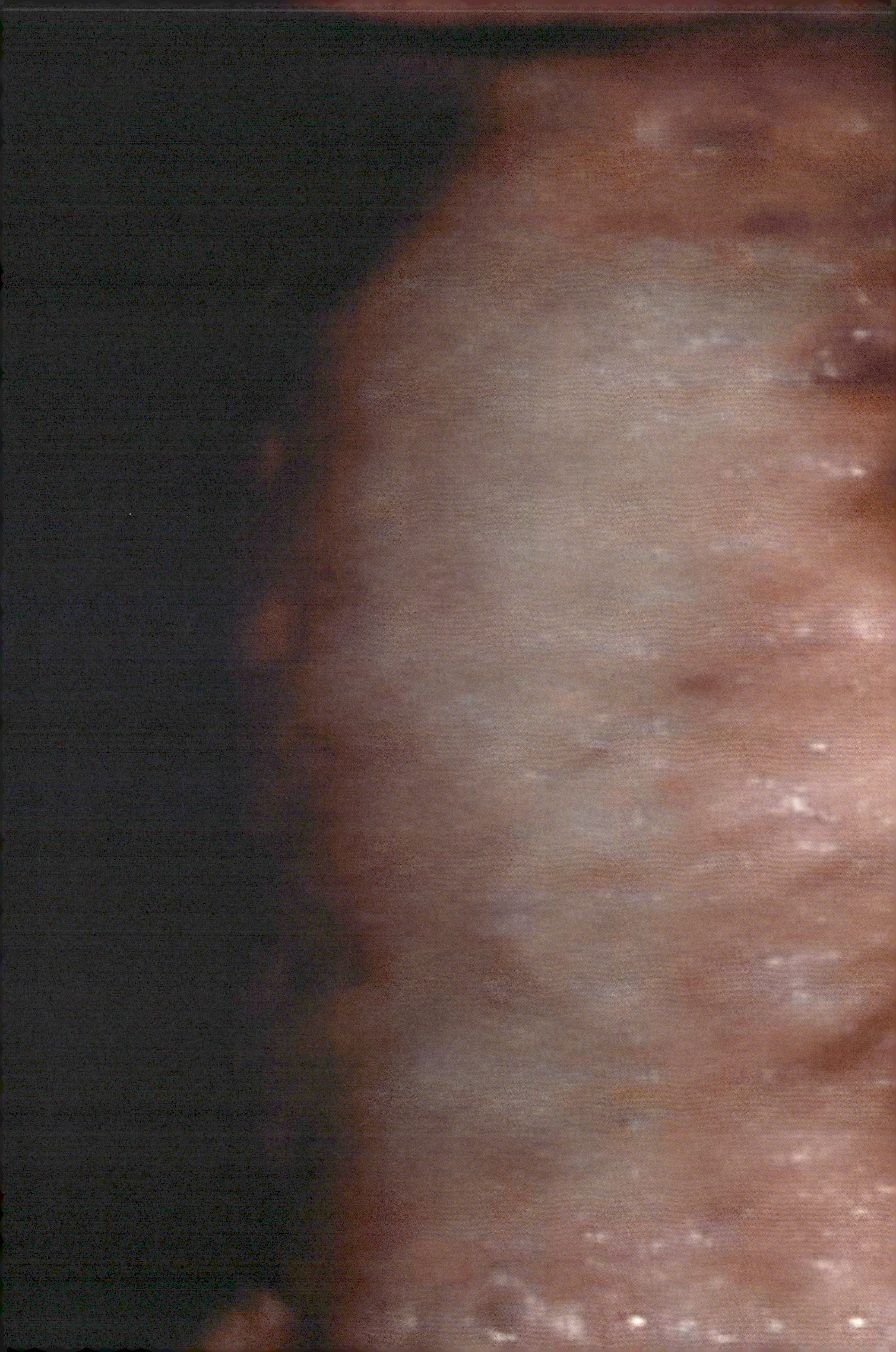

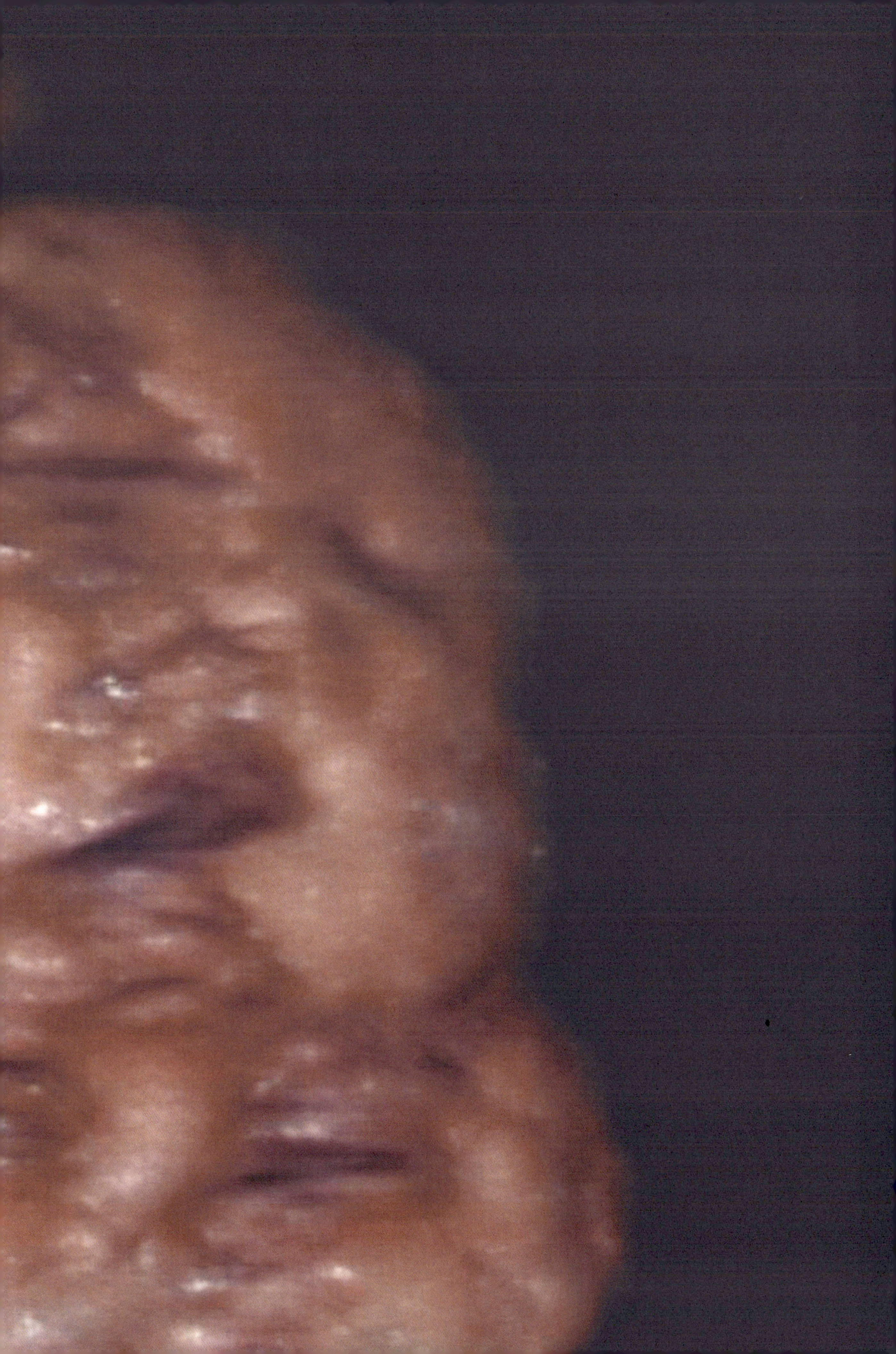

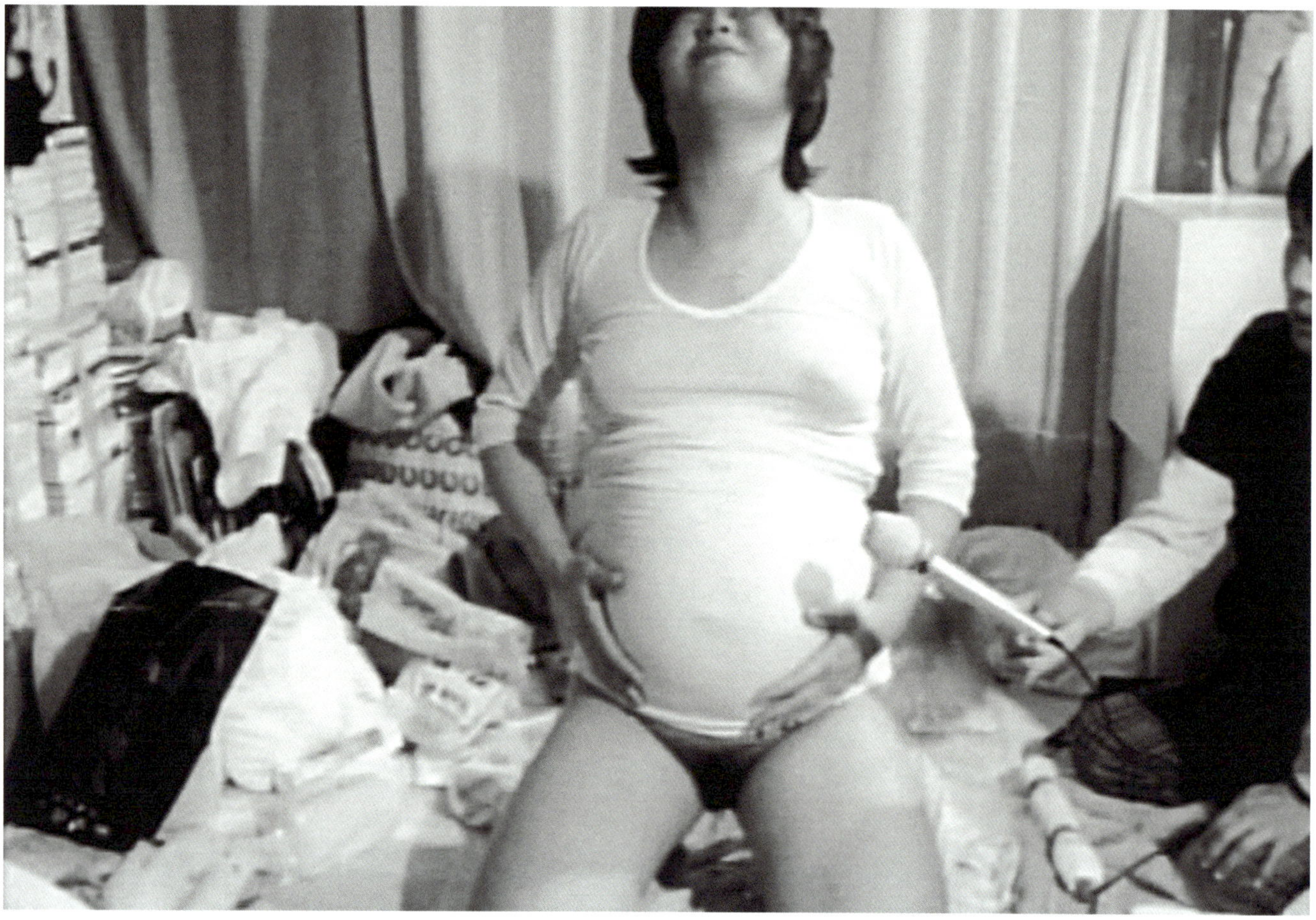

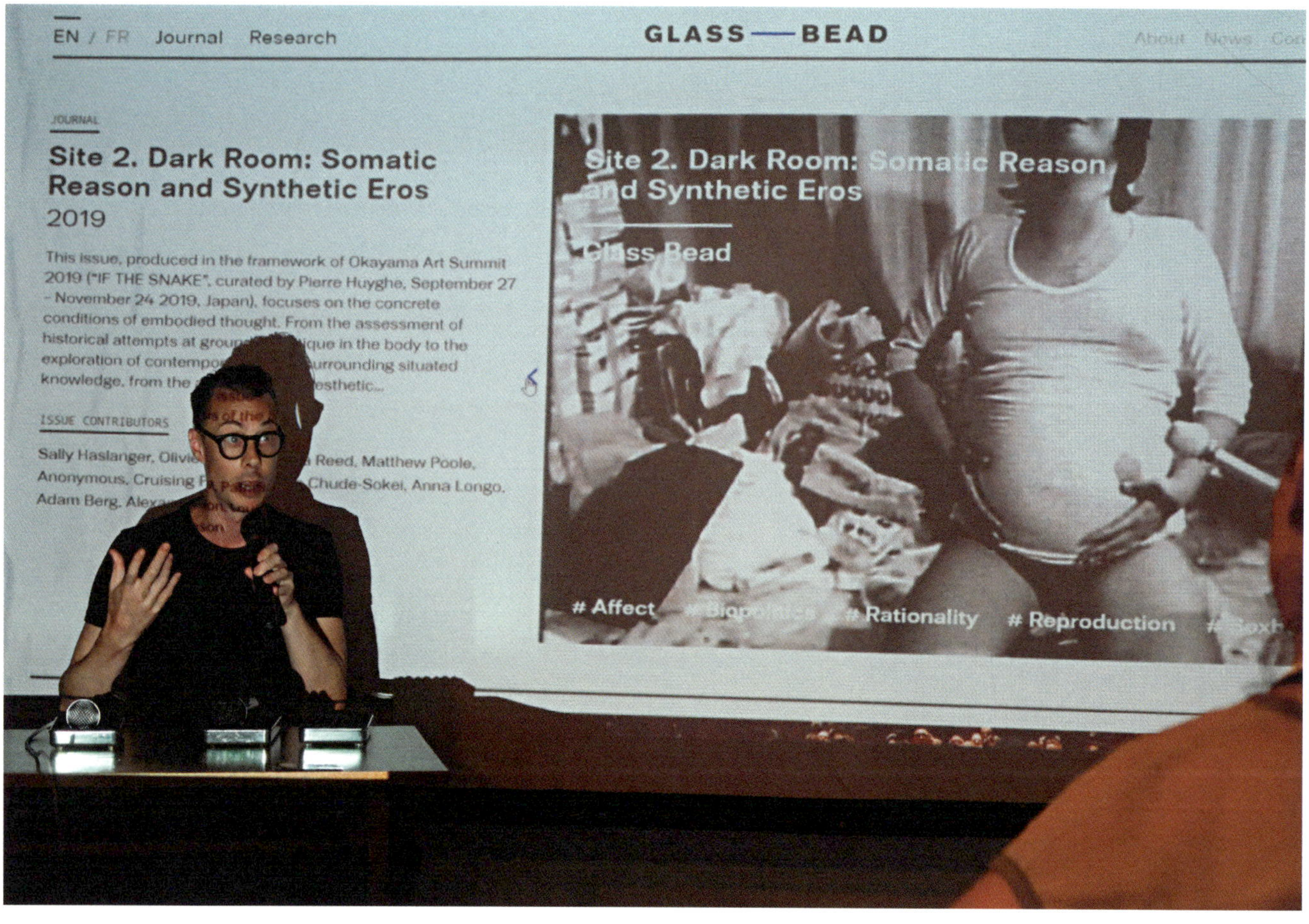
EN / FR Journal Research
GLASS—BEAD
About News
JOURNAL
Site 2. Dark Room: Somatic Reason and Synthetic Eros
2019
This issue, produced in the framework of Okayama Art Summit 2019 ("IF THE SNAKE", curated by Pierre Huyghe, September 27 – November 24 2019, Japan), focuses on the concrete conditions of embodied thought.
ISSUE CONTRIBUTORS
Site 2. Dark Room: Somatic Reason and Synthetic Eros
Glass Bead
Affect
Rationality
Reproduction

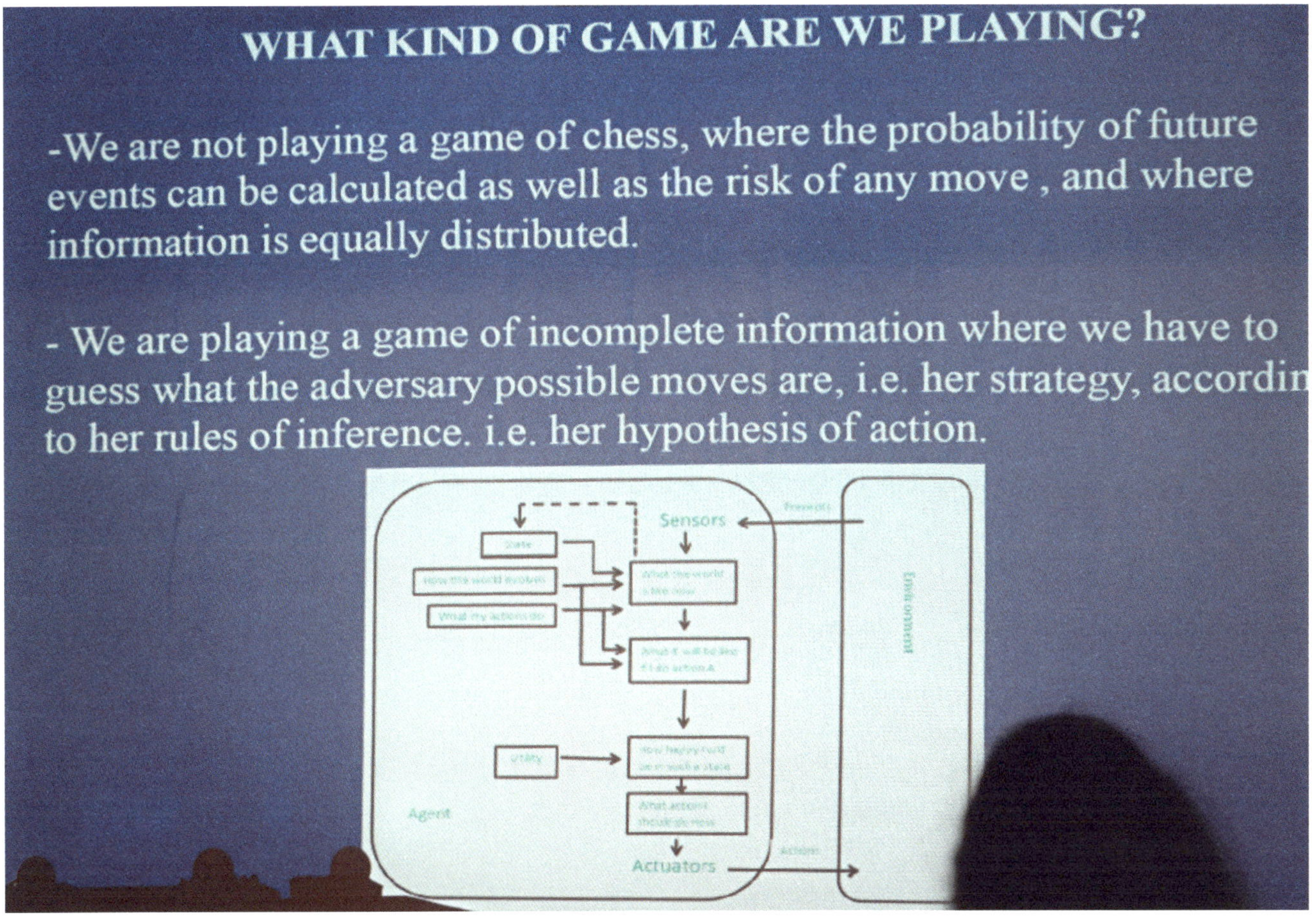

WHAT KIND OF GAME ARE WE PLAYING?

-We are not playing a game of chess, where the probability of future events can be calculated as well as the risk of any move , and where information is equally distributed.

- We are playing a game of incomplete information where we have to guess what the adversary possible moves are, i.e. her strategy, accordin to her rules of inference. i.e. her hypothesis of action.

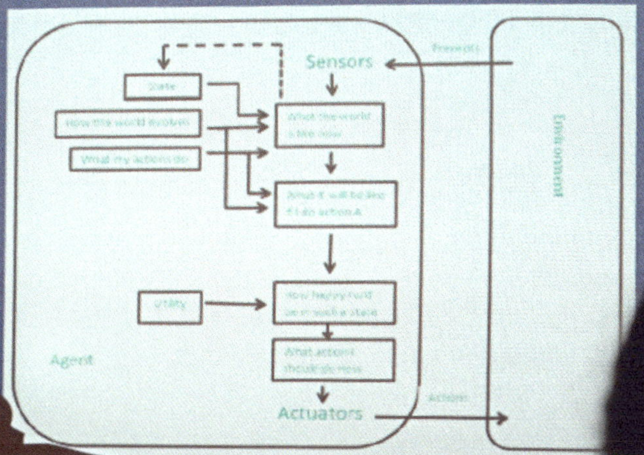

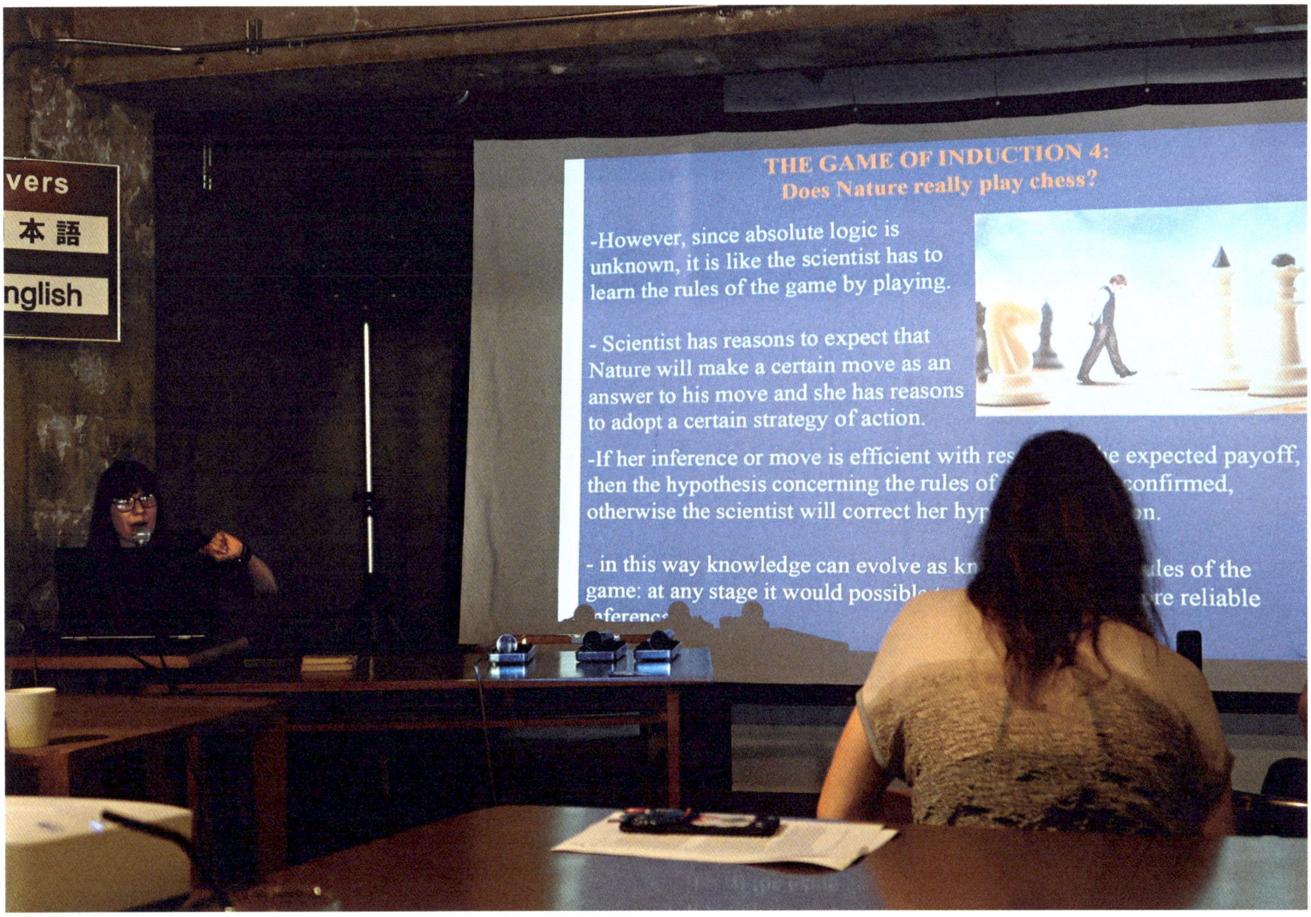

vers
本語
nglish

THE GAME OF INDUCTION 4:
Does Nature really play chess?

-However, since absolute logic is unknown, it is like the scientist has to learn the rules of the game by playing.

- Scientist has reasons to expect that Nature will make a certain move as an answer to his move and she has reasons to adopt a certain strategy of action.

-If her inference or move is efficient with res e expected payoff, then the hypothesis concerning the rules of confirmed, otherwise the scientist will correct her hyp n.

- in this way knowledge can evolve as kr les of the game: at any stage it would possibl re reliable

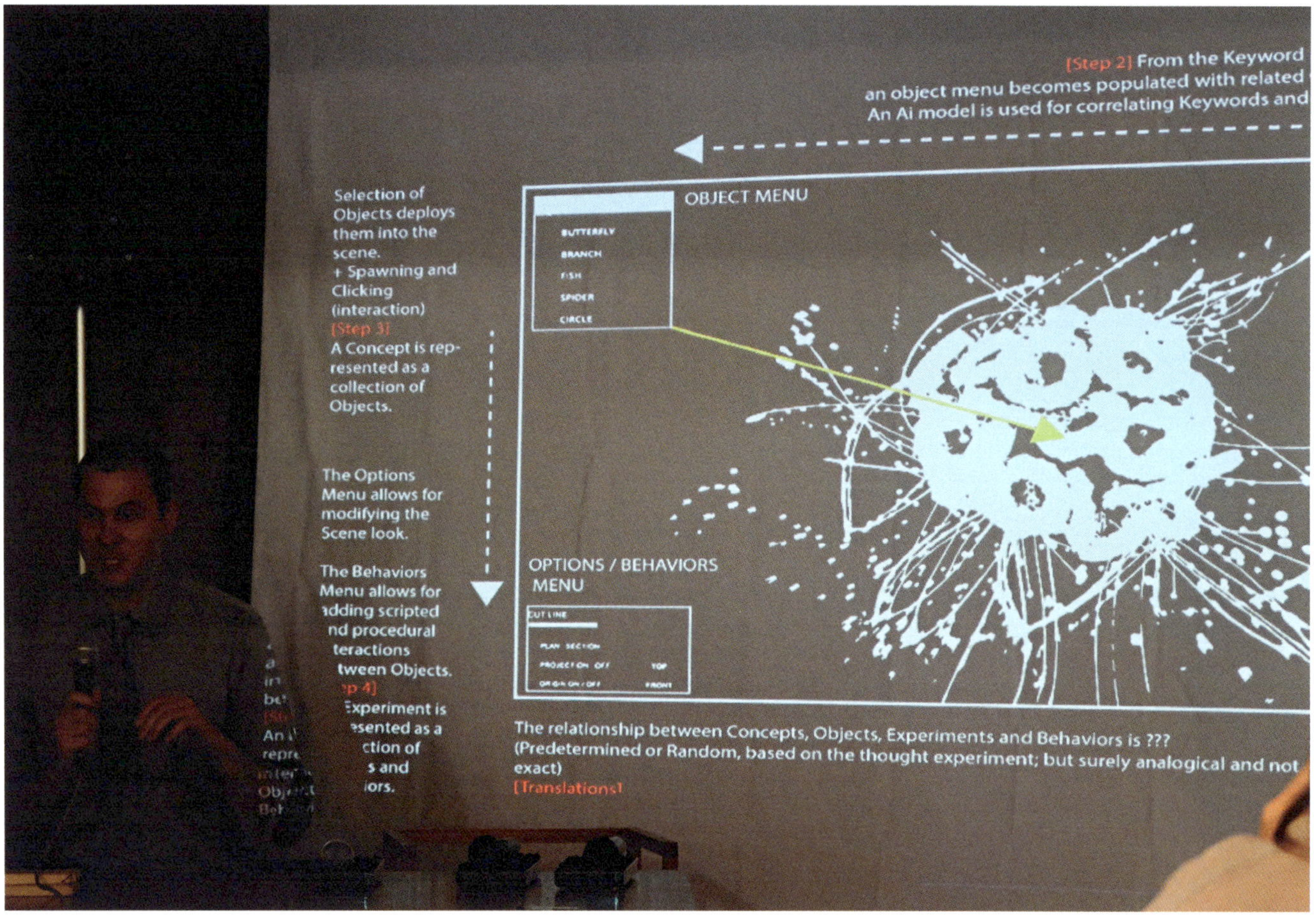

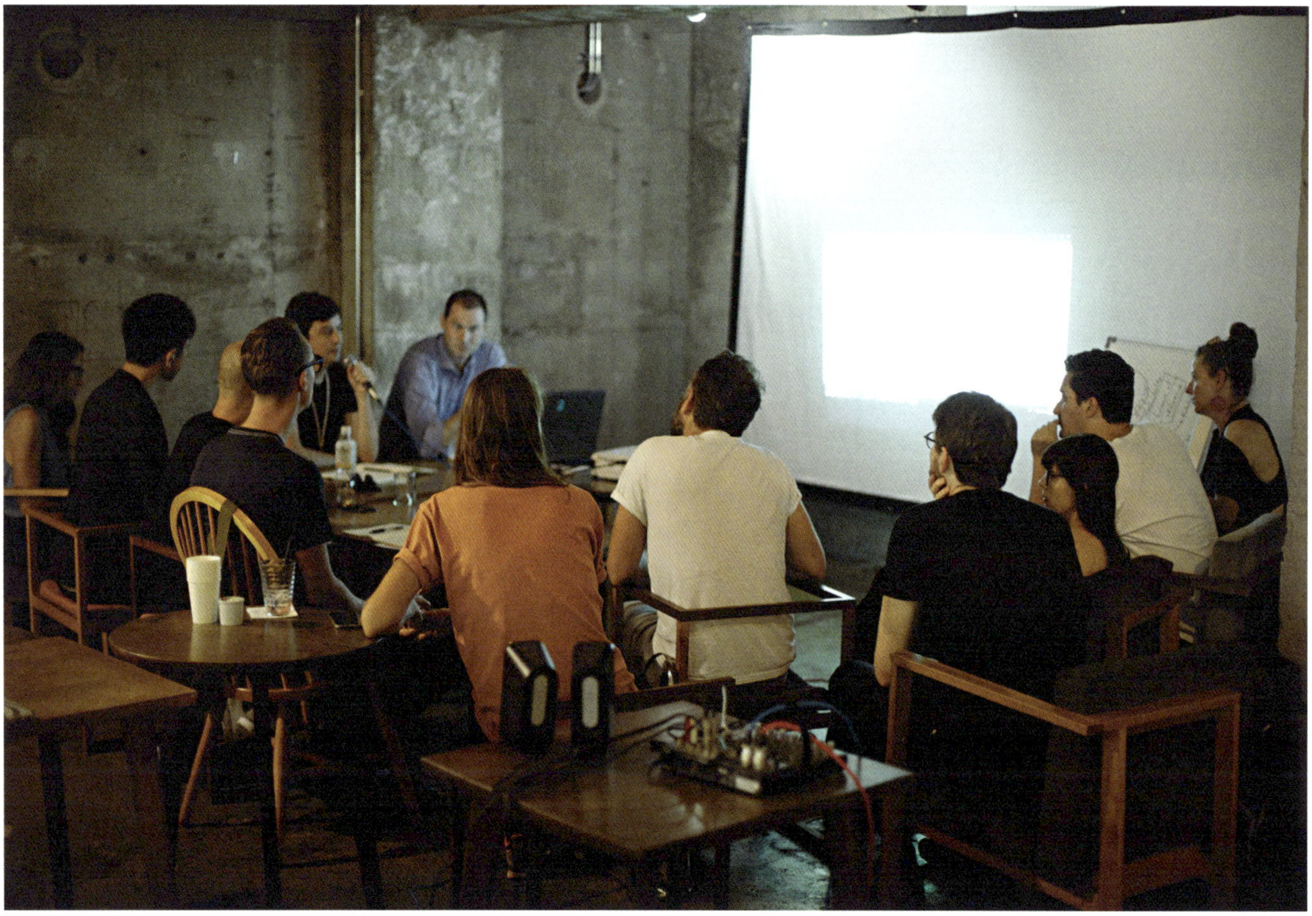

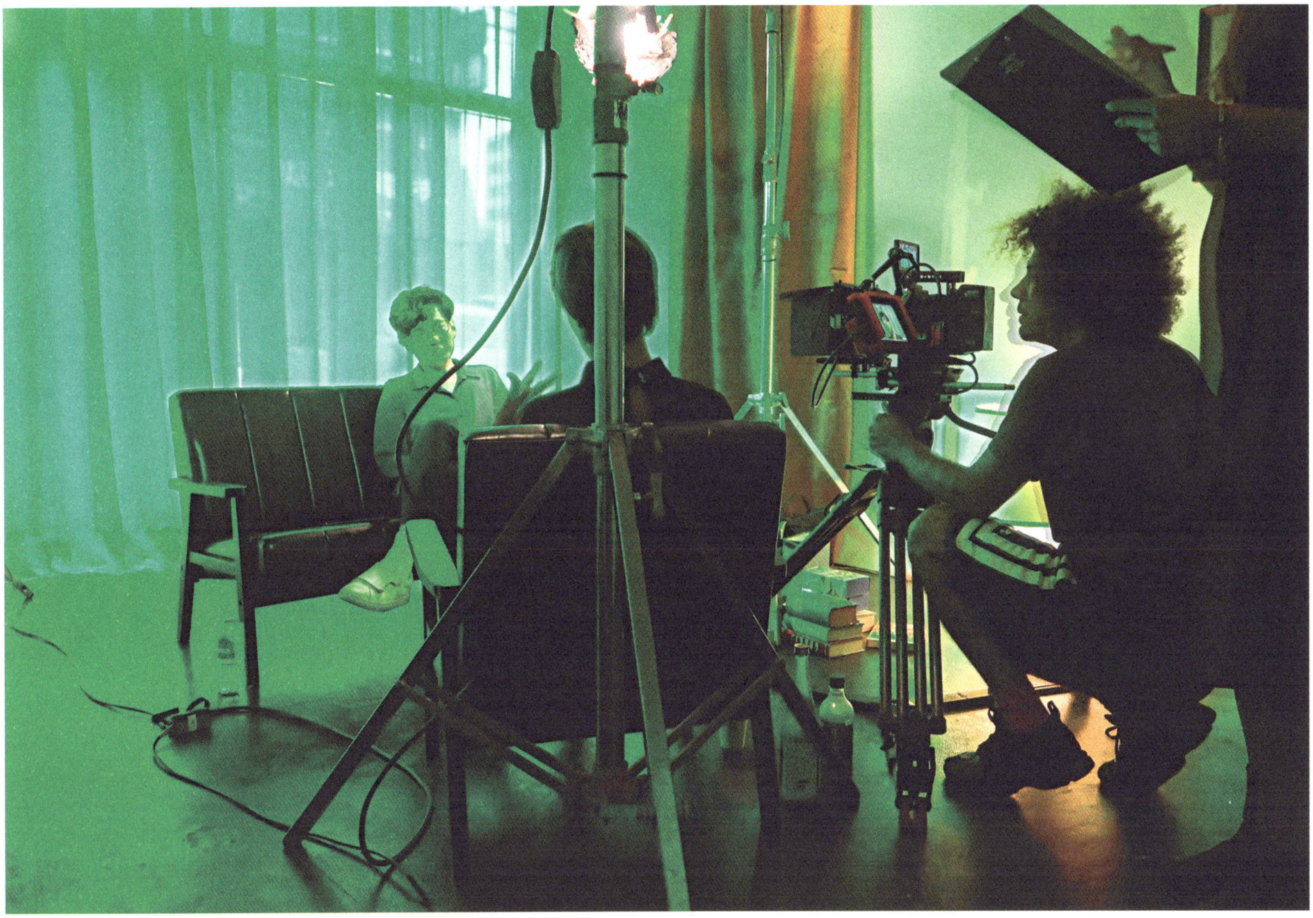

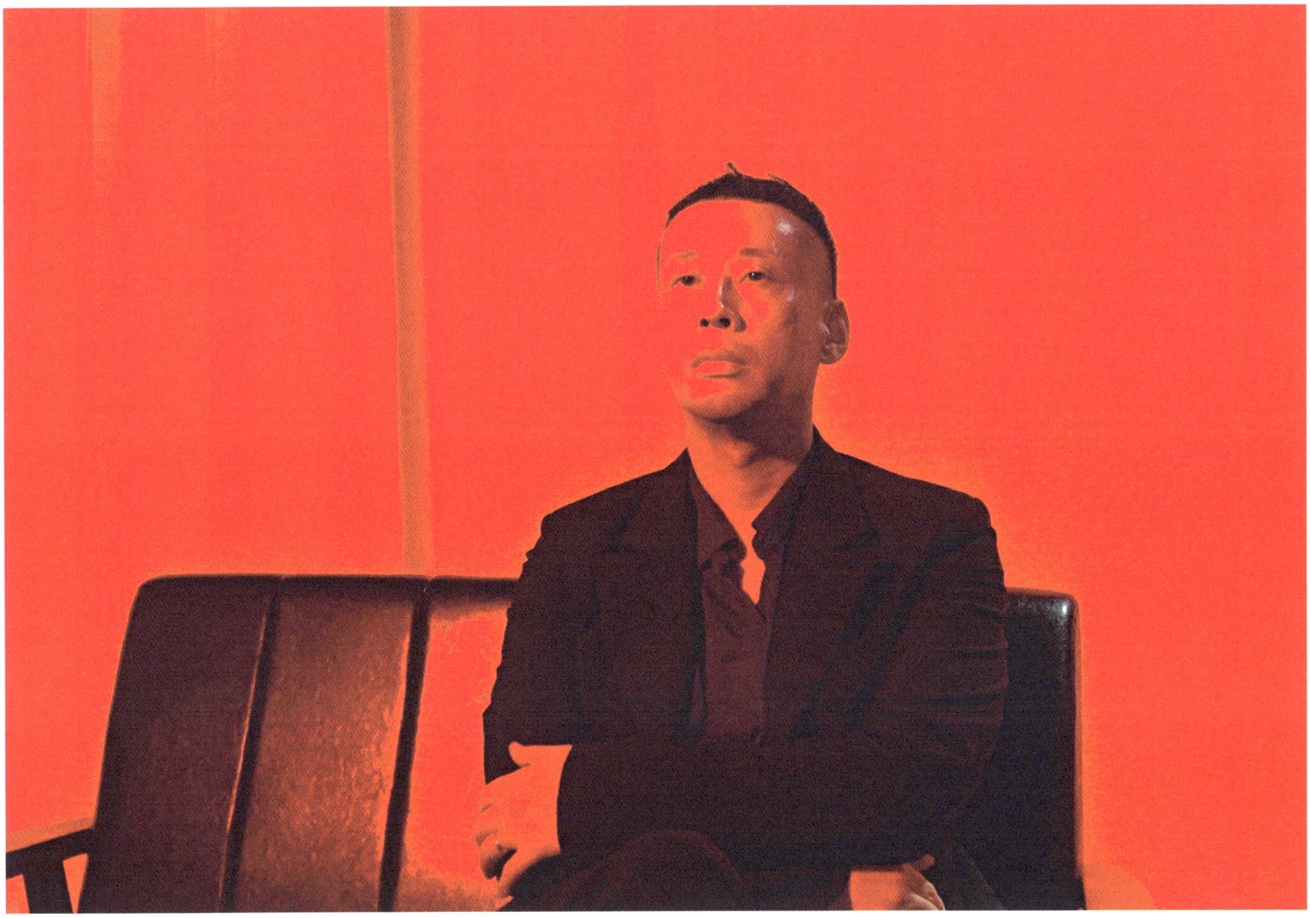

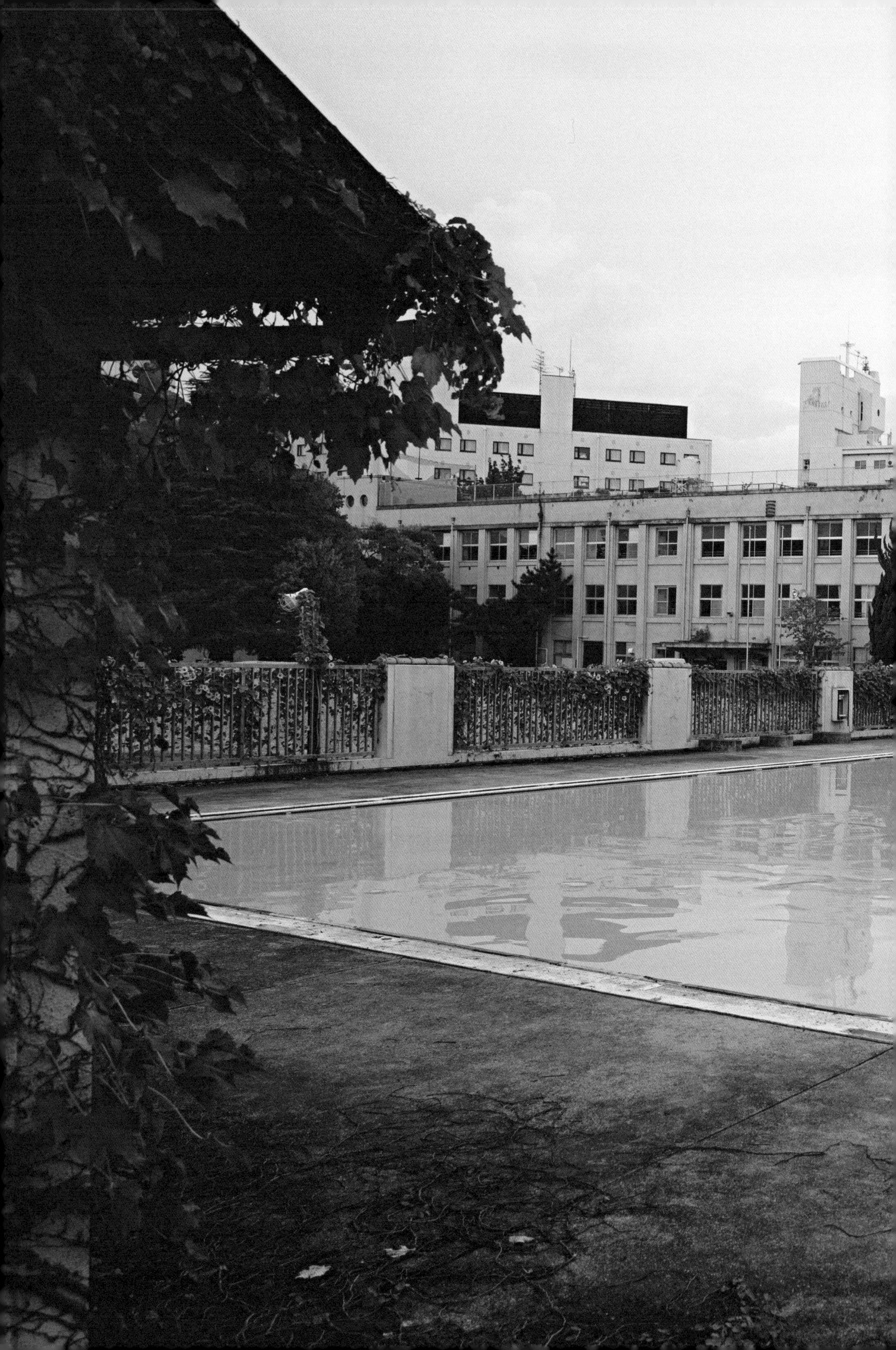

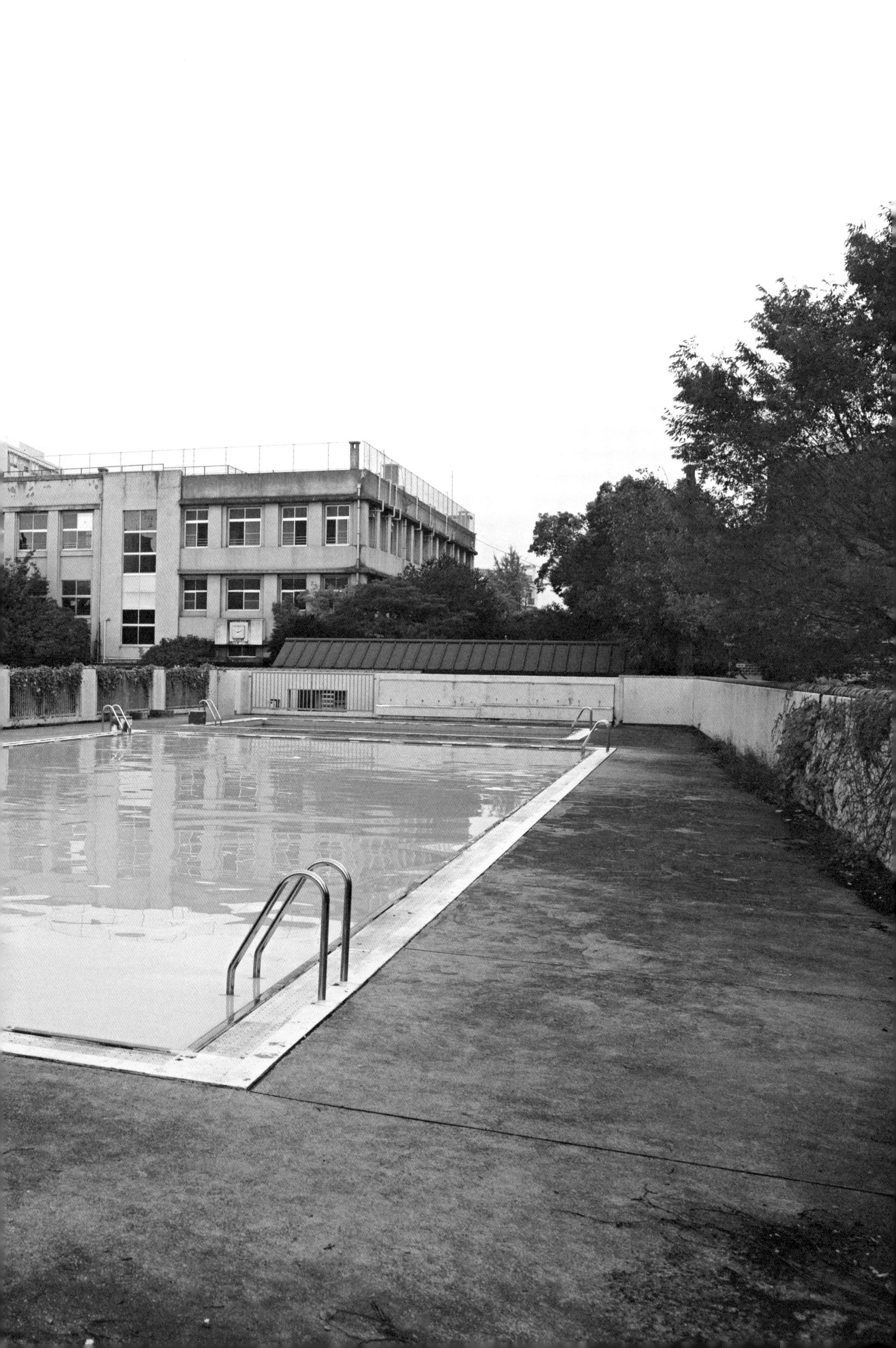

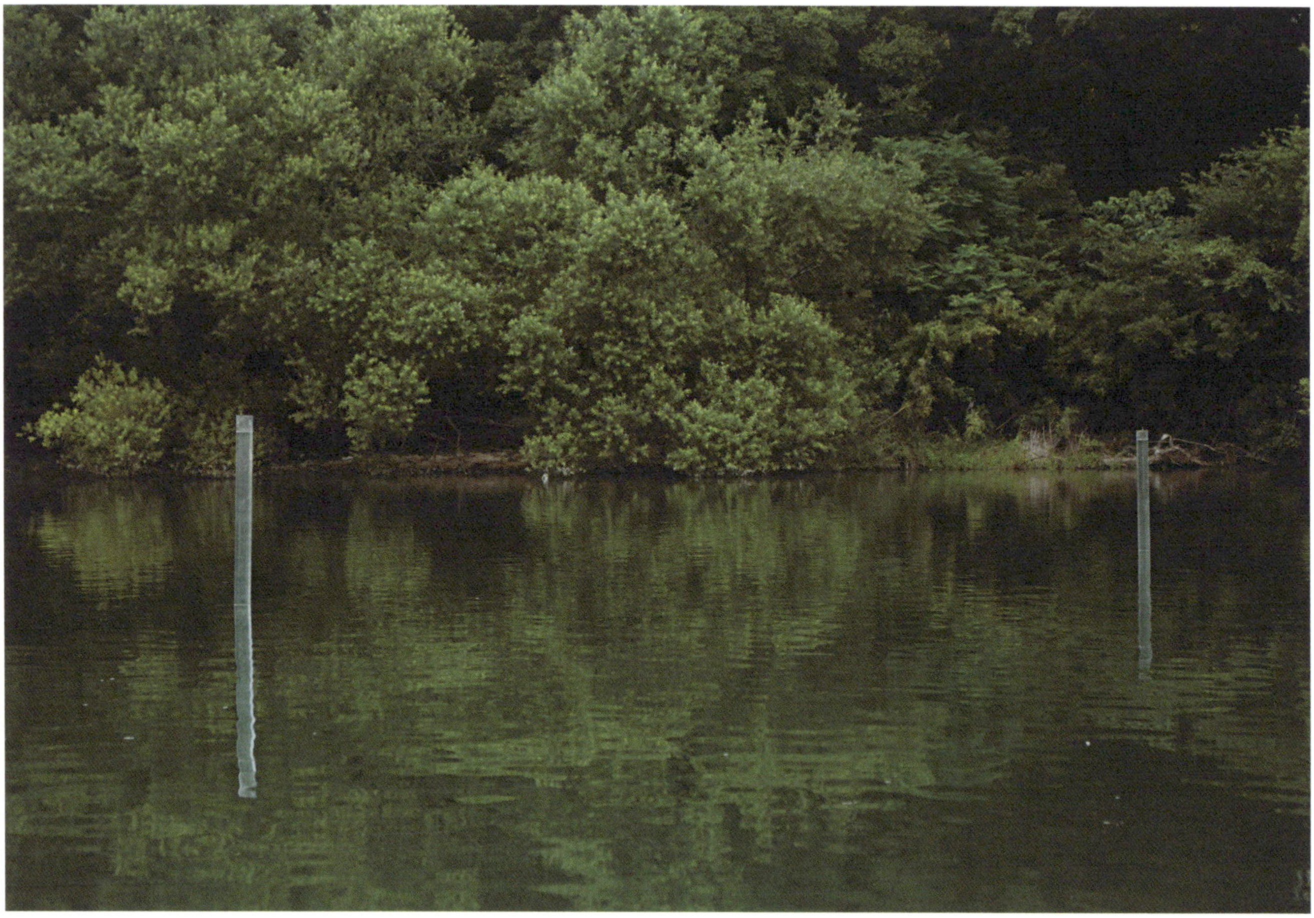

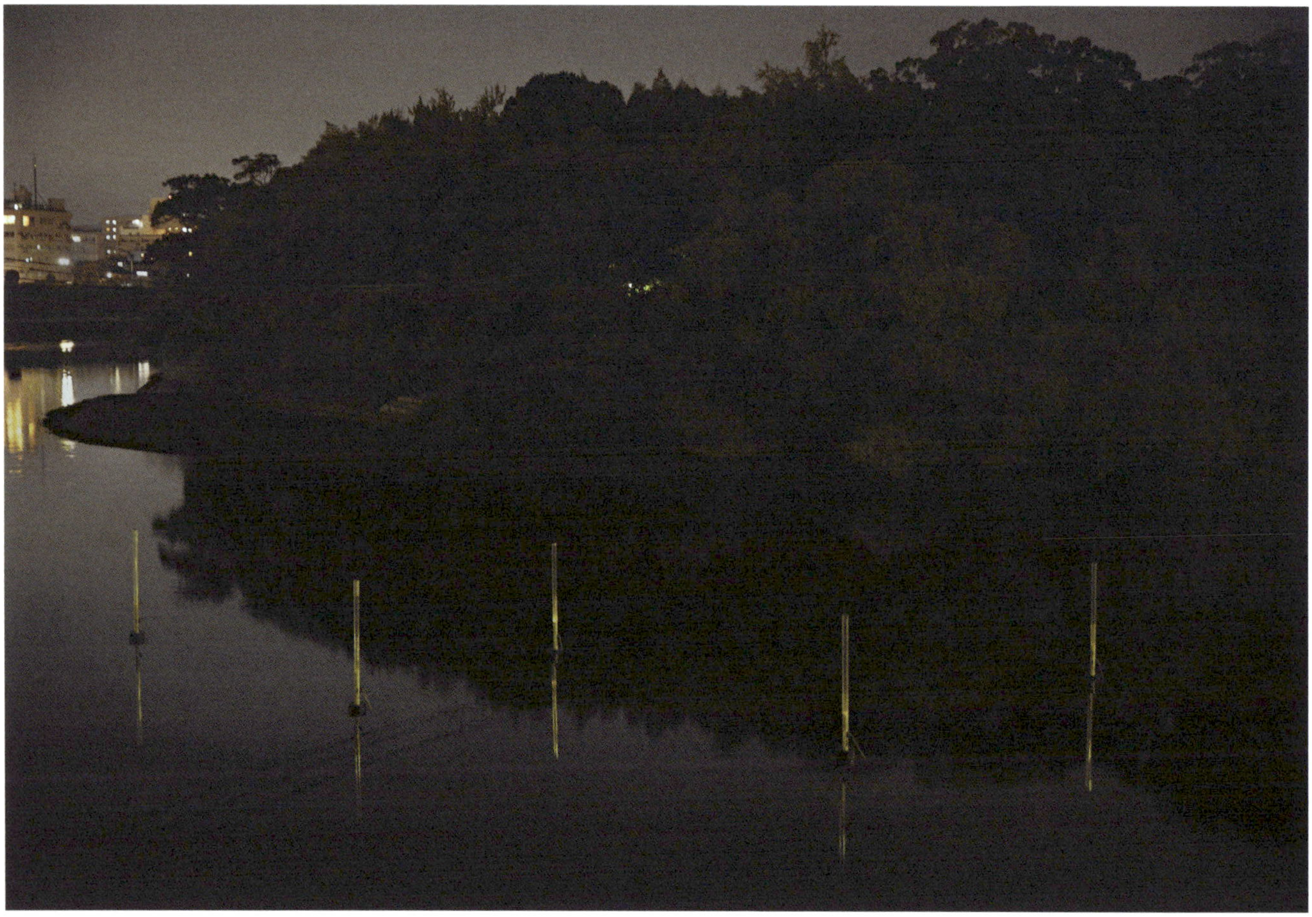

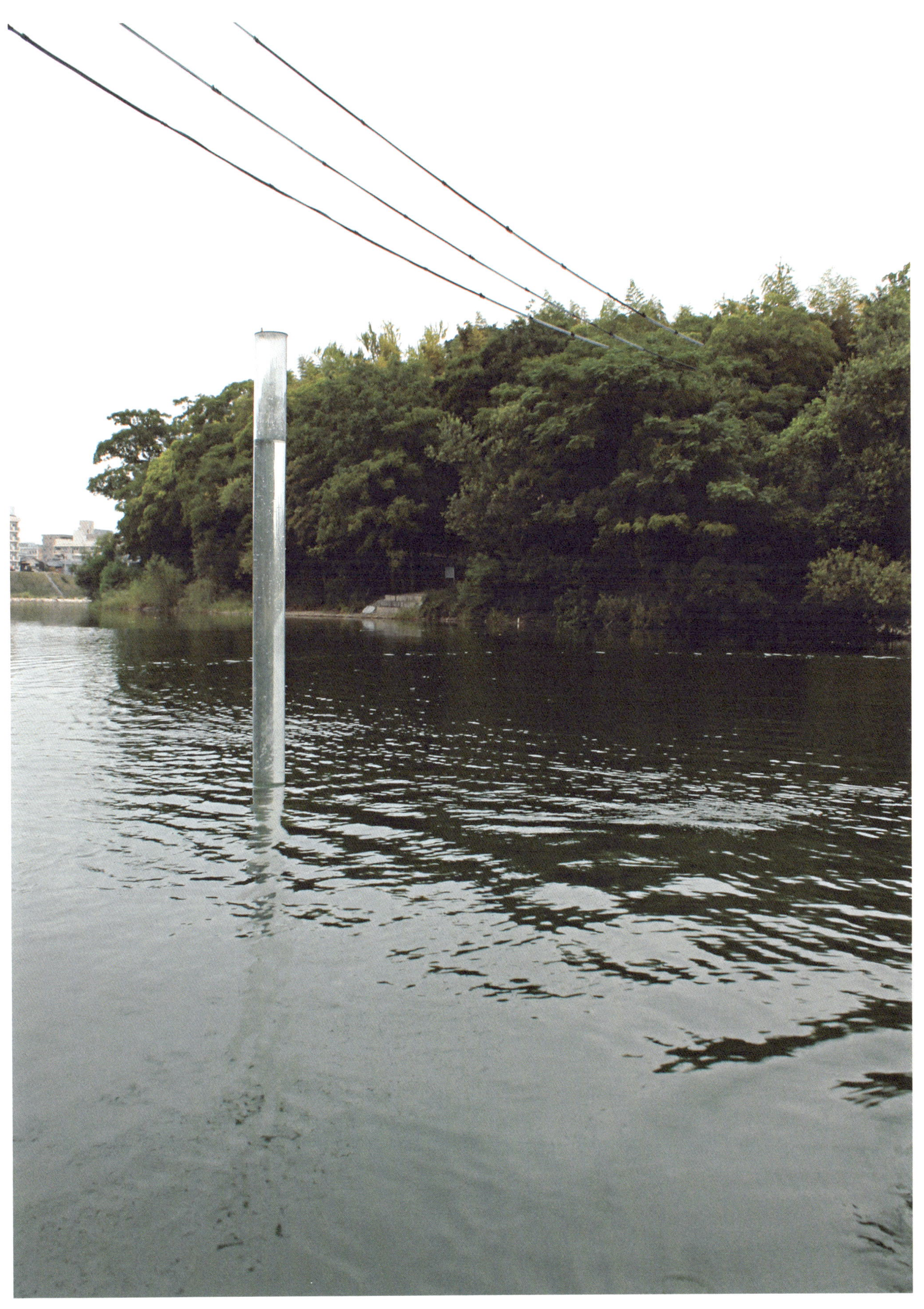

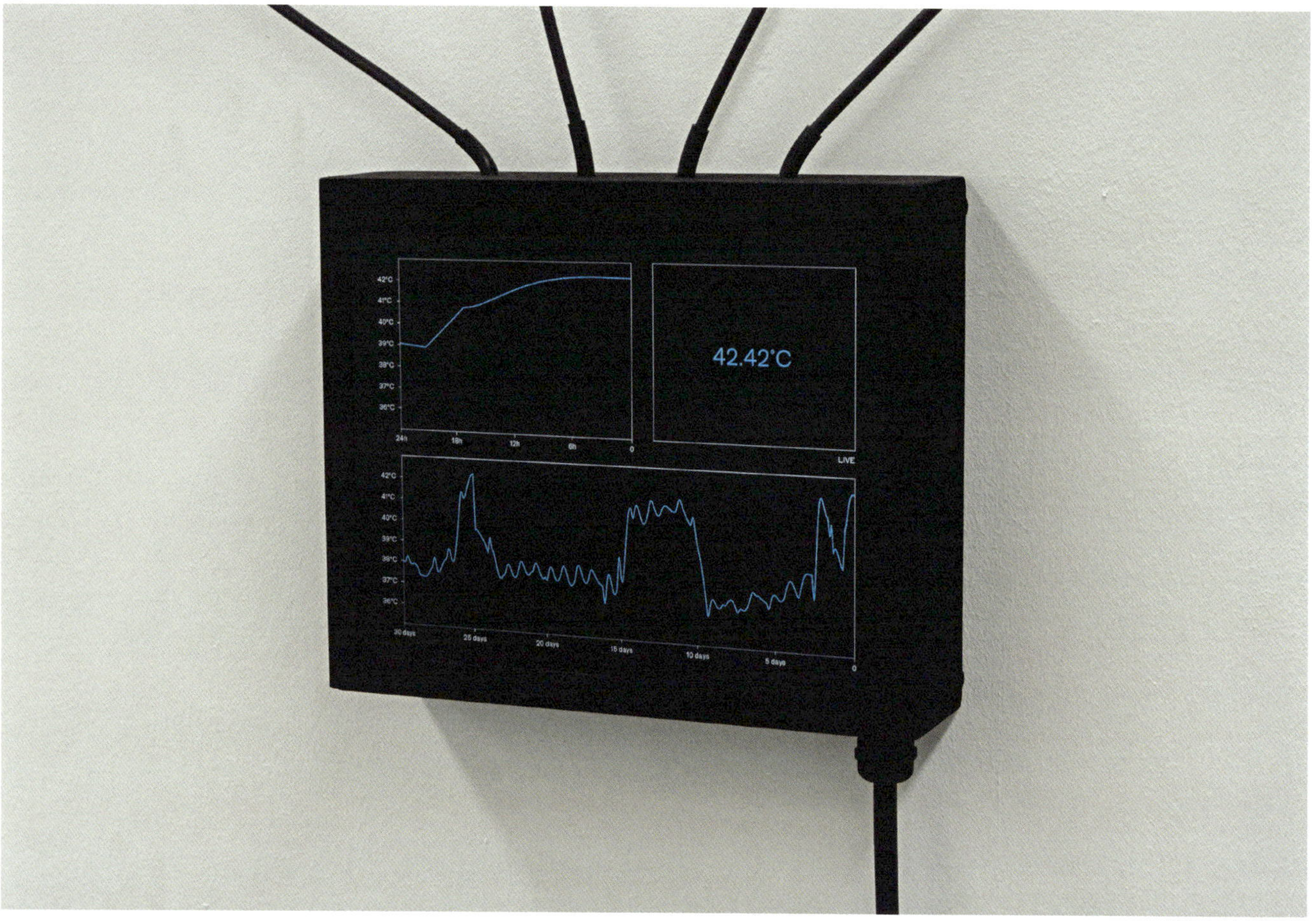
42°C
41°C
40°C
39°C
38°C
37°C
36°C
24h
18h
12h
6h
0
42.42°C
LIVE
42°C
41°C
40°C
39°C
38°C
37°C
36°C
30 days
25 days
20 days
15 days
10 days
5 days
0

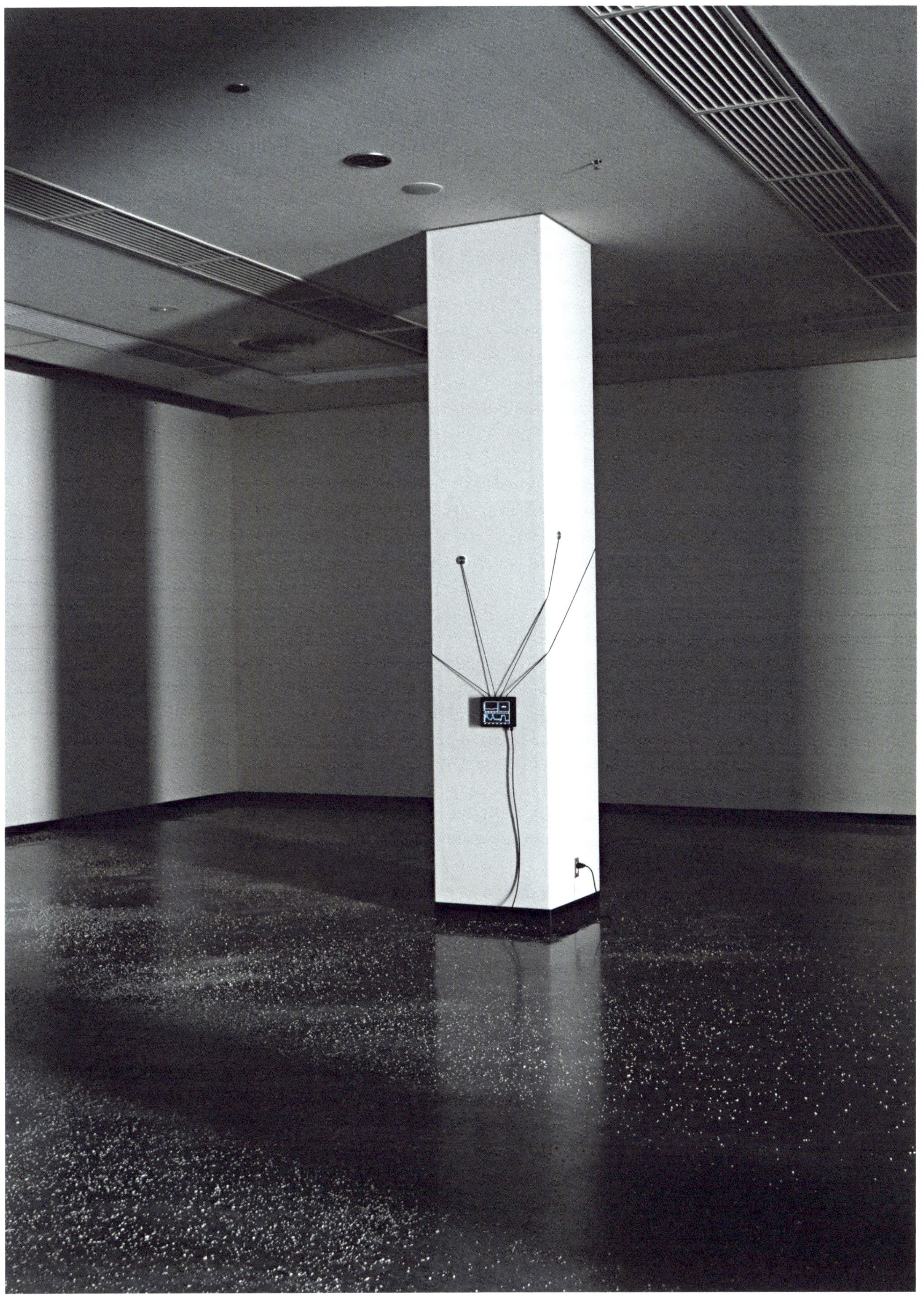

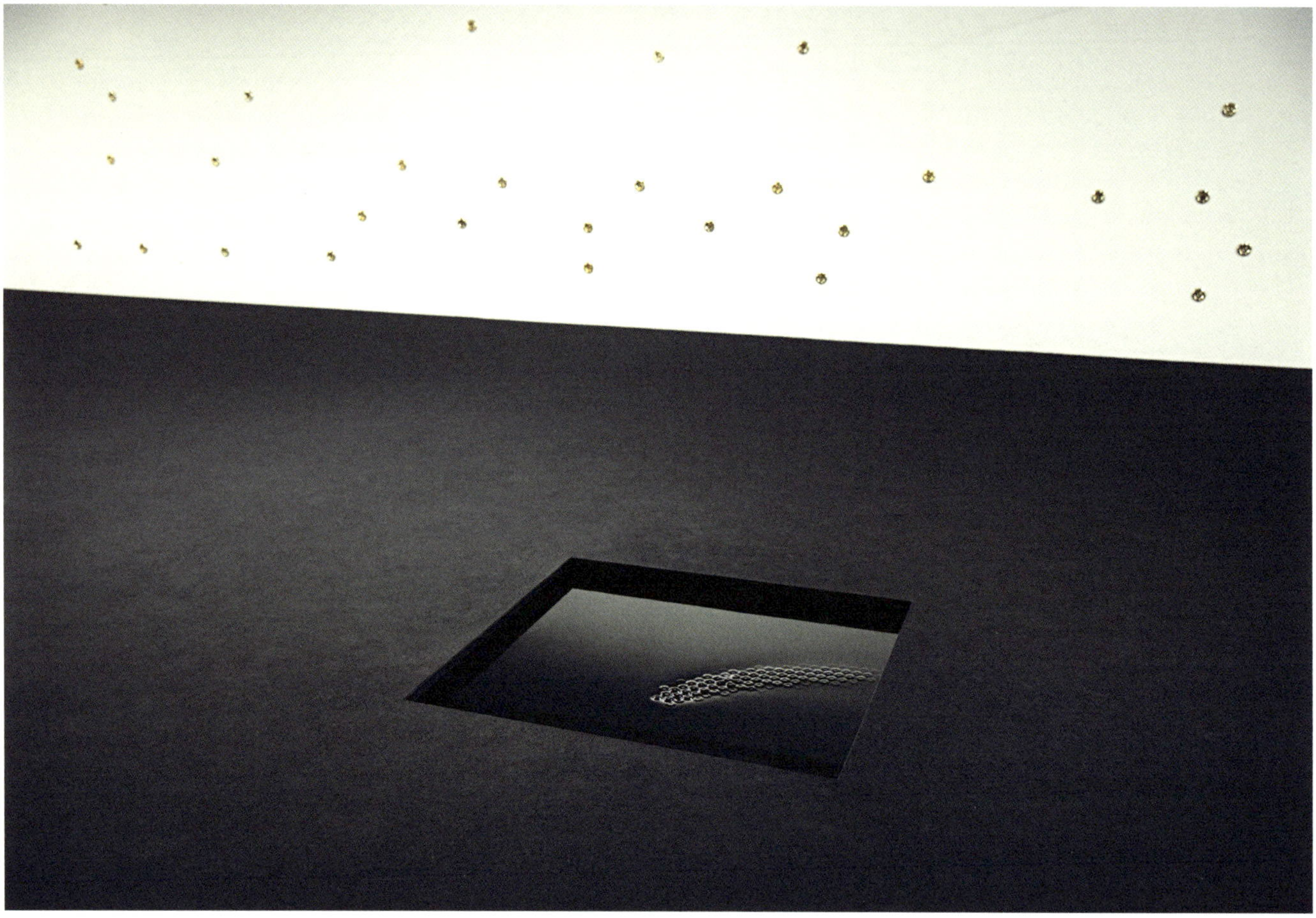

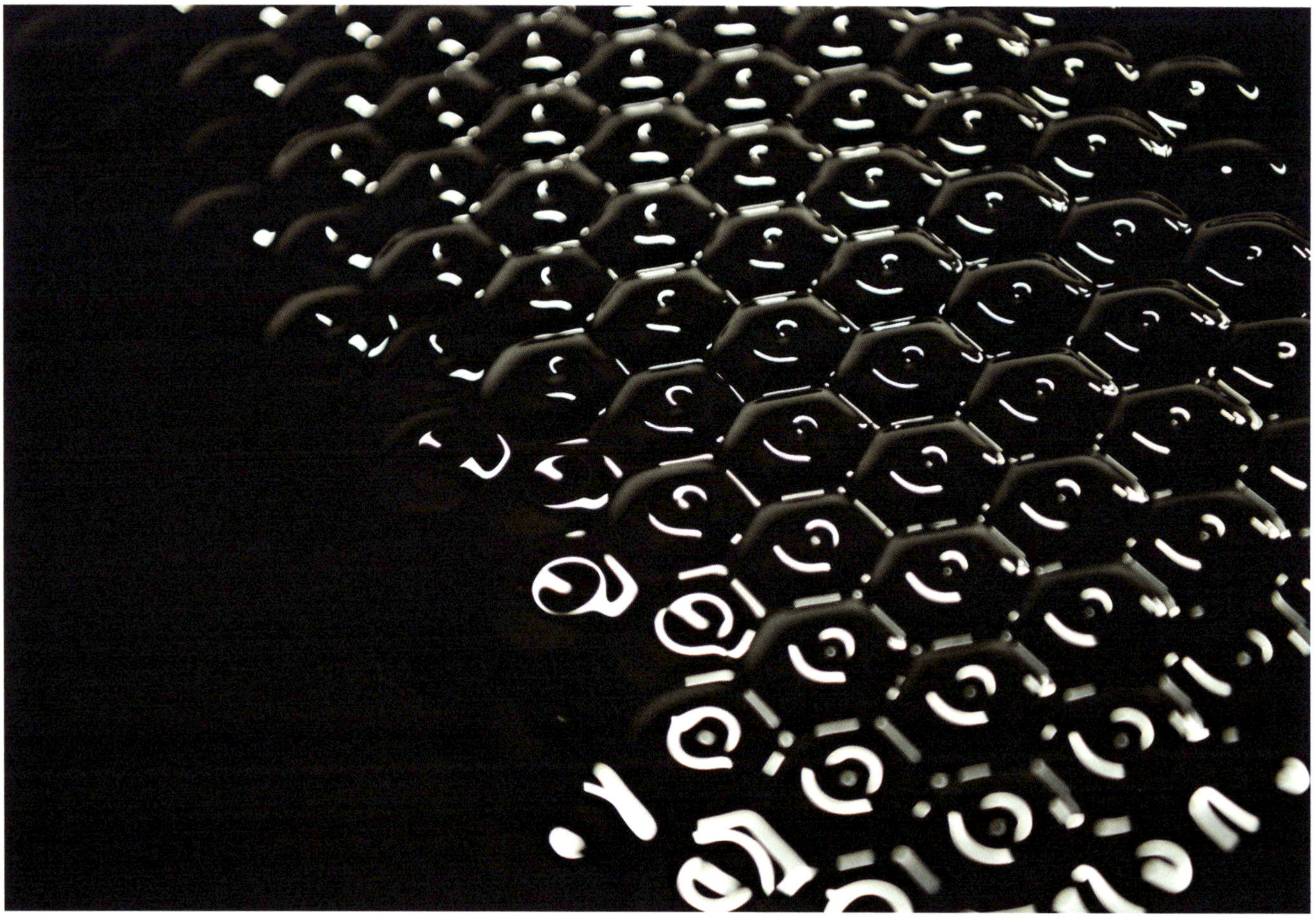

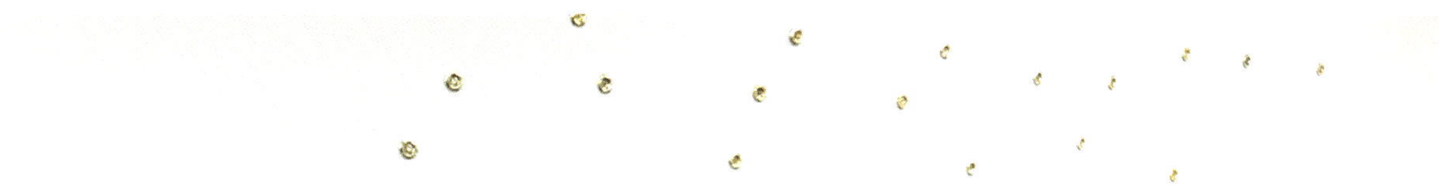

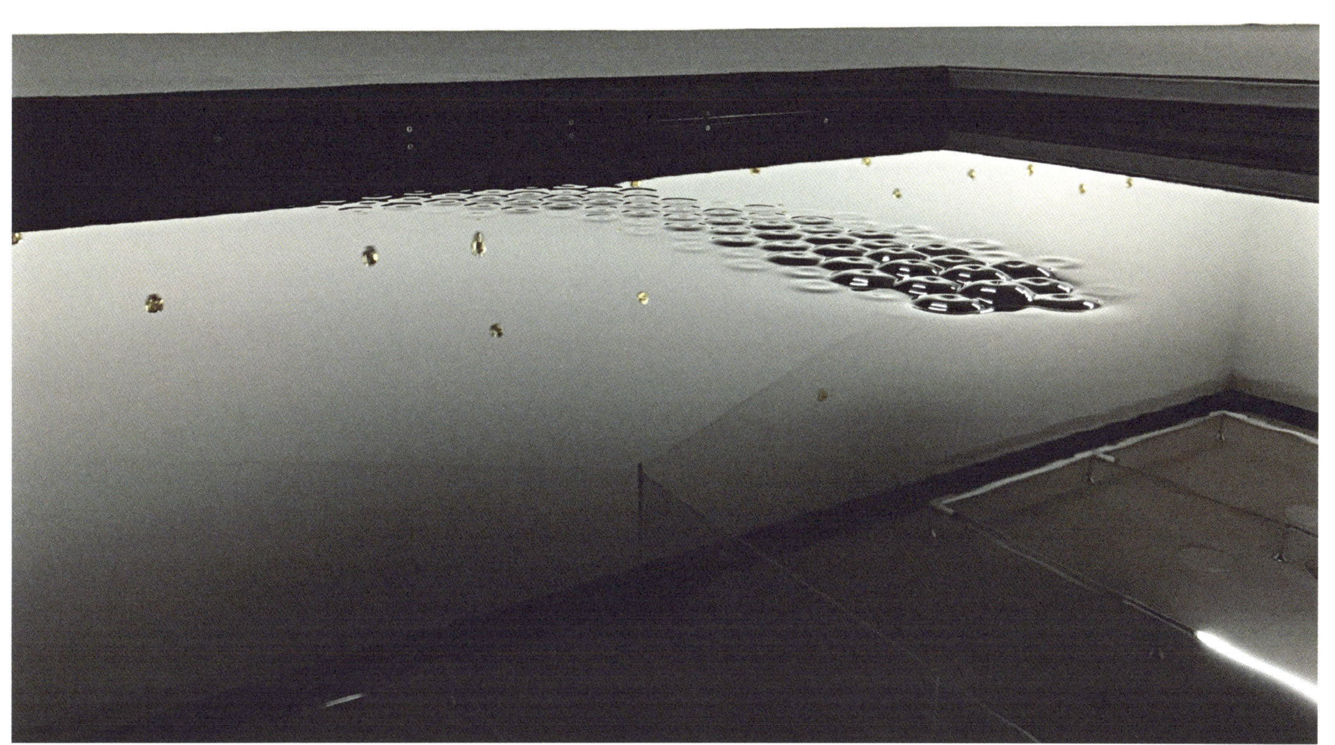

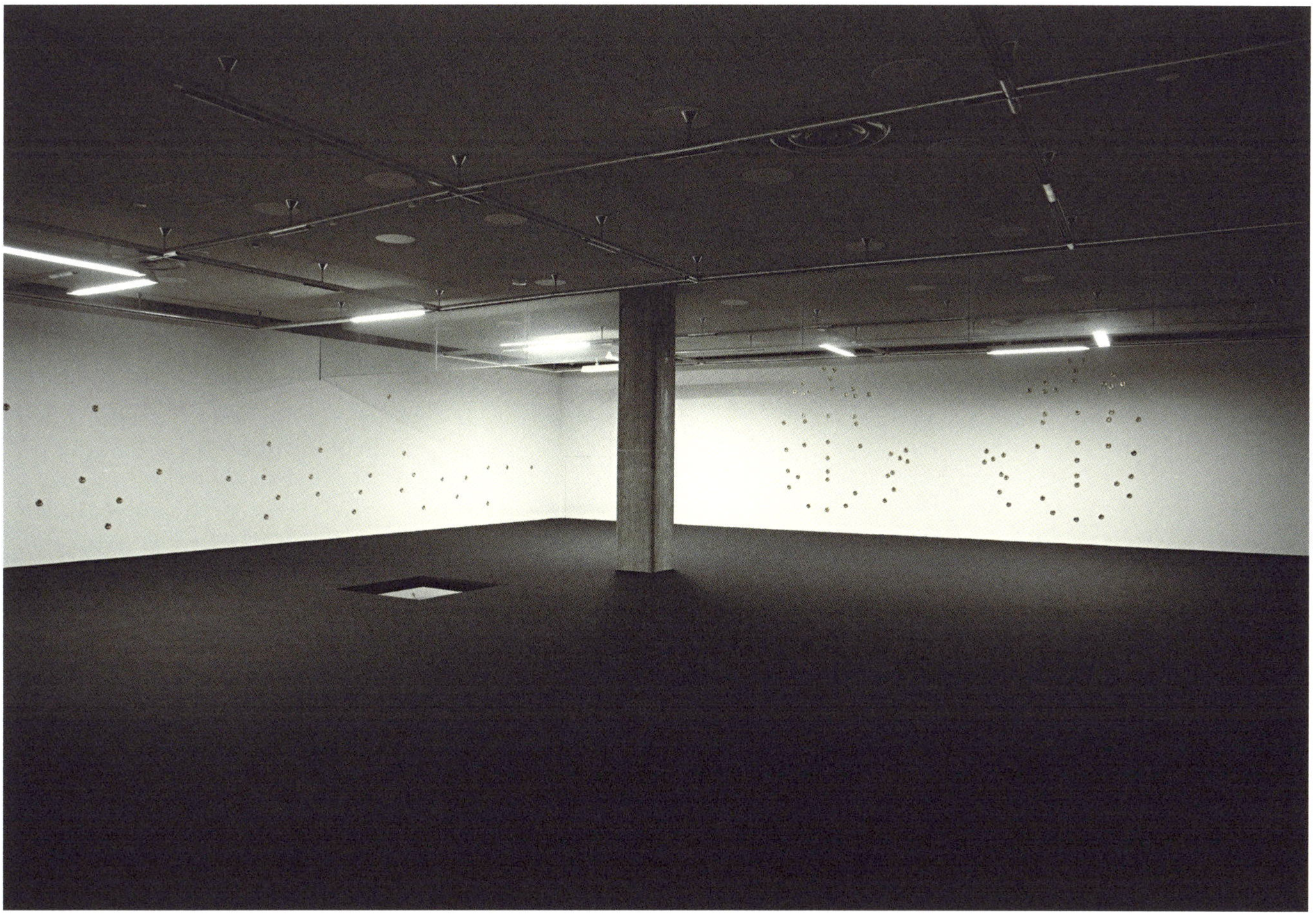

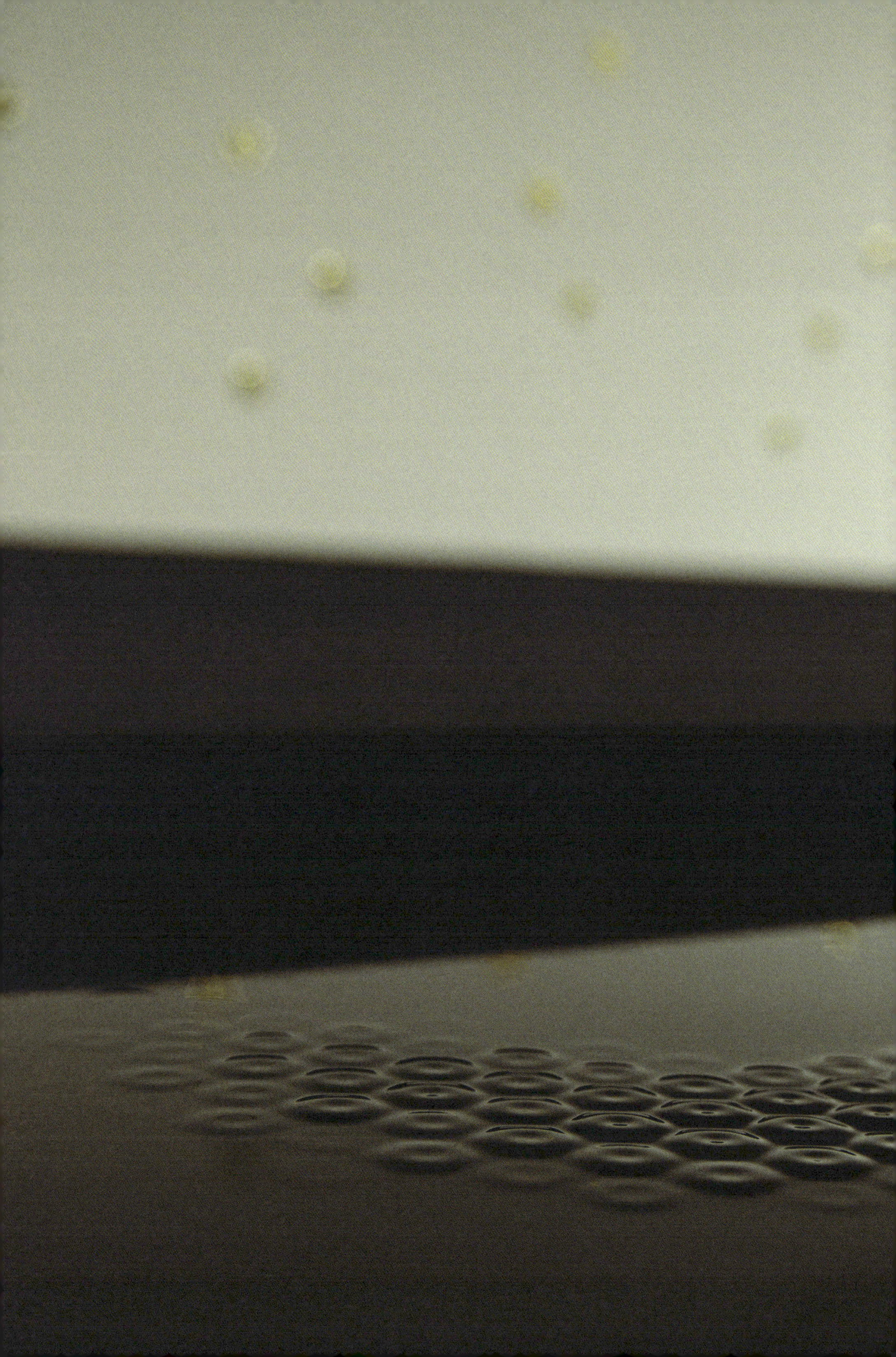

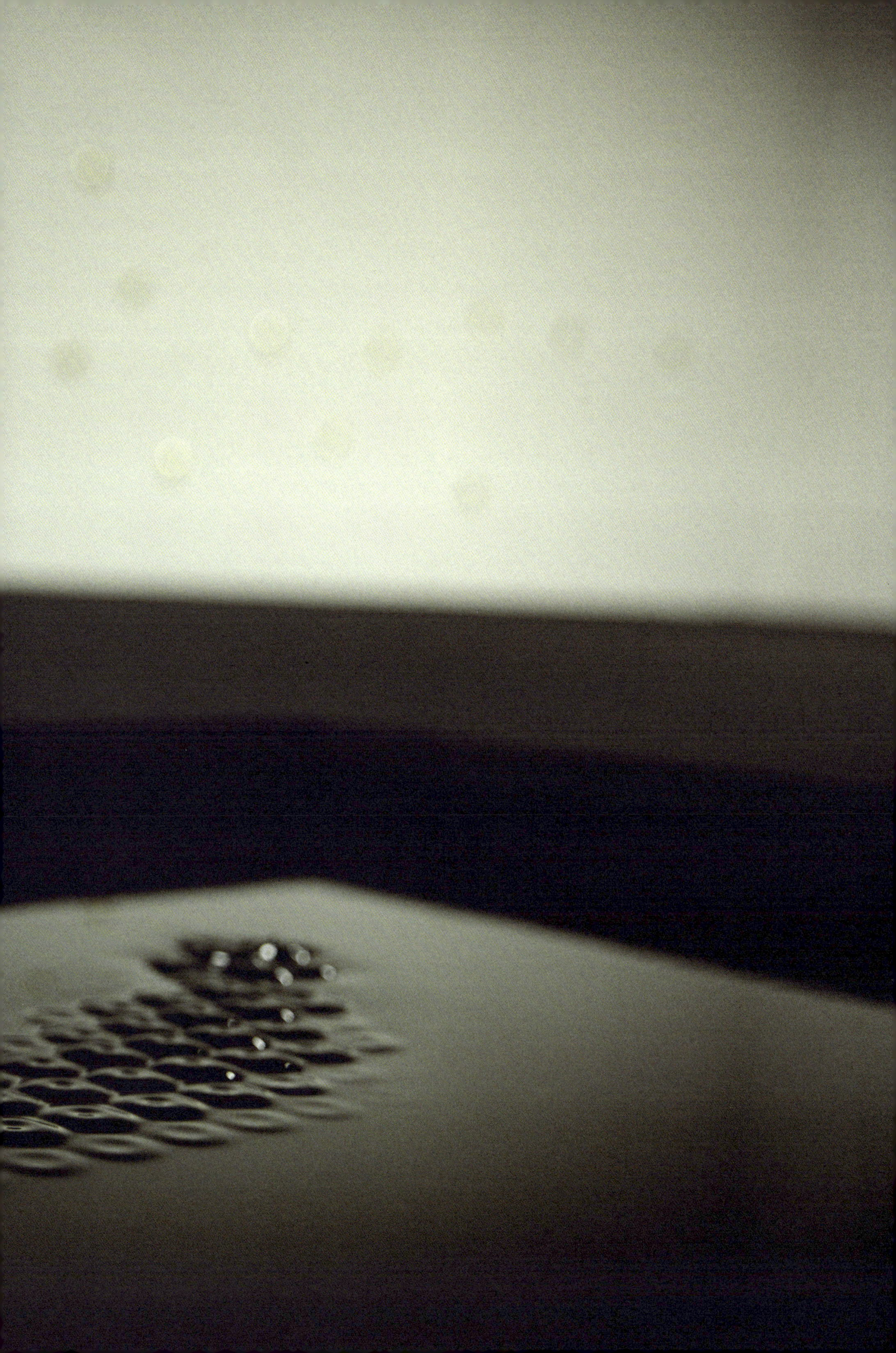

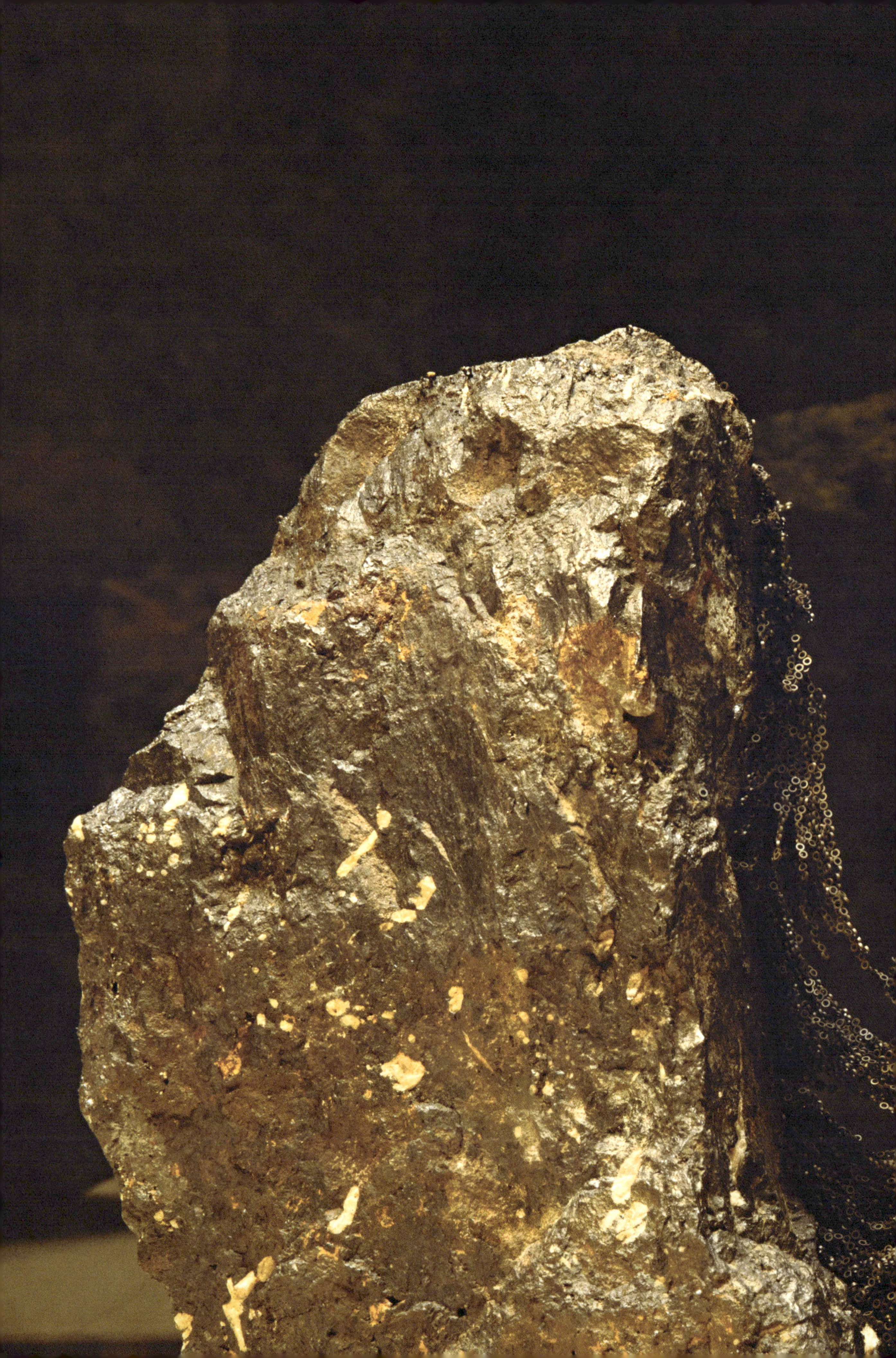

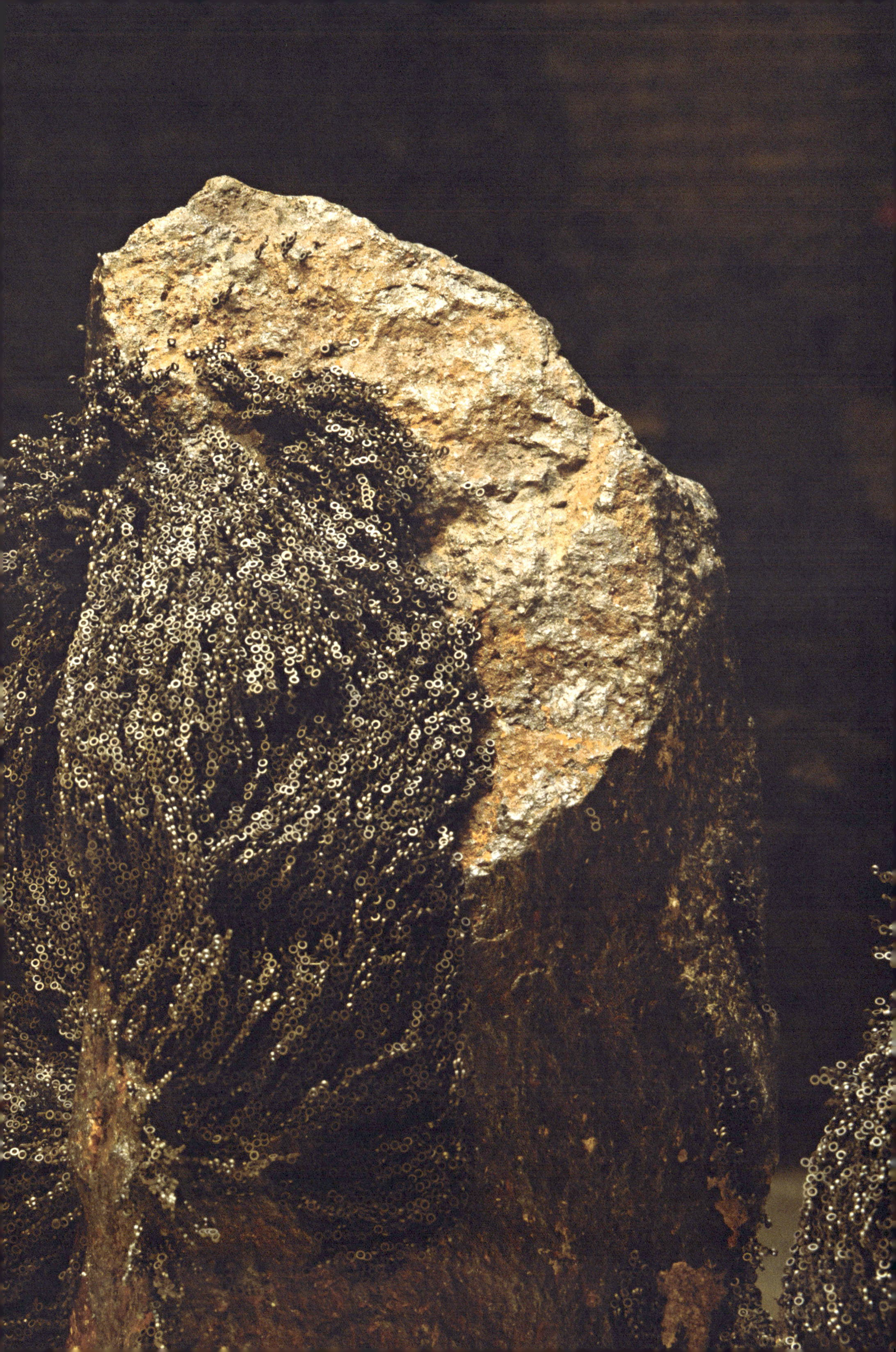

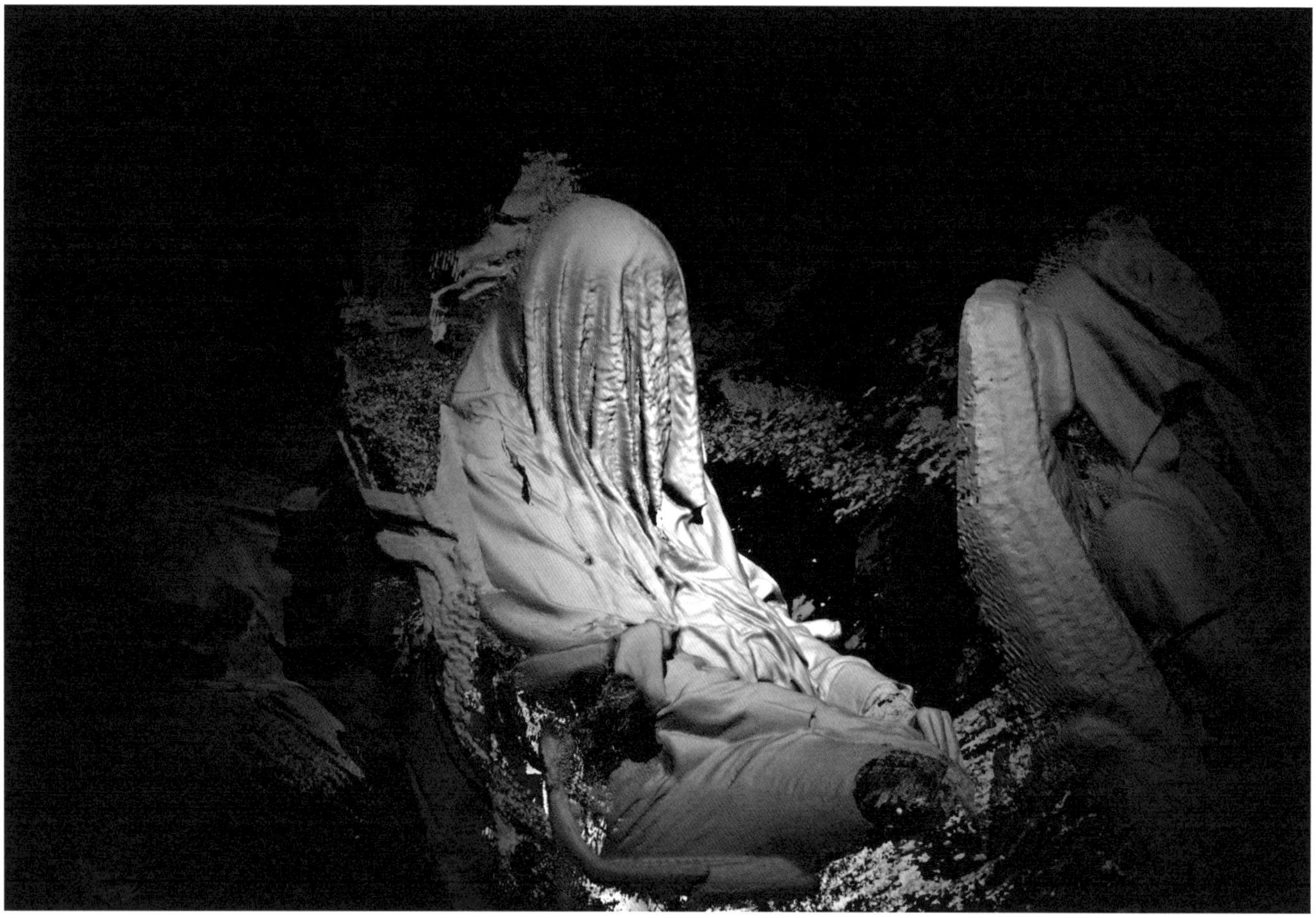

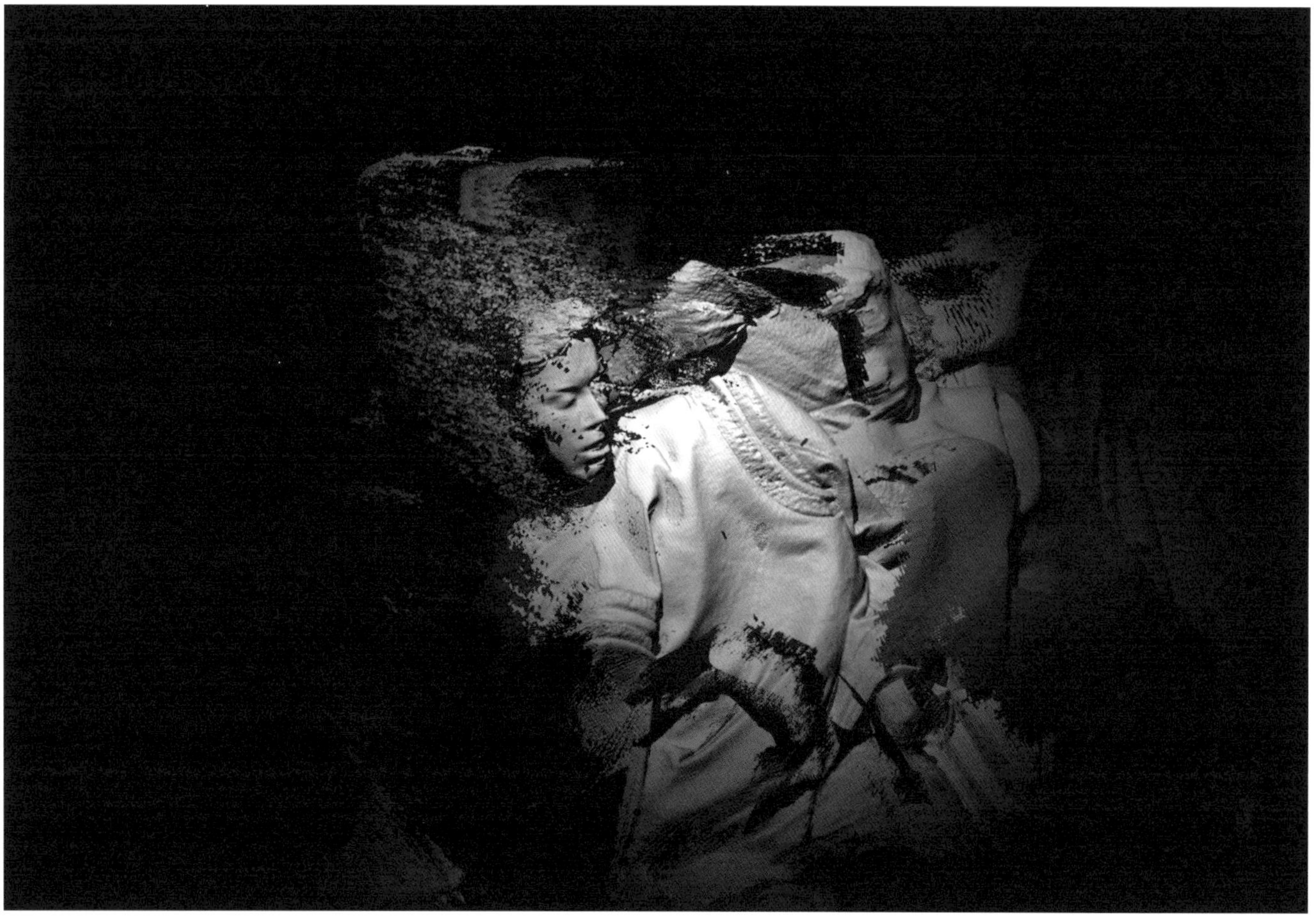

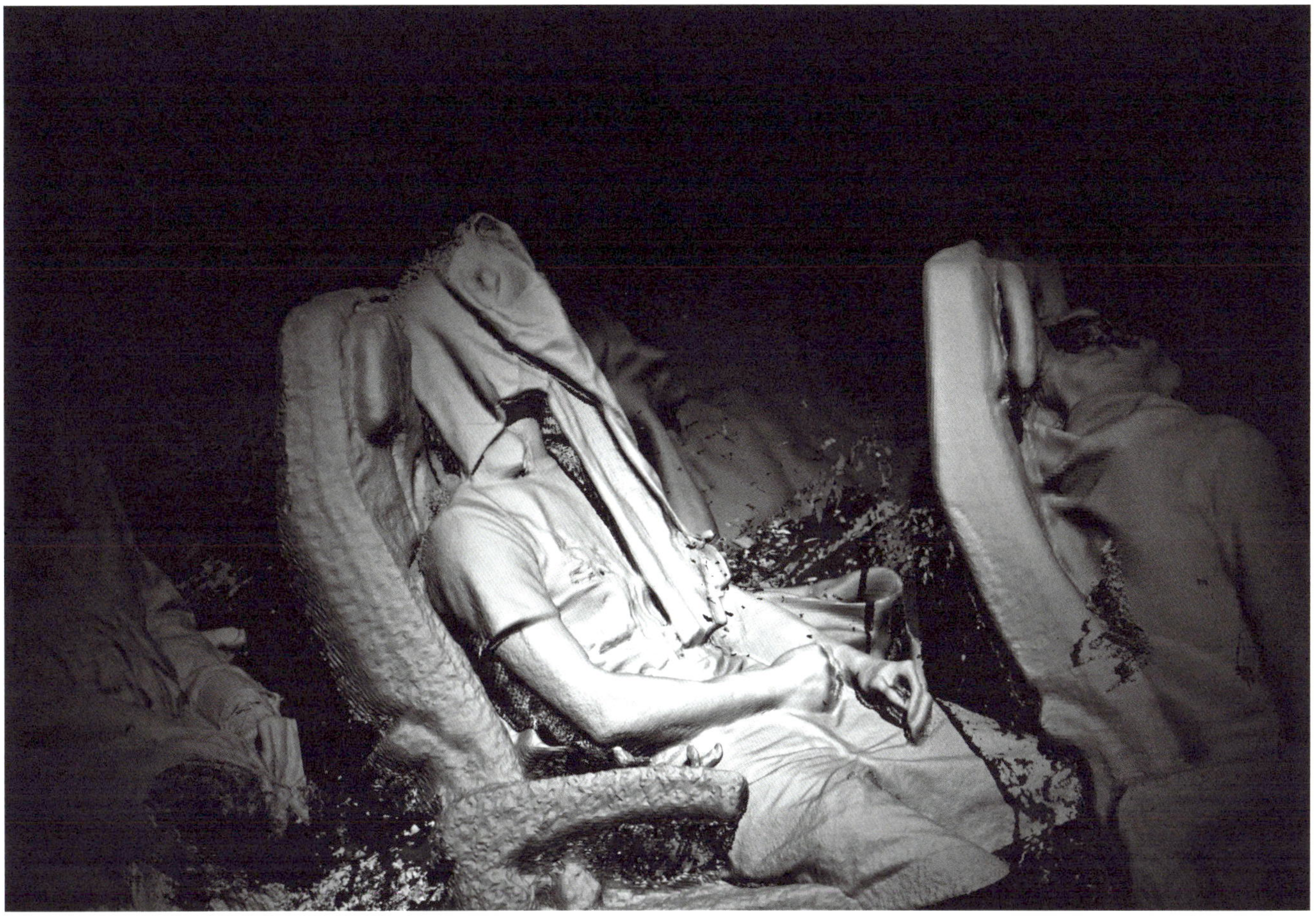

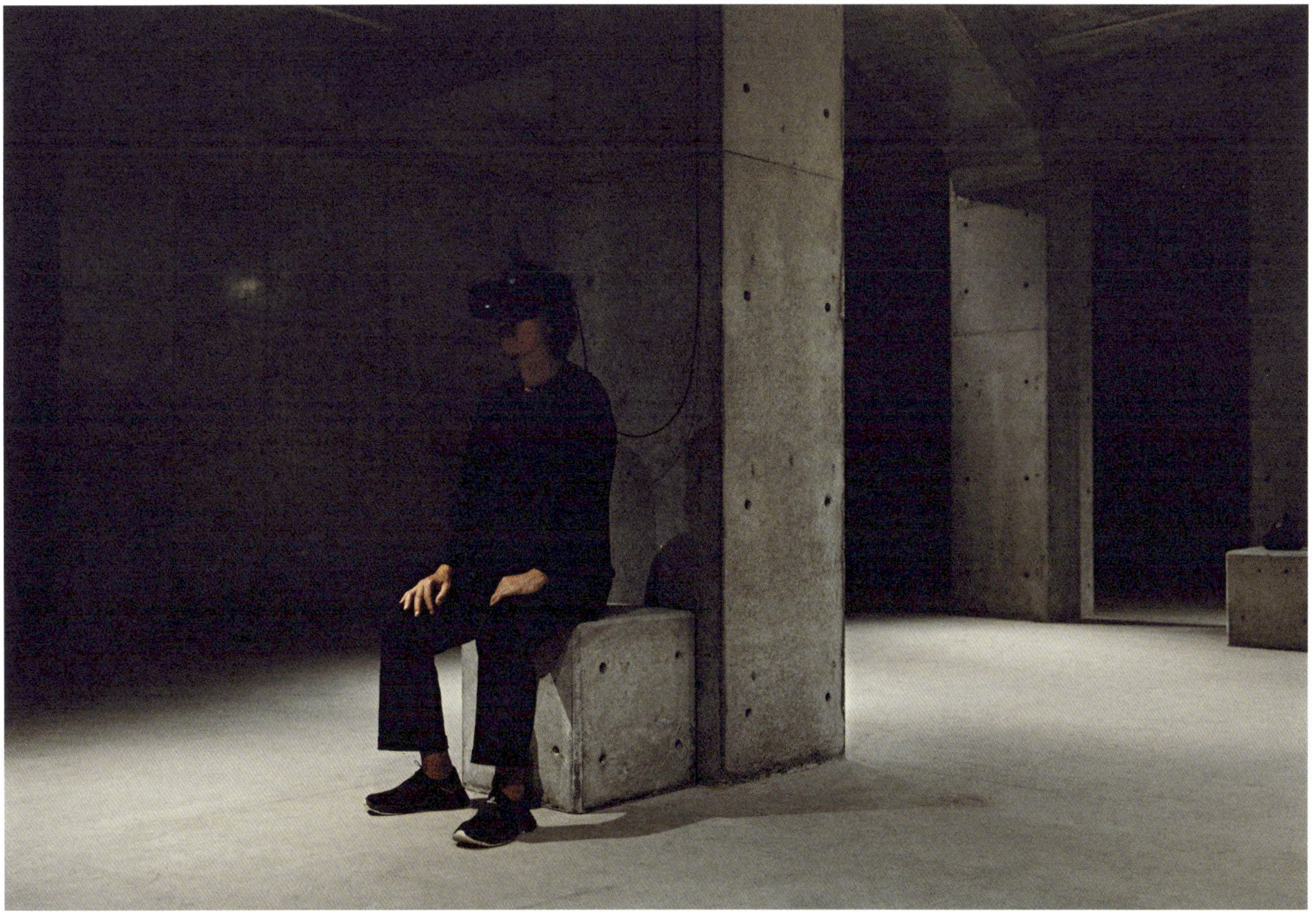

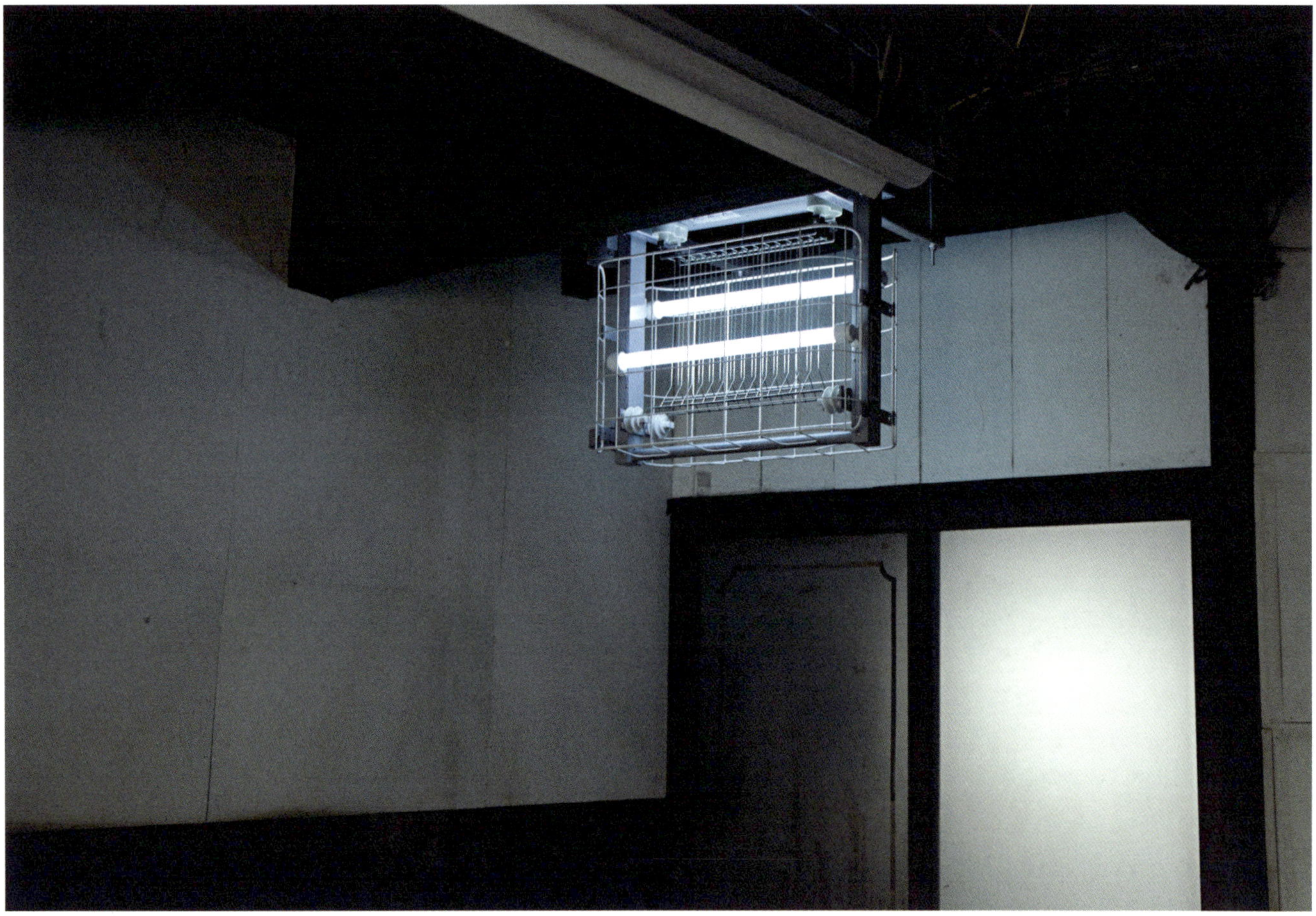

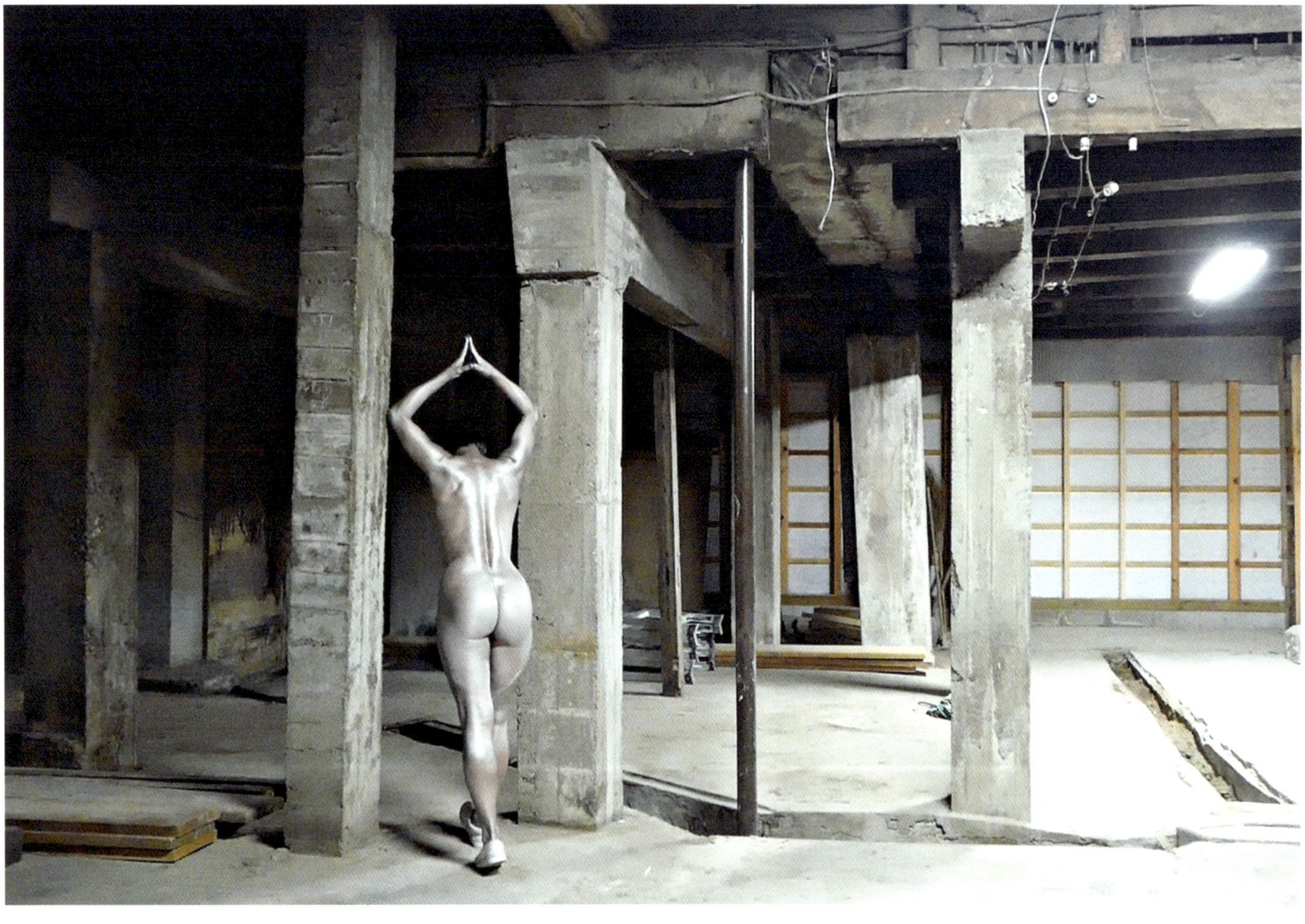

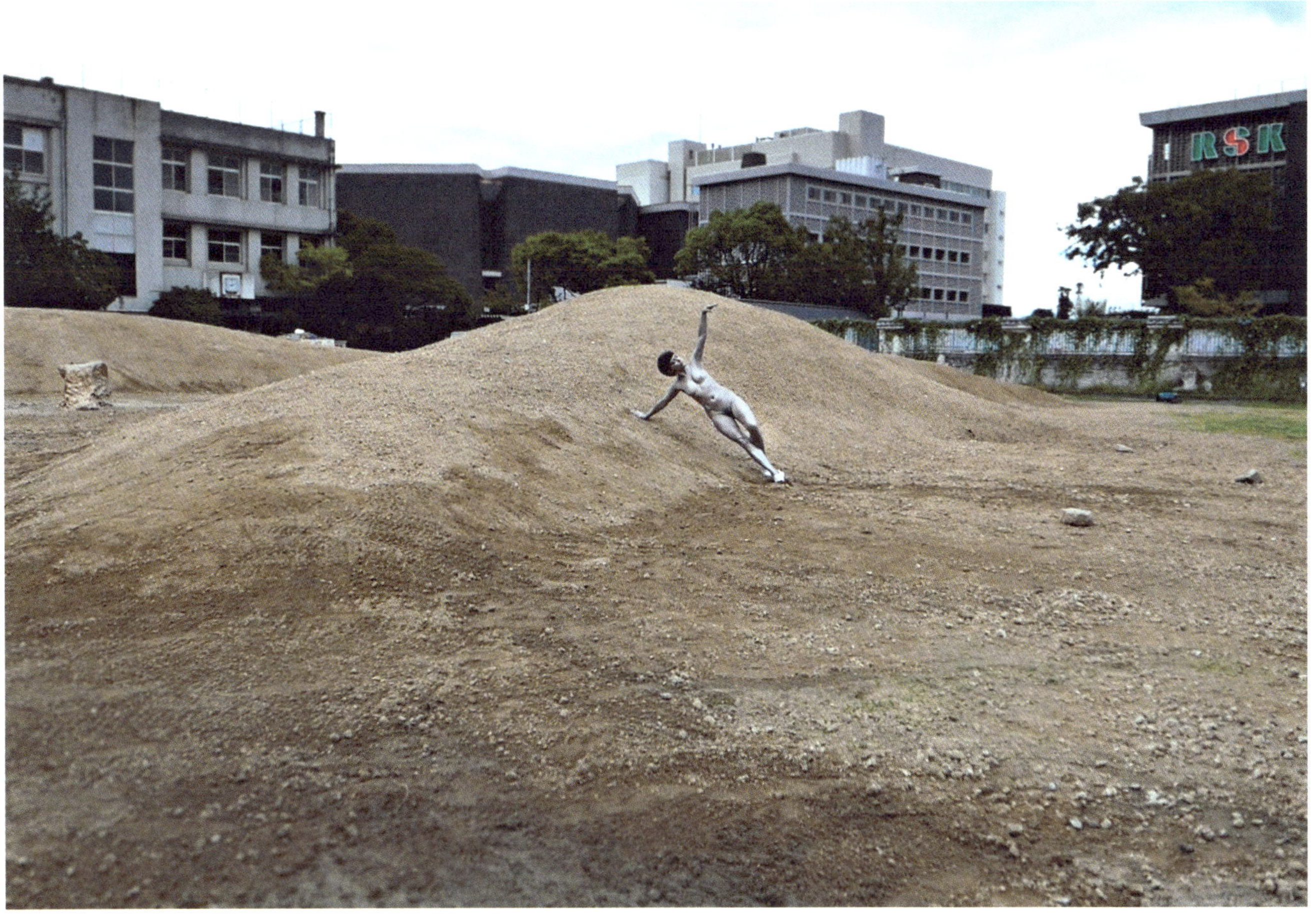

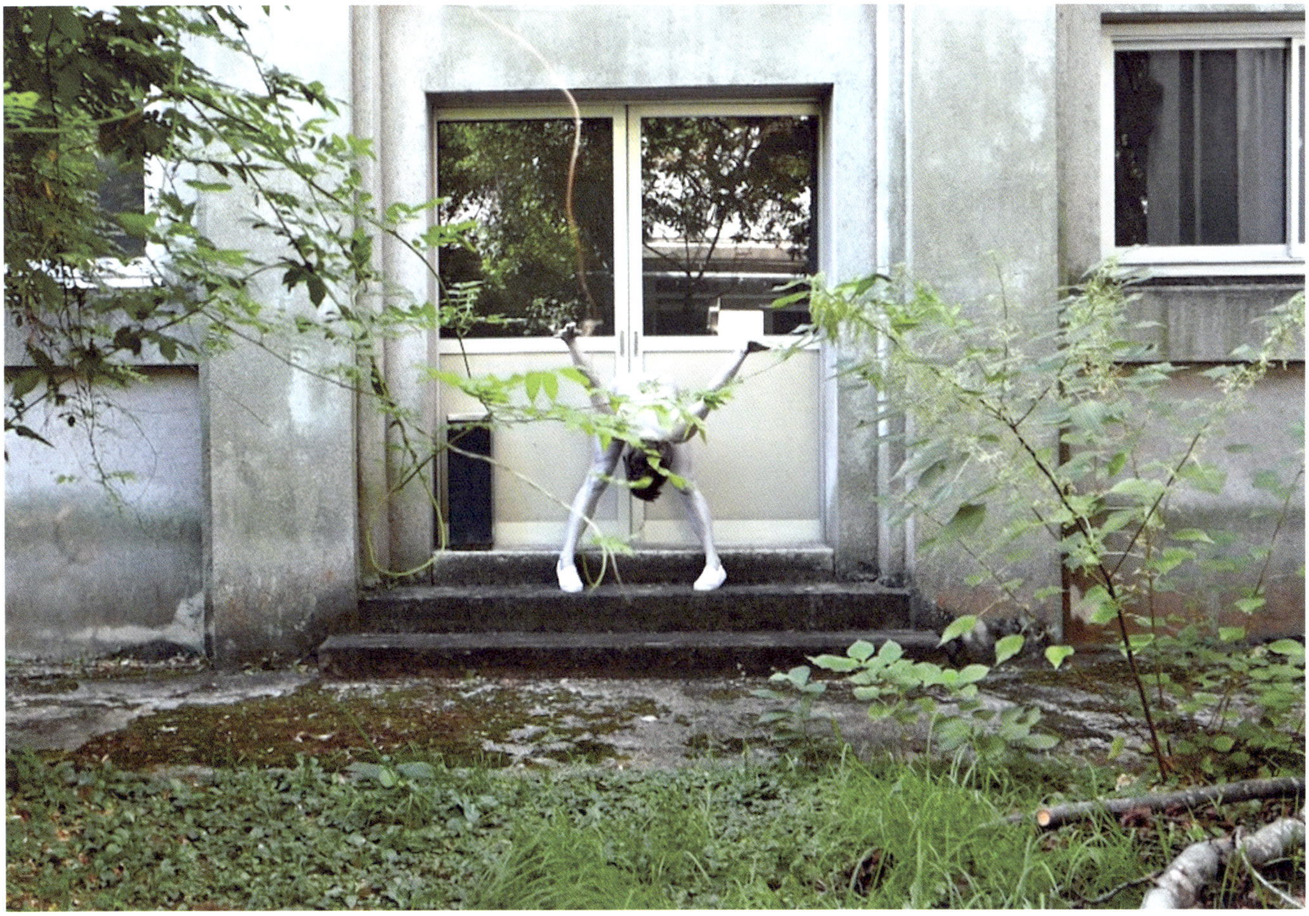

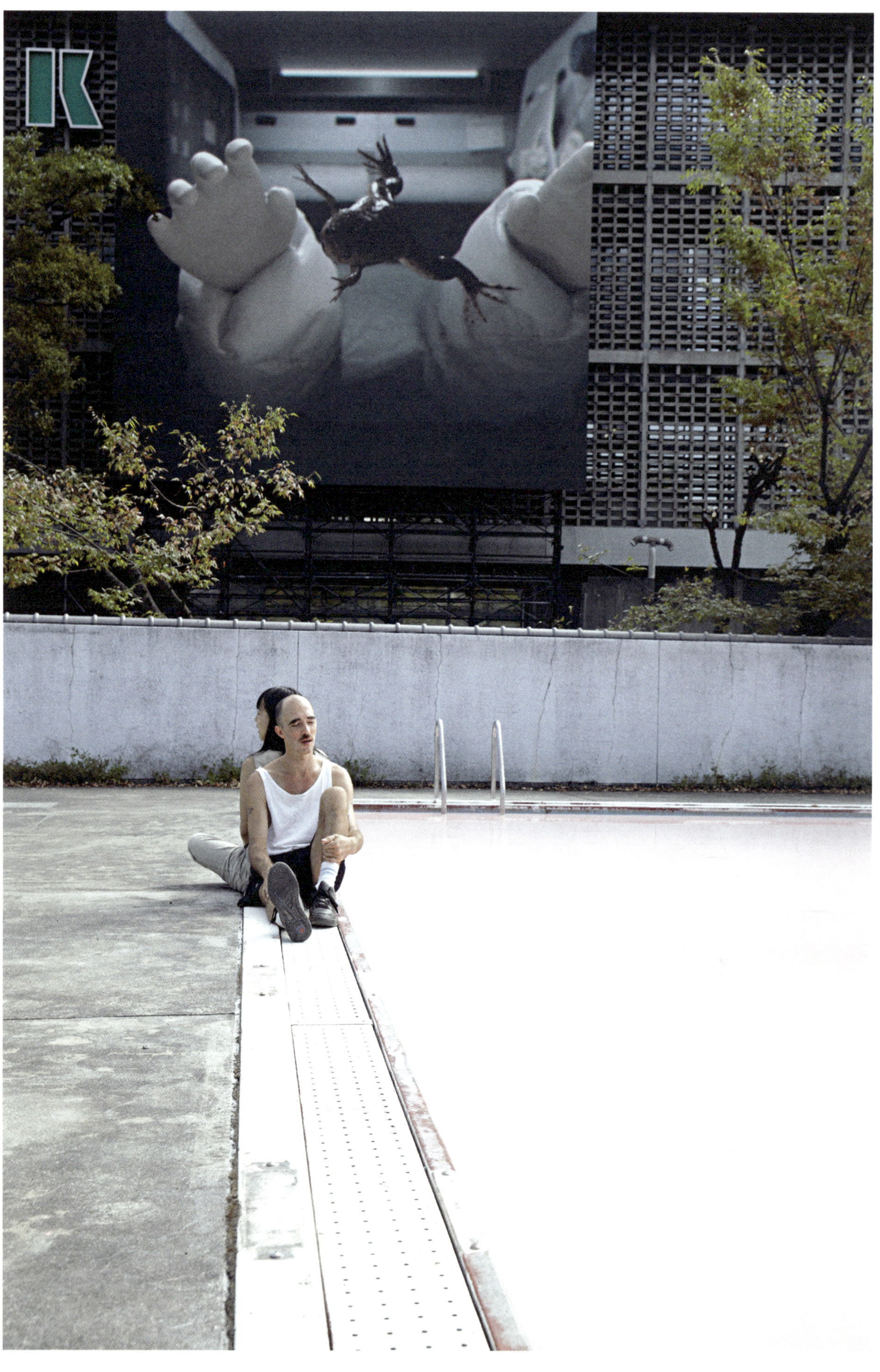

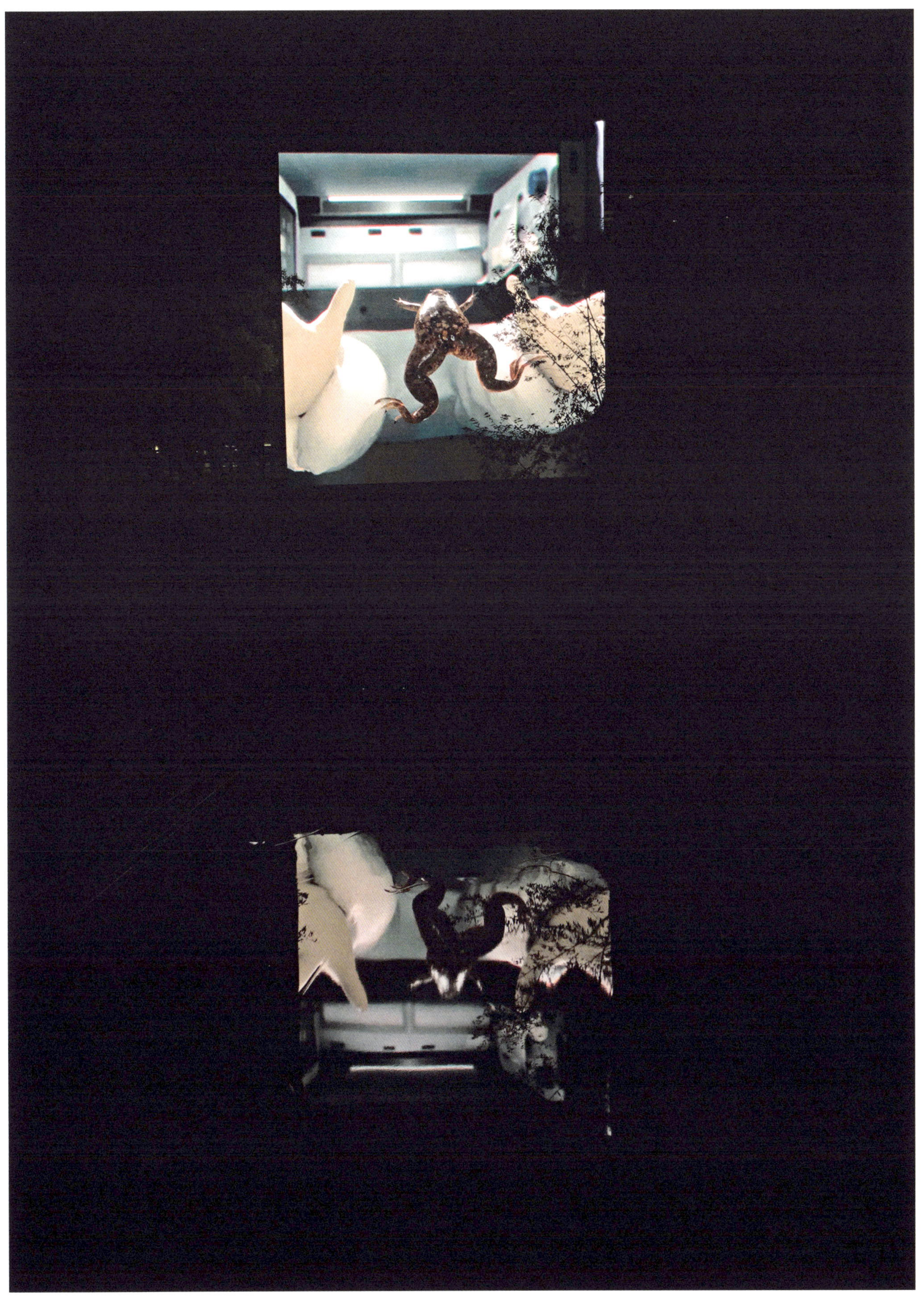

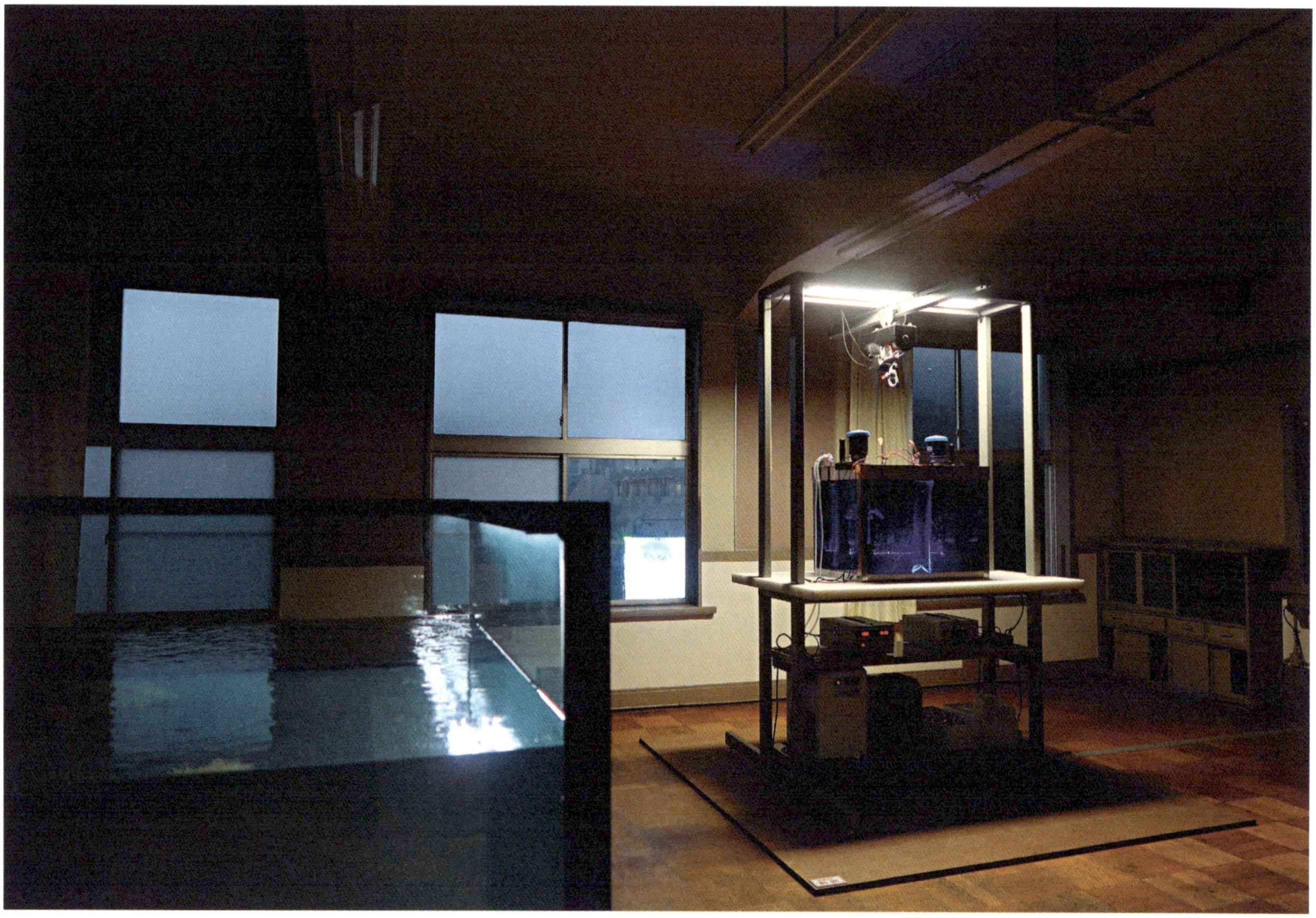

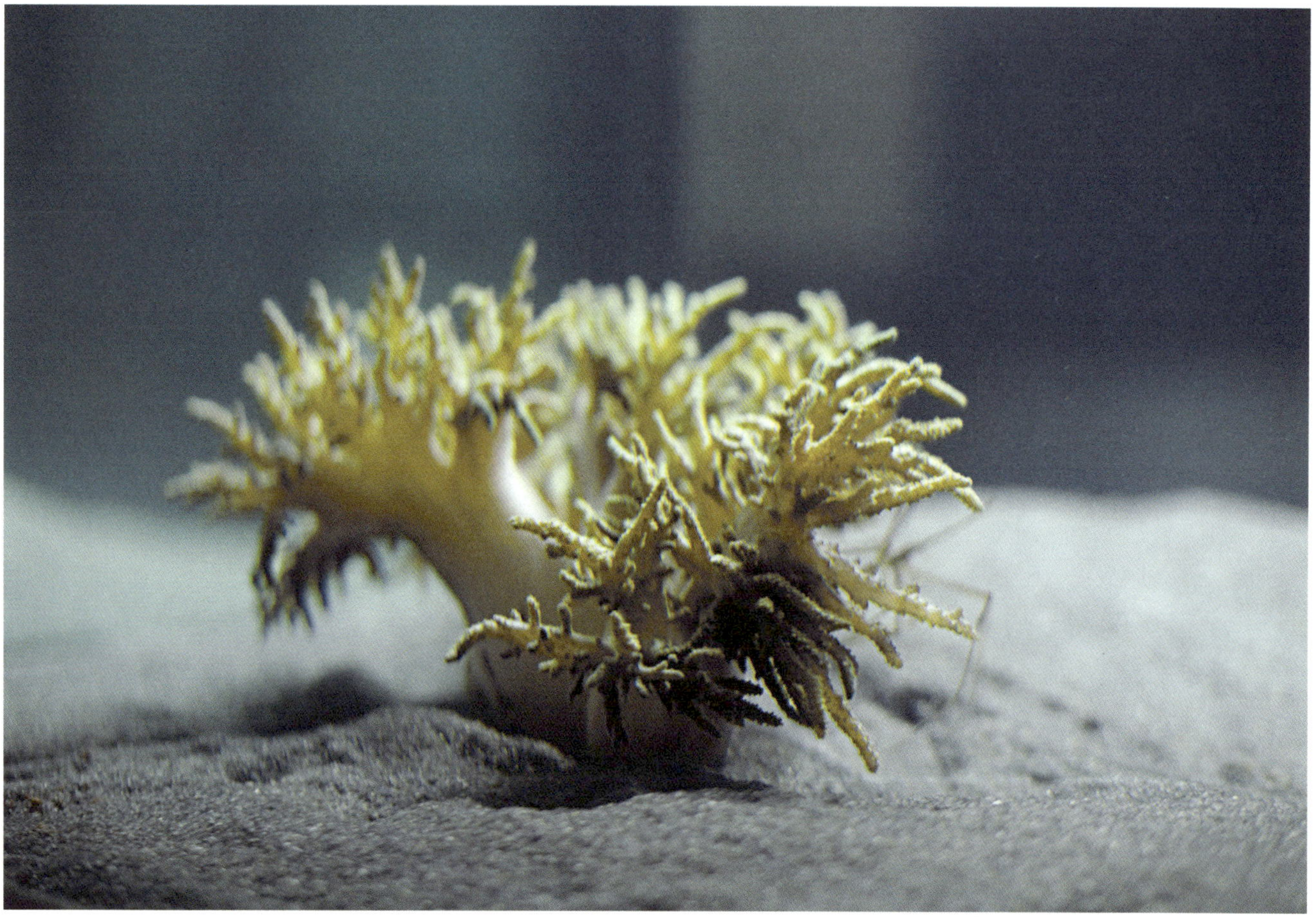

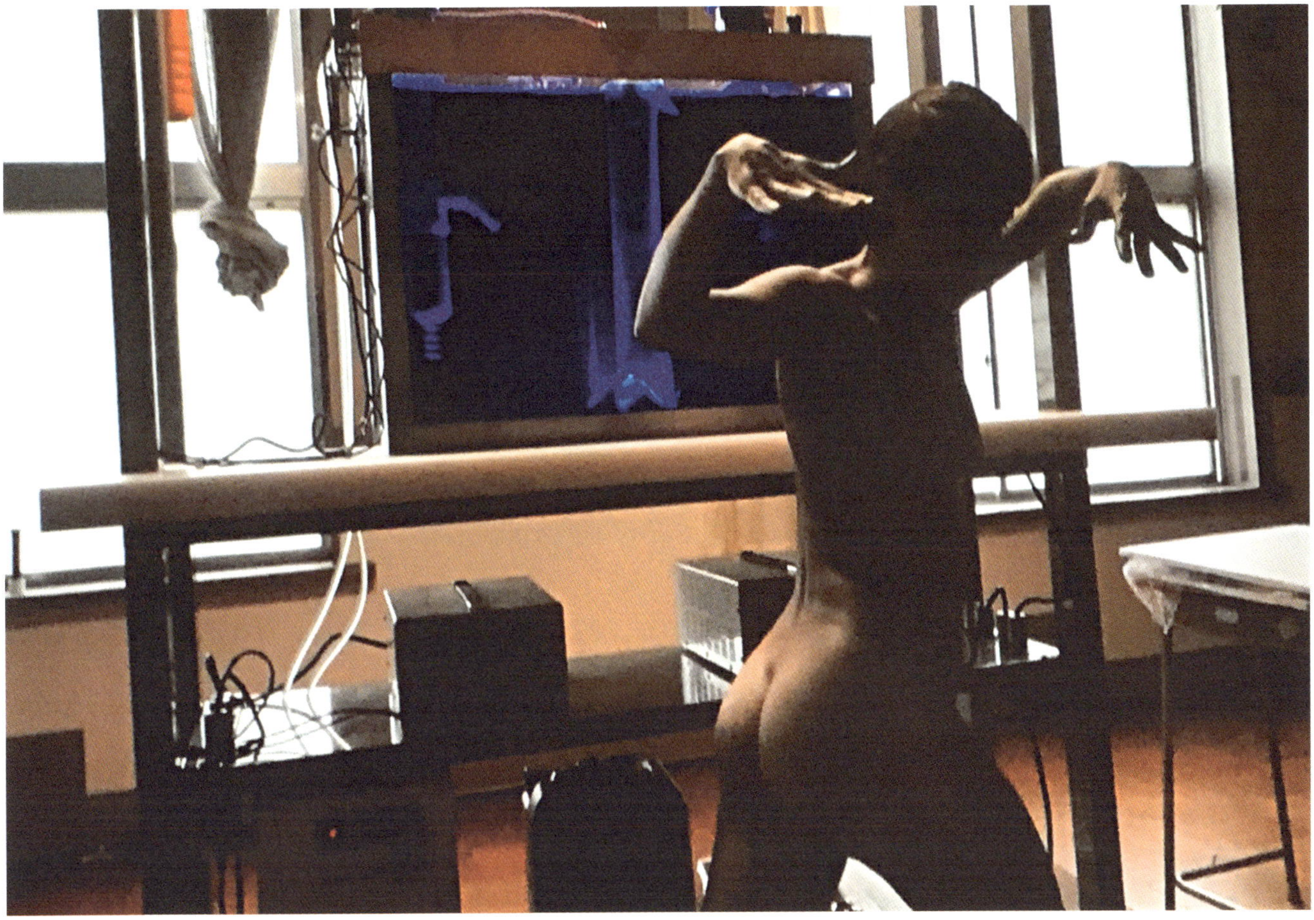

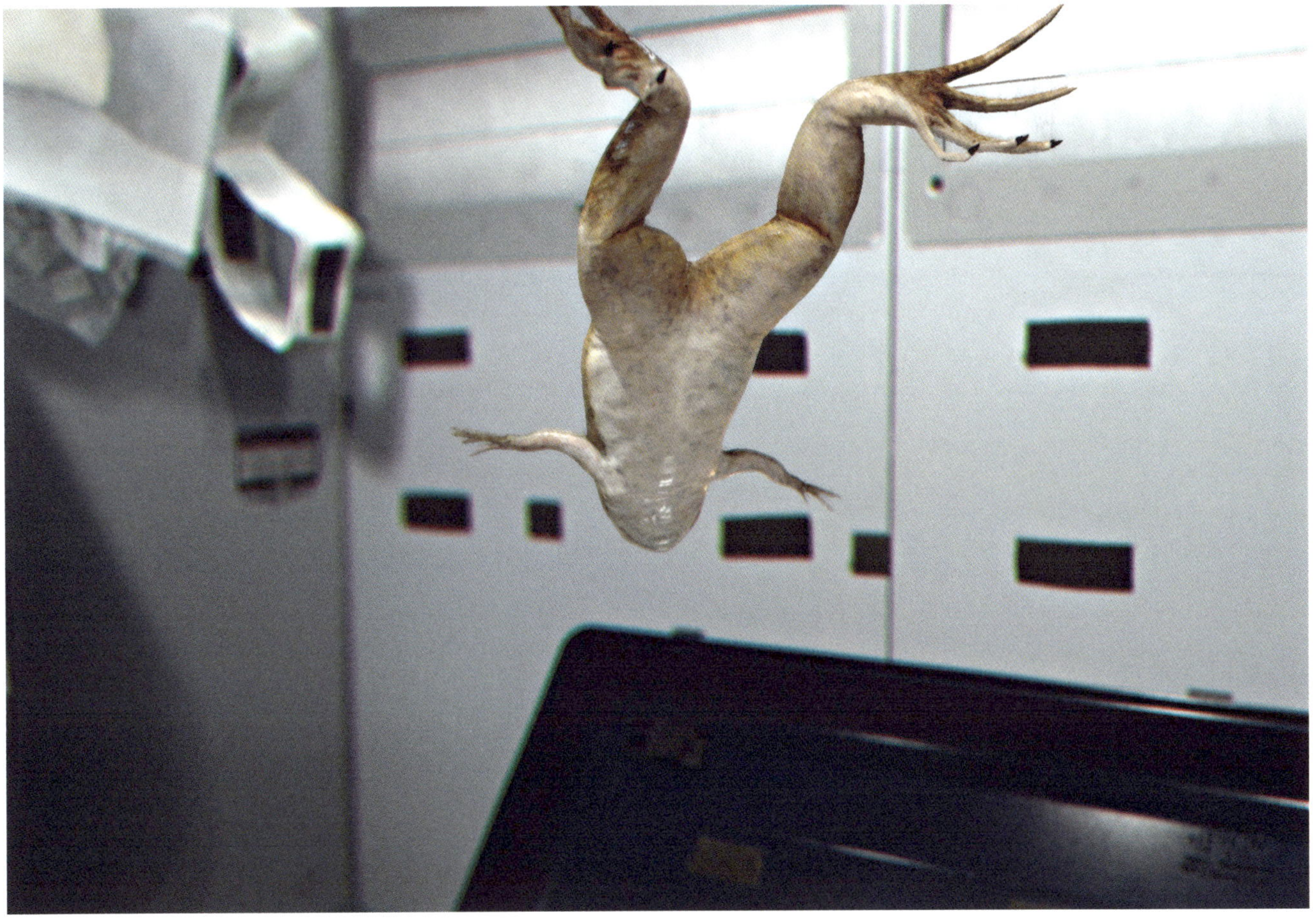

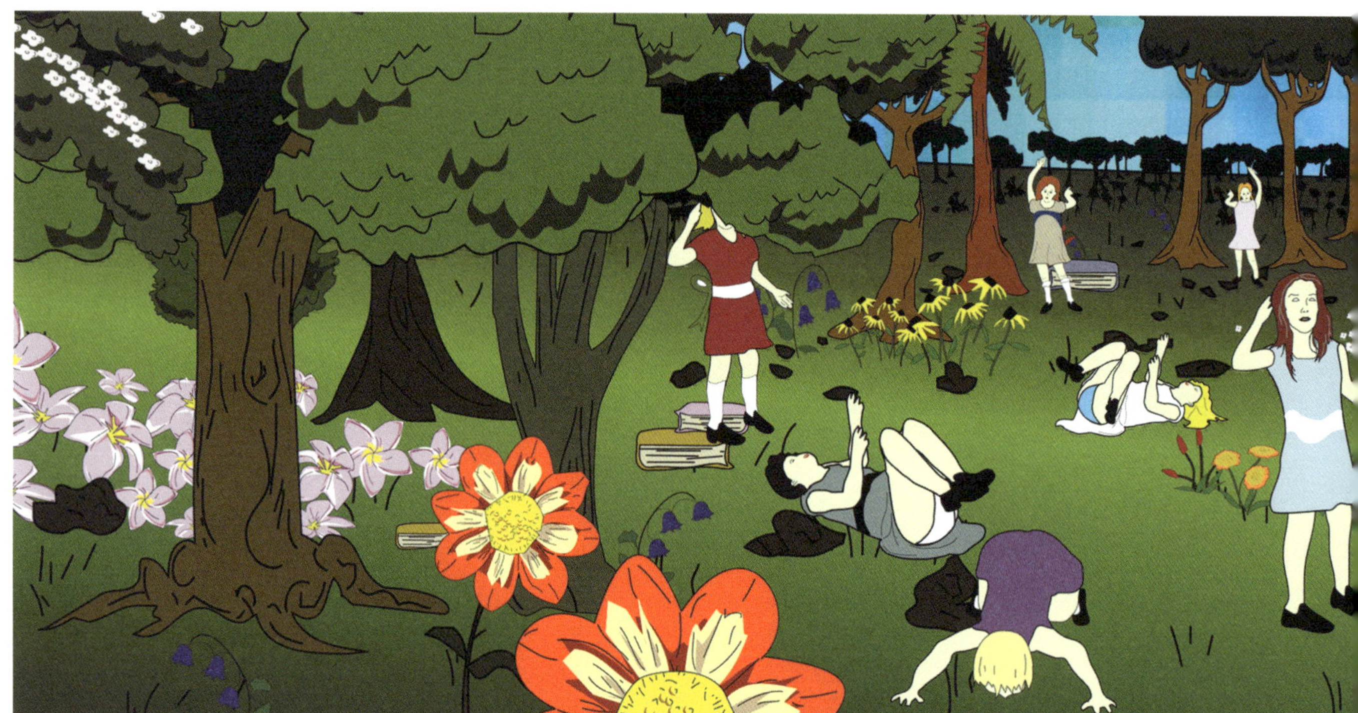

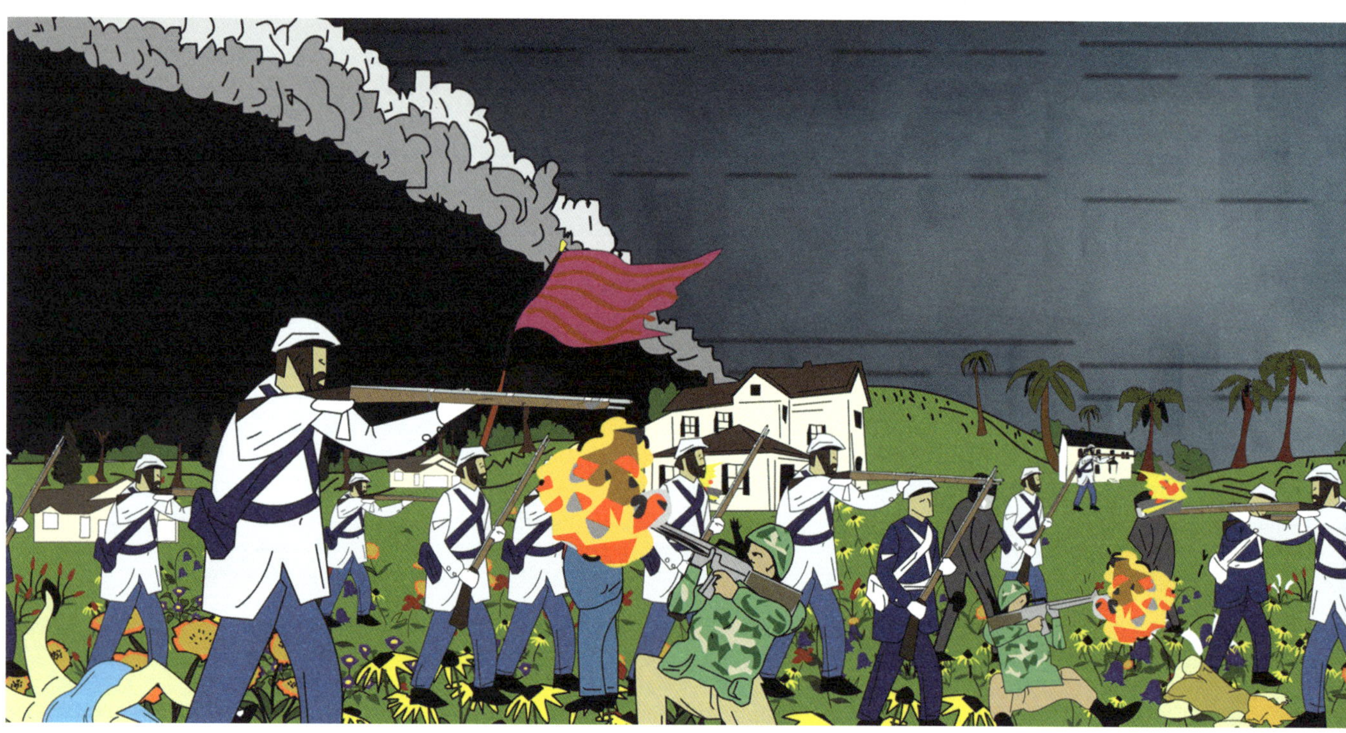

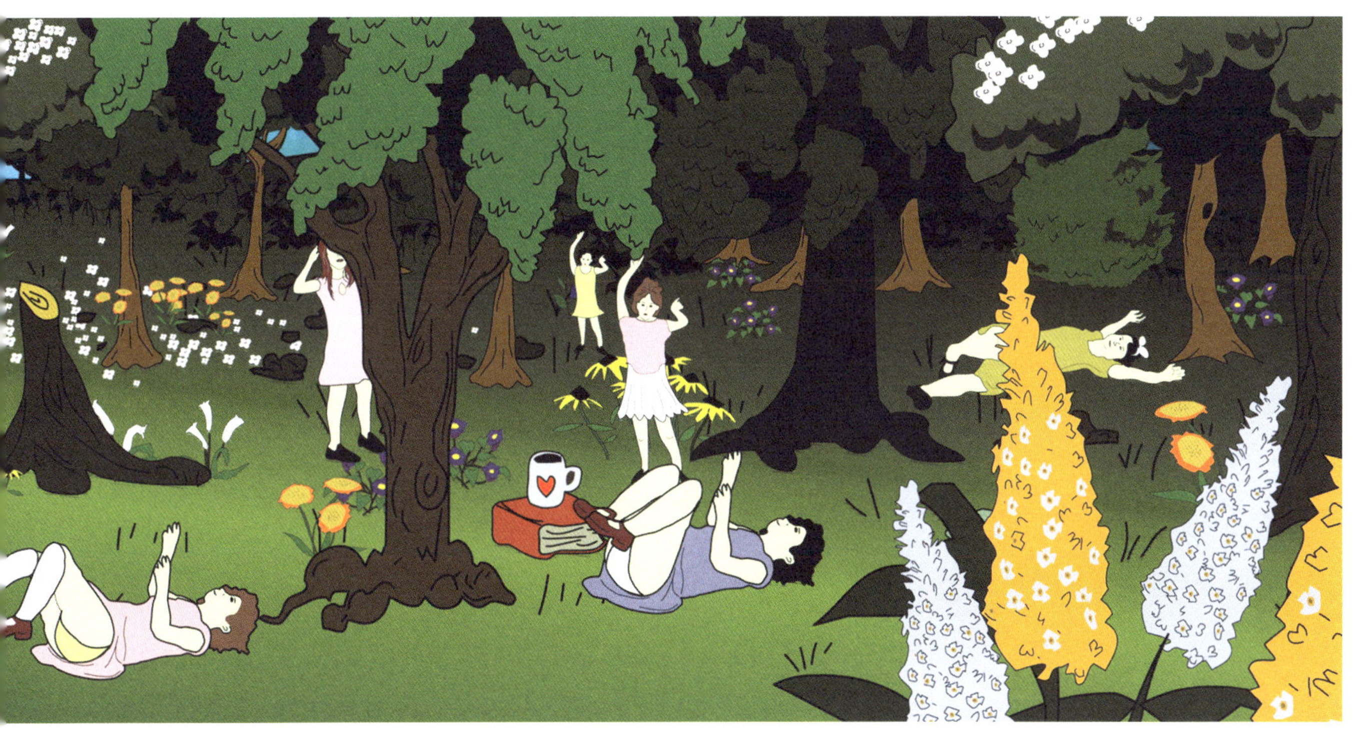

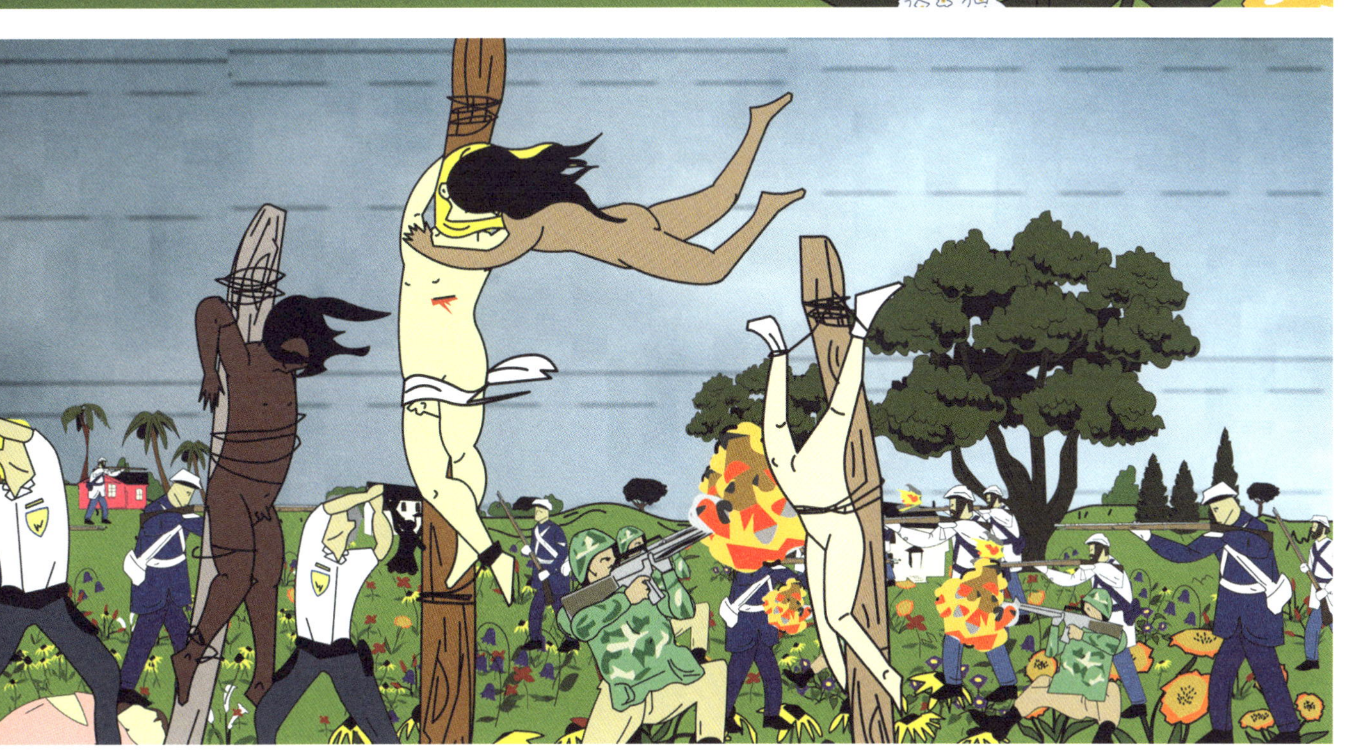

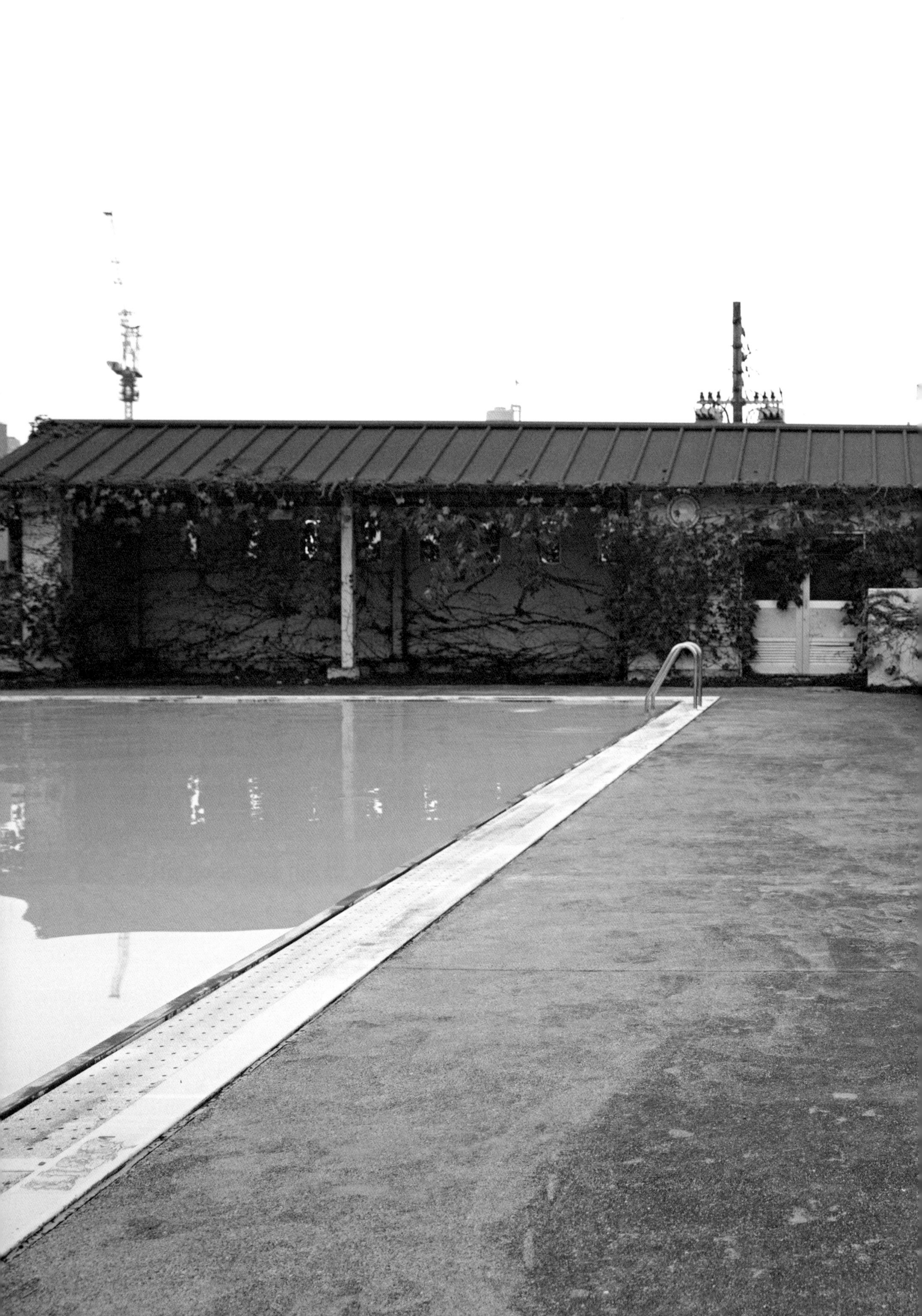

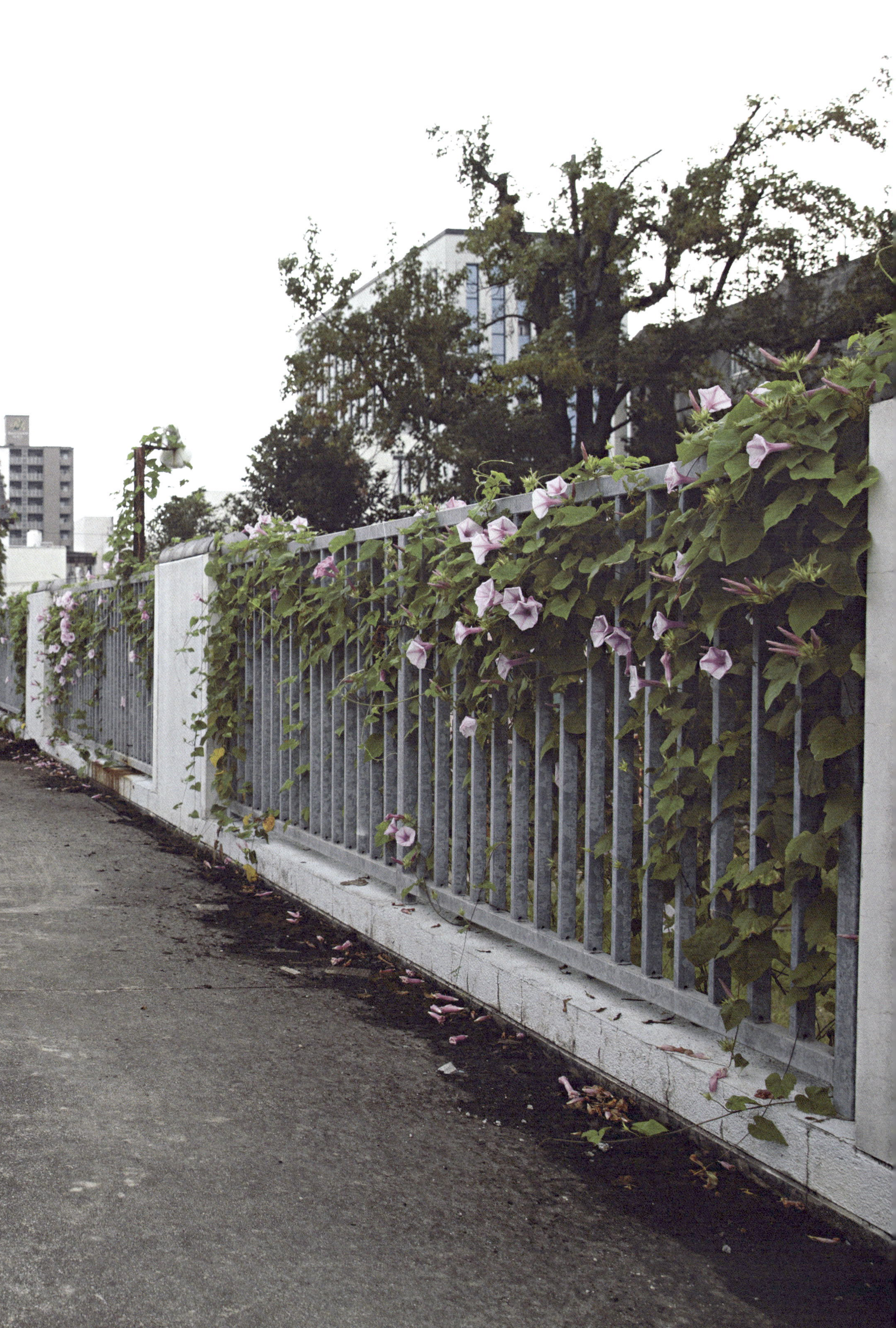

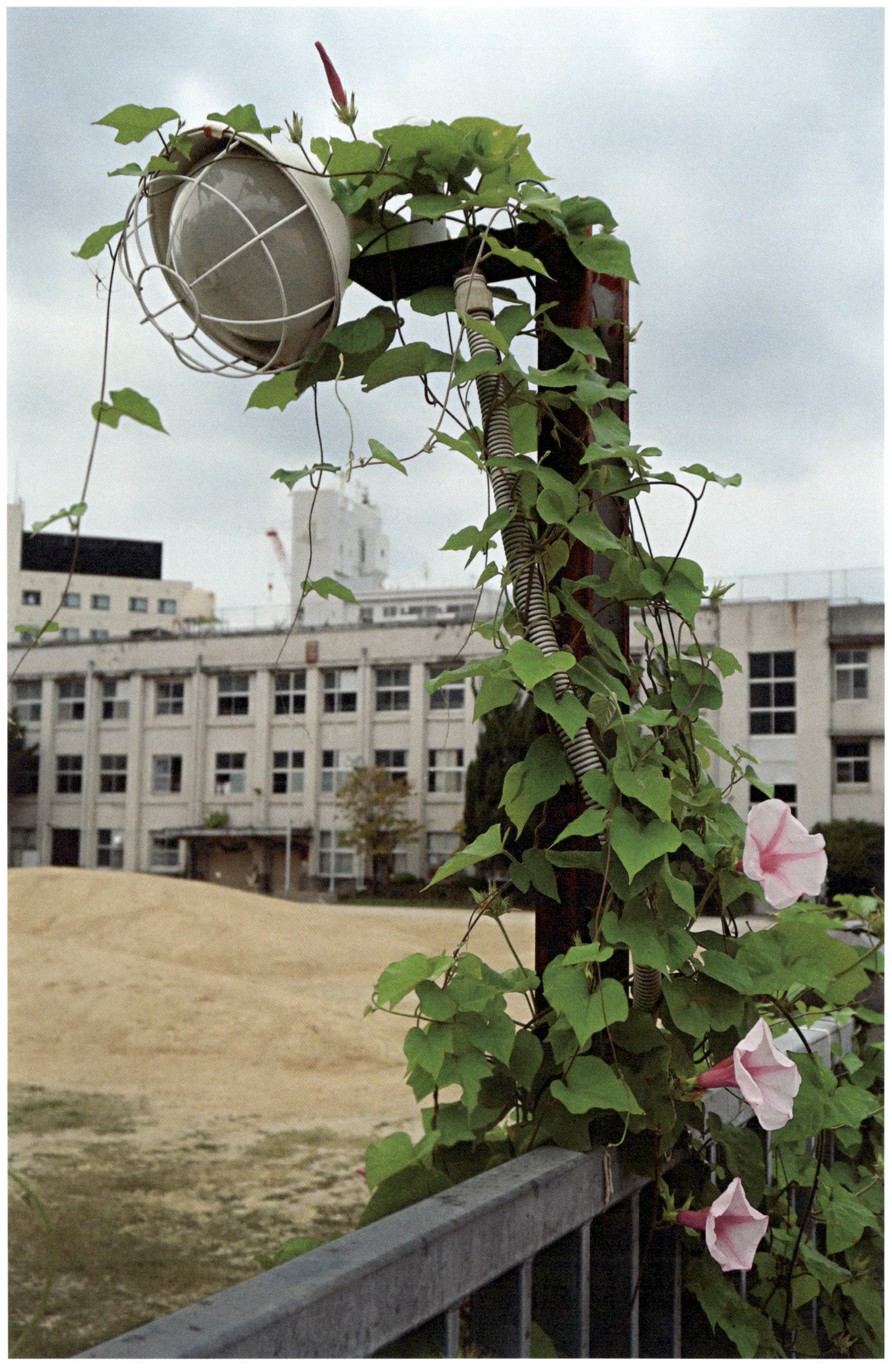

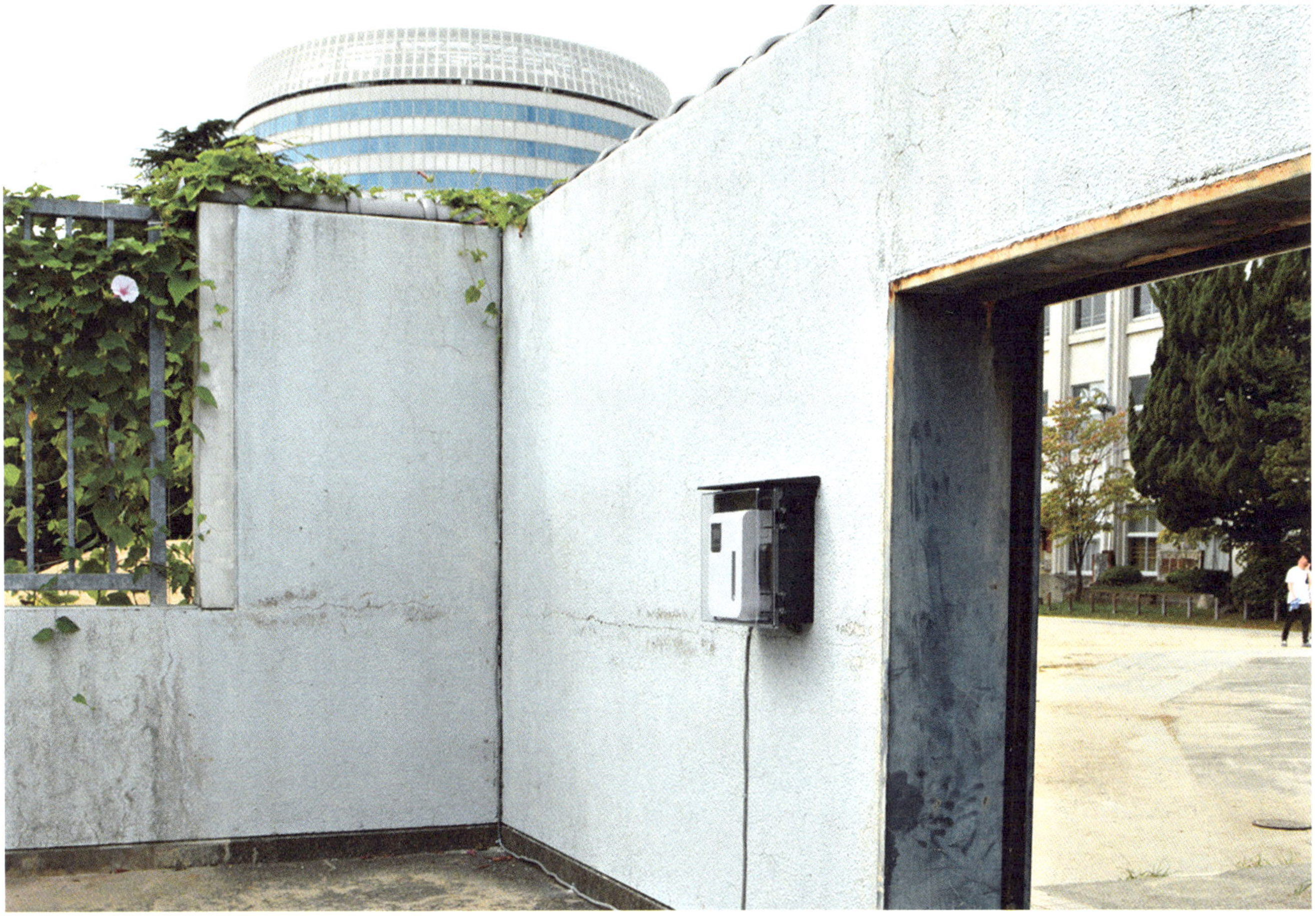

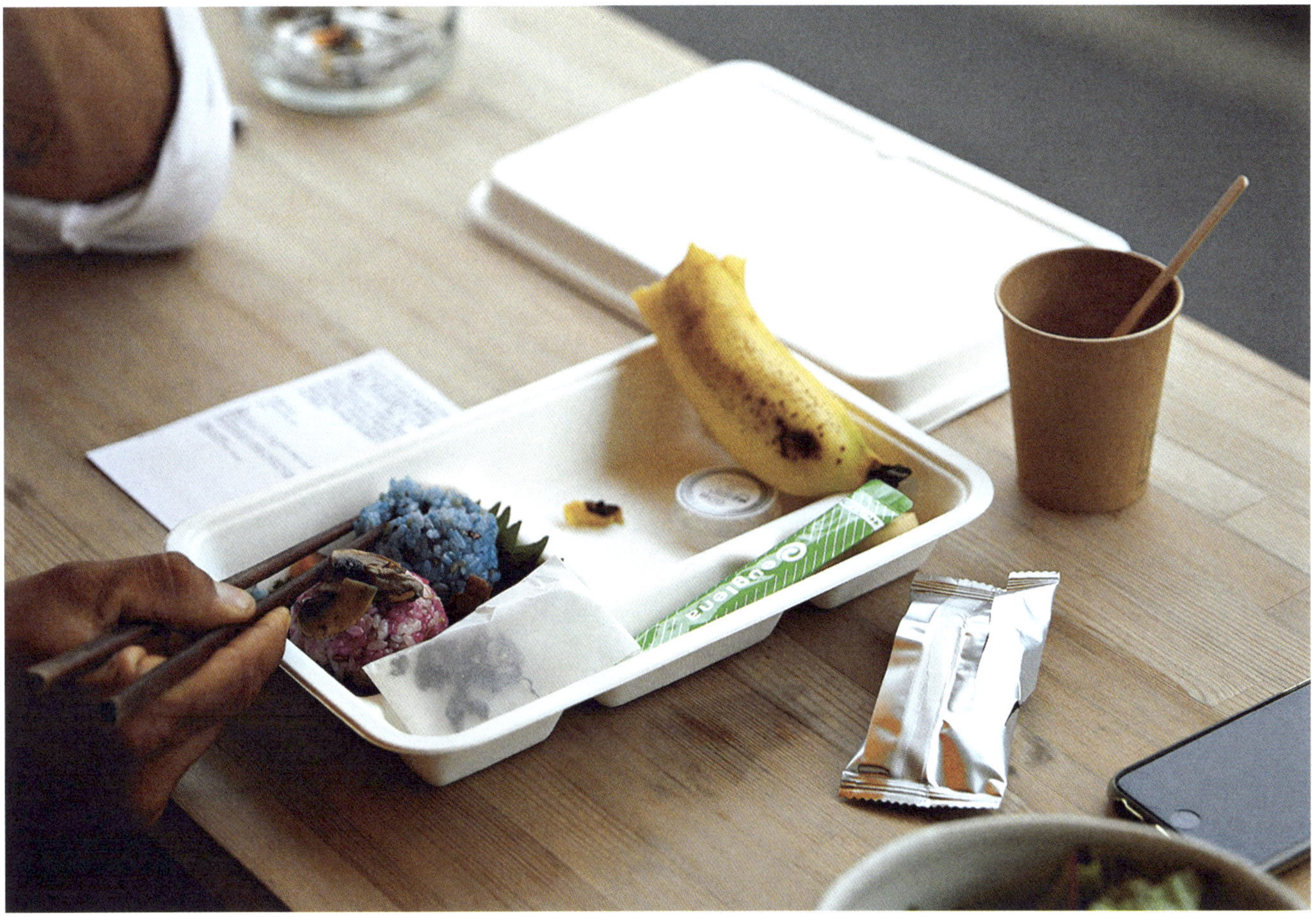

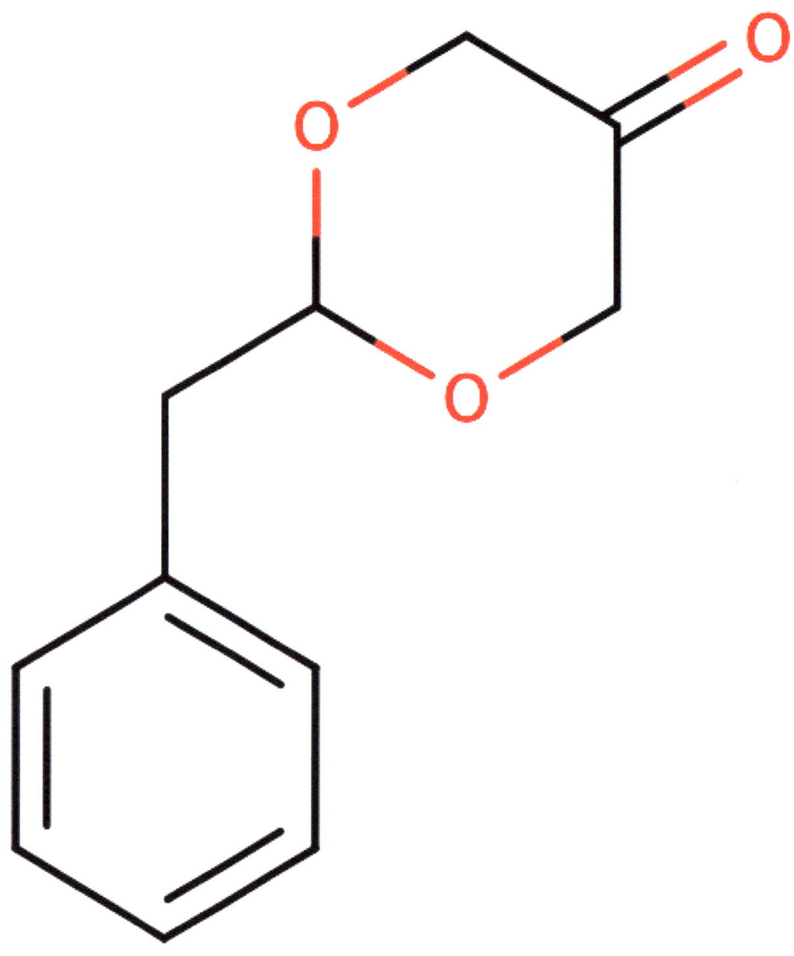
O
O
O

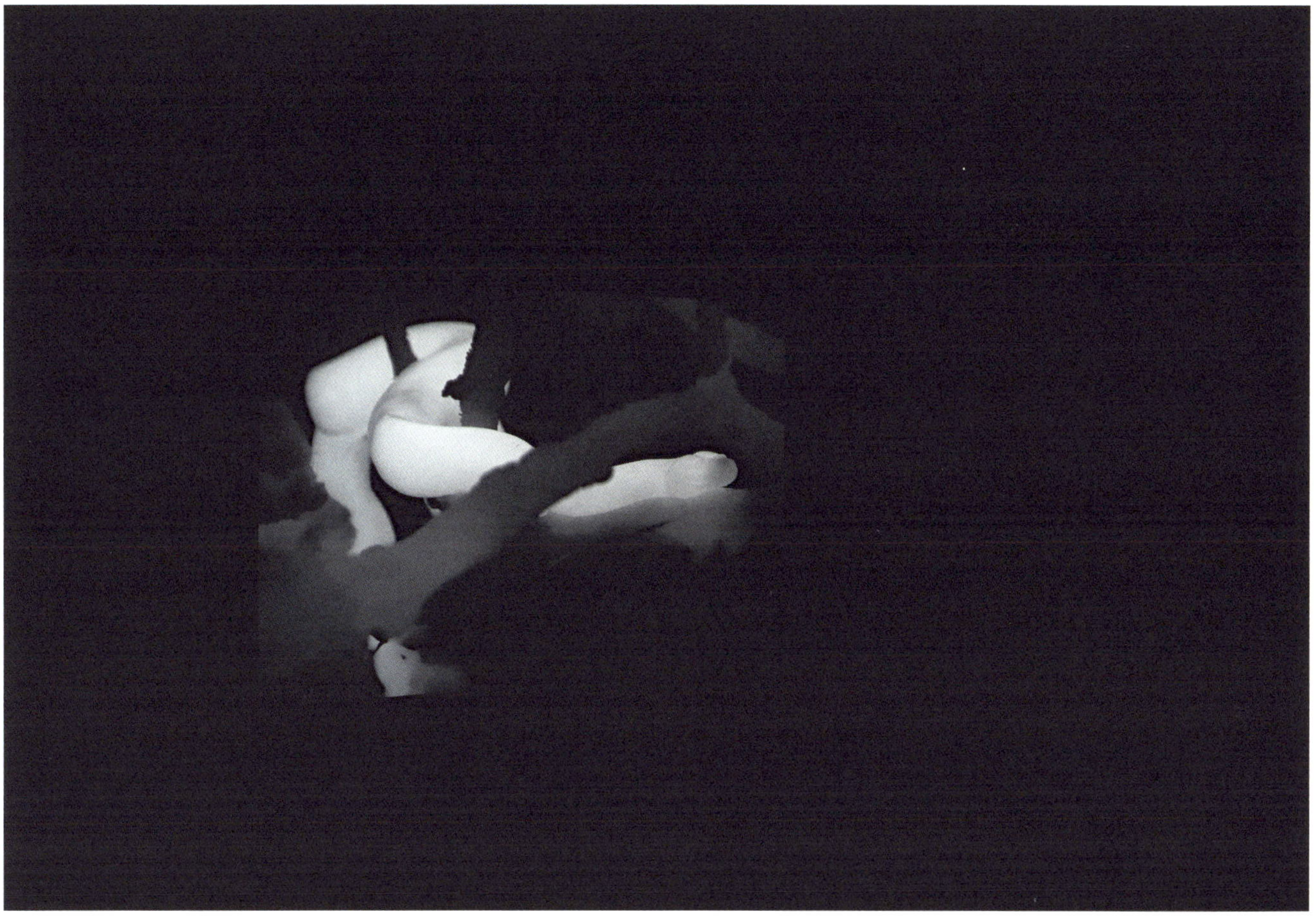

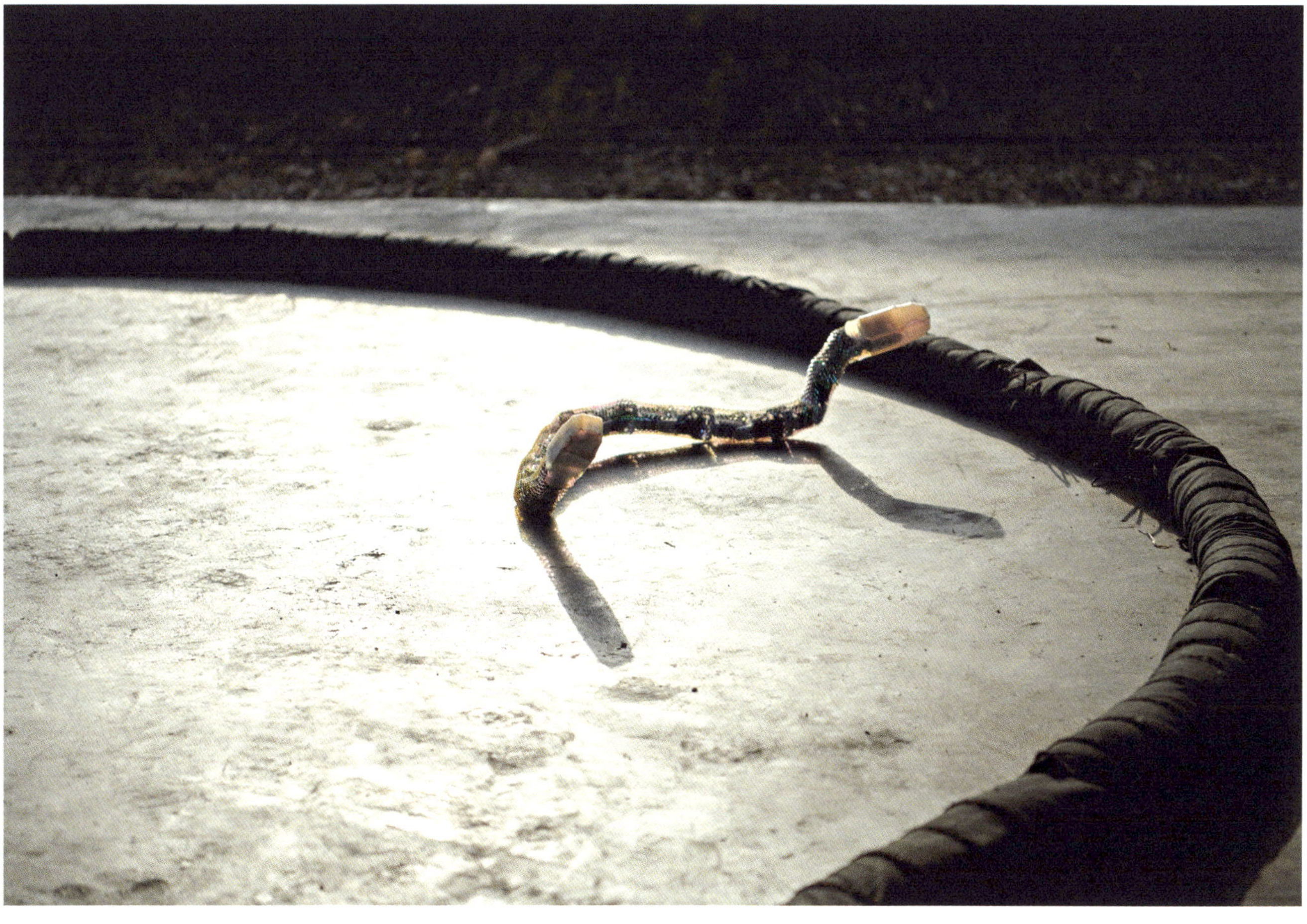

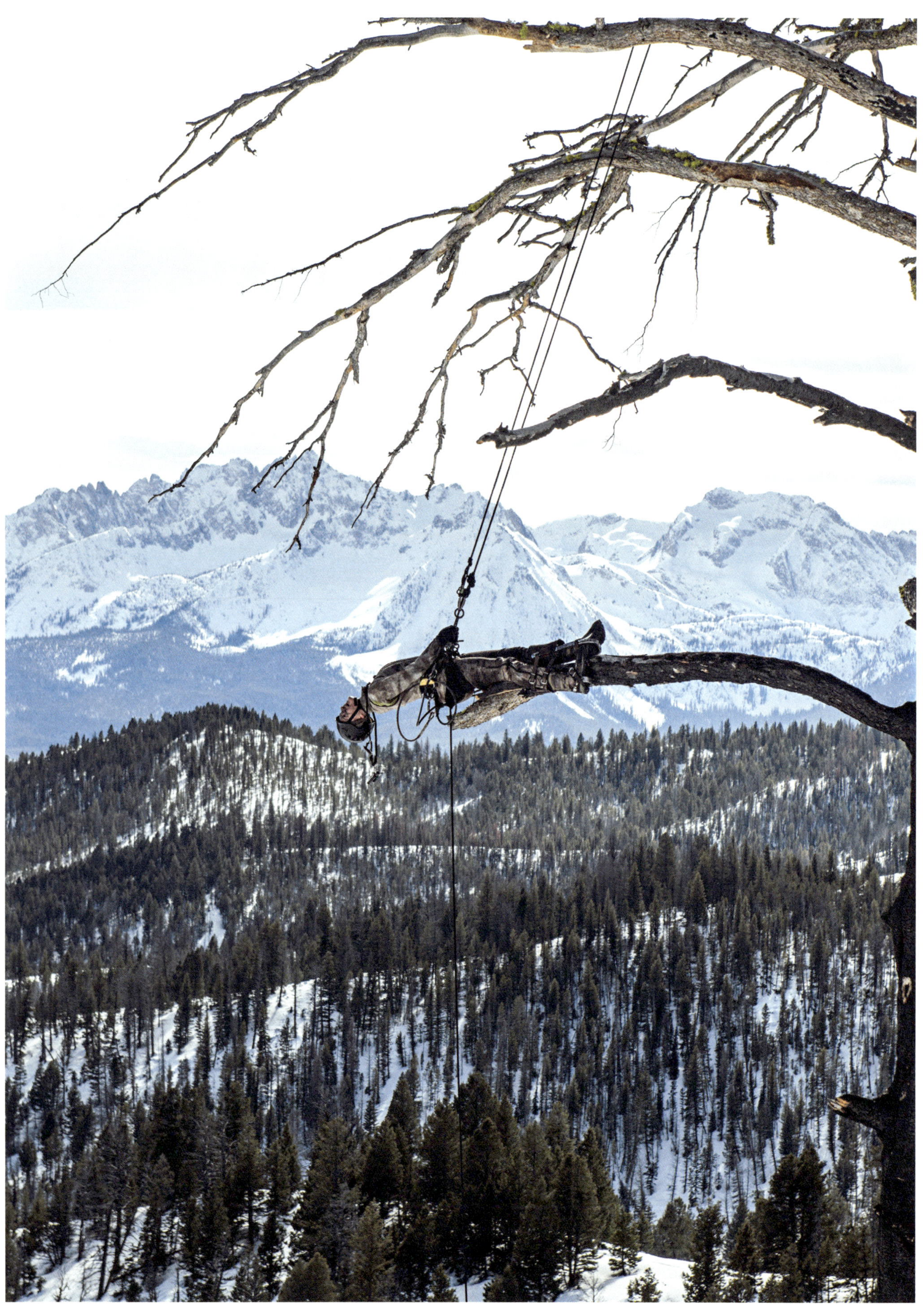

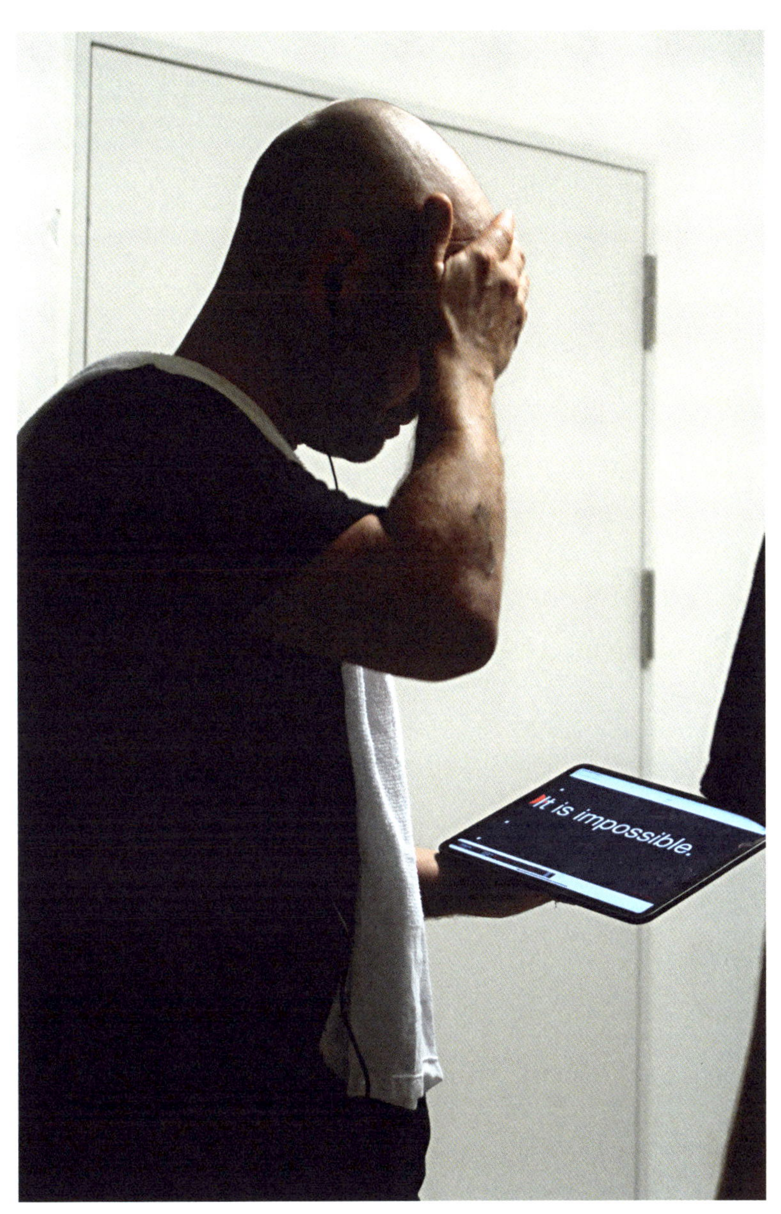
It is impossible.

IMAGE CREDITS

Listed by appearance
from left to right on pages

9

Okayama City
Photo credit: Ola Rindal

Melissa Dubbin
& Aaron S. Davidson
Delay Lines, 2019
Collection of Ishikawa
Foundation, Okayama
Courtesy of the artists
Photo credit: Pierre Huyghe

10–11

Melissa Dubbin
& Aaron S. Davidson
Delay Lines, 2019
Collection of Ishikawa
Foundation, Okayama
Courtesy of the artists
Photo credit: Ola Rindal

12–14

Fabien Giraud & Raphaël Siboni
The Everted Capital (1971–4936),
The Unmanned, Season 2,
Episode 2, 2019
Collection of Ishikawa
Foundation, Okayama
Courtesy of the artists
Photo credit: Pierre Huyghe

15

Pierre Huyghe
View IF THE SNAKE, 2019
Photo credit: Pierre Huyghe

16

Pierre Huyghe
View IF THE SNAKE, 2019
Photo credit: Pierre Huyghe

John Gerrard
X. laevis (Spacelab), 2017
Courtesy of the artist
and Pace Gallery
Photo credit: Pierre Huyghe

Etienne Chambaud
Calculus, 2019
Collection of Ishikawa
Foundation, Okayama
Courtesy of the artist, Labor,
Mexico, and Esther Schipper,
Berlin / Paris / Seoul
Photo credit: Pierre Huyghe

17

Pierre Huyghe
View IF THE SNAKE, 2019
Photo credit: Pierre Huyghe

John Gerrard
X. laevis (Spacelab), 2017
Courtesy of the artist
and Pace Gallery
Photo credit: Pierre Huyghe

Pamela Rosenkranz
Healer (Waters), 2019
Courtesy of the artist,
Karma International,
Miguel Abreu Gallery,
and Sprüth Magers
Photo credit: Marc Asekhame

18–19

John Gerrard
X. laevis (Spacelab), 2017
Still
Courtesy of the artist
and Pace Gallery

20–21

Pierre Huyghe
View IF THE SNAKE, 2019
Photo credit: Ola Rindal

22

Pierre Huyghe
View IF THE SNAKE, 2019
Photo credit: Ola Rindal

Etienne Chambaud
Calculus, 2019
Collection of Ishikawa
Foundation, Okayama
Courtesy of the artist, Labor,
Mexico, and Esther Schipper,
Berlin / Paris / Seoul
Photo credit: Ola Rindal

23

Ian Cheng
BOB (Bag of Beliefs), 2018–2019
Collection of Ishikawa
Foundation, Okayama
Courtesy of the artist, Pilar
Corrias, and Gladstone Gallery
Photo credit: Ola Rindal

Mika Tajima
Human Synth (Istanbul), 2018
Still
Courtesy of the artist
and TARO NASU

24–25

Ian Cheng
BOB (Bag of Beliefs), 2018–2019
Collection of Ishikawa
Foundation, Okayama
Courtesy of the artist, Pilar
Corrias, and Gladstone Gallery
Photo Credit: Ola Rindal

Life After BOB (First Tract), 2019
Collection of Ishikawa
Foundation, Okayama
Courtesy Pilar Corrias,
and Gladstone Gallery

26–27

Pamela Rosenkranz
Healer (Waters), 2019
Courtesy of the artist, Karma
International, Miguel Abreu
Gallery, and Sprüth Magers
Photo credit: Ola Rindal

28

Matthew Barney
Cathode in Refugium, 2019
Courtesy of the artist
and Gladstone Gallery
Photo: Peter Strietmann

29

Matthew Barney & Pierre Huyghe
Not yet titled, 2019
Courtesy of the artists
and Marian Goodman Gallery
Photo credit: Ola Rindal

30

Matthew Barney & Pierre Huyghe
Not yet titled, 2019
Courtesy of the artist and
Marian Goodman Gallery
Photo credit: Ola Rindal

31

Matthew Barney & Pierre Huyghe
Not yet titled, 2019
Courtesy of the artist and
Marian Goodman Gallery
Photo credit: Ola Rindal

Matthew Barney & Pierre Huyghe
Not yet titled, 2019
Courtesy of the artist and
Marian Goodman Gallery
Photo credit: Pierre Huyghe

32

Matthew Barney & Pierre Huyghe
Not yet titled, 2019
Courtesy of the artist and
Marian Goodman Gallery
Photo credit: Shinichiro Uchida

33

Matthew Barney & Pierre Huyghe
Not yet titled, 2019
Courtesy of the artist and
Marian Goodman Gallery

Pierre Huyghe
Of Ideal, 2019–ongoing
Courtesy of the artist, TARO NASU,
Marian Goodman Gallery,
and Hauser & Wirth
Photo credit: Shinichiro Uchida

34–35

Pierre Huyghe
Of Ideal, 2019–ongoing
Courtesy of the artist, TARO NASU,
Marian Goodman Gallery,
and Hauser & Wirth
© Kamitani Lab / Kyoto
Photo credit: Ola Rindal

36

Pierre Huyghe
View IF THE SNAKE, 2019
Photo credit: Ola Rindal

Etienne Chambaud
Calculus, 2019
Collection of Ishikawa Foundation, Okayama
Courtesy of the artist, Labor, Mexico, and Esther Schipper, Berlin / Paris / Seoul

John Gerrard
X. laevis (Spacelab), 2017
Courtesy of the artist and Pace Gallery
Photo credit: Ola Rindal

Paul Chan
Triosophia, 2016
Courtesy of the artist
Photo credit: Masayuki Saito

37

Pierre Huyghe
View IF THE SNAKE, 2019
Photo credit: Pierre Huyghe

Fabien Giraud & Raphaël Siboni
The Everted Capital (1971–4936), *The Unmanned*, Season 2, Episode 2, 2019
Collection of Ishikawa Foundation, Okayama
Courtesy of the artists
Photo credit: Pierre Huyghe

38–39

Etienne Chambaud
Calculus, 2019
Collection of Ishikawa Foundation, Okayama
Courtesy of the artist, Labor, Mexico, and Esther Schipper, Berlin / Paris / Seoul
Photo credit: Ola Rindal

40

Etienne Chambaud
Calculus, 2019
Collection of Ishikawa Foundation, Okayama
Courtesy of the artist, Labor, Mexico, and Esther Schipper, Berlin / Paris / Seoul
Photo credit: Ola Rindal

41

Etienne Chambaud
Calculus, 2019
Collection of Ishikawa Foundation, Okayama
Courtesy of the artist, Labor, Mexico, and Esther Schipper, Berlin / Paris / Seoul
Photo credit: Etienne Chambaud

Pierre Huyghe
View IF THE SNAKE, 2019
Photo credit: Ola Rindal

42

Pierre Huyghe
View IF THE SNAKE, 2019
Photo credit: Ola Rindal

John Gerrard
X. laevis (Spacelab), 2017
Courtesy of the artist and Pace Gallery
Photo credit: Ola Rindal

Etienne Chambaud
Calculus, 2019
Collection of Ishikawa Foundation, Okayama
Courtesy of the artist, Labor, Mexico, and Esther Schipper, Berlin / Paris / Seoul

Pamela Rosenkranz
Healer (Waters), 2019
Courtesy of the artist, Karma International, Miguel Abreu Gallery, and Sprüth Magers
Photo credit: Shinichiro Uchida

43

Pierre Huyghe
View IF THE SNAKE, 2019
Photo credit: Ola Rindal

John Gerrard
X. laevis (Spacelab), 2017
Courtesy of the artist and Pace Gallery
Photo credit: Ola Rindal

Etienne Chambaud
Calculus, 2019
Collection of Ishikawa Foundation, Okayama
Courtesy of the artist, Labor, Mexico, and Esther Schipper, Berlin / Paris / Seoul
Photo credit: Ola Rindal

44–45

Pierre Huyghe
View IF THE SNAKE, 2019
Photo credit: Ola Rindal

46

Pierre Huyghe
View IF THE SNAKE, 2019
Photo credit: Ola Rindal

Sean Raspet
Ipomoea indica (morning glory): IRBli Light Blue x IRBli Silver Blue, 2019 (first generation)
Special thanks to the Institute of Radiation Breeding, Japan, Fukukaen Nursery & Bulb Co., Ltd., and Joel Keunnen
Photo credit: Ola Rindal

Pamela Rosenkranz
Skin Pool (Oromom), 2019
Courtesy of the artist, Karma International, Miguel Abreu Gallery, and Sprüth Magers
Photo credit: Ola Rindal

John Gerrard
X. laevis (Spacelab), 2017
Courtesy of the artist and Pace Gallery
Photo credit: Ola Rindal

47

Pierre Huyghe
View IF THE SNAKE, 2019
Photo credit: Ola Rindal

Pamela Rosenkranz
Skin Pool (Oromom), 2019
Courtesy of the artist, Karma International, Miguel Abreu Gallery, and Sprüth Magers
Photo credit: Ola Rindal

48

Pamela Rosenkranz
Skin Pool (Oromom), 2019
Courtesy of the artist, Karma International, Miguel Abreu Gallery, and Sprüth Magers
Photo credit: Ola Rindal

John Gerrard
X. laevis (Spacelab), 2017
Courtesy of the artist and Pace Gallery
Photo credit: Ola Rindal

49

Pamela Rosenkranz
Skin Pool (Oromom), 2019
Courtesy of the artist, Karma International, Miguel Abreu Gallery, and Sprüth Magers
Photo credit: Pierre Huyghe

Sean Raspet
Ipomoea indica (morning glory): IRBli Light Blue x IRBli Silver Blue, 2019 (first generation)
Special thanks to the Institute of Radiation Breeding, Japan, Fukukaen Nursery & Bulb Co., Ltd., and Joel Keunnen
Photo credit: Ola Rindal

50–51

Pierre Huyghe
Of Ideal, 2019–ongoing
Still
Courtesy of the artist, TARO NASU, Marian Goodman Gallery, and Hauser and Wirth
© Kamitani Lab / Kyoto

52

Pierre Huyghe
View IF THE SNAKE, 2019
Photo credit: Ola Rindal

Pierre Huyghe
Of Ideal, 2019–ongoing
Courtesy of the artist, TARO NASU, Marian Goodman Gallery, and Hauser & Wirth
© Kamitani Lab / Kyoto
Photo credit: Ola Rindal

Pierre Huyghe
Two Minutes Out of Time, 2000
Courtesy of the artist
Photo credit: Pierre Huyghe

53

Pierre Huyghe
Two Minutes Out of Time, 2000
Still
Courtesy of the artist
Photo credit: Pierre Huyghe

Pierre Huyghe
View IF THE SNAKE, 2019
Photo credit: Pierre Huyghe

54

Ian Cheng
BOB and Ann Lee for IF THE SNAKE, 2019
Courtesy the artist

55

Pierre Huyghe
View IF THE SNAKE, 2019
Photo credit: Shinichiro Uchida

Ian Cheng
BOB (Bag of Beliefs), 2018–2019
Collection of Ishikawa Foundation, Okayama
Courtesy of the artist, Pilar Corrias, and Gladstone Gallery
Photo credit: Shinichiro Uchida

56–57

Ian Cheng
BOB (Bag of Beliefs), 2018–2019
Collection of Ishikawa Foundation, Okayama
Courtesy of the artist, Pilar Corrias, and Gladstone Gallery
Photo credit: Masayuki Saito

58–61

Melissa Dubbin & Aaron S. Davidson
Delay Lines, 2019
Collection of Ishikawa Foundation, Okayama
Courtesy of the artists
Photo credit: Pierre Huyghe

62–63

Tarek Atoui
Glitter Beats and Wild Synths / the wave, 2019
Courtesy of the artist and Galerie Chantal Crousel
Photo credit: Pierre Huyghe

64

Fernando Ortega
Untitled, 2003
Courtesy of the artist and kurimanzutto
Photo credit: Pierre Huyghe

Tarek Atoui
Glitter Beats and Wild Synths / the wave, 2019
Courtesy of the artist and Galerie Chantal Crousel
Photo credit: Ola Rindal

65

Tarek Atoui
Glitter Beats and Wild Synths / the wave, 2019
Courtesy of the artist and Galerie Chantal Crousel
Photo credit: Pierre Huyghe

66–67

Tarek Atoui
Glitter Beats and Wild Synths / the wave, 2019
Courtesy of the artist and Galerie Chantal Crousel
Photo credit: Ola Rindal
Photo credit: Masayuki Saito

68–74

Fabien Giraud & Raphaël Siboni
The Everted Capital (1971–4936), *The Unmanned*, Season 2, Episode 2, 2019
Collection of Ishikawa Foundation, Okayama
Courtesy of the artists
Photo credit: Ola Rindal
Photo credit: Shinichiro Uchida

75–77

Fabien Giraud & Raphaël Siboni
The Everted Capital (1971–4936), *The Unmanned*, Season 2, Episode 2, 2019
Stills
Collection of Ishikawa Foundation, Okayama
Courtesy of the artists

78

Fabien Giraud & Raphaël Siboni
The Everted Capital (1971–4936), *The Unmanned*, Season 2, Episode 2, 2019
Still
Collection of Ishikawa Foundation, Okayama
Courtesy of the artists

Fabien Giraud & Raphaël Siboni
The Everted Capital (1971–4936), *The Unmanned*, Season 2, Episode 2, 2019
Collection of Ishikawa Foundation, Okayama
Courtesy of the artists
Photo credit: Ola Rindal

79–80

Fabien Giraud & Raphaël Siboni
The Everted Capital (1971–4936), *The Unmanned*, Season 2, Episode 2, 2019
Collection of Ishikawa Foundation, Okayama
Courtesy of the artists
Photo credit: Ola Rindal

81

Lili Reynaud-Dewar
I Want All Of The Above To Be The Sun (If The Snake), 2019
Stills
Courtesy of the artist

82–83

Fabien Giraud & Raphaël Siboni
The Everted Capital (1971–4936), *The Unmanned*, Season 2, Episode 2, 2019
Still
Collection of Ishikawa Foundation, Okayama
Courtesy of the artists

84

Kazuo Hara
Kyokushiteki Erosu Koiuta 1974
16 mm film, black & white, 92'
Still

84–86

Glass Bead
The Glass Bead Game: Views from the Anti-World
Talks and workshop with Futoshi Hoshino, Damjan Jovanovic, Anna Longo, Patricia Reed, and Casey Rehm
Courtesy of Okayama Art Summit executive committee
Photo credit: Ola Rindal

87

Lili Reynaud-Dewar
Rome, November 1st and 2nd 1975, 2019
Courtesy of the artist
Photo credit: Pierre Huyghe

88–89

Pamela Rosenkranz
Skin Pool (Oromom), 2019
Courtesy of the artist, Karma International, Miguel Abreu Gallery, and Sprüth Magers
Photo credit: Ola Rindal

90–91

Elizabeth Hénaff
Drift, 2019
Courtesy of the artist
Photo credit: Elizabeth Hénaff
Photo credit: Ola Rindal

92

Etienne Chambaud
Fever (Deep Sky Borreliosis), 2019
Courtesy of the artist, Labor, Mexico, and Esther Schipper, Berlin / Paris / Seoul
Photo credit: Etienne Chambaud

Etienne Chambaud
Salted Space, 2019
Courtesy of the artist, Labor, Mexico, and Esther Schipper, Berlin / Paris / Seoul
Photo credit: Etienne Chambaud

93

Etienne Chambaud
Fever (Mustard Malaria), 2019
Salted Space, 2019
Courtesy of the artist, Labor, Mexico, and Esther Schipper, Berlin / Paris / Seoul
Photo credit: Etienne Chambaud

94–97

Mika Tajima
New Humans, 2019
Developed with the support from WArt, Cornell Tech, and Ferrotec
Collection of Ishikawa Foundation, Okayama
Courtesy of the artist and TARO NASU, Tokyo
Photo credit: Ola Rindal

Force Touch (Corporis), 2019
Collection of Ishikawa Foundation, Okayama
Courtesy of the artist and TARO NASU
Photo credit: Ola Rindal

98–99

Melissa Dubbin & Aaron S. Davidson
Core (1), 2017
Courtesy of the artists
Photo credit: Ola Rindal

100–101

Eva L'Hoest
Under Automata, 2017
Courtesy of the artist
Photo credit: Ola Rindal

102

Fernando Ortega
Untitled, 2003
Courtesy of the artist and kurimanzutto
Photo credit: Ola Rindal

Lili Reynaud-Dewar
I Want All Of The Above To Be The Sun (If The Snake), 2019
Still
Courtesy of the artist

103

Lili Reynaud-Dewar
I Want All Of The Above To Be The Sun (If The Snake), 2019
Stills
Courtesy of the artist

104

Pierre Huyghe
View IF THE SNAKE, 2019
Photo credit: Ola Rindal

Pamela Rosenkranz
Skin Pool (Oromom), 2019
Courtesy of the artist, Karma International, Miguel Abreu Gallery, and Sprüth Magers
Photo credit: Ola Rindal

John Gerrard
X. laevis (Spacelab), 2017
Courtesy of the artist and Pace Gallery
Photo credit: Ola Rindal

105

John Gerrard
X. laevis (Spacelab), 2017
Courtesy of the artist and Pace Gallery
Photo credit: Pierre Huyghe

106

Matthew Barney & Pierre Huyghe
Not yet titled, 2019
Courtesy of the artist and Marian Goodman Gallery
Photo credit: Pierre Huyghe
Photo credit: Ola Rindal

107

Lili Reynaud-Dewar
I Want All Of The Above To Be The Sun (If The Snake), 2019
Still
Courtesy of the artist

John Gerrard
X. laevis (Spacelab), 2017
Still
Courtesy of the artist and Pace Gallery

108–109

Paul Chan
Happiness (Finally) After 35,000 Years of Civilization (after Henry Darger and Charles Fourier), 2000–2003
Stills
Courtesy the artist and Greene Naftali, New York

110–111

Pamela Rosenkranz
Skin Pool (Oromom), 2019
Courtesy of the artist, Karma International, Miguel Abreu Gallery, and Sprüth Magers
Photo credit: Ola Rindal

Sean Raspet
Ipomoea indica (morning glory): IRBli Light Blue x IRBli Silver Blue, 2019 (first generation)
Special thanks to the Institute of Radiation Breeding, Japan, Fukukaen Nursery & Bulb Co., Ltd., and Joel Keunnen
Photo credit: Ola Rindal

112–113

Sean Raspet
Ipomoea indica (morning glory): IRBli Light Blue x IRBli Silver Blue, 2019 (first generation)
Special thanks to the Institute of Radiation Breeding, Japan, Fukukaen Nursery & Bulb Co., Ltd., and Joel Keunnen
Photo credit: Pierre Huyghe

Sean Raspet with Shengping Zheng
Hyperflor© (2-benzyl-1,3-dioxan-5-one), 2018–2019
2-benzyl-1,3-dioxan-5-one molecule

Sean Raspet
Untitled (meal kit), 2019
Distributed through STAND6-10, CCCSCD by CIFAKA, Okayama
Photo credit: Ola Rindal

114

Sean Raspet with Shengping Zheng
Hyperflor© (2-benzyl-1,3-dioxan-5-one), 2018–2019
2-benzyl-1,3-dioxan-5-one molecule

115

Fabien Giraud & Raphaël Siboni
The Everted Capital (The Axiom), The Unmanned, Season 2, Prologue, 2018
Still
Courtesy of the artists
Photo credit: Pierre Huyghe

Pamela Rosenkranz
Healer (Waters), 2019
Courtesy of the artist, Karma International, Miguel Abreu Gallery, and Sprüth Magers
Photo credit: Masayuki Saito

116

Matthew Barney
Redoubt, 2019
Still
Courtesy of the artist, Gladstone Gallery, New York and Brussels, and Sadie Coles HQ, London
Photo credit: Peter Strietmann

117

Pierre Huyghe
View IF THE SNAKE, 2019
Photo credit: Pierre Huyghe

LIST OF WORKS

TAREK ATOUI

Glitter Beats and Wild Synths / the wave
2019
Composition for Litophones, Lymaçons, Rotators, Duo Fluctus, Sub-ink, Ourobouros, and Horns of Putin
Variable dimensions
Courtesy the artist and Galerie Chantal Crousel

MATTHEW BARNEY & PIERRE HUYGHE

Not yet titled
2019
Electroplating tank containing an engraved copper plate with asphaltum ground
Aquarium, live marine ecosystem (arrow crab, horse shoe crabs, anemone, coral), sand, and life support system
Courtesy the artists and Marian Goodman Gallery, New York

MATTHEW BARNEY

Cathode in Refugium
2019
Engraved copper plate with asphaltum ground in high density polyethylene frame
17 ¾ by 20 ¼ in
4K video with 7.1 sound
Courtesy Matthew Barney, Gladstone Gallery, New York and Brussels, and Sadie Coles HQ, London

Redoubt
2018
4K video with 7.1 sound
Courtesy Matthew Barney, Gladstone Gallery, New York and Brussels, and Sadie Coles HQ, London

ÉTIENNE CHAMBAUD

Fever (Deep Sky Borreliosis)
2019
Computer simulation, heating device, sensors, cables
Variable dimensions
Courtesy of the artist, Labor, Mexico, and Esther Schipper, Berlin / Paris / Seoul
Courtesy of the artist and Labor, Mexico

Salted Space
2019
Bone powder
Variable dimensions
Courtesy of the artist, Labor, Mexico, and Esther Schipper, Berlin / Paris / Seoul

Calculus
2019
Bronze
82 × 91 × 98 cm
Collection of Ishikawa Foundation, Okayama
Courtesy of the artist, Labor, Mexico, and Esther Schipper, Berlin / Paris / Seoul

PAUL CHAN

Triosophia
2016
Nylon, wood, concrete, shoes, fans
120 × 120 × 84 in / 305 × 305 × 213 cm
Courtesy the artist and Greene Naftali, New York

Happiness (Finally) After 35,000 Years of Civilization (after Henry Darger and Charles Fourier)
2000–2003
Digital video projection on screen (color, sound)
17'20"
Courtesy the artist and Greene Naftali, New York

IAN CHENG

Life After BOB (First Tract)
2019
Duratrans, lightboxes
Each lightbox 166.0 × 112.0 × 1.8 cm
Collection of Ishikawa Foundation, Okayama
Courtesy Pilar Corrias, London and Gladstone Gallery, New York

BOB (Bag of Beliefs)
2018–2019
Artificial lifeform
Collection of Ishikawa Foundation, Okayama
Courtesy the artist, Pilar Corrias, and Gladstone Gallery

MELISSA DUBBIN & AARON S. DAVIDSON

Delay Lines
2019
Water from subterranean Asahi River, borosilicate glass, overclocking water-cooled computer, soft robot manta, simulation, temperature sensors, compressor, control system, metal, plastic, wood, filter, silicone tubing, and power supplies
Variable dimensions
Collection of Ishikawa Foundation, Okayama
Courtesy the artists

Core (for Okayama)
2019
Lodestones and 135,000 ferrite core memory toroids
Variable dimensions
Courtesy the artists

JOHN GERRARD

X. laevis (Spacelab)
2017
Simulation
Variable dimensions
Producer: Werner Poetzelberger
Programmer: Helmut Bressler
3D Modeler: Max Loegler
Rigging and posing: Michael Buettner
Installation development and technical design: Jakob Illera / Inseq Design
Game Engine: Unigine
Collection of Ishikawa Foundation, Okayama
Courtesy of the artist and Pace Gallery

FABIEN GIRAUD & RAPHAËL SIBONI

The Everted Capital—The Axiom.
The Unmanned, Season 2—prologue
2018
HD Video; Merlin SLX Thermal camera, animal, vegetal and mineral used as a currency in Human history, clay globe
24 hours
Courtesy the artists

The Everted Capital (1971–4936)
The Unmanned, Season 2, Episode 2
2019
HD video, 24-hour filmed performance, edited in real-time by an artificial intelligence
24 hours
Collection of Ishikawa Foundation, Okayama
Courtesy the artists

The Form of Not (Infantia)
The Unmanned, Season 3, Episode 2
2019
Sculptures formed by Deepfake; various materials, Artificial Intelligence
Courtesy the artists

GLASS BEAD (FABIEN GIRAUD, JEREMY LECOMTE, VINCENT NORMAND, IDA SOULARD, INIGO WILKINS)

The Glass Bead Game: Views from the Anti-World
Talks and workshop with Futoshi Hoshino, Damjan Jovanovic, Anna Longo, Patricia Reed, and Casey Rehm
Journal Site 2 with essays by Blindfield Collective, Louis Chude-Sokei, Luca Fraser, Sally Haslanger, Anna Longo, Reza Negarestani, Matthew Poole, Patricia Reed, Olivier Surel, "Three Billions of Perverts" archive, and conversation with Cruising Pavilion and Rebekah Sheldon
Film by Kazuo Hara, Kyokushiteki Erosu Koiuta 1974 / (Extreme Private Eros: Love Song 1974)

ELIZABETH HÉNAFF

DRIFT
2019
DNA, paper, flotation device, metagenomic analysis
Courtesy the artist

EVA L'HOEST

Under Automata
2017
VR Game
Courtesy of the artist

PIERRE HUYGHE

Of Ideal
2019–ongoing
Deep image reconstruction, sensors, sound
Collection of Ishikawa Foundation, Okayama
Courtesy the artist and TARO NASU
© Kamitani Lab / Kyoto

Two minutes Out of Time
2000
Animation film, color, sound
4'
Courtesy Marian Goodman Gallery, New York

FERNANDO ORTEGA

Untitled
2003
Fly electrocutor device
Courtesy the artist and kurimanzutto, Mexico City

SEAN RASPET

Ipomoea indica (morning glory): IRBIi Light Blue x IRBIi Silver Blue
2003 (first generation)
IRBIi Light Blue and IRBIi Silver Blue mutant varieties of morning glory developed through gamma radiation mutation by the Institute of Radiation Breeding, Japan; planted in proximity to allow for cross-pollination
Variable dimensions; 81 individual plants with a 1:3.76 ratio of IRBIi Silver Blue to IRBIi Light Blue
Special thanks to the Institute of Radiation Breeding, Japan, Fukukaen Nursery & Bulb Co., Ltd., and Joel Keunnen

SEAN RASPET WITH SHENGPING ZHENG

Hyperflor© (2-benzyl-1,3-dioxan-5-one)
2018–2019
2-benzyl-1,3-dioxan-5-one molecule
Diffused via electronic diffuser
Special thanks to Sihan Li and Hunter College, CUNY

SEAN RASPET WITH INTEGRICULTURE INC./ SHOJINMEAT PROJECT; EUGLENA CO. LTD.; AVANT MEATS COMPANY LIMITED; D&T FARMS, OKAYAMA; NONFOOD; CCCSCD-CIFAKA, OKAYAMA, AND OTHERS

Untitled (meal kit)
2019
Meal kit
See nutrition facts for calorie, vitamin, and mineral information
Distributed through STAND6-10, CCCSCD by CIFAKA, Okayama
Special thanks to Nao Yamoto

LILI REYNAUD-DEWAR

ROME, NOVEMBER 1ST AND 2ND 1975
2019
Performance
With Ichiro Fukano, Koichiro Osaka, Satoshi Ukai, Lili Reynaud-Dewar, Victor Zébo
Text by Pier Paolo Pasolini and Furio Colombo
Courtesy the artist

ROME, NOVEMBER 1ST AND 2ND 1975
2019
Film
With Ichiro Fukano, Koichiro Osaka, Satoshi Ukai, Lili Reynaud-Dewar, Victor Zébo
Text by Pier Paolo Pasolini and Furio Colombo
Courtesy the artist

I Want All Of The Above To Be The Sun (If The Snake)
2019
Color video, HD
Courtesy the artist

PAMELA ROSENKRANZ

Healer (Waters)

2019

Robot, circuit board control units, battery, LED light, 3D Printed Head and Tail, Kirigami Skin
Collection of Ishikawa Foundation, Okayama
Courtesy the artist and Karma International, Zurich / Los Angeles, Miguel Abreu Gallery, New York, and Sprüth Magers

Skin Pool (Oromom)

2019

Liquid, thickeners, coloring, pumps
Courtesy the artist and Karma International, Zurich / Los Angeles, Miguel Abreu Gallery, New York, and Sprüth Magers

TINO SEHGAL

2019

Ann Lee

2011

Collection of Ishikawa Foundation, Okayama

MIKA TAJIMA

New Humans

2019

Generative algorithm using machine learning (GAN, T-SNE) and fluid simulation (Navier Stokes), user profile data caches (DNA, fitness, and dating), Ferrofluid, custom electromagnet matrix, custom PCB control system, computer, steel, polycarbonate, wood, aluminium
Developed with the support from Art, Cornell Tech and Ferrotec
Courtesy of the artist and TARO NASU, Tokyo

Force Touch (Corporis)

2019

Gold chromed Jacuzzi jets, fans
Variable dimensions
Courtesy of the artist and TARO NASU, Tokyo

Human Synth (Okayama)

2018

Custom predictive sentiment analysis program, gaming engine, Alienware VR PC, Twitter API; video, color; endless duration
Variable dimensions
Courtesy of the artist and TARO NASU, Tokyo

Negative Entropy (Kurozumikyo Shinto Shrine, Dawn Meditation, Red, Single)

2019

Cotton, polyester, nylon, wool, wool acoustic baffling felt, and wood
36.9 × 27.4 × 2.1 in / 937 × 696 × 53 cm
Courtesy the artist and TARO NASU, Tokyo

Negative Entropy (Stripe International Inc., Accounting Department, Mint, Single)

2019

Cotton, polyester, nylon, wool acoustic baffling felt, and wood
36.9 × 27.4 × 2.1 in / 937 × 696 × 53 cm
Courtesy the artist and TARO NASU, Tokyo

OKAYAMA ART SUMMIT 2019 IF THE SNAKE

PERIOD
September 27, 2019 to November 24, 2019

LOCATIONS
Former Uchisange Elementary School
Former Fukuoka Soy Sauce Factory
Tenjinyama Cultural Plaza of Okayama Prefecture
Okayama Orient Museum
Okayama Castle
Cinema Clair Marunouchi
Hayashibara Museum of Art
Other locations in Okayama City

ORGANIZER
Okayama Art Summit Executive Committee

CHAIRMAN
Masao Omori, Mayor of Okayama City

VICE CHAIRMAN
Kenrou Satou, Vice-Governor, Okayama Prefecture
Hisashi Matsuda, President, Okayama Chamber of Commerce and Industry

ADDITOR
Masato Miyanaga, President, Chugoku Bank

PRODUCER
Yasuharu Ishikawa,
President, Ishikawa Foundation
President and CEO, Stripe International Inc.

DIRECTOR
Taro Nasu, TARO NASU Co., Ltd. / Art&Public Co.,Ltd.

ARTISTIC DIRECTOR
Pierre Huyghe

CURATORIAL ADVISOR
Anne Stenne

PUBLIC PROGRAM DIRECTOR
Chieko Kinoshita, Associate Professor, Co-Creation Bureau, Osaka University

LEARNING PROGRAM DIRECTOR
Masako Hosoi, TARO NASU Co., Ltd. / Art&Public Co.,Ltd.

ADVISORS
Masahiko Urakami, Chairman, Okayama City Council
Takamasa Koshimune, Chairman, Sanyo Shimbun
Hiroshi Makino, President, Okayama University

AMBASSADORS
Yasushi Akimoto, Lyricist
Takeo Obayashi
Masamichi Katayama, Wonderwall, Inc.
Yukiyasu Kamitani, Professor at Graduate School of Informatics, Kyoto University
Kengo Kuma, Kengo Kuma and Associates
Nobuhiro Nishitakatsuji, Chief Priest, Dazaifu Tenmangu
Kenya Hara, Nippon Design Center, Inc.
Yoshiko Mori, Chairperson, Mori Art Museum
Takashi Yamashita, Member, House of Representatives

AFFILIATED ENTITIES
Okayama City
Okayama City Board of Education
Okayama Prefecture
Okayama Chamber of Commerce and Industry
Okayama Vistor & Convention Association
Okayama Culture Zone Liaison Council
The Consortium of Universities in Okayama
Sanyou Shinbun
RSK Sanyo Broadcasting Co., Ltd.
Okayama Broadcasting Co., Ltd.
Setouchi Broadcasting Co., Ltd.
Okayama Bus Association
Okayama Taxi Association
Okayama Branch of West Japan Railway Company
Chugoku Bank
Ishikawa Foundation

OKAYAMA ART SUMMIT EXECUTIVE COM- MITTEE OFFICE

CHIEF OFFICER
Manabu Kishi

ASSISTANT CHIEF OFFICER
Masashi Ogawa

OPERATION STAFF
Satomi Muraguchi
Katsumi Azuma
Nobuyuki Satou
Yoko Akagashi
Tomochika Hirooka
Eri Miura
Misato Nakai
Kayo Sakamoto
Riho Shishido
Yoko Abe
Meikei Han

OPERATION PR
Takeshi Tanaka
Mai Sugano
Masako Taira
Akihiro Mochizuki
Kanoko Tamura
Ai Yoshida
Hideaki Hara

CURATORIAL STAFF
Shino Ozawa
Mao Hashinoguchi
Yasuhisa Kawada

PRODUCER SUPPORT
Hiroyuki Isobe
Taiji Okada

OPERATION SUPPORT
Tsutomu Harigae, Yoshiko Ishikawa, Shuntaro Sugiura, Shigehiro Okada, Jun Shimamoto, Tomoko Yamashita, Ayumi Mizutani, Sayuri Okuda, Sanae Otsuki, Jun Kamiyama, Rika Nagase, Saki Kawazoe, Yuya Ishiwata, Mayumi Nakamura, Tomoko Okumura, Tetsuo Tachibana, Takamichi Kataoka, Mouri Yoso, Fumihiro Kobayashi, Masato Okada, Go Omoto, Ataru Yoshida, Yusuke Inagaki, Yui Fujii, Futaba Sawada, Ayumi Uemoto, Yumi Suyama, Keita Arai, Kyoko Iikawa, Waon Ieda, Tomoko Koizumi

COLOPHON

IF THE SNAKE
PIERRE HUYGHE

ISBN: 978-3-7533-0678-0

CONCEPT
Pierre Huyghe

WORKS BY
Tarek Atoui, Matthew Barney, Etienne Chambaud, Paul Chan, Ian Cheng, Melissa Dubbin & Aaron S. Davidson, John Gerrard, Fabien Giraud & Raphaël Siboni, Glass Bead, Elizabeth Hénaff, Eva L'Hoest, Pierre Huyghe, Fernando Ortega, Sean Raspet, Lili Reynaud-Dewar, Pamela Rosenkranz, Tino Sehgal, Mika Tajima

EDITOR
Anne Stenne

RESPONSIBLE EDITOR
Helene Gamst, Roulette Russe

TEXT
Pierre Huyghe

GRAPHIC DESIGN
deValence

IMAGE PROCESSING
Arciel Graphic

PRINT
Cassochrome, Belgium, 2024

WITH THE GENEROUS SUPPORT OF
Galerie Chantal Crousel, Marian Goodman Gallery, Hauser & Wirth, TARO NASU, Esther Schipper

SPECIAL THANKS TO
Pierre Huyghe Studio

DISTRIBUTION

Europe:
Buchhandlung Walther König
Ehrenstraße 4
D-50672 Köln
GERMANY
T +49 (0)221 / 20 59 6 53
verlag@buchhandlung-walther-koenig.de

UK & Ireland:
ART DATA
12 Bell Industrial Estate
50 Cunnington Street
London W4 5HB
UNITED KINGDOM
T +44 (0)208 747 10 61
F +44 (0)208 742 23 19
orders@artdata.co.uk

Outside Europe:
D.A.P. / Distributed Art Publishers, Inc.
75 Broad Street, Suite 630
USA – New York, NY 10004
T +1 (0) 212 627 1999
orders@dapinc.com